"I myself am a savage, owing no allegiance but to the King of the Cannibals, and ready at any moment to rebel against him."
- Herman Melville, *Typee*

Me, the Boat and a Guy Named Bob

C. E. BOWMAN

Copyright © 2019 C.E. Bowman
All rights Reserved

Published by Tradewind Publishing
20 Bristol Avenue, Bicton
Western Australia, 6157
www.tradewindpublishing.com

 A catalogue record for this book is available from the National Library of Australia

Author: Bowman, C.E.
Title: Me, the Boat and a Guy Named Bob
ISBN: 9781925 171501 (paperback)
Subjects: Biography- Adventure Travel - Bob Dylan – Non-fiction

Cover artwork by Peter Carr

Excerpts of lyrics from: *A Hard Rain's A Gonna Fall*, *When the Ship Comes In*, *Chimes of Freedom*, *Not Dark Yet* and *Most of the Time* are used with the permission and courtesy of Bob Dylan.

"How Bad Do You Want To Get To Bequia" first appeared in *Sail* magazine in slightly different form.

The descriptions, the experiences and the words of this story are the authors own.

All rights reserved. No part of this publication may be reproduced, stored in a retrieval system or transmitted in any form or by any means, electronic, mechanical, photocopying, recording or otherwise, without prior written permission of the copyright holder.

The scanning, uploading, and distribution of this book via the Internet or via any other means without the permission of the publisher is illegal and punishable by law. Please purchase only authorized electronic editions, and do not participate or encourage electronic piracy of copyrighted materials. Your support of the authors rights is appreciated.

This book is dedicated to Life...
in all of its Manifestations.

Prologue

Story: the telling of a happening or connected series of events, whether true or fictitious.
- Webster's New World Dictionary

Life is full of stories. Everyone's got one, and this is mine. Be patient, bear with me, and you will see how the happenings I am about to describe ARE connected…sometimes by only a spider's web of cosmic filament…and about as true as I can remember. Life is also full of characters, and drifting through these pages you will find a rogue's gallery of penny stock hustlers, magicians, sea-gypsy philosophers, master boatbuilders and even a few rock stars, all of whom in one way or another play their part. It is the tale of a special island and an exceptional time, a pinpoint in history filled with extraordinary people, who through the magic of the universe came together for one last hurrah. A key player in this story is the enigmatic musician Bob Dylan. "I'm usually either in New York or on the West Coast or down in the Caribbean. Me and another guy have a boat down there," he once said. Who was this "other guy", what was this boat, and whatever happened to it? Over the years there has been lot of conjecture and misunderstanding going around concerning all of this, and after forty years I'd like to finally set the record straight. After all, that long dark cloud is rolling down, or at least it's looming over the horizon somewhere and will be here eventually, so it's about time I make the effort to tell this tale before those of us who had anything to do with it are pushing up daisies on Boot Hill. And like so many other stories, it wouldn't have happened without a few simple twists of fate…

- C.E. Bowman
Autumn, 2019

~ BOOK I ~

ME

1
Hawcon

Oh, where have you been, my blue-eyed son?
Oh, where have you been, my darling young one?
I've stumbled on the side of twelve misty mountains
I've walked and I've crawled on six crooked highways
I've stepped in the middle of seven sad forests
I've been out in front of a dozen dead oceans
I've been ten thousand miles in the mouth of a graveyard
And it's a hard, and it's a hard, it's a hard, and it's a hard
And it's a hard rain's a-gonna fall
- Bob Dylan, "A Hard Rain's A-Gonna Fall"

Somewhere near Mombasa on the Kenya Coast, November 1972…

Late afternoon, and the monsoonal rain tumbled down, pouring off the thatched roof in sheets. I lay in the top bunk, watching the ceiling fan turn slowly overhead, stirring the heavy equatorial air like a thick goat curry. From my vantage point I could see through the open doorway, where something outside in the tropical gloom caught my eye. A figure clad in a bright yellow oilskin jacket and white canvas hat emerged from the emerald jungle, entered the hut, and shook the rain off. Picking the bottom bunk across from me, he dropped his small pack down and proceeded to open up a long cylindrical tube he had been carrying under his arm. I propped myself up on my elbow, curiously watching. From out of the tube he extracted some sort of white roll, which he proceeded to spread out onto his bed. From where I was these items appeared to be maps of some sort. I had never seen anything like them. Unable to contain my interest, I cleared my throat. "What are those things, if you don't mind me asking?" I cautiously enquired.

The man looked up at me with a start, obviously unaware of my presence. "You scared the shit outta me, man! Who are ya'll, the Cheshire cat?" he asked with a Texas drawl.

"Sorry - I didn't mean to startle you," I apologized. Sitting up, I swung my legs over the side of my bunk and jumped down onto the hard dirt floor. I looked the fellow over. Shoulder length grey hair hung from under his canvas sun hat. He sported a peppercorn beard. But what immediately attracted my attention were his eyes, which were an almost neon, aquamarine blue. "My name's Chris," I said, holding out my hand.

"Gatlin Mitchell," he replied, squeezing my hand with a long, brown paw. "These here are nautical charts," he said, nodding at the bed. "Me and a partner of mine have a sailboat out in the Seychelles and I came to Mombasa to buy these charts for the next part of our voyage."

I bent over and looked at the top map. *Gulf of Aden and the Arabian Sea* it said. "Interesting. So, what are you guys doing - sailing around the world or something?" I innocently asked.

"Yeah. Something like that," the Texan replied, looking up at me with those laughing iridescent eyes. "And what's your story? How did you end up out here, so far off the beaten track?"

"Oh, I'm just hanging out waiting to catch the mail boat from Mombasa to the Seychelles. It's not easy, as you probably know. There's only one a month and it's hard to book a passage."

He looked me over with the wisdom of a man twice my age. "Well, it's definitely worth the wait," he finally said.

"If there was ever a paradise on earth, then that's where it would be. If you ever do get out there you look us up, you hear? Name of the boat is *Hawcon*. Bout the only sailing boat anchored in Port Victoria. Can't miss us."

And that is how I met the raw-boned Texan Gatlin Mitchell. In the jigsaw puzzle that is one's life, there are key moments, innocuous incidents, off handed decisions, and seemingly fortuitous happenings which become important link-pins that tie the future together. From my present vantage point I can see now this chance meeting would become a key piece of the puzzle. I just didn't know it at the time.

Ah, the Seychelles! My romance with that place started two years earlier back in my hometown of Laguna Beach. It was a late night at my friend's pad smoking weed and drinking cheap white wine when I first heard about those mysterious islands. In those days, Laguna was full of interesting characters, and Snake was one. Snake rented a very strange room, a converted garage, which was somehow ten feet square and about twenty feet high. Every morning at first light he crossed Pacific Coast Highway to be the first person combing the beach. "You never know when you might find a Rembrandt washed up on shore," he explained. He once paid a guy three hundred bucks for an 'authentic' map of the Lost Dutchman Gold Mine, and then almost died fossicking through Arizona's arid Superstition Mountains in a futile search to find it. So, it was at Snake's place on this late night that the tall, bearded, blond-haired hippy tossed a dog-eared copy of National Geographic into my lap. "Once I strike it rich," he said, "this is the place I'm going to retire. Just kick back in a hammock under the swaying palms and be tended to by my nubile Creole harem." The article described a place lost in time; a tropical paradise of twenty-four lofty granite isles located a thousand miles off the East African Coast in the heart of the Indian Ocean, and with no airport could only be reached by the monthly mail boat from Mombasa, Kenya. The photos were breathtaking. High, cloud covered peaks, turquoise waters, coral-white beaches, colorfully clad smiling dark-skinned women, surf lashed reefs, Tradewinds and palm trees. My twenty-year-old brain was mesmerized.

"You might retire there one day, but when you do, you'll be meeting me there, 'cause I'm going!" I said as I leafed through the pages once more. I borrowed the magazine and looked at it every night for weeks. The Seychelles became my quest, my goal in life. Snake might talk about it, but I had made up my mind. "Show me, don't tell me!" is how Coach Stuetz, my Saddleback College football coach, used to put it. I would make sure to send Snake a postcard.

For several years I had supported myself by selling flowers from my own flower stand, which I set up on a vacant lot on the corner of Pacific Coast Highway and Bluebird Canyon Road, just a stone's throw from Snake's pad. An hour south of Laguna was the small coastal town of Encinitas, proudly proclaimed as "the Flower Capital of the World". Nearly every weekend I would make the early morning trek south in my old VW bus, visiting the many commercial flower growers there, where I would cheaply purchase second and third grade carnations, chrysanthemums, roses and other seasonal flowers. Upon returning home I would arrange the flowers in buckets of water, put them back in my van, and go set up my stand. CARNATIONS $1.00 A DOZEN, my hand-painted signs said. It wouldn't be long before cars would turn out of the steady flow of weekend traffic to purchase one of my fresh bouquets. Over the four years in high school and college that I ran my little business, I never lost money, nearly always doubling my investment every weekend. The holidays were always good earners, and so it was on Mother's Day in the spring of 1972 that I made my biggest haul, and not long afterwards made my getaway. I was twenty years old with a one-way ticket to London, cashed up, and off to see the world.

The rust streaked freighter *Nordvaer* pounded into the southeast Trades, and I was "spewin' me guts" as Terry, the Liverpudlian first mate would say. It had been a brutal three days. I couldn't eat, and my sleep was marred by bizarre nightmares. "If we ever reach land I'm going to stay there forever," were my thoughts as I battled through another seemingly endless night of seasickness in my small, stuffy cabin. The steward's knock came punctually at six a.m., bringing me my morning tea. As I went to the door, I could tell something was different. I didn't stagger; wasn't thrown violently about. I made my way to the wheelhouse where Captain Larsen, a heavyset Dane, stood steadfast next to the wheel. Through the wheelhouse windows appeared a vision of Homerian proportions. The sea was like a millpond, and as we steamed east "the rosy tinted hands of Dawn spread over a flawless wine dark sea into a brazen sky, brightening for the immortal gods and for mortal men, who plow the earth and perish," is how Homer might have described it. Off the starboard bow a dark shape slowly began to emerge beneath a mass of motionless pink clouds.

"Silhouette Island," the captain said. "You're in the Seychelles now."

As the bow of the old coaster relentlessly cleaved the mirror-like surface, the dark shadow slowly began to take shape. The towering cloud-wrapped mountains became defined. Colors morphed from violet to blue to a vivid green. Valleys and headlands, bays and coves and finally palm-fringed beaches became clear as our course took us over the north point of the island. The sun climbed into the eastern sky and the sea lightened into a turquoise blue. Silhouette dropped astern and the rugged outline of Mahé and her surrounding isles stretched out before us. By mid-morning the engines had slowed to a stop and we were moored to the large yellow quarantine buoy which lay outside the entrance to Port Victoria.

I stood in the stern of the small wooden Customs launch flying the red British ensign as we motored towards shore. Heavy grey clouds enveloped the high granite peaks towering before me, their slate grey outcroppings cascading rainwater as they pushed through the emerald green vegetation. A couple of freighters lay idly alongside the wharfs in front of us as the small boat cut through the mirror-like calm. The island of Mahé sits at three degrees south of the equator, and the oppressive heat and humidity was almost suffocating. It wasn't long before my shirt was soaked through with perspiration.

Stepping ashore, I wandered away from the concrete dock area into town. I was headed for Captain Tregarden's Guesthouse, which I only knew to be "up the hill somewhere." The town was busy, the narrow streets bustling. Colorfully clad black women sold tropical fruits from wooden stalls, haggling in their French Creole with islanders doing their mid-day shopping. Weathered, tin-roofed wooden buildings jumbled on top of each other, interspersed with mango and papaya trees, coconut palms and other rich fauna. I ducked into a gloomy shop run by a Chinaman selling everything under the sun to ask directions. Dodging rain-filled potholes, I climbed a narrow street up the hill, the grey-black clouds overhead threatening an immanent downpour. Rickety wooden shacks loomed out of the tropical foliage, the smell of cooking fires mixing with the moist, musky scents of the rich vegetation as the islanders went about their day-to-day business.

Climbing on I finally reached the guesthouse, a ramshackle six-room affair. Captain Tregarden, a heavyset Creole in his seventies with deep blue eyes, iron-grey hair and a rolling gait, showed me to my room. As I stood at my window, catching a glimpse of the sea through the trees far below, the rain came - the sound of a thousand drummers pounding on the tin roof overhead. I lay down on my narrow bed, hands behind my head, wondering what would happen next. The room wasn't cheap, and from what I had seen in town the price of food wasn't either. My money wouldn't last long at this rate. I'd have to find that guy and his boat, and quick. After a while the rain stopped and I headed back down the hill.

My enquiries around the port led me nowhere. A couple of people knew of *Hawcon*, but no one seemed to have any idea where she had gone. There were conflicting stories of the boat having sailed both for South Africa and for the Red Sea. Finally, I spoke to an English yachtsman who thought they had only left for a short trip to the islands and would be back. I walked back to the Captain's guesthouse that evening anxiously hoping the man was right. Later that night, as I lay on top of my sweat-soaked sheets amid the smoky scent of a burning mosquito coil, I found it odd that now I had finally reached my goal, I had no idea what I was going to do next. For whatever reason, this boat was important to me. I fell asleep wondering what tomorrow might bring.

After a couple of days of aimless wandering, I ran into Terry from the *Nordvaer* at the Pirates Arms, one of the few portside bars. As we chatted over a cold Tusker beer, I was given some hope. "I don't know if it's the boat you're looking for," Terry said encouragingly, "but I noticed a ketch motor in this afternoon just around sunset. They're moored stern-to out where the new harbor extensions are being done." As I walked back up the hill that night amidst the massive trees and foliage obscuring the simple dwellings from where the sounds of laughter and guitar music drifted, I hoped Terry was right. I couldn't afford to stay at the Captain's much longer. I was running out of options.

The following morning, I was up bright and early. It was a fine, clear day. I walked down the hill and made my way through town towards the eastern side of the harbor. There, moored on its own, lay a two-masted yacht. As I stood on the rocky shore wondering what to do next, a shirtless, skinny, curly haired fellow wearing plaid shorts appeared in the hatchway. Looking up, he spotted me standing on the shore.

"Hello!" I shouted. "Is Gatlin Mitchell aboard?"

After looking me over for a moment he turned and called down below. Moments later Gatlin emerged from the cabin, looked ashore and waved. He jumped into the small dinghy tied alongside and pulled himself along the stern rope tied to the rocks. I scrambled down the big granite boulders and stepped gingerly into the small plywood pram.

"How's it goin', Chris?" Gatlin asked with his Texas drawl. "I was wonderin' if you were goin' to make it."

"Well it took me a while. I've been here a couple of days," I said as I gingerly sat down. "I thought I might have missed you."

"Oh, we just went out to Cerf Island to clean the bottom," he said over his shoulder as he pulled us back out to the boat. Once alongside, we lifted ourselves up over the lifelines and I put my feet onto the solid teak decks of *Hawcon* for the first time. "Welcome aboard. This here's my partner Ross. How about a cup of tea?"

An hour or so later I was on my way back ashore to collect my gear and check out from Captain Tregarden's. I didn't know it then, but I had just stepped aboard the vessel that would become my home for the next twelve months.

2
Strange Days

"In this life you must scheme...or you must louster."
- Cornish adage

I know exactly where I was when I heard *Blonde on Blonde* for the first time. It was 1966, I was fifteen years old, in ninth grade, and was spending the night at a friend's place. His mom had just bought the album and let us listen to it. The kid also had a Playboy magazine. It was an eye-opening night. He lived in a trailer at Paradise Cove at the south end of Point Dume in Malibu. I was living on the Point at the time, and we were classmates at Malibu Park Junior High School. I don't recall much more about the night, except there wasn't much parental supervision and we could go to bed whenever wanted. Anyway, we sat around that night looking at Playboy and listening to Dylan's new record. I held the album in my young hands, looking at the blurred cover, seeing a guy with disheveled hair standing against a brownstone wall wearing a heavy overcoat and a black and white checkered scarf. Of course, I had heard his music on the radio before, but I didn't have a record player or own any albums, so the smell of a new album, the texture...everything about it was an excitingly new experience to me.

    I had listened to plenty of other records over the previous years, usually at some friend or the other's house. Early on it was mostly the Beach Boys, a bit of Elvis, then the Beatles. But this music was very different. These weren't catchy pop tunes. These songs had mysterious messages that painted pictures in my mind of Arabian drums and sad-eyed ladies and river boat captains and judges walking on stilts and getting stoned...whatever that meant. And the songs were long. One took up the whole side of one disk. Which was another thing. This was a double album - it had two records in it. It was the first of a kind, I think. My favorite song was "Visions of Johanna". It conquered my mind.

I walked home along the beach the next day, past the surf breaks of the Rock and the Gully, Middle Reef, the Point and Outer Reef. It was a sunny day, one of those special crisp Malibu mornings. I walked around the rocky point of Little Dume, and set out through the soft sand towards Big Dume. No one ever surfed it back then, although rumor had it a local named Kenny Lynn paddled out there once. Finding a path, I climbed to the top the cliff and crossed Cliffside Drive. We lived in a very funky place in those days, which sat on the corner. It took up the whole block, and there were corrals and horses. The house had been stables at one time, but had been converted into two...a...um ...don't know what you'd really call them. Dwellings I suppose. That land would be worth a fortune these days, I bet.

My best friend back then was Rick Murray. He lived around the corner and was the son of the famous sports writer Jim Murray, who wrote a column for the LA Times. Their house was ranch style too, but a bit more up-market than ours. We used to play one-on-one basketball in his driveway sometimes. His old man's office was separate from the house, and the backboard was on the garage not far away. For a man who wrote a funny column, he was certainly short tempered. He used to come out and yell at us and chase us off if we were making too much noise. I think he suffered from the gout, which might explain it. I went to a Dodger game with him and Rick once. Sat in the press box, met Vin Scully. We even went down into the locker room where I met Don Drysdale and Maury Wills. Heady stuff. The album Rick liked most was the Byrds, with David Crosby and Jim (later Roger) McGuinn which featured several Dylan songs, including the hit "Mr. Tambourine Man" and my personal favorite "Chimes of Freedom". Why do I mention all of this? You'll see…you'll see.

***

The Malibu ranch house was just one of many locations we lived at when I was a kid. We moved so many times I'd struggle now to count all the different places. More than a year in one spot was remarkable. This leads me to my old man, Ramon. He was certainly a unique individual who moved to the beat of his own personal drum. He used to proudly proclaim he was a man who never had a job, and as far as I know, he was right. Ray had struck it rich once, back in the early fifties in Salt Lake City. He and his father and his younger brother Ralph rode the crest of the burgeoning uranium wave. They had put together a penny stock company called Standard Uranium, leased huge tracts of uranium-laden land in southern Utah and Colorado, and flogged it Over-the-Counter out of New York. The stock went from two cents to a dollar overnight. And of course, they all had millions of shares. Ray bought a house on a few acres of land outside Salt Lake and didn't hold back remodeling it. We had underfloor heating, a swimming pool, a tennis court and an orchard. My parents went to Vancouver and bought a truckload of antique furniture. Ray and Ralph even owned a plane. I was five when the shit hit the fan. Some trading irregularities attracted the attention of the Securities and Exchange Commission, who stepped in and shut them down. I stood in the driveway one cold and cloudy afternoon with my little sister and brother holding my Mom's hand as we watched strange men go in and haul everything away. Ray loaded the five of us and all we could carry into our Chevy station wagon and headed south, over the border into Mexico.

My memories of Mexico start in Guaymas, where I saw the sea for the first time. We went sport fishing and I got seasick - a portent of the future - and caught a fish, a shimmering green one with a big square head which I know now was a Dorado or Mahi-Mahi. We drove on south along potholed roads through dusty villages where animals were herded through the streets to shady Guadalajara, pushing on until we finally reached Acapulco, playground of fifties jet-setters and movie stars. Of our driving experiences in Mexico, Ray would later relate, "I know what happened to Kamikaze pilots who made it through the war - they went to Mexico and became bus drivers!" He had firsthand experience with Kamikazes when he was a gunnery officer on an aircraft carrier in the Pacific during the war, where the gun emplacements were always the enemy's first targets. He must have had nerves of steel. He definitely had a sense of humor.

Ray was a wheeler dealer, an entrepreneur, a promoter, a penny-stock hustler, and yes - a schemer. He sailed close to the wind, and we were his crew. He made fast money and spent it quicker, had good ideas and lousy ones. Usually he made ends meet, sometimes he didn't, but somehow, we survived. From Acapulco we went to Mexico City, where we lived with a well-to-do business associate of Ray's. It wasn't the last time the five of us would invade someone else's household. At bullfights the seats are sold on location. The cheap seats are in the sun (sol), choice seats are in the shade (sombra). Who knows how, but somehow Ray got involved in raising money for a restaurant he called the *Sol y Sombra*. Great name, but like so many of his deals it didn't work out, and so after a year in Mexico we climbed back into the Chevy and headed north, trekking the thousand miles over dusty roads back across the border to Los Estados Unidos, finally rolling to a stop in Houston, Texas, where I started school. It would be my first of many.

Through all of this my mom, Jean, was a saint, a trooper, a faithful lieutenant and co-pilot, a loving mother, and a sad-eyed lady who never lost belief in her husband. She looked after her three kids, always making us feel safe and warm no matter how weird the situation became. And there were plenty of weird ones, believe me. My sister Joan was a year and a half younger than me, and my brother Rick five. It must have been so hard for my mom to keep the faith, but somehow, she did. Of course, Ray never ran out of confidence. We were always on the verge of striking it rich. "This deal's going to be bigger than IBM," he would say, or "soon we'll have more money than God!" And we always believed him.

And so began our late fifties sojourn across the Great Southwest. Like itinerants we went from city to city and apartment to motel, like the ancient Spanish conquistadors in search of the Seven Cities of Cibola - the lost cities of gold. From Houston we headed north until we caught Route 66, finally stopping in Tucson, Arizona, where we lived in a little poolside apartment. The telephone was Ray's main tool of choice. Everyone laughed when I did an imitation of my Dad on the phone. "I'm gonna make fifty thousand bucks on this Gylsonite deal!" I mimicked. Gylsonite, by the way, "is a bitumen-impregnated rock (asphaltite) mainly found in the Uintah Basin of Utah and Colorado," according to Wikipedia. The Gylsonite deal didn't work out, and so we moved on to Phoenix, another apartment and another school, and not long after to Scottsdale, where I began third grade. By this time I was a hardened newcomer, a kind of professional "new kid". I learned to be wary of the first boy to want to befriend you and to stand up for myself. For Joan it was different. Boys will grudgingly accept you if you can play football, but for girls I think it's tougher to break into closed circles. Especially if you live in a motel. This insecurity would play a huge part in the development of her psyche. She would never get on top of it.

Arizona in 1959 wasn't the place for Ray to make his next million, and so we packed up and lit out for the real land of milk and honey - California! And more specifically, the Mecca of all that epitomized the Great American Dream…LA. There is a photo imprinted in my mind's eye. It is a color photo, or perhaps more of a flickering short movie. It is a chilly but sunny February day, and our little family is standing at the end of the Santa Monica Pier where Route 66 runs into the Pacific Ocean. A light wind is drifting in off the sea, rustling my Mom's dyed blond hair. We are holding onto the railing, looking north towards the blue silhouette of Point Dume. There are a few surfers in the water, sitting on their long, balsa surfboards. Ray takes a deep breath of the pungent sea air, turns and looks over our heads towards the megalith that is LA and says, "This is it, kids. This is the place. One day we are going to own this town, you mark my words." And we didn't doubt him.

From a Wiltshire Boulevard motel, we invaded the home of an associate of Ray's with the probable assurance it would only be for a week or so. I think we camped out there for a couple of months. To say after a while things got a little testy around that Pasadena household would be an understatement.

As I said, Ray was a promoter, and he had a nose for deals. He knew how to meet people and raise money. As long as I knew him, he always had a few balls in the air. He took me to Burbank once to meet a guy who had invented a 3D movie camera which you could watch without glasses. Another deal he had going was a Hawaiian Punch-flavored wine. I'm sure there were lots more, every one of which was going to be the biggest thing since sliced bread. He was the world's biggest optimist, and his belief was infectious. Most of his deals showed great potential; many were well ahead of their time. Unfortunately, his home run shots usually fell just short of the fence and turned into routine outs.

The early sixties were the formative years of Ray's biggest deal - Thermal Dynamics. And to give him credit, he did take it to the brink of success. Through his links with his brother Ralph in Salt Lake City, Ray took an invention that made charcoal out of coal and turned it into a patented industrial process that turned high-Sulphur coal into clean burning char while recovering most of the valuable coal tar. The "Bowman Process" (U.S. Patent 3,475,279) was going to be the answer to all of the world's energy needs. "There's enough coal in Utah alone to run the U.S. for the next thousand years!" he would say. He started calling himself "Big Daddy Coal Bucks". In 1963, oil was in abundant supply. But pollution was a major problem in the big cities where coal was burned to generate electricity, and acid rain was a destructive by-product. These poisons would be removed from the atmosphere using the Thermal Dynamics process. Ray was going to revolutionize power generation. "For every ton of coal we pass through the retort we get a barrel of oil!" he would say. "Out of the other end we get clean, pure char, or carbon, and the only by-products are the natural gasses that fill the retort, which we siphon off to run the process, and Sulphur, which we pile outside. It's like a god-damned perpetual motion machine! It's like having a license to print money!"

    Assisted by a genius chemical engineer by the name of Clyde Berg, who worked for Union Oil, Ray took the Bowman Process to within a hair's-breadth of fruition. By this time, we had moved into a sprawling house atop Hasting's Ranch in Pasadena. The Angeles National Forest started in our back yard. You couldn't get any higher up the hill. At night the zillions of twinkling lights of LA spread out below us. On a clear day we could see Catalina Island. They took my Mom's antiques out of storage. We even had a player piano. You had no trouble figuring out which house was ours, because my Dad rented a spray gun and compressor and painted it pink, much to our neighbor's consternation.

Ray went out and raised money. Using the old Standard Uranium template, he and his brother put together a shell company, in which they naturally held millions of shares. They went to see all of the big construction companies like Ralf Parsons and Lummis. They made deals with giant power consortiums like Consolidated Edison in Chicago to take their product. In the small town of Helper, Utah, they leased a disused coal mine and built a small-scale prototype that could process a few tons a day. It worked a treat. The char was devoid of Sulphur, the oil from the retort dripped down and filled the barrels below, just like it was supposed to, and there was so much natural gas being produced "we've got to flare the son-of-a-bitch", Ray would say. It wouldn't be long before several fifty-thousand-tons-a-day plants would be built across the USA. He'd done it! We'd made it! Ray didn't hold back. He acquired two flashy cars, bought us all new clothes and held big parties. In a matter of a few short years we were exactly where he predicted, sitting right on top of the City of Angels. "When Thermal goes" was a mantra we heard almost daily. "When Thermal goes, I might buy us an island. How does Australia sound?"

When Thermal goes…

And then, on the brink of taking the company public, disaster struck. Ralph had pulled some dodgy investors into the deal from Canada. They had their own company, and they made a take-over bid. There was a proxy fight. Shareholders had to decide whether to stay with Thermal Dynamics and go down the legitimate road - not making the same mistakes as Standard Uranium - or go with the Canadians. The Canadians won the vote by a whisker, promptly ran the stock up on the Toronto Exchange, dumped it for as much as they could get, and when they were busted ran for the hills. All for a quick buck. The plant in Helper was dismantled and dumped in Ralph's front yard. It didn't take long for the tsunami to hit us in our Pasadena palace. The telephone was cut off first, then the electricity, and finally the water. We couldn't even flush the toilets. I remember seeing my Dad climb the electricity pole to see if he could turn the power back on. And then the moving vans turned up and the antiques were put back in storage. It would be a long time before they would see the light of day again. Our cars were repossessed, and so Ray bought an old clunker, a red Ford station wagon he nicknamed the "Red Dragon". We packed it up and moved into a motel in nearby Sierra Madre so that we could finish our year in school. The dream was shattered, yet we had to move on. This was LA, after all. There was no sympathy for losers on those mean sidewalks. "Your picture in yesterday's newspaper and a dime will get you a cup of coffee anywhere," is what Ray used say.

Pasadena had given our family the sense of normalcy. We went to the same school for three years. I played little league baseball. We became part of the neighborhood, part of a community. The first sign of a storm on the horizon was my parents' heavy drinking. When Ray drank scotch, he turned into a red-faced beast. There were arguments and fights, screaming and yelling. As a twelve-year-old kid I had no idea what was going on. And then the

C'MON AL SETTLE DOWN—Catcher Chris Bowman calls a conference with pitcher Alan Armour at crucial moment in Little League game at Sierra Madre. Independent

rug was pulled out from under us and we were living in a motel. It would have been in July of 1964 when we made our next move. I know because my grandparents saved a photo of me off the front of the sports page of the local Independent Star-News dated July 5, 1964. I'm in my last year of Little League in my catcher's gear, at the mound and giving my pitcher some sound twelve-year-old advice.

From Pasadena, Ray decided to head for the coast. It is hard to know how he made the connection, but the next thing we knew we were in Santa Monica, just south of the pier, and moving into a couple of rooms at the old Monica Hotel. Built on the edge of the Pacific Ocean, this Art Deco monstrosity loomed over the famous "Muscle Beach", where oily weight lifters and gymnasts pumped iron and worked out on the beach just outside our doorstep. The beachside regulars were muscle-bound, suntanned and weird. A bald ex-wrestler with a big waxed moustache named Honest John rented beach chairs and surf mats and that summer we were his best customers. For six weeks we lived the ultimate California Dream. We spent every day in the surf, riding our mats. I can still smell the corndogs and French fries and Coppertone and sea air.

As kids we had the run of this rag-eared relic of the Roaring Twenties. We found secret passageways, an old ballroom with balconies and rotating panels leading to hidden rooms, and an indoor swimming pool. And the Monica's occupants were equally as strange. Most were regulars at its shady cocktail lounge. Alcoholic stuntmen, part-time actors and extras, two-bit script writers, and ex-cops became drinking companions of my parents. Those were innocent times, free from paranoia. The three of us kids ran out on to the beach in the morning and came back when we were hungry.

We spent six weeks or so there, living through the heart of summer. But all good things must come to an end sometime. The new school year was just around the corner.

We packed up the Red Dragon and wound our way north along Pacific Coast Highway to Malibu, where we settled into a small motel on the edge of Point Dume. For the next three years we would make that area our home. Ray's business fortunes fluctuated from high and hopeful to near rock-bottom, and we shifted several times until we finally settled into the horse stables across from Big Dume. Those years were tough, but they were good. Rick and I learned how to surf at the pristine break at Little Dume. It was fresh, clean country living. There was always wholesome food on the table, even though we were tip-toeing on the thin razor's edge of survival.

Eventually living so far from the action caught up with us, and the landlord chased us from his ranch. We moved into yet another motel and were eating our breakfast at the Malibu Inn before school. Ray had had enough of Malibu, so we hit the road again, finally settling south of Los Angeles in the seaside village of Laguna Beach. I was in the middle of ninth grade, and went from being student body Vice President of Malibu Park Junior High to just a new kid at Laguna Beach High School. It was a big step for me and my little brother, but for my sister it would prove to be life-changing.

3
The Most Far-out Place in the Universe

"Laguna Beach, man...it's the most far-out place in the Universe!"
       - Raisin Head, Laguna acid freak

On July 29, 1966 Bob Dylan crashed his Triumph T-100 motorcycle on a winding Woodstock road, which laid him up and took him out of the public eye for several years. Dylan wouldn't come out with anything new for a while, but the year of '66 was awash with ground-breaking sounds, and this burst of awakening creativity was driving a new generation in directions that were inconceivable even a year earlier. Musical limits were being pushed, and so were cultural boundaries. The growing war in Vietnam represented all that was wrong with the conventional teachings of previous generations. We didn't know it then, but in December of 1966 the fuse had been lit, and in a few short months the world would shake from the explosion.

The flowering of this revolution didn't happen everywhere on the planet at the same instant, but slowly began to manifest itself in different places and in slightly different ways. London was one, Greenwich Village another. It had well and truly taken hold in Berkley and San Francisco. Little did we know as we desperately drove south in the Red Dragon that we were about to jump right into the maelstrom and encamp ourselves smack-dab in the middle of one of these counter-cultural hotspots. Because although not as famous, and perhaps not on as grand a scale, the quaint 1930's artist colony of Laguna Beach was on the verge of becoming the

Height-Ashbury of the south. This was dramatically brought home on my very first day of school, when the whole of the student body went out on strike with a "sit-in" protesting dress code regulations and hair cut standards. Welcome to Laguna High.

    Within a few days Ray had convinced a realtor to rent us a house in the exclusive gated community of Emerald Bay. It was wintertime and rentals were cheap. It didn't take me long to make friends. Sport was always an easy way in for me. There was a park with a basketball court, and within a week or so I had made a handful of new friends. For my sister it was a different story. Teenage girls need to fit in. She was very attractive, had a great figure, and looked older than her thirteen years. Appearance meant everything to Joanie, and that also included our home life. Her new friends all had money, but we lived in a rental and drove a wreck of a car. No one knew our past, but the last thing she needed was any kind of embarrassment. It wasn't long before the boys started to show an interest - usually older ones who had their own cars. My Dad wasn't impressed. There were plenty of arguments and slamming of doors. And this was just the beginning.

Our stint in Emerald Bay didn't last long; we were out before the jacked-up summer rental rates kicked in. Soon we were checking into another motel. One upside Laguna had was there were plenty of motels. Malibu had only about six, and we were well acquainted with all of them. Our tenure at most of these establishments usually ended in robust discussions concerning the bill, and woe be it to the poor manager who had the courage of knocking on our door after Ray had a few stiff scotches under his belt. We spent most of the summer of '67 at a motel not far from the epicenter of Laguna Hippiedom. The "Summer of Love" was raging up in the Height, and we had our own version.

Just after the Pacific Coast Highway topped the hill south of the old Hotel Laguna, it descended into a hollow before climbing up to the traffic lights at Thalia Street. This quarter of a mile was an area the locals dubbed "Hip Dip". On any given summer's night, the sidewalks would be packed with hippies flaunting all of the typical gear - long hair (real and wigs), tie-dye shirts, beads, headbands, bandanas, bangles, capes, bell-bottoms, buckskin jackets and other American Indian gear. What spawned this influx of young searchers was a "head shop" called Mystic Arts World. It was owned and operated by a mysterious spiritual organization called The Brotherhood of Eternal Love. The high-priest and guru was Timothy Leary, whose goal in those heady years was to spread love, peace and happiness to an "uptight" world. This alternative book store and meditation temple became a meeting place for local hippies and artists. It also became the headquarters of one of the biggest suppliers of marijuana, hashish and LSD in all of the USA.

And it was into this smoky caldron my sister wandered. I wasn't interested. I was looking forward to my first year of varsity football. None of my friends were hippies; we were surfers and played beach volleyball. If I was ever offered a joint, I turned it down. I would never have even contemplated dropping acid. But Joanie was the perfect fit for the sixties flower child - young, pretty, disillusioned with home life and easily led. The first night she turned up with a long-haired boyfriend - a blond surfer named Gly Cooper - Ramon exploded and sent him running down the motel steps. "You bring another long-haired son-of-a-bitch home like that and I'll beat his ass down the street with barbed wire!" he thundered. And she never did.

To most people, all of these shenanigans must seem unreal, but to be truthful we were so used to it that to us so-called "normal" lives seemed weird. To Ray, living in a suburban house with a mortgage and going to work at the same job every day was tantamount to being in jail, and we were brought up believing this as gospel. Because when you were around Ray, you had no choice but to be caught up in his aura. His personality was all-encompassing. He just had a way, a magnetism that drew you in. My friends loved him - his jokes, his quick wit, his view of life. Ray had a good heart, a gift of the gab, and strong opinions on everything, which he had no problem changing if the situation called for it. He was an extrovert, and encouraged his kids to follow in his footsteps. Money was like water to Ray; there was an endless supply out there and you just had to know how to open the tap. Saving or putting away for a rainy day did not compute. When he had it, he spent it, and when it was gone, he would just go out and find more. I don't know how he did it, but there was always another deal around the corner and he knew how to locate it. Ramon's gravitational pull was impossible to resist, like being sucked into a quasar. And somehow my mother stayed with him and put up with it all.

A big part of my life in those days was sport, and especially football. The Laguna Beach "Artists" (yes...we even had a pallet and paint brush logo on our helmets!) had a proud tradition, and I played three years of varsity football there. The season of my junior year was especially memorable because we were undefeated. I went on to play two seasons at Saddleback College, where I developed friendships that have lasted a lifetime. In fact, I can actually credit the sport for saving my life, but that is further on down the track.

Another huge influence on my youthful view of the world was the mind-blowing new music that seemed to be appearing almost daily. Although I steered clear of the hippie scene, I couldn't help but get into the revolutionary sounds of those times. One of my first friends to get a car was a guy named Pierre. He had a maroon Chevy Corvair, and we used to cruise around in it everywhere. The car had an eight-track car stereo, and Pierre had three tapes... *the Best of Mose Allison, Fresh Cream*, and *the Doors*. I don't know how many times we listened to those tapes. It wouldn't be long before I bought my own stereo, and became a weekly visitor to Sound Spectrum...probably one of the coolest record stores on earth. Jimmy Otto looked everything like Jerry Garcia of the Grateful Dead, and his store always had the latest in underground music. I used to buy a record a week, and at $2.99 they were a pretty good deal. Sometimes I would simply buy an album because of the cover. One I recall was a high-contrast black and white picture of a Zeppelin crashing and burning. It was an amazing image. The music wasn't bad, either.

1969 was the summer of Woodstock and men walking on the moon. I don't recall which deal Ray had cooking back then, but it was paying off because we had moved into a nice new condo in South Laguna in a complex called Blue Lagoon. As I mentioned before, when Ray had money in his pocket, he spent it, and the summer of '69 was no exception. His attorney at the time owned an apartment on the beach on the big island of Hawaii just outside of Kailua-Kona, and he told us we were welcome to use it for the summer. So, we packed our surfboards and got ready to go. Joanie, however, was torn between a Hawaiian summer and going on a school-sponsored excursion to Europe. She played it cool, I'll give her that. One minute she was coming with us, and the next she wanted go to Europe. Finally, she made up her mind to join Dr. Colomoro, our school's ancient philosophy teacher, and the dozen or so other students on the culturally enriching trip to the United Kingdom, France and Italy. So off we went in different directions. Little did we know the surprise Joan had in store for us all.

It was a magical time in Hawaii; surfing and skin diving and cliff jumping and drinking Primo beer with our Hawaiian friends on the beach at night. The Kona Coast was sparsely populated, had only one or two hotels, and had a perfect climate. Kailua was a small village where everyone knew everyone. My best friend from the Malibu days was Ben Burkhalter, and he came with us for the summer. Ben would play a major part in this story down the track, by the way, but there was no way we knew it then.

A month later, Ray had to return to the mainland on business. Back in Laguna he went to the bank, where the first thing the manager asked was, "Have they found your daughter yet, Mr. Bowman?"

"Excuse me?" he responded. "What the hell are you talking about?"

"You haven't heard the news? Oh dear…"

It turned out my sweet little sister pulled a fast one on everyone. After only two days in London, she ran away from the tour. Interpol was called in along with the British police to try and track her down. Dr Colomoro, the chaperone, was completely distraught. The tour was wrecked and no one could locate us to tell us the news. Ray stormed out of the bank and straight into The Whitehouse, a local watering hole, and started hammering down scotch on-the-rocks. As he parked his car at the condo a few hours later, Mike Dearraux, our next-door neighbor, wandered out in his monogrammed bathrobe and casually inquired, "Aloha Mr. Bowman…how was Hawaii?"

"Aloha my ass you cocksucker!" was Ray's famous response.

And so, while we were having the time of our lives in the islands, my old man was on a Scotch-fueled bender at home. My mom was completely shattered when she found out. She had put up with so much over the years, and this was just another burden she would have to bare. It would be six months before we received any news from Joan - a letter sent to us through an intermediary in Milwaukie - and by then my mom was a chain-smoking wreck. She was in India, the letter said, and she was fine. Everything was my parent's fault because they didn't understand or love her, but now she was with someone who did. All she wanted was for us to get Interpol off her back and leave her to live her own life. Joanie was fifteen at the time, and would be gone for over two years. Her boyfriend was twenty, and a member of the Laguna Brotherhood. It would be years before we heard the real story, about how they drove to Afghanistan, lived with a prince and warlord, and began smuggling hashish back to Laguna. But that is another tale…

It was around this time I started selling flowers. This would provide me with my own income, and eventually a means to make my escape from what I had finally begun to see was madness. There would be more moves, more motels, more late-night runners, debt collectors and repo-men before it would happen. I moved out, lived on my own, and saved my pennies. And when the time was right, I made my move and flew the coop. Bob Dylan would've said, "Don't look back". And I didn't.

4
The Straights of Bab-el-Mandab and Other Tales

"Now that bird is maybe two hundred years old, Hawkins, they lives forever mostly, and if anyone's seen more wickedness it must be the Devil himself. She's sailed with England, the great Cap'n England the pirate. She's been at Madagascar and at Malabar and Surinam and Portobello. She was at the fishing up of the wrecked plate ships. It was there she learned 'Pieces of eight!', and little wonder…three hundred and fifty thousand of 'em Hawkins! She was at the boarding of the Viceroy of the Indies out of Goa she was, and to look at her you'd think she was just a baby. But you smelt powder, didn't you Cap'n Flint?"
- Long John Silver

As a kid, *Treasure Island* was my favorite book. Robert Rodgers, my grandfather, hailed from Kirkaldy in Scotland, a small town on the Firth of Forth. There were many summers when we would drive up from California and visit my grandparents in their old Victorian house in the leafy suburbs of Salt Lake City. There was a beautiful antique clock on the wall with a painting of a clipper ship under full sail on it, and my grandfather wound it at the same time every day. I used to wish I was sailing aboard that ship. In the basement was a workshop where he repaired antique furniture for people as a hobby. Amongst the scent of varnishes and shellacs and wood shavings we built pirate cutlasses and crutches and small wooden boats and painted them and rigged them for sail. I always wanted to go to the Caribbean, and could picture myself bounding down the main into a golden sunset towards tropical isles, much like Gardner McKay did on his schooner *Tiki* in the famous TV show *Adventures in Paradise*. My grandfather and I used to always chat about building a real boat together one day. Years later my Grandma Louise showed me a letter I had written to him when I was ten. I'd drawn a picture of the boat we were going to build. It was a schooner. Somehow I must have known something, even back then. I had never had the chance to go sailing, though. Until I reached the Seychelles.

It didn't take me long to settle into life aboard *Hawcon*. I didn't know much about boats, but even I could tell she was a sturdy vessel. Built on the Thames from solid teak for a British yachtsman in the 1930's, she was forty-two feet long, could accommodate six people, had a large galley, comfortable main saloon, and with her polished teak interior and brass fittings exuded the warmth and character of a proper British yacht. "She ain't no racin' boat, but she will get you where you want to go," is how Gatlin put it.

I wasn't on board much more than a week when the question was put to me. "As you know, we're getting ready to sail north, and we need a crew," Ross said. "It takes three people minimum to sail the ol' girl. An Aussie backpacker sailed with us from Penang, but she jumped ship as soon as we arrived here, so we're looking for crew. What do you think? Are you interested?"

Crossroads. Forks in the road. Decisions. Do I stay or do I go? The question didn't surprise me - there had been hints over the previous few days. But now that it was official, I had to do some soul searching. Did I really come half-way round the world to simply join a boat and leave? How important were the Seychelles to me? Once I left, I knew it would be a long time before I returned. But when would I get another chance like this? It was a heavy decision. I thought about it overnight; by breakfast I'd made up my mind. "Where do I sign the Ship's

Articles, shipmates?" I asked. It was official. I was crew aboard *Hawcon*.

In the couple of weeks before our departure we worked on the boat preparing it for our upcoming voyage. One morning we woke up to find a new neighbor tied up close bye. It didn't take us long to meet Bob Taylor and his crew aboard the yacht *Freedom*. Bob hailed from Newport Beach in California, had sailed his boat through the South Pacific to Australia, and from there on to India. As the years passed, I began to hear tales from other sailors concerning this outlaw renegade. I won't go into the details because that would make a book all on its own. Taylor would weave his way in and out of my own story over the years as he continued to ply the oceans of the world, the last time at a crucial moment which helped avert imminent disaster. That would be many years and a couple of oceans away. Suffice it to say Bob Taylor and I first crossed paths in the Seychelles, and we'll leave it at that.

On the tenth of March, 1973 we watched Bird Island, the northernmost of the Seychelles group, slowly slip into the sea astern. And I was as sick as the proverbial dog. This was the season of the north-east monsoon, and we were pounding straight into it, seemingly going in the opposite direction of our first intended landfall, which was the Horn of Africa close to fifteen hundred miles away. Ross was the navigator, and in order for us to get a good angle on the wind (or lay line) we needed to sail in an easterly direction for three days. And for those three days I couldn't keep anything down, not even water. I was spewing green bile every fifteen minutes. I received no sympathy from my shipmates either. I still had to stand my watches, which were four hours on and eight off. And they were murder.

Eventually the time came for us to make our turn north. We came about onto the starboard tack, and the transformation was almost immediate. As we moved away from the equator the weather moderated, and as if by magic my seasickness disappeared. Once we set our new course and trimmed the sails, we found we didn't even have to steer. We tied off the helm and *Hawcon* virtually sailed herself. Every morning prior to sunrise and every evening just after sunset Ross would come on deck with his sextant and "shoot" his stars; the readings from which he could, through some sort of alchemy, transcribe to our position on the chart. The stars were his guides, and they went by mysterious names like Arcturus, Betelgeuse, Aldebaran, Pollux, Regulas, Sirius and Rigel, to name a few. I found the process fascinating.

The so-called Horn of Africa, the easternmost point of the African continent, appeared on the horizon off our port bow on the morning of our fifteenth day at sea - exactly when it was supposed to. As the day wore on and we sailed closer, details began to emerge. It was a rugged, forlorn, desolate spot. Not the sort of place one would care to take a holiday. That evening the sun set red into the dust and shimmering heat over Africa as we left the Indian Ocean in our wake astern.

The Gulf of Aden is a rectangular bit of water roughly two hundred miles wide by five hundred miles long. It is bordered by the Arabian Sea to the east, Yemen to the north and Somalia to the south. As we slipped past Africa and entered the gulf our course changed, and as it did our pleasant existence of the previous two weeks was shattered. Our destination was the entrance to the Red Sea, which lay at the northwest end. The sea conditions, which had been so ideal, now became choppy and confused. The boat broached and rolled in the uneven swell; the sails and booms slatted and banged about disconcertingly. Worst of all, my "mal de mer" returned, and I was back to my fifteen-minute puking schedule.

On we sailed, and the further west we went the stronger the wind became. The morning of our fifth day in the Gulf of

Aden broke sunny and clear with a gale blowing straight up our backside. We had our hands full with only the tiny storm jib flying. The Straights of Bab-el-Mandab are like something out of a science fiction movie. Barely thirty miles across, they form a bottleneck where the Red Sea and the Gulf of Aden meet. Desolate, remote, and skirted by high rocky cliffs, the Arabic translation is the "Gate of Tears", which is a fairly accurate description. The wind was now blowing well over fifty knots, and the current was flowing like a river behind us. It was as close to sailing a twenty-ton yacht down rapids as you could get. The old girl had probably never moved so fast. We flew past Perim Island, which sits near the straights center, and reached the Hanish Islands eighty miles away well before sunset. The further we moved away from the Straights the calmer it became, until soon we ran out of wind completely and were motoring over a flat calm sea. Finally, after twenty-four days and close to two thousand four hundred miles of ocean, we anchored off the dusty port city of Massawa, which in those days was still part of Ethiopia.

    Not a bad introduction to sailing. There had been some good days, and there had been trying days when my spirit was severely tested. We didn't know it at the time, but the worst was yet to come.

5
Stars, Planets and Magic Castles

Astrology: the divination of the supposed influences of the stars and planets on human affairs and terrestrial events by their positions and aspects.
- Webster's New World Dictionary

I'm no expert on the subject of astrology, but I find it interesting. As I understand it, as the celestial bodies such as the sun, moon, planets and stars skip along on their merry way through the Universe, their relationship to each other as it corresponds to their observed location from earth at a precise moment in time has a profound effect on human affairs. It is known to have been studied as far back as the second millennium BCE, and has been called "the language of the heavens speaking to learned men." I doubt the greatest astrologer of all time could have predicted how Bob Dylan's star-studded orbit and mine would ever become intertwined, but somehow, they did. As I sat aboard an old teak ketch anchored in the stinkingly hot, arid Red Sea backwater of Massawa, Ethiopia, Bob's star was reaching new heights with the release of one of his greatest songs: 'Knockin' on Heaven's Door'. We were still a number of years away from crossing paths, but our trajectories were inexorably locked on to a collision course nevertheless.

My dad used to tell a joke. "Once there was a guy standing on a street corner hitting himself in the head with a hammer. When asked why he was doing it, he replied, 'because it feels so good when I stop!'" That pretty much describes the feeling we had on those first days in Massawa. As much as we were enjoying the tranquility, the fact remained that we had to move on. We expected headwinds in the northern portion of the Red Sea, and the longer we tarried the worse they would get. So, after stocking up with fuel, water and whatever provisions we could find we headed up the road. We motored out of Massawa on a calm, sunny morning. Sailing the Red Sea is not for the faint hearted. Treacherous reefs reached out from each shore, where dhow-sailing pirates were said to skulk in secluded anchorages. There were few ports to head for in case of emergency. Most of all, there was the nagging thought in the back of our minds that turning back was not an option. Where do you run to? The other end of Africa and the Cape of Good Hope? It was eleven hundred miles from Massawa to Eilat, Israel, our next port of call, and the equation was simple. We had no other choice but to get there.

An astute student of geography might ask why we were bound for Eilat, and not the Suez Canal. The reason was the Canal was blocked by ships sunk during the Six Day War of 1967, and was yet to be reopened. While in the Seychelles the boys had heard through the sailing grapevine it was possible to bypass the canal by trucking the boat across Israel, so the route north was chosen over the hard slog around southern Africa. We would cross that "land bridge" when we came to it. First, we had to get to Eilat.

The morning of our second day out of Massawa the sun rose into a dirty, ominous sky. Not long afterwards the weather we had been anticipating stampeded down upon us like a herd of wild beasts. The sea rose with the wind, and soon we were slamming into large cresting waves, the decks awash with breaking white-water. There was no chance of *Hawcon* making any headway against this fresh gale with the sails alone, so the engine was turned on, and under a double reefed mainsail we began to motor-sail against it. It was nine hundred miles from Massawa to the entrance to the Gulf of Aqaba, and we pounded and thrashed and clawed every inch of the way.

Slowly, but surely, we made progress until on our twelfth day we reached the Straights of Tirane, our off-ramp from the Red Sea. We entered the Gulf of Aqaba, with Eilat only ninety miles away. We had made it! In the afternoon Ross popped open a bottle of Champagne, which proved to be a little premature. Not long afterwards we were approached by a heavily armed Israeli gunboat. As it drove circles around us Ross stood on the foredeck waving the American flag. The helmeted gunners aiming their menacing weapons at us were deadly serious, but finally, after their third pass, the vessel turned away and left us alone. As it receded towards the high, barren mountains of the Sinai we heard a horrible sound. With a sputter and a cough, the engine died. We were out of fuel.

The Gulf of Aqaba is a narrow finger of water that divides the Sinai Peninsula to the north from the Arabian Peninsula to the south. High, rugged mountains skirt each coast, and the wind, which if anything had grown only stronger, now funneled down the gulf against us, threatening to blow us right back out to where we came from. With our storm sails up we began to tack into it. The gulf was barely twenty miles across at its widest point, and as we slowly reached from shore to shore, we visually noted our progress in landmarks which didn't seem to move. There is an old yachting adage: "Gentlemen don't sail to windward", and *Hawcon* had surely been built with that in mind, because it took us six days to cover ninety miles. At long last, after eighteen horrible days at sea, we reached Eilat. Never did the punchline of Ray's old joke ring truer. It feels so good when you stop.

Ross returned to the boat having done his official duty of clearing us in through customs and immigration. The authorities were exceedingly helpful and friendly. As rare as it was for a yacht to clear into Eilat, it just so happened one had arrived a week before us, and it was now on the dock awaiting transport to the Mediterranean. Ross had wandered over to meet the captain.

"What a character!" said Ross. "The name of the boat is *Magic Castle,* home port Hollywood, California, and the owner is a magician. It's a big motor yacht, and this guy travels around the world doing magic shows. There are just three of them aboard - he, his Singaporean wife and a little Chinaman. Wait until you meet him! I told him what we want to do and he has already got it all worked out. Trucking company, permits, cranes, the works. I said we'd have some breakfast and then come in and have a chat with him."

And that is how we met John Calvert. His yacht was blocked up on the main wharf. The day was beginning to warm up, and we found him in the shade under his vessel giving orders to Charley, his Chinese crew. John was tall and lean and fit. He wore a white boiler suit and captain's hat, and even though he was in work mode he looked dapper and distinguished. His mirthful eyes were crystal blue, and he sported a pencil-thin moustache over a perfect, flashing white smile. John Calvert was a throwback to a bygone era, and once you met him you came under his spell. We shook hands and were hypnotized.

John showed us around the sixty-foot *Magic Castle*, which he had built in Singapore entirely of teak to the highest of standards. He moved quickly and talked fast. "I've been doing magic my whole life. In the thirties I went to Hollywood and starred in several movies. Have you ever heard of "The Falcon" detective series? I played the part of Michael 'the Falcon' Watling. Big movies back in those days."

He showed us a black and white photo of himself escaping from a strait jacket whilst dangling from the end of a crane. In the main salon there was an electric organ, and he sat down and played us a quick tune. "I've made a living doing many things in my life," he told us. "Before I got into the movies, I was a stunt man. I worked on tuna boats. I sold used cars; I traveled the world with my own circus. By the way, if you need a hand taking your masts down, I'm your man. I've put big tops up and down so many times I couldn't count 'em all."

From Singapore he had worked his way through India, the Persian Gulf, and Saudi Arabia, doing magic shows in every port he came to. The previous night he had done a show in Eilat. "You see this gold Rolex? A prince from the Arab Emirates gave it to me. All and all, the trip has been quite good, although the last leg in the Red Sea was a bit tough."

John then got down to business. He said if we would give him a hand painting the antifouling onto the bottom of his boat, he would in turn organize getting us across Israel to the Mediterranean. The deal was struck. The next day we turned up for work and he got us straight into scraping and sanding. A sixty-foot power boat has a lot of surface area, and it didn't take us long to figure out that we might have drawn the short end of the stick. As for John, he was a whirling dervish of a man. He had boundless energy, and seemed to be everywhere at once. After three days of working on his boat, John lived up to his end of the bargain. He came aboard and helped us lower the masts before arranging for the harbor crane to haul us out and place us on a low-loader. After only a few days in Israel, we were ready to set off for the Med.

Friday is the day of the Sabbath in Israel, and that was the day the two boats were to travel as the roads were mainly clear. Shifting boats from one coast to the other was a matter of routine in Israel since their coastal patrol craft were designed to be moved from one side of the country to the next within hours. Early on Friday morning our small convoy drove out of Eilat. We drove past the Dead Sea, where of course we had to stop to take photos. At mid-day we stopped in the town of Ber-Sheba for lunch.

The restaurant was crowded and noisy, and no one paid much attention to us as we entered; that is until John walked in with the ship's cat on a leash - a fully grown cheetah he had acquired in the African port of Djibouti! As we sat down at our table, the place became silent. Several people left. The waiter came and took our orders. "And could I also have a whole chicken, please," John finished. "Don't cook it…bring it raw. It's for the cat." The waiter returned a few minutes later to say they only had frozen ones. "That's okay. Bring it anyway," John replied. The waiter brought the chicken. John led the cheetah to a corner and gave the frozen chicken to her, whereupon she proceeded to lie down and gnaw on it enthusiastically. There was an immediate scraping of chairs as the lunchtime crowd made quickly for the exits.

"It seems everyone needs to be somewhere else all of a sudden," John chuckled.

The Port Captain of the Mediterranean port of Ashdod was a very friendly fellow. Two foreign yachts travelling across the desert were obviously a rarity in his port, so he treated us as honored guests. *Hawcon* needed a lot of maintenance, so we were given an area on the hard where we could work on the boat. *Magic Castle* was put straight into the water, and a few days later motored off, heading for 'the Lebanon' as John called it. "Our show should do well there, I think. The people around here could do with a little magic," he said, flashing his trademark smile.

This was the last I ever saw or heard of John Calvert and his magic boat until I tracked him down with the help of a new kind of magic - the internet.

After two weeks of sanding and scraping and painting and varnishing, *Hawcon* was lifted into the Mediterranean Sea with a port crane. The harbormaster didn't charge us a shekel. Not for the crane lifts, not for the time on the hard, not for the gallons of paint he gave us, not even for the Arab shipwright he sent over to do some caulking. We sailed from Ashdod with a good feeling in our hearts. We had met some great people in Israel.

      Ross set a course for Paphos, located on the southwest tip of the island of Cyprus, which lay two hundred and fifty miles away to the northwest. We spent a week hanging out in that beautiful port surrounded by Homerian spirits, Roman ruins, biblical chapels and Ottoman forts before heading off for the Greek island of Rhodos. A light breeze filled our sails, the sea was calm and blue, and the high green island faded away astern. Overnight the wind grew in strength and soon we found ourselves crashing into yet another gale, this time the fickle wind known to the Greeks as the "Meltemi", which rears her ugly head through the Aegean Islands anytime between May and October. On the morning of the third day out we fought our way through the same harbor entrance where thousands of years earlier stood one of the Seven Wonders of the World, the Colossus of Rhodos. Hundreds of yachts lay moored in the calm amphitheater of a harbor. We anchored and backed in stern first to the logjam of sailboats of every size and description, finally making fast three-deep to the busy quay. It was the beginning of summer, and I didn't know it yet, but I was in for quite a ride.

6
Odesseyan Summer

*"Who are you strangers? Where are you sailing from,
and where to, down the highways of sea water?
Have you some business here? Or are you, now,
reckless wanderers of the sea, like those Corsairs
who risk their lives to prey on other men?"*
- Homer, *The Odyssey*, translated by E.V. Rieu

It had been a year since I left Laguna, and I'd covered a bit of ground. I had hitchhiked around England, ridden a bicycle through Wales, lived in a fifteenth century farmhouse in Bavaria nestled on the Danube while working in a metal fabrication company when I couldn't speak German and I couldn't weld, driven an old VW combi through Yugoslavia to Athens where I sold it to some Syrian black-market smugglers, spent a couple of months carousing on the Greek islands smoking hash, drinking wine and playing chess before flying off to Kenya and catching a tramp steamer to the Seychelles...and you know the story from there. My flower money had stood me in good stead; all sixteen hundred bucks. But upon reaching Rhodos the well had run dry. The boys on the boat lent me a few drachmas, but that was a stopgap measure. Until then I had never made any plans and I hadn't considered the future, but now being broke had me more than a little concerned.

These were the days when the internet was as real as a Dick Tracey two-way wrist radio. My only means of communication with home were those thin, blue, all-in-one aerograms which I bought at post offices and sent along the way. Destinations were chosen specifically as collection points for future mail, and Poste Restante was always the first stop upon arrival. I had written home from Israel after sailing up the Red Sea (as a parent THAT would have been a letter to receive), where as an addendum I asked Ray if he would lend me a couple of hundred dollars to get by. Once in Rhodos the first thing I did was check my mail, but there was nothing. I wandered back to the boat, a cloud of disappointment hanging over my head.

The previous year I had found my way to the south coast of Crete to the village of Agia Galini, a remote spot where a small colony of young travelers had taken over the town. The locals loved us. The mayor danced on the tabletops of the local taverna, drank retsina and smashed plates with us; the guest houses, or "pensions", did a roaring trade, the food was cheap, the Fix beer excellent, and the autumn weather intoxicating. All in all, it wasn't a bad place to hang out. Amongst this collection of European freaks, American draft dodgers, hard partying Geordies and California surfers was a mystical Dutchman who lived in a cave somewhere in the mountains. He kept to himself, moving like a specter. All we knew was that he had traveled to the East, and if he liked you, he might sell you some hash. One night I passed the test. Sitting around a campfire in a remote olive grove, I sampled his wares with a couple of his friends. Picture the cover of the first Jethro Tull album, or a scene from Lord of the Rings. Anyway, this pundit told me something that night which has stuck with me ever since. As he ceremonially packed his chillum he said, "Don't let the blind people fool you. Magic does happen if you let yourself go. The Universe will look after you if you put your trust in Her. And you will always know when you are on the right track when things fall into place."

That day a year later in Rhodos was a perfect example of this philosophy at work. Making my way down the crowded wharf I dejectedly climbed back aboard *Hawson*. For the first time since I left home my future didn't look so rosy. Then Ross popped his curly head out of the cabin. "Hey Chris," he said, "Good thing you're back. There was an English guy here just five minutes ago looking for crew for his charter boat. He has apparently been doing the rounds, and someone sent him to us. Sounds like he's offering good money, too. The boat is *La Desirade* and his name is Mike. I told him you would probably be interested."

Interested?!!! I flew ashore and down the quay, my heart in my mouth, hoping no one had beat me to it. I found the boat and was hired on the spot. We would leave in two days and the pay was ten dollars a day. Yeee Hawww!!! The Universe was indeed looking after me. The next day a letter from my folks arrived. Things were tough back home, but Ray had sent me twenty-five bucks, bless him. Now I had a job, money in my pocket, and was off on another adventure.

My sailing apprenticeship began on *Hawson*, and a good introduction it was, too. Joining *La Desirade* would represent another segment in my quickly-advancing learning curve. Mike Crocket was a tall, easygoing English yachtsman who had sailed virtually all his life. He had raced dinghies; he had raced yachts. He and his wife Liz had done a circumnavigation on his first boat, and now they were on a second extended voyage on their new yacht, which they had recently built. Mike had taken the job as skipper for the summer on *La Desirade* to help make ends meet. A group of the French owner's friends had just departed in Rhodos, and now my job was to help Mike get the boat back north to the island of Samos, where another group was set to join her. The Meltemi was still howling when we set off, prowling the Aegean like a malevolent goddess, and we would be bashing into it for the next two days. This was a far different sailing experience than my previous three thousand miles, however. The only similarities between

Hawcon and *La Desirade* were that they were both boats, they each had two masts and they were built of teak. Long and sleek, the black hulled *La Desirade* was a thoroughbred designed by the legendary American firm of Sparkman and Stevens, and she cut like a hot knife through butter as we cleaved through the water to windward. Late in the afternoon of our second day we were motoring past the breakwater into the quiet fishing village of Pythagorean, Samos.

Pythagorean was as picturesque and quaint little harbor as you could imagine. Inside the two rocky breakwaters sat a semicircular quay adorned with colorfully painted traditional caïques, nets strung out drying in the hot, summer sun. Lying behind the wide, cobblestone quay were several shady, waterfront tavernas, tables and chairs set out under vine-covered trellises. The whitewashed village climbed up the hill, looking out over the harbor and across the blue Aegean to the high, soaring mountains of Turkey just a few miles away. For the next week I worked on *La Desirade*, interspersed with long quayside lunches and even longer dinners. It was all very civilized.

It was at one of these late-night affairs when Mike introduced me to Misha, the hard-drinking Croatian wild man. With *La Desirade* due to leave with a new set of guests, I decided to go to Athens to collect my mail. Misha owned an old caïque, and said he could use a hand to sail it to the island of Spetses, which was quite close to Athens, so I took him up on the offer. Mike said if I returned to Pythagorean, I would always have work on *La Desirade*, so it was agreed to meet up back in Samos in a couple of weeks' time. He also said that in September he would be delivering her back to the south coast of France, and I could join on as crew if I wanted, which sounded great to me.

La Desirade sailed out with her guests, and after saying goodbye to Liz and the kids I sauntered down the quay to where the heavy double-ended *Agia Maria* sat tied to the dock.

Misha was on deck busily pumping diesel fuel out of a red forty-four-gallon drum into his fuel tanks with a hand pump. He was a big, powerful, coarse sort of fellow with long sandy hair and deep blue eyes. Barebacked and brown from the sun, he wore a greasy pair of khaki shorts and looked as rough and ready as his boat.

"Hey Krist how you go!" he bellowed. "Don't stand and wait for invite…this not some fucking yacht! Throw your shit in wheelhouse and give me hand. When we finish this drum, we get going."

It was just after mid-day when we motored out of the harbor, the noisy diesel engine thumping a regular beat. Misha stood at the helm in the little wheelhouse aft, a cigarette hanging loosely from his lips as I busied myself coiling ropes and tidying the deck. Once past the breakwater we turned right and headed out across the calm Aegean Sea. Spetses lay in a small group of islands just to the southwest of the main port of Piraeus, about one hundred and fifty miles away. Our course would take us right through the heart of the Cyclades archipelago; past Mykonos, Siros and Kea.

"Hey Krist, you ever been to Beirut?" Misha yelled over the noise of the engine. "No? Well you should go. I love it there. I take *Maria* there plenty of times. Beautiful women. Great hashish. Much money to be made there, if you know what I mean," he winked. Misha never told me specifically what he did with his boat, but Mike had mentioned rumors of gun-running and other nefarious deeds. "Once we get to Spetses we can talk, eh? Maybe I could use good sailor like you. We can do good business."

I just nodded. "Sure," I said. "No harm in talking."

The early part of the trip was rather uneventful as we took turns at the wheel. It got dark and the nighttime horizon was filled with flashing navigation lights marking various islands and rocks. It was around midnight and I was at the wheel. Misha had gone below to make some coffee when I heard the shout. "Jesus Christ we're sinking!"

I ran to the hatchway and looked below. Sea water was sloshing over the floorboards! I went back to the wheel as Misha charged into the engine room. Now *Agia Maria* was not the tightest of vessels to begin with; two bilge pumps had been running continuously from the time we'd left Samos. This latest development, however, was a bit of a worry, especially since the old caïque carried no lifeboat. I peered down the engine hatch to see Misha rushing around like a madman. Finding the hand bilge pump, I began furiously pumping. After a while Misha jumped up on deck.

"The belt to one of fucking pumps broke but I don't want to stop engine to fit new one so I rigged sea water intake to motor to act as pump. Hope this works...otherwise big trouble!" He disappeared back down into the engine room. I didn't really want to know what the ramifications of 'big trouble' meant. It was quite frantic for a couple of hours with much cursing in Serbo-Croat and other languages before Misha finally got the water level inside the boat down, and with all pumps running we were just able to pump more water out than was coming in - always a good idea when on a boat.

Late in the afternoon, and without any further mishaps, we motored into the anchorage and backed onto the quay at Spetses. Leaving me to watch the pumps, Misha rushed off to make arrangements with the local boatbuilder to get his boat out of the water. Not long afterwards he turned up with a big electric pump, and finally we could relax. It had been a slightly stressful eighteen hours, to say the least.

"Hey Krist, let's go find a taverna. I don't know about you, but I could use a fucking drink. And no messing around - we going straight for the Raki!" It didn't take us long to find what we looking for. For the uninitiated, Raki is a clear high-octane firewater distilled from grapes to which Ouzo is a poor second cousin. Later we met up with some artist friends of

Misha's and carried on into the early hours of the morning. I was still a little wobbly when I climbed aboard the ferry to Piraeus the next day. Misha didn't bring up the idea of going to Beirut with him again, and I wasn't going to remind him.

Athens was a home away from home for me; I had spent a lot of time there the previous summer and knew the place by heart. I stayed at the Pension Dianna, whose owner Georgios told every traveler without fail the rock star Joni Mitchell was his most famous guest. I slept on the rooftop and it cost next to nothing, lived off cheap cups of rice pudding and yogurt and honey sold at the corner shop; ate plenty of souvlaki and Greek salad, and drank my fair share of retsina wine. Poste Restante was at the American Express office at Syntagma Square, a place where virtually every young traveler passing through Athens visited at some point or other. It was a hang out, meeting point and message center where invaluable traveling information was exchanged.

Checking my mail, I received a letter from my former Saddleback College football teammate Mark Padbury. We had played a season together there, and had become very close friends. The two of us connected immediately. Although from completely dissimilar backgrounds, we viewed the world in a harmonious way. When I left Laguna, I turned over my flower stand to him. Mark was writing from Berlin, saying he was thinking of coming to Greece. I had written back straight away, encouraging him to come. "You'll love the place." I said. "There might even be a sailing job for you." I told him I would be sitting in front of the American Express office between twelve and three for three days, starting in two weeks' time. I mailed the letter and left for Piraeus. I had to catch the ferry to the island of Thera to meet up with *Hawcon*. I was a busy boy.

Ross and Gatlin sailed into the crater-like bay of Thera right on schedule, and I joined them for a ride to the

Peloponnesus. I'd left the bulk of my traveling gear aboard and I needed to retrieve it before they sailed west for France. We sailed on and anchored the next day at the near-by island of Ios, and when I went ashore to buy bread. I bumped into Geordie McLeod, who I'd last seen in East Africa. It's a small world indeed. "Bill-O and a few of the other boys are here and we're heading out to the country for a party. It's a full moon tonight, mate. You gotta be there," he said to me in his heavy Newcastle brogue. I delivered the bread and Gatlin rowed me straight back ashore. I wouldn't miss this party for the world.

The crowded central square was filled with young revelers drinking wine, wildly cavorting and carrying on. The Greek waiters and proprietors were smiling and laughing and joining in the fun; there seemed to be no 'us' and 'them'. Everyone was enjoying themselves. The boys were all standing against the far wall. "Those that dies'll be the lucky ones!" I shouted as I hugged my old friend Bill O'Brien. We all had our own adventures to share since our last night around the campfire drinking "pombe" on a deserted Kenyan beach. Bill was a lover of Long John Silver quotes, which endeared him to me from the first time we met. With him and Geordie around, it was bound to be an interesting night.

"Open yer mouth and stick out yer tongue Chris lad...we've got a wee treat for you," Bill said with a twinkle in his eye. I did as he ordered. He placed a small piece of paper on my tongue. "Just a wee something to help you through the night," he grinned. It was Bill himself who had once told me, "Takin' acid is like goin' in yer head with a shovel an throwin' the shit outta yer ears." I was about to find out. This would be my first time.

Soon after leaving town we found ourselves walking single file along a small track guided by the fluorescent light of the full moon overhead, resembling nothing less than a ragged band of pirates. Eventually we reached a little whitewashed stone cottage surrounded by fig trees and sweet-smelling honeysuckle. The rest of the night is a bit of a blur as the electric flashes of the drug began to come on. There was incense and strong hash and plenty of wine and stories from travelers who had lived on houseboats in Kashmir and ridden on top of trains across the Sudan and hiked to the Mountains of the Moon in Rwanda. Not to mention sailing up the Red Sea. Eventually I found myself on the rooftop listening to the buzzing of bees and the tinkling of goat bells as the morning of a new day began. It was time for me to go. Still flying, I said goodbye to my friends and followed a path down the valley to the sea. First light found me sitting on the beach watching the moon set behind the anchored *Hawcon*. Gatlin came on deck, noticed me and rowed ashore. After breakfast we pulled up anchor and headed west.

Sleep was out of the question as I tried to maintain my composure. I mentioned my condition to Gatlin and he smilingly understood. The boys were in no hurry as the wind was light and the seas calm. The effects of my trip were softening around the edges but still amazingly pleasant. Soon the high cliffs of the tiny island of Foligandros loomed into view. The place looked interesting so we decided to stop and have a look. Gatlin and I rowed ashore, and after pulling the dinghy high up on the sand of a beautiful little beach, we found a small path and scrambled up the hill, where we stumbled upon an immaculately laid cobblestone road. A lonely white lighthouse appeared off in the distance, a solitary sentinel standing high above the blue Aegean Sea. We followed this remarkably well-made road (built by convicts from the local prison, we discovered later) as it wound its way across the windswept, treeless landscape. There was not another soul in sight. We made our way up the hill towards a village in the distance turned pink by the sunset. Reaching the top of a rise we stood in silence and watched the sun disappear into the waters of the west while the full moon simultaneously rose in the east.

Nearing the village, we could see it was a cluster of clean, whitewashed stone houses dramatically built on the edge of a cliff. It was dark as we walked into the small central square, which was abuzz with townspeople. The whole of the island's population, it seemed, was in the square this night. The smell of wood smoke and cooking food filled the air. Tables laden with bread and fruit and wine were spread around the edges of the plaza. The two of us were noticed immediately and greeted with friendly smiles and gestures. My smattering of Greek which I had been taught by an old man in Paphos came in handy now. We had wandered into an island full moon festival, and the party was just beginning! And still the remnants of my previous night's ingestion continued to have their hallucinatory effects.

Space was made for us at a long table covered with all types of food. A thin, wiry, grey-haired man with a huge silver moustache, a mirthful grin and sparkling eyes sat at the head of the table. He stood and greeted us graciously, then motioned for us to sit down next to him and help ourselves to the enticing spread. Old women dressed in their traditional black dresses served us plates laden with lamb carved from the turning spit. Our glasses were filled with white wine and never allowed to go empty. Toasts to America, and to George McGovern, and to Anthony Quinn and Nikos Kazantzakis and Charles de Gaulle, and any other non-Fascists who could be thought of were held. Grapes hung from the trellises overhead, the night wrapped around us like a warm blanket, and the sweet wine had my head in a spin.

And then, with the feasting over, the music began. Three ancient gentlemen sat down at one end of the square and started to play what I can only describe as Organic Bouzouki. One man played a lute-like stringed instrument; one beat his hands on a goatskin drum, while the third played a Greek version of the bagpipes. The music was simple and exotic and rhythmic. It wasn't long before the mayor had us all up and dancing in the center of the square. With arms wrapped around each other and can-can like, we stumbled through the steps, laughing and clapping and then drinking more wine. The old guy on the pipes was hitting notes John Coltrane would've been proud of. The music didn't stop and neither did we, until finally, in the early hours of the morning, Gatlin and I pulled ourselves away from our gracious hosts and started the long trek back to the boat.

It had been an action-packed two days for me. Halfway to the beach I hit the wall. Like a Spitfire struck by enemy fire over the channel, it took all the determination and resourcefulness I could muster to limp back with my engine smoking to base. Finally, we reached the dinghy and rowed back out to the ketch floating peacefully under the stars. I climbed over the lifelines and made for my bunk, where I virtually blacked out, not waking until the middle of the following afternoon to find us moored stern-to at the neighboring island of Milos.

The following day, we sailed on to the small port of Pilos located at the end of the hand-like Peloponnesus peninsula, the ancient home of Sparta. *Hawcon* was sailing on to the south coast of France to take advantage of an invitation from a friend met in the Seychelles who owned a seafood restaurant there. I was going to catch a bus back to Athens, hopefully meet up with my friend Mark, and then head back out to Samos to re-join *La Desirade*. "Well Christopher, make sure you look us up when you get to France, you hear?" Gatlin said as we shook hands on the quay. "We're hoping to clear out of the Med before the weather gets too cold; then we'll be headin' out across the Atlantic to the Caribbean, and you-all are welcome to come back aboard anytime." I shook hands with Ross and headed off down the quay. At the corner I stopped and took a last look, wondering if I would every lay eyes on the salty old ketch again. I didn't tarry too long. My life was speeding on, and I had to sprint just to keep up.

7
Movin' On Up

Mistral: A strong, cold north-westerly wind that blows through the Rhône valley and southern France into the Mediterranean, mainly in winter.
- The Oxford Dictionary

"C.E. Bowman! What's happening?" The shout came from out of the midst of the throng of young travelers hanging about Syntagma Square. I was sitting in front of the American Express on the third of the appointed days, and time was running out. And there he was, Markos himself. Wild beard, out of control mop of hair on top of a huge head, big white teeth flashing through his hairy face. A wiry, strong, lumberjack-line-backer wolfman of a friend.

I jumped up and we laughed and shook hands and hugged and punched each other, and then sat down and marveled at how he had just made it in the nick of time. Hitchhiking from Berlin to Athens was a tricky proposition at the best of times, but a deadline made the degree of difficulty even more extreme. After standing for hours without catching a ride near a small village halfway down the Dalmatian Coast, Mark conceded he had almost given up hope when a mad Frenchman and his girlfriend picked him up in their Citroën. It just so happened they were going to Athens, and they were in a hurry. They drove like maniacs, which was lucky, because otherwise he would never have made it on time. Having driven those same narrow, twisting roads myself, it sounded as if he was lucky to have made it to Athens at all.

After a couple of days in Athens we caught the ferry out to Samos. Within the first few minutes of meeting Mike, we knew Mark's gamble of making the trip to Greece had paid off. Both yachts needed delivering to Port Grimaud in France for the winter, and crew would be required for each of the two trips. It was decided - I would go with *La Desirade* and Mark would help Mike and Liz sail *Reeve* to France afterwards. For the next couple of weeks we settled into the rhythm of the Pythagorean lifestyle: fresh bread and strong coffee for breakfast, long, lazy lunches and dinners at our favorite quayside taverna interspersed with a modicum of work on the two boats.

It was the end of August when *La Desirade* sailed for the south of France. As we motored past the bleached white breakwater of Pythagorean, I looked back one more time on the picturesque port. Mark stood on the foredeck of *Reeve* with naked little Barnaby cradled in one arm as four-year-old Sophie and Liz waved goodbye. They were still waving as we turned right and they disappeared from view. I wondered when Mark and I would cross paths again. As we motored across the calm, windless Aegean I could never have guessed that scenario would unfold on an island floating somewhere in the distant future neither of us, even in our wildest dreams, believed existed.

The smoggy, noisy port of Piraeus dropped quickly astern as we motored west on a hot and windless morning. Two days later we entered the Sicilian port of Messina, where we refueled and took on provisions. The next day bright and early we rounded the northernmost tip of the island of Sicily, and steering a northwesterly course entered the Tyrrhenian Sea.

"Looks like a bloody Mistral is blowing up," Mike said the following afternoon as we skirted the northern end of the island of Sardinia. Seeing my confusion, he explained. "The Mistral is what the French call their northerly wind which comes screaming down the central plains of France and out onto the Gulf de Lyons this time of year. It can blow really hard and is something which should be avoided if at all possible." After looking at the chart it was decided to head for the port of Bonafacio, which lies at the southern tip of the island of Corsica.

We spent six cold and rainy days in Bonifacio waiting for a good weather report. Finally, we got a break and set off for the French coast. That night we were unexpectedly belted by a full-strength Mistral. It was a wild night of freezing gale-force winds and blown-out sails as we fought tooth and nail to claw ourselves off the treacherous Corsican shore. At first light Mike turned the boat downwind and we ran in past the still flashing light perched on top of what in French were known as Les Îles Sanguinaires - the Bloodthirsty Isles. On a wet and frigid morning, we limped into the port of Ajaccio. Mike jumped into a taxi and went off to find a sailmaker to repair our tattered sails as the rest of the crew got busy putting the boat back together. The sail repairs were done quickly and we left bright and early the following morning. The foul weather had passed, and the last hundred miles turned into an easy, comfortable sail. Now the passage was nearly over my mind went on to *Hawcon* and where she might be. Would I be able to find them? Were the boys still in France, or had they moved on? What would my next move be? As the coastline slowly came into focus the myriad of possible futures anxiously played out in my mind. In the end, however, I didn't have to waste my energy.

Just before we left the Seychelles, we made a short trip around the nearby islands. A couple of English girls who lived on Mahé would be our guests, and they asked if they could bring some friends along. One was Lolo, an extrovert French restaurateur with a wicked sense of humor who owned one of the best seafood eateries on the Riviera. He was so impressed with Ross and Gatlin's hospitality he insisted they stop at his restaurant La Marine on their way through the Mediterranean so he could return the favor. Port Grimaud was not only *La Desirade's* home base; this also happened to be the location of Lolo's restaurant. As we rounded the breakwater on that sunny autumn day the first yacht I spotted, out of the thousands located in the south of France, was *Hawcon,* moored directly in front of La Marine. The familiar form of my old shipmate Gatlin was working on deck, and he looked up and waved as he watched us sail in.

Restaurant La Marine closed its doors at the beginning of October, and Lolo took off for the Seychelles. Winter was around the corner and it was time to make a move. I rejoined *Hawcon* along with Jacques, a young Basque sailor. It was a brisk, clear autumn morning when we let go of our lines and motored out through the breakwater, and with a cool northerly wind filling our sails we plotted a course across the Gulf de Lyons. After spending two days in trendsetting Ibiza, we sailed for the British enclave of Gibraltar, the gateway to the Atlantic Ocean.

November in Gibraltar and it rained for ten days straight. Our six-cylinder Perkins diesel engine lay in pieces, scattered about the floor of the main saloon. It was wet and cold and damp, and we couldn't wait to get the hell out of there. The parts for the engine finally arrived, Gatlin fired her up, the weather cleared and we made a break for it. We were bound for Casablanca, it was the end of November, and our goal was to be in the Canary Islands by Christmas. The scuttlebutt running around the Gibraltar cruising fleet made getting out of the straights sound almost impossible. We were inundated with harrowing stories of unfavorable tides, strong currents and winter storms. Maybe we were just lucky, but after an easy crossing we found ourselves rocketing down the African coast.

We sailed into to the bustling city of Casablanca, and after of a couple of days exploring this exotic port we sailed on, taking advantage of fair weather to get south. Our next stop was the walled city of Essaoura, about three hundred miles away. Rumor had it Jimmy Hendrix wrote "Castles Made of Sand" while hanging out in Essaoura, and it would have been cool to spend a bit more than a day exploring the old gated city and surrounds, but we were on a mission, so we shoved off and continued on for the port of Agadir, which would be our jumping off point for the Canary Islands and the open Atlantic Ocean.

The Canaries are a Spanish archipelago consisting of seven volcanic islands which lay about two hundred and fifty miles off the coast of Africa. After stocking up the boat for the Atlantic crossing in the duty-free port of Las Palmas, we sailed for the neighboring island of Tenerife, where we anchored in the little fishing harbor of Los Christianos. The boys wanted to clean the bottom of the boat and paint it before heading off on the twenty-nine hundred-mile voyage to Barbados and the Caribbean. The plan was to tie up alongside the wharf and use the several meter tidal fall to help us accomplish this. It was in the midst of this operation when things exploded aboard the boat, and I felt it was time to jump ship. Living aboard any boat, no matter how big, has a potential for personal differences to arise. It is a small space for four people to coexist, and everyone has their own idiosyncrasies. Tensions had been brewing aboard *Hawcon* since I rejoined in France, and during our haul-out it came to a head. Ross and Gatlin had an argument which almost came to blows. Rather than stay on in this uncomfortable environment, I grabbed my pack and said goodbye to my old mates, trusting in my ability to find another boat to join to sail across the Atlantic. And I did find a boat. Oh, did I ever find a boat.

8
O Youth!

*"O youth! The strength of it, the faith of it, the imagination of it!
I think of her with pleasure, with affection, with regret — as you would
think of someone dead you have loved. I shall never forget her...
pass the bottle."*
- Joseph Conrad, *Youth*

In March, 1974, Los Christianos was just a sandy fishing village with a fun surf break out the back. No high rise, no Brit-Tours, no time share. I'd rented a cheap room in a pension, and with a hundred bucks in my pocket it didn't take a mathematical genius to figure out I wouldn't be able to afford to stay there very long. I needed to find another boat, and quickly. My problem was there were no other yachts anchored in the bay - none that I noticed, anyway. And then one day I met this character walking up the street with a surfboard tucked under his arm. Short, stocky, with balding blond hair and missing a front tooth, he went by the name of Cisco. It turned out he had a boat and was looking for a crew to sail across the Atlantic with him. "Perfect!" I thought. "Thank you, Universe!"

We walked down to the beach and gazed out into the harbor. I pointed out *Hawcon*, explaining briefly the miles we had covered over the past year, and all the sailing I had done. Other than fishing boats, the only other yacht I could see was a tiny fiberglass boat anchored near shore. "Dat's my boat, the little blue one. I call her *Tyree*." Cisco was Mexican but he spoke with a Hawaiian accent developed from years living in the islands.

"Pretty small boat," I nodded. "How big is she?"

"Twenty-three feet." It looked small. Tiny. About the length of three surfboards. "Still, she got me here from the Atlantic coast of France. I salvaged her off da beach when I was surfing in Biarritz, sailed single-handed down the coast of Spain and Portugal, across the Straights of Gibraltar to Morocco, and then over here to the Canaries. I want to sail home to the Yucatan in Mexico, but I can't do it alone...not 'cross the Atlantic. I met a guy who said he'd go with me, and we left, but he freaked out after a day, and we had to come back," he said.

"From France to here is a long way to come on your own."

"Yeah, I guess," he shrugged.

"Looks okay, though."

"Uh huh."

I stood there on the beach and considered my options. The boat really was small. Not much longer than a big dinghy. But I thought, with all the bravado and wisdom of youth, that it was only the Atlantic Ocean. It was two thousand, nine hundred miles, but downwind all the way...like riding a bike downhill. A hundred miles a day, twenty-nine days - no problem! After what I'd been through it would be a cakewalk...right? I thought long and hard about it, looking at it from every angle. For all of two minutes. "I'll go with you," I said. "I can stand a watch."

Cisco turned his pale blue eyes on me and gave me a penetrating stare. Then his round face broke into a gap-toothed grin. "Okay bruddah...let's go!" he said, extending his hand. I grasped it, returning the stare of solidarity. I had found a boat.

I think there is another old saying which with a few more years under my keel I might have considered - be careful what you wish for. Sometimes the Universe deals with requests at a more literal level. Or perhaps She just has a dark sense of humor.

During my summer in Kona on the Big Island of Hawaii we had one huge swell come through. My buddy John Keanaaina took us to Hapanha, one of the local's secret breaks. In the middle of a lava strewn cove was a reef that only broke when it was really big. By that I mean Hawaiian big. It was a gnarly wave, a towering "A" frame that jumped out of the Pacific with little warning, not like in California where you could see the lines of a set coming for ages. Sitting in the take-off zone, the water boiled and swirled, streaming up the face of the wave as it sucked over the reef creating a steep, hollow drop. It was the biggest surf I had ever experienced, and needless to say, my heart was in my throat. John, his brother Duane and his cousin Jerome were carving it up, tackling the huge waves with no fear. As I stroked over a monster the next one towered over my head, and I knew I was in the perfect spot. John was paddling alongside me, and as he glided towards the shoulder, he turned his head and gave me some advice I've never forgotten. "Don't think about it brah - just go!" I whipped around and stroked into the monster, and when I kicked out, I was screaming. What a ride! And he was right. When you do those kinds of things there is only one speed - full ahead, with no thought of failure or consequence, no time to hesitate or think twice.

So now, two weeks after joining Francisco, we sat in San Sebastian de La Gomera, the same port from which Columbus set off from on his first voyage to the Americas, and we figured we were ready. Sitting there on the brink, staring off into the infinite blue Atlantic stretching on forever, we knew it was time; John's mantra "Don't think about it brah - just go!" ringing in my ears.

The morning dawned clear and blue, the high green mountains and deep valleys of Gomera looking vibrant and fresh. A crisp, clean, flower-scented wind blew down the valley. We awoke, and knew this was it. A little later, around noon, we hoisted sail, picked up the hook, and were gone. We planned to sail to the Caribbean in tandem with *Hawcon*, and so the two boats left together. Clearing the breakwater, we were off, flying downwind, riding the northeast Tradewind two thousand, nine hundred miles across the Atlantic to the Caribbean.

In the two weeks before we left, we had a few minor details to sort out. Like navigation and drinking water and food. Although I had left *Hawcon*, there were no bad feelings between us, and they did all they could to help us get ready. Cisco had a cheap plastic sextant on board, a good transistor radio, and a Nautical Almanac. Ross showed me how, using only those three tools, I could find both longitude and latitude. It was a crude, basic system, but it was simple and fairly accurate. For extra water the boys also gave us three old eight-gallon jerry cans they had been carrying extra fuel in, which along with the *Tyree's* inbuilt twenty-five-gallon water tank gave us the fifty gallons of drinking water we thought we needed to carry – a gallon a day for fifty days (just in case, in the highly unlikely scenario, we had something go wrong). And for food, well, to start off with I need to explain a little bit about Francisco. This guy was a survivor. Whenever Cisco had money, and he had literally no money when I met him, he stocked his boat up with brown rice, oats, tea, sugar and powdered milk. He claimed these were the basic ingredients of a macrobiotic diet promoted by followers of Zen Buddhism, and you could live almost forever on it. With the small amount of money I had left I helped top up his stores. The night before we left, we went ashore with some guys off a French yacht and pinched some tomatoes and a stock of bananas from a local farm to give us something fresh to eat. We were also planning to catch some fish along the way.

The wind was behind us and Gomera quickly disappeared astern. Near sunset, Hierro, the last of the Canaries, was just visible on the horizon behind. *Hawcon's* three sails could be seen ahead of us in the distance. We both knew there was no turning back. It was at this point Cisco decided to smoke the last of his hashish. He lit up a pipe and passed it over. It didn't take long for the paranoia to set in. As I steered the little boat into the sunset, and looked at the vanishing island astern and those white-capped waves marching up behind, and finally paid attention to the scant eighteen inches of freeboard we had above the water, the reality of our situation sunk in. It was a bit late, but in my altered state of consciousness I began to have serious doubts. "Are we crazy?" I blurted out. "What the hell are we doing out here? Look at this endless ocean, and the size of this boat! We might as well be going into outer space! We have no radio, nobody knows we're out here, and they couldn't save us if they did! We don't even have a dinghy, let alone a life raft! This really is insane..." I ranted on like this for a while. Cisco just sat there, scrunched up against the cabin, watching me with hooded eyes from underneath his woolly hat.

"Hey man," he finally said, disdainfully shaking his head, "if you can't handle it, don't smoke!"

Over the first six days we got into the rhythm of things. But in no way was it easy. This was just a little day-sailor with a fin keel and a spade rudder. An experienced Southern Californian sailor would think twice before taking her to Catalina Island. There was no way that you could get her to steer herself, so we had to physically keep a hand on the tiller every minute of every day. Early on we tried all sorts of watch systems. Six hours on, six off. Four on and four off. Finally, we decided on three on, three off. Needless to say, we weren't sleeping much. We still had to cook and navigate and make running repairs in our time off. Being so small we were constantly being thrown about. You couldn't let go of the boat for a second, even to change shorts (try that one handed!). And the food got old really quick. Porridge in the morning, brown rice at night. Porridge in the morning, brown rice at night. Day after day after day. At least we were keeping up with our friends on *Hawcon*, which gave us some reassurance. They were a security blanket, of sorts. In the afternoons we could sail in close and Ross would call over our latest position so I could compare it to mine. At nighttime we kept in touch, their kerosene hurricane lamp hanging from the backstay a reassuring beacon in the night. And then about a week into the voyage the wind began to shift to a new direction, our courses changed and our friend's hurricane lamp faded into the distance, flickering in and out of sight before finally disappearing into the darkness altogether. In the morning they were nowhere to be seen. I can still remember that sinking feeling. It was the final realization. Our umbilical cord had been severed, and we knew we really and truly were on our own.

In the first week, we not only had to get used to the constant motion, the fatigue, and the relentless pace of existence, we also had to get used to each other. Early on, Francisco set his ground rules for communication on board. He was a disciple of Meher Baba, the Indian swami who claimed to be the "Avatar" and who had taken the code of silence, spending the last fifty years of his life not speaking, which might have given me a clue as to what was about to come. "Listen, brah," he said in his simple and direct manner, "I don't like to do much talking, and I don't like to listen to a lot of bullshit either. Unless there is something important to say, it's better not to say anything at all." So rarely did we speak, quietly slipping past each other like two silent ships in the night.

Cisco's view on navigation also differed from my own. His system was even more primitive than the one I was using. It basically entailed sailing into the void in a westerly direction, and when we got close to the islands on the other side use the transistor radio to find land. This is done by "nulling out" the transmission from a given station by turning the radio from side to side. The direction in which it goes silent gives the bearing from where the signal is coming from. Needless to say, this is a fairly inexact science. I was far more comfortable knowing approximately where we were on a more daily basis for a number of very obvious reasons. Like how far north or south we were, and how far to our destination - just to mention a few minor details. So not only did I have to deal with all of the aforesaid complications, I also had to cope with Francisco's disdainful daily shaking of his head whenever I did my navigation.

The best trans-Atlantic route Ross had garnered in Gibraltar from other cruisers was to sail a south-westerly course towards the Cape Verde Islands from the Canaries. Somewhere around eighteen degrees north we'd been told we should pick up the NE Trades. At fourteen degrees we would then turn right and sail due west "running down the latitude" as it was called, which would take us straight across to the West Indies. (One old saying went "sail south 'til the butter melts and then turn right"). It was about as simple as it gets. On the tenth day out, we skirted north of the Cape Verdes, made our turn and ventured out into that vast blank space of open ocean that looked so forbidding on the chart. We had done close to a third of the trip, the wind had swung around to the northeast as predicted, and even though we'd lost contact with our friends, we were feeling very good about ourselves.

It was around that time when we began to pick up a big, rolling swell which seemed to grow larger by the hour. We both knew there was a cause for this large swell - there was something coming behind it. It didn't take long for the wind to begin to build. It rapidly grew in strength, and before long we had a full-blown gale howling up our backside. The waves were huge, and now the wind was causing them to break. We shortened down to our tiny storm jib and were soon surfing down these mammoth waves, trying to keep ahead of the churning foam which occasionally rolled right through the cockpit. The days were manageable because you could see what was coming; night time was a virtual nightmare, especially listening to the sounds on deck when trying to sleep. The sea was chaotic and confused, and our only hope was to keep the bow downwind. It was crucial not to get caught broadside by one of these monsters where we could broach, roll over, fill up and sink. We were surfing the biggest waves of our lives, but this time if we wiped out there was no swimming to shore. We were sailing on the edge, and there was no time to lose concentration. After three days, the gale started to ease off, and we began to relax. The last of the storm finally passed, the weather became fair, and soon we had more sail up and were doing one hundred forty miles a day - not bad for such a small boat. At that rate I figured we'd be in Barbados in another ten days. Reaching the halfway mark, we felt buoyant. We'd passed the test, been through the fire, and now we could almost feel the warm Caribbean sand sifting between our toes.

Tradewind sailing at its best is a mystical experience. Alone in the cockpit you are surrounded by the natural universe. The world of man is lost, except what exists on your little island. You live by the rules of routine. Time rolls by, the waves hiss and boil. The days are hot and clear and blue, one blurring into the next as they slowly slide past. The sun sets, stars come out, constellations dance across the clear night sky. Darkness melts into light, the sun rises, the wind keeps on blowing, another day starts, and it happens all over again.

On our chart, the seemingly endless blank space between old world and new was slowly being traversed by the plotted 'x' marks showing our daily position. On our eighteenth day out we had our best run of one hundred forty-two miles in twenty-four hours - close to a six-knot average. With two jibs set up on whisker poles we were flying straight downwind. We were fit, hardened, and healthy. Nine hundred miles to go and we could be in Barbados within a week.

It was my watch and it was getting close to midnight on a moonless, star-filled night. I looked forward to my three hours of sleep. "I'll give him a shout in five," I drowsily thought to myself as I looked at the two billowing sails in front of me, the feel of the wooden tiller in my hand. And then it happened. In an instant the boat broached to windward, sails and poles flailing wildly in the night. I pulled the tiller to bring her back on course, but there was no response. I concluded immediately we had no rudder. "Cisco! Cisco! The rudder's gone!" I yelled down the hatch as I instinctively rushed forward to drop the flogging sails. After getting the foredeck sorted, I moved quickly aft to find Francisco sitting in the cockpit holding the tiller connected to what was left of our rudder shaft. I looked at the hole through the deck where only moments earlier our rudder had been. Holy shit. Now what?

We sat in the darkness. The boat was laying side-on to the swell which was now smashing violently into us as we rolled from gunnel to gunnel.

"Can you see why it broke?" I finally asked, taking the shaft and turning it around in my hands.

"Oh yeah man, I know why the fucking thing broke," he answered as he got up and jumped down through the hatch. I followed him, sitting down on my bunk as he lit a lamp. Stunned and silent, we stared into the yellow flame. I took off my jacket and woolly hat. Cisco examined the stainless-steel tube in the flickering light, turning it around in his calloused hands.

"See here," he said, pointing to the edge of the sheared tubing. "I was sailing into a river-mouth on the north coast of Spain and ran aground on a sandbank. The rudder shaft got bent, so I took it to a welder in the nearest village to straighten. He was supposed to press a steel rod inside the tube to strengthen it where it bent, but obviously the rod didn't get past the bend. He told me he did it and I believed him. All he did was make the tube weaker because it had a hard edge to work against."

"Yeah, and this is a great place to find out - in the middle of the fucking Atlantic Ocean," I said. "The guy should be shot."

"Don't worry about that guy, brah. Karma will take care of him. Let's get some sleep so we can get sailing again tomorrow."

I blew out the lamp and we lay back in our bunks, and although we had lost our rudder, neither of us had hit the panic button. In the morning we'd simply get up and make a new rudder. It couldn't be that hard. After all, we only had to go downwind. No problem...right?

It was the fourth day of floating sideways, and this was our third attempt at making a rudder. Getting any boat to sail straight downwind is not as easy as it sounds; the natural motion of any vessel is to screw around sideways once put in motion by a wave. It is the rudder which keeps a boat on course and for three days our attempts at making one either big enough or strong enough ended in failure. This one had to work - we were running out of material. We had ripped up the plywood bunk top from the forward berth and shaped it into a rudder blade, then lashed it to a piece of wooden whisker pole, carved down to fit through the rudder tube. At the top of our new shaft we would connect the tiller. To get it to enter the rudder tube wasn't easy. Our new rudder was made of wood, and wood obviously floats. It was my job to go over the side and try and guide the shaft into the tube. I'd been in the water several times in the previous days, but those experiences didn't reassure me. Big fish swim in the deep ocean, and I was hoping they were all busy somewhere else. Putting on my mask and snorkel, I jumped over the side. Below me was nothing but blue and deeper shades of blue reflecting light waves into the abyss. Being suspended in this soundless void of nothingness was sort of hypnotic. As I surfaced for air I awoke to the reality of wind and waves and foam. Even in the short time of being submerged, the boat had drifted several meters, and I had to swim to catch up with her. Cisco handed me the rudder. Previous experience with our first attempts taught us to lash a weight to the bottom of the blade to hold it down; there were also guidelines Francisco used to help center the rudder from on deck. After several lung-bursting attempts, I finally got it entered, and with one last mighty heave I rammed the shaft up in to place. After a final dive down to remove the weights I got back aboard as quickly as possible - not wanting to tempt fate any longer than necessary. Now came the moment of truth. We lashed the tiller in place, and I went forward to hoist our smallest sail. Slowly the bow fell away downwind and we were moving! I was just about to give a huge shout of joy when I heard the crack. Our thin wooden shaft had no hope of handling the strain on it, and snapped like a toothpick. I threw myself down onto the deck and stared into the sky. What do we do next?

  Sitting down below, we ate our porridge in silence. Our situation was beginning to look dire. I'd calculated it would take us at least fifty more days to drift the nine hundred-odd miles we had left, and there was no way our food and water would hold out that long. In all our days at sea we hadn't seen one ship, so our chances of being rescued were non-existent. Suddenly, Cisco reached into the pouch behind him and pulled out a National Geographic magazine. After flipping through the pages, he tossed it over to me. "Take a look at this," he said. It was an article on the "Ra" expedition, when Norwegian adventurer Thor Heyerdahl took a straw raft across the Pacific from Peru to Polynesia. Hanging off the back of the raft was a series of giant steering oars. "It might work, brah," he said. "I got that big oar on deck. It might be our last chance."

Somewhere in his travels Cisco had salvaged a giant oar which he used to scull the boat along in a calm. We finished our food, jumped up on deck and quickly lashed the oar onto the stern. Using it in a sculling motion we actually turned *Tyree's* head downwind, and we held her like that for a while before a wave overpowered us and she broached sideways once more. We tried again, this time hoisting our storm jib to give us some speed. We were moving! It was hard work to hold her on course, but we were going in the right direction and a lot quicker than drifting. The next day we fashioned a simple square sail out of a tarp folded over the last of the broken whisker poles and hoisted it behind the mast. Now we were cooking with gas! At long last the water was foaming behind us again. Once we got into the groove, we made some good runs; our best being just over eighty miles in twenty-four hours. It was physically demanding, but at least we were making progress. We had been at sea for twenty-one days. It hadn't been easy, but we could see the light at the end of the tunnel. Things weren't exactly great, but they were about to get a whole lot worse.

Me, the oar, and the broad Atlantic.

It was mid-morning as I took over the oar. Francisco wanted to make breakfast, and our daily water jug was empty. We had filled it the day before with the last of our water from the inbuilt tank up forward, which showed our consumption was about as I had figured - a gallon a day for cooking and drinking. We were storing the remaining twenty-four gallons of drinking water in three big blue plastic jerry cans the *Hawcon* had given us, which were chocked in the cockpit in front of me. Cisco lifted the first jerry can up on the seat and cracked the lid. A gaseous noise blew out of the opening. Not a good sign. He bent over and gave the interior of the container a sniff and jerked back his head immediately. "Fuck me! It smells just like diesel!" he exclaimed, looking at me with wild eyes. He poured some water into a cupped hand and sipped, but spit it out straight away. "And it tastes like it too!"

"Try opening another one," I suggested hopefully. Same thing. The third one seemed worse than the first. Cisco poured some water out into our day jug and went to make some tea. He brought me a cup. It tasted foul, just like boiled diesel. After drinking the tea, I had a migraine for three hours. How did this happen? Obviously, the fuel the boys had been carrying around in those jugs had soaked into the plastic. Even though we had washed them out with Clorox, the residue had remained, slowly leaching out into our drinking water over twenty-one days of sloshing around. It might have been prudent for us to drink that water first or at least check the containers after a couple of days. That would have been the smart thing to do. But as my dad used to say, "If the little dog hadn't stopped to take a piss, he would have caught the rabbit." The best we could do to remedy this situation was to pray for rain, but once again the gods weren't in any mood for being generous.

As our position gradually moved closer to Barbados there were signs to show we were nearing our destination. Flying fish were constantly taking off from our bow wave, and every morning we would find at least a couple on deck. For two thousand miles we had towed a fishing line, and never had a bite; now the water was teaming with tuna and we were easily catching one or two a day, which added some variety to our daily menu.

The water situation on board had become critical. Of the three jerry cans, only one was at all drinkable, and we had finished it. We had no choice but to use the remaining water, which was done in small sips and only when desperate. We were forced to cook our food in seawater, which made our thirst even worse. The headaches still came, but the rain didn't. We hopelessly watched as passing rainsqualls dumped their loads all around, but never on top of us. Our cooking gas was running out; it was doubtful it would last the journey.

And then one morning we had company. Occasionally breaking through the crests of the following sea was a big, black dorsal fin. Shark. El Tiburon. The Man in the Grey Suit. And it was a big one. As we steered, we could occasionally see the fin poke through the surface as the shark cruised along behind us. The following day it was still there, sometimes well back, sometimes quite close. Once it came so near to our stern that Cisco pulled the oar in. "Don't want dat fuckah chewin' up our oar!" he said.

On the morning of our thirty-fifth day at sea I threw on my trusty Ethiopian sombrero and jumped up into the cockpit. Our grey-suited friend hadn't been sighted that morning, which made us breathe a little easier. Just as I came on deck a tuna hit our line, so I pulled him in. The fish beat and wriggled and shook its strong body until I smacked it in the head with our rusty hammer, and I started to scale and clean it. After tossing the head and guts overboard, I reached under the lifeline with our yellow bucket to dip some seawater with which to wash out the cockpit. As I scooped up the passing water, like we did many times a day, the bucket ripped out of my hand. It wasn't tied on. Jumping up, I yelled, "Oh no…the bucket!"

"Jump fo' da fuckah!" was Cisco's quick response.
And I did.

It was a reflex action. It was our only bucket, and we would need it to catch rainwater. For some illogical reason I believed I could jump overboard, grab the bucket, and still have time to catch onto the stern of *Tyree* as it slipped by. It was insane. As I hit the water, I spotted the bucket through the bubbles. It was sinking, and fast. I dove down and grabbed it, and as I surfaced *Tyree* was already ten meters away and moving quickly.

"What the hell am I doing here?" is the first thought which sprang to mind. As I began to sidestroke towards the quickly disappearing boat, I watched Cisco rush forward and get the sails down. The second question I asked myself was, "I wonder what happened to that shark which has been following us for the last three days?" We hadn't seen him in a while, but was he still in the area? Maybe he was just hanging back where we hadn't noticed him. All I could do was remember what the Hawaiians had told me; sharks are attracted to the vibrations of struggle in the water, so swim strong and natural and try to act like a big fish. Which was a little easier said than done, because 1) I was dragging a bucket behind in one hand which was trying to carry me to the bottom of the sea, and 2) my sombrero was still on the top of my head, and with the Atlantic Ocean breaking over me it was a bit difficult to keep my head above water.

Now that sombrero meant a lot to me. You don't simply find a handmade Ethiopian hat like that just any ol' where. There was no way I was going to lose the hat, so I pushed it off my head so it hung on by my chin string. It choked me and dragged in the water and made it a hell-of-a-lot harder for me to swim, but I was keeping the hat, hell or high water!

The bucket was a far more serious problem. I immediately discovered pulling a bucket through water actually weighs quite a lot, and it is incredibly difficult to swim with. I was struggling, but there was no way I was leaving that bucket behind. After all, it was the reason I was in the water in the first place. I remembered hearing someplace that sharks were attracted to yellow. Our bucket was yellow - just one more thing to worry about. I side-stroked onwards as calmly as I could, but with each stroke I looked at my scissoring feet through the bubbles behind, expecting to see a wild set of rolled up eyes and a gapping mouth full of razor-sharp teeth streak out of the blue depths and chomp down at any moment on my extremities.

With the sails down *Tyree* was still drifting at a good clip, and at first it seemed like I wasn't making any headway. But on I swam, as calmly as the situation allowed. Dragging a yellow bucket and soggy sombrero, and remembering I had only recently thrown a bucket of shark chum over the side before deciding to take a swim, I was expecting to become fish food myself at any moment. Despite swallowing seawater and choking and gasping for air as waves broke over my head, I still tried to project the vibe I too was a big fish. There wasn't much Francisco could do. He tried tossing the end of a line to me several times, but I was no way near close enough to grab on to it.

Slowly I began to see my efforts were paying off. Stroke by sputtering stroke the boat was indeed getting closer. Cisco kept chucking the rope until finally I caught hold of it and he pulled me in as fast as he could. I came alongside and after tossing the bucket aboard practically flew up onto the deck, even at the last second expecting those fierce jaws to clamp down onto my legs. But they didn't! I made it! I lay down on the cockpit floor, totally spent.

My shipmate said nothing. A scowl and a shake of the head were about the only acknowledgments I received. He went forward and hoisted the sails, then returned to the oar and got us moving again. I was wasted, but I had to keep moving. It was almost time to do my navigation. I slowly rose and went below, carefully taking our precious yellow bucket with me.

As if things couldn't get any worse, with a little under two hundred miles to go our last gas bottle fizzled out and died, which left us subsisting on a diet of uncooked oats lubricated with diesel milk supplemented with raw fish. I said Francisco was a survivor, and he came up with the idea of marinating the tuna we were catching in apple cider vinegar, so we were not reduced to Gollum-like desperation, but in physique we probably weren't that far away from the nasty creature. I had never heard of sushi back then, but I guess that's what we were eating.

  And then late on the afternoon of our thirty-sixth day out it finally came. Big and black, it stretched clear across the windward horizon. A rainsquall! And there was no way this one was going to miss us. As it rolled down on us, we prepared ourselves. We dropped the square sail, covered the cockpit with a tarp, and grabbed every type of receptacle we had that could hold water. And yes, we now had the all-important bucket! Standing on deck, we watched with anticipation as the giant squall slowly drew towards us, the dark grey lines of rain slanting down into the water. At first there were only a few windblown drops, but then it came thundering down, like the gods had finally turned a massive tap on. Francisco held on to the edge of the jib and funneled torrents of water into the bucket which I held. We filled it up in a matter of minutes. As quickly as it came the squall passed, rolling on its way off to leeward. We drank the water out of that bucket like desert survivors who had just found an oasis, like men possessed, like two guys who hadn't had a good drink of water for over two weeks.

On we struggled, eating our raw oats and sushi. And we couldn't even make a hot drink! The music and sounds over the radio were as strange and exotic to me it was if they were coming from outer space. "Relax yourself wit' a Guinness, mon," a deep voice said in a lyrical accent. Visions from my youth of the West Indies ran before my eyes.

Steering a boat alone for long periods, especially at night, allows your mind to wander to a million different places and explore countless future scenarios. Looking at the chart and reading the exotic names of the islands before me excited my imagination even more. What would I do when I finally got there? After this last sailing experience, maybe I would retire to some sleepy hamlet on the French island of Martinique, sipping rum in my white linen suit beneath a slow-turning fan and writing novels like Ernest Hemmingway. I had no idea what would actually transpire, but I had a lot of dreams.

Slowly we crept towards Barbados. The only chart we had showing anything of the West Indies was a British Admiralty chart of the North Atlantic, which covered an area from Senegal to South America and from Trinidad to Nova Scotia. Barbados was not much more than a dot on a giant cream-colored sheet of paper. It showed the main town of Bridgetown lay at the southwest corner of the island, and there were two navigation lights. Most mariners would have a detailed chart of their landfall destination, but not us. We had no idea of reefs or rocks, approaches, hazards or anchorages - just some of the minor details prudent sailors use to navigate their vessels to safety. And what were we looking for? The name Barbados hinted at a high, volcanic, jagged-peaked island, and as we got within sixty miles that was what we were on the lookout for. We both had seen the high Canary island from such a distance, so on the morning of our thirty-seventh day out our eyes were straining towards the horizon ahead for the first sight of land.

The more I stared, the more I was sure I could see land. Then there it was! A dark purple shape emerging through the clouds. I was steering and called Francisco from below. "Land ho, shipmate!" I shouted.

Cisco climbed up onto the cabin top, bracing himself against the mast. After a moment he turned to me and asked, "Where?"

"Right there, dead ahead. You can't tell me that isn't land!"

After a few moments he turned around, shaking his head. "Man, don't call me again unless we are about to go ashore. Your navigation is up to shit." he said in passing as he returned to our little cubbyhole down below.

My latest plotting of our position showed we were forty miles out. Ross had always said a plotted position should fall within a fifteen-mile radius of accuracy. In other words, we should have been seeing land. Cisco's high-tech radio system said the island was dead ahead, but how far? It was upsetting that we hadn't seen anything yet. Sunset passed with still no sign of land. Could we have sailed past it? Were we now out in the broad Caribbean heading for Panama? I handed over the oar and went below to an anxious sleep. We couldn't continue on much longer like this. We just had to be close!

"Hey Chris! Come up here. You gotta see this!" Cisco's voice shook me from a fitful dream. I sleepily climbed up into the cockpit.

"What is it?" I asked.

"Just look over there," he replied, pointing forward. I turned around and couldn't believe my eyes. Lights! Dancing on the horizon dead ahead were the sparkling lights of Barbados. I howled into the wind with joy as I performed a little jig. We'd made it! Well - almost.

Navigation lights were flashing from both ends of the island before us. We made the decision to steer for the northern end, which would then put the wind astern as we sailed down the lee side of the island towards Bridgetown. Sunrise came and a low, flat, pancake of an island lay before us. No wonder we hadn't seen it earlier. Gradually the land grew near, until finally we rounded the northern end and on a beautiful, sparkling day we finally changed our course and steered south down the lee side of the island. The pungent, verdant smell of land wafted over us. After all those days at sea it was sensory overload. The Tradewinds were now on our beam, so we dropped the square sail, put up a larger jib, and reached along in the smooth, flat water past glittering white sand beaches lined with waving coconut palms. Not really knowing where we were going, we finally anchored near a little sloop off a quiet looking beach. It was early in the afternoon of our thirty-eighth day at sea.

Since we didn't have a dinghy (Francisco had traded his rubber raft to *Hawcon* for those blighted jerry cans), we swam ashore holding our shirts and valuables over our heads. We emerged from the surf and staggered ashore like two pieces of sun-bleached driftwood washed up with the tide. Parched, weary, hungry, and brown as two old coconuts we wandered up the beach in search of a place where I could cash a traveler's check. We were told we had to go into town for that, which was five miles up the road. We started walking.

As we neared Bridgetown, we noticed a familiar-looking yacht sail out past the breakwater. It was *Hawcon*! For an instant we looked at each other, thinking, "Do we sprint back to the boat and try and catch them?" It was only a fleeting thought, however. If we had only sailed on along the coast a bit further, we would have crossed tacks with them. Standing in the shade at the edge of the road we watched the sails grow small as she sailed off into the west. It was the last time I ever saw the old ketch. (It would be forty-five years before Ross and I would connect again and he would discover what actually happened to us. They had waited for us for ten days before finally deciding to leave).

The hustle and bustle of the busy West Indian port exploded in our faces. Wandering around like lost boys we eventually found a Barclays Bank only to discover it had just closed, which meant we had no local money. Barebacked, machete-wielding vendors pushed wooden carts laden with green drinking coconuts, and we didn't even have twenty-five cents to buy one. As we wandered aimlessly through the crowded streets we stumbled upon some luck. An Aussie cruising sailor we had met in Gomera shouted us from across the street, and when we told him of our plight, he loaned us five Barbados dollars, which we treated as a Godsend. "What should we buy?" we asked ourselves. We ended up getting some tomatoes, a papaya, a couple of mangos, a loaf of bread, and a bottle of Guinness. It was near sundown by the time we got back to the boat. The two of us sat down in the sand, opened the Guinness and passed it slowly back and forth, savoring every drop. It was a brilliant sunset, and we sat silently on the beach and watched the cat's paws blow gently across the water as the sun disappeared behind the silhouette of *Tyree*. Eventually we swam back aboard and enjoyed the different flavors of the food we had bought.

Lying in my bunk that night was as close to paradise as I had ever been. We weren't moving! The boat swung gently to her anchor as the soft breeze whispered through our now peaceful cabin, carrying the spicy smells and gentle sounds of the island. Looking up through the open hatchway I gazed at the glittering stars overhead until my eyes slowly closed, and I slept through the night for the first time in thirty-eight days.

9
Good Fortune, Destiny or Chance?

"There are no accidents."
- Hindu Verse

Tyree was tied up alongside the Grenadines Wharf in Kingstown, St. Vincent. Francisco and I shook hands and exchanged brief goodbyes. Life had not been easy aboard the small yacht since our arrival in Barbados, and although I had no idea where I would be going or what I would be doing, I was glad to leave. A friend of Cisco's who owned a service station in East LA had sent him twenty-five bucks, and he had used his money and some of mine to get a steel rudder fabricated in Bridgetown. We had sailed to the Grenadines, a group of tiny islands that lie ninety miles west of Barbados. We'd anchored behind the reef in the deserted, pristine Tobago Cays and lived off conch we collected from the sandy bottom and fish we speared off the fabulous reef. But Cisco was on a mission to get home to the Yucatan, and I was now in his way. After a brief stop in Bequia, the northernmost of the group, we carried on to St. Vincent, where my shipmate in his diplomatic way told me to leave. "I like to live on my own, and you're taking up too much space," is pretty much how he put it.

On the wharf young kids in khaki shorts surrounded me. "Hey skip I'll dive fo' a dollah!" they shouted. Little did they know I only had a few bucks to my name. Cisco pushed off immediately. I paused at the end of the wharf and watched him sail out before turning and walking into town with my pack on my back and surfboard under my arm. The area around the Kingstown docks was seedy and rough. After finding a room at a shabby place not far from the wharf, I dropped my pack on the floor and took stock of my situation. I was down to my last fifty dollars and had zero prospects on the horizon. I was on a strange island where I had so far found the vibe quite aggressive. In my brief stay I hadn't seen another white man, and the locals seemed to think my pockets were filled with money and weren't backward in asking me to give them some. I did have one lead, however. At the front desk I had gleaned the information that there was an anchorage up the coast called Young Island where "all de yachts did anchor". It was already after three in the afternoon and I thought about waiting until the next morning to visit the place, but something told me not to delay. I locked my door and headed up the road.

    I jumped aboard one of the colorfully painted buses parked in a square near the markets, and we wound up the hill. St Vincent is a high, volcanic island - the complete opposite of Barbados. Lush and green, it is covered in dense foliage and painted with the floral colors of the tropics. In the late afternoon we lurched and bumped along the potholed road alive with colorful activity. The old Bedford truck stopped and started. Passengers jumped on and off amidst laughter and continual conversation in a language I hardly understood as English. We passed the coconut oil factory, which produced a thick, overpowering odor. We drove across the local airstrip littered with grazing cows. Finally, I was dropped by the side of the road and told by the driver to simply "go down de road to de sea." Walking down the narrow lane, butterflies flitted through my stomach as I pondered what lay in store for me. Near the bottom of the hill I could see the tops of tall masts through the trees. Stepping on to the narrow beach I looked out over the anchorage, which was not really a bay as such but more of a channel between the mainland and a small island a couple of hundred meters offshore. Laying at anchor in the late afternoon sunshine were close to a dozen large sailing yachts, all of them having the look of rather plush charter boats.

As I stood there on the sand, how could I ever have envisioned one day in the not too distant future I would be standing with my partner on the same beach waiting to go aboard our own schooner laying outside at anchor. Or that partner would be Bob Dylan? I couldn't have, and I never would have believed the seer who told me it would happen. At that moment, Bob Dylan and owning schooners were the furthest things from my mind. I had more pressing issues at hand.

My plan was vague but simple. If I could hitch a ride to one of the more popular islands north, I might be able to find a boat heading back to the States, where I would have a chance to earn some money. But how would I get out to those yachts to even ask them? As I stood at the water's edge a small red boat drifted down the shore with the wind. Stopping in front of me the oarsman shouted, "Need a ride out, Skip?" Crudely lettered in white down the side of the roughly hewn dinghy were the words LEO WATER TAXI and SNUCKLING (which I took to mean snorkeling). Leo's white captain's hat, shirt and shorts were in sharp contrast to his jet-black skin. He turned the boat and backed the transom in towards shore, and I stepped aboard.

"I'm not actually on one of those boats. I just want to go out and see if any of them need crew," I said.

"No problem, Skip. It'll cost you a dollah." I nodded and Leo leaned into his oars.

The first boat we stopped at was a large catamaran. The captain was a gruff, unfriendly American with a flattop haircut who quickly answered no when I asked if he needed crew. Our next stop was alongside a big maroon ketch flying an enormous British ensign off the stern. The portly Englishman who peered down from the rail was equally as rude, most likely because I disturbed him from his afternoon gin and tonic. Leo was patient and actually quite sympathetic as he rowed me from boat to boat. But things weren't looking good.

Our last stop was alongside a huge white American schooner Leo called "de Shearwatah". We shouted out and waited, hanging on to the boarding ladder. Eventually a young couple appeared on deck. After explaining my situation, I was answered by a friendly young American with an impressive walrus moustache. "I'm sorry I can't help you. I'm just the mate, and you'll need to ask the captain. He's ashore at the Mariner's Inn having an afternoon cocktail. His name is Jim Shearston."

"How will I recognize him?" I asked.

"Just look for the guy who resembles John Wayne," the tall blond girl standing behind the mate said with a smile.

"Thanks," I said as we pushed off for shore.

"Good luck," called the mate, and the two gave a wave.

Leo dropped me on the jetty and I paid him his "dollah". As I walked up the shore, I noticed two long haired white guys with sea bags over their shoulders striding purposefully in the same direction. They looked like they knew where they were going, so I followed along behind. The bar at the Mariner's Inn was packed. I stood in the background, surveying the scene. It was the most people I had been around in a long time, and I must admit I was suffering from a bit of culture shock after spending so much time with the stoic Francisco. The two guys had gotten themselves drinks. I wandered over and struck up a conversation. I found out they were about to join *Shearwater* and were sailing in the morning for Antigua and Race Week, which was the biggest party of the year for sailors in the Caribbean. My heart sunk. If these two had just signed on, then surely the skipper wouldn't need any more crew. "Do you think they might need anyone else?" I shouted over the music and noise from the bar.

"I doubt it, mate," one of them answered in a broad English accent. "I think we were lucky to get aboard. They have a full crew."

"Thanks," I said. I dejectedly slipped away from the crowd and looked out towards Young Island. I felt like leaving. But then what would I do? It was the end of the charter season, and all of the boats were heading north for the summer. I had no money, and no other options. "What the hell," I thought. "I've come this far and I'm this close, what have I got to lose? I might as well ask the question and see what happens. All he can say is no."

I pushed through the raucous crowd to the bar, which was built out of the hull of an old fishing boat. The captain did look like John Wayne. Tall and distinguished, he would have been in his mid-fifties. I introduced myself, and briefly explained my situation. "I just sailed across the Atlantic," I told him, "and left the boat here in St. Vincent. I'm trying to get to Antigua where I hope to find a boat sailing to the States. Would you happen to need any crew?"

Jim Shearston stared down at me with pale blue eyes. After what seemed like an eternity he asked in a slow, Waynesque drawl, "Do you have a passport?" I nodded yes excitedly. "Well then be aboard by ten tomorrow morning."

I walked back over to the English guy and his blond cohort and informed them of my good fortune. I muscled my way back to the bar and ordered myself a rum punch. Hang the expense…I had to celebrate. I wandered back out to the stone wall overlooking the anchorage and watched the sun slip into the sea. Off in the distance the silhouette of a gaff schooner sailed south towards the Grenadines. It hadn't taken very long, I thought, but it seemed as though I was off on another adventure. I couldn't believe my luck.

Days start early in the Caribbean. In the cool of the tropical morning I was up and moving. I checked out of the hotel and made my way back to the Young Island anchorage. After finding the ever-present Leo, I went aboard *Shearwater,* where the mustachioed mate met me at the boarding ladder. Once on deck I introduced myself. "Vin Cleary," he said, shaking my hand. "Follow me. I'll show you where to stow your gear. You're lucky," he said over his shoulder as we descended the steps of the main companionway. "The crew's quarters in the fo'c'sle are full, so we have put you in one of the charter cabins. Your berth is right here, across from the captain's cabin."

The cabin was magnificent, with its perfectly varnished mahogany furniture contrasting beautifully against the ivory paintwork of the bulkheads and deck. "Hey, I don't need all of this! Sleeping on deck would be fine with me," I said, dropping my backpack onto the oriental carpet.

"Don't worry about it. It's only for the passage north, which shouldn't take more than a couple of days," Vin said matter-of-factly. "We're sailing as far as Martinique tonight, and won't be leaving until late this afternoon. Make yourself at home." And with that the mate left me to settle in.

As I stowed my gear, I tried to come to grips with the change in direction my life had taken in the last twenty-four hours. The day before I was in survival mode with no idea what was going to happen next, and now here I was with my own private cabin aboard one of the classiest charter vessels in the Caribbean!

Shearwater was an immaculately maintained yacht. She was gifted to the University of Pennsylvania by a rich alumnus, spent the summers chartering the New England coast and the winters plying the waters of the Caribbean. A seventy-five-foot stays'l schooner, she was a brilliant combination of teak and mahogany and polished bronze. While the rest of the crew was ashore shopping, I had a good look around. I checked out the spotless engine room, looked through the well-appointed galley, and climbed up to the spreaders of the towering wooden mainmast. Sitting on the foredeck I watched a little blue sloop tack into the anchorage. As Francisco sailed *Tyree* past the bow of *Shearwater*, I gave him a shout. He looked up, and a hint of surprise flashed across his face, but only for a moment. Recovering his stony stare, Cisco continued on, giving me nothing more than the slightest of nods. He anchored far to windward of us, tucked behind the reef well away from everyone else, as was his style.

We sailed at sunset and anchored in Martinique at sunrise, where we spent the day taking on provisions. From there we sailed straight for English Harbor in Antigua, mooring stern-to the quay at the famous Nelson's Dockyard amongst the glamorous fleet of charter boats that worked the Caribbean during the months of the northern winter. We went straight into work mode, sanding and varnishing as much as we could before Race Week, which had been started a few years earlier by a group of charter boat captains who wanted to mark the end of the season with a big party. It had grown quickly, and racing yachts from all over the sailing world made their way to Antigua for the festivities. In the evenings the pub at the Admirals Inn was packed with the crews off these yachts, and it didn't take me long to get into the swing of things.

Amidst the rum-soaked partying of Race Week the swirling, foggy outlines of possible futures began to emerge before me. *Shearwater* would be sailing to New England for the summer, and among other things would be attending the America's Cup in Newport. Vin and his girlfriend Sally Erdle would be leaving the boat, and so it became known the mate's job would be up for grabs. At one point, Jim questioned me as to my future plans, and offered me a crew position for the trip north. It seemed if I stayed aboard, I had a good chance at the mate's position.

There was something else happening that week. A strange undercurrent of hush-hush secrets drifted through the big schooner. It didn't take long for the story to come out. Vin and Sally owned a thirty-six-foot cruising yacht they had bought cheaply from an elderly couple in Grenada who had grown tired of the sailing life. They found a young American to look after the boat and deliver it to Antigua for the end of the season. He had done so, but when he entered Antigua customs had searched the boat and busted him for possession of pot. He was being immediately deported, the yacht was to leave the island, and they were now looking for someone to take their boat back to Grenada and look after it. They offered me the job. The pay would be one hundred US dollars per month and any charters I could hustle would be split fifty-fifty. I told them I would think about it.

My ever-meandering path had led me to another one of those challenging forks in the road, and both directions looked inviting. On the one hand I could sail up to the States, perhaps get the mate's job, see the America's Cup, and probably make some good money. Or... I could become skipper of a well-appointed cruising boat where I'd have the chance to spend more time sailing through the islands I had only had a glimpse of but really wanted to see. What would I do? Which path would I take? It was a tough choice.

What ifs. Defining moments. Turning points. Alternative realities. Every now and then I wonder what would have happened if I had stayed on *Shearwater*. Anything is possible, I suppose. I could have been struck by lightning or married an heiress or become a taxi driver. But I didn't. I took the job on *Muiden Maid* and sailed south. I did see Francisco one more time, though. Race Week had finished and English Harbor had become a ghost town. We were stern-to and I was doing something on the foredeck when he paddled up to the quay on his surfboard. "Hey Cisco!" I shouted. "How's it going amigo?" I was genuinely happy to see him.

He walked over and asked me what I was up to, and I told him. "And what about you?" I queried.

"I'm sailing for Puerto Rico tonight. They speak Spanish there so maybe I can find some work."

As I looked at my old shipmate, I could see the signs of a desperate man. It went without saying he was down to his last few dollars, if he had anything at all. "When you're done looking around come back and let's have a drink. We can even cook something up," I suggested.

"Yeah...okay. I'll see you later," he said as he walked off, surfboard under his arm. I never saw him again.

Antigua dropped slowly astern, the Tradewinds blew, the warm tropical sunshine reflected like diamonds off the deep blue sea, the purple silhouettes of St. Kitts, Nevis and Monserrat lay off to starboard, and the high, cloud covered mass of Guadeloupe loomed dead ahead. For the first time I was in charge of my own boat and I felt as if I was the luckiest man alive. There was no pressing schedule, no appointment to keep, no reason to get anywhere in a hurry. I had inherited my two crew members - Ken Pearson, a South African about my age, and a young Vincentian named Ronnie -who had been aboard on the yacht's trip north. It was the beginning of May 1974, I'd been on the road for two years, and for the first time in a long while I could take a deep breath and relax.

Vin and Sally had chosen the secluded anchorage of L'Anse aux Pines, or Prickly Bay on the south coast of the island of Grenada as the home port for their little yacht, and over the next few months I settled in to the place. The pace was slow and sleepy, and over time I began to meet the locals.

On a rocky point overlooking the bay sat a beautifully constructed house which blended pleasingly into the landscape. Every evening just before sunset, the owner would swim past the stern of my boat, and eventually we became acquainted. His name was Bob Macintosh, a wealthy New Englander who not only owned this fine bayside home but also a huge plantation. on the island's west coast. When my brother Rick turned up on his way home from his guitar studies in Spain, Bob Macintosh became captivated with his story and invited him to stay in his guest cottage. What a score! It was the perfect place for a classical guitar student to study and practice. I used to love to sit in the cockpit and listen to the golden notes of Bach or Villa-Lobos drift across the anchorage.

In August, Rick and I sailed to Carriacou for the annual Regatta, which was a carnival of local boat racing, rum drinking, and full on West Indian *bacchanal*. The shore was lined with people who came from the neighboring islands to enjoy the two days of racing. Boats of all sizes, from dinghies to fishing sloops to whaleboats, competed against each other in different classes as they raced around Hillsborough Bay. The forty-foot sloops were the most exciting. Moving through the water like magnificent seabirds, these roughly hewn gaff-rigged sloops were built by hand on the beaches of Carriacou and Petite Martinique, and every year the competing island's boatbuilders would try and come up with a faster model. Island pride and a year's bragging rights were at stake. The racing was serious, there was big prizemoney involved, and ashore odds were laid and bets were made. For me it was like finding a pearl in an oyster shell. The regatta finished, the overloaded ferries carried their weary revelers back home to their islands, but I had stumbled upon something which had a lasting effect on me. More and more one thing was becoming clear...I wanted my own boat.

10
Corsair

"I'm a great believer in luck. I find the harder I work, the more I have of it."
- Thomas Jefferson

The late afternoon sun canted towards the western horizon, casting cool evening shadows across Prickly Bay. I sat in the cockpit of *Muiden Maid* and watched Bob Macintosh methodically stroke through the calm surface as he partook in his daily swim. At the stern of the boat he made his usual stop, treading water while we chatted. This day the subject was the little wooden sloop hauled up on the beach underneath the coconut trees. I had been looking over the neglected boat since the day I had sailed into the bay, and over time had learned it was owned by Mr. Macintosh. Some lobster divers from the Grenadine island of Bequia were living down the beach, and several times I had chatted with one by the name of Kingsley over the merits of the little yacht.

"I noticed someone earlier today having a good look at your sloop on the beach," I said. "Are you thinking about doing something with it?"

"Oh yes, I'm fed up with seeing the thing just rot away, so I'm negotiating with a fellow to burn the boat. He will be paid with the material he salvages. It's a shame, but what else can be done?" he replied as he continued on with his swim.

The trap was set. And I took the bait. Early the next morning I rowed ashore to have another look at *Corsair*. Despite being full of rainwater, leaves, sand and neglect, to my untrained and extremely biased eye the boat looked to be in fairly good shape. The mast and rigging seemed sound and I knew Bob had the sails up at his house. I'd learned the boat had been originally built in Antigua and Bob had used it as a day-sailor around the bay. Unfortunately, the boat leaked so badly that one day she sank at her mooring. Bob had her hauled up onto the sand, and she'd remained there ever since.

My time on *Muiden Maid* was coming to an end. Vin and Sally were due in November when the charter season started, and when they came would be moving aboard their yacht. I needed to find another boat to live on, and the *Corsair* might be just the one. She was small, but I had crossed the Atlantic on something not much bigger. If the boat was only going to be burned, perhaps I could get it cheaply. I sat down in the shade of a coconut tree and thought about it. I stood and walked up the hill to the house to have a word with Mr. Macintosh.

"If you are going to simply burn the boat then I'll take it off your hands," I offered. "How much would you want for her?"

"As long as you fix her up and get her off the beach you can have her for nothing," he replied.

My dreams had come true! I now had my own boat. I returned to the beach and started work immediately. After standing her upright and cleaning her out I surveyed the work needed to be done, and on closer inspection saw there was more than I had anticipated. I had no tools, limited resources, and very little experience. I did have a Swiss army knife, though.

The first thing to do was repair the broken and rotten ribs in the boat. I didn't have a clue where to begin. I decided to try and find someone who could help me make a start. Asking around the waterfront in St. George's I was directed to a boatbuilder located up the leeward coast of the island who built fishing boats. I jumped on a bus and went to find him.

George Paris turned out to be the perfect man for the job. A big, strong man in his early thirties, he immediately impressed me with his stature and presence. Alongside his neatly painted house on the hillside was a small yard where several double-ended fishing boats were either under construction or repair. It was obvious George Paris hadn't had many visits from strange white men before, but gradually he lost his initial reserve and listened to what I had to say. We made a time for him to visit Prickly Bay and have a look at the boat.

A few days later George came to the boat, and after taking a good look gave me a quote for repairing or replacing the broken ribs, as well as re-caulking the hull. I admit I was on a bit of a fishing expedition as I only had the small amount of cash I'd saved from my monthly wages, but when his quote was far less than I was expecting I readily accepted. It would send me broke, but what else was new? He was keen to start as soon as possible. Early the following Monday morning George arrived with a crew of workers on the back of his brightly painted Bedford lorry, and immediately his men sprang into action. With crowbars and hammers ribs began to be removed. He brought with him slabs of a local timber called white cedar which were grown perfectly to the shapes we would need. Templates were made, wood was sawn, and the new ribs were shaped and fitted using only hatchet, hand plane and spoke shave. I had no idea what to do but jumped in and helped where I could. In the center of the action stood the big frame of George Paris, who commanded this hurricane of activity.

By the end of the week George's work was done. The boat had been re-ribbed and re-caulked. Luckily, we found the planking still to be in perfect shape. George didn't know what kind of wood it was, but it was hard, and even after all the years of being soaked with rainwater showed no signs of rot. He packed his lorry back up, we shook hands, and he and his men trundled off home.

I used the last of my savings to buy a couple of gallons of paint, along with enough brown rice and oats to keep me from starving. I had no idea where the next money was coming from, but was hopeful something would turn up. So, there I was, squatting on my haunches late one hot afternoon, despondently chipping huge flakes of rust off the pigs of iron ballast, when I was startled out of my hypnotic work by the appearance of two American tourists standing in front of me. The people over at the charter office at the marina had sent them to see me. There had been a mix up and the boat they had chartered wasn't available and they wanted to know if I was interested to take them to the Grenadines for two weeks on the *Muiden Maid*. They would pay me the going charter rate plus expenses. I told them the boat had no engine but she sailed well. That didn't bother them, they said, as long as we had enough ice to keep the drinks cold. We quickly made a deal. It turned out they were newspaper reporters from the Chicago Tribune. We sailed as far north as Bequia, drank copious amounts of rum, and had a fantastic time. Not only that, I now had a pocketful of cash.

The sultry hurricane season slowly passed and my work continued on *Corsair*. As the charter season approached, the anchorage at L'Anse-Aux-Pines started to see the arrival of yachts from every point of the compass. It was late November, and the windless, humid, rainy-season days and nights gave way to sunshine and the return of the Tradewinds. The Red Crab, the English style pub located a stone's throw down the road, began to fill up with hard drinking sailors. My time on *Muiden Maid* came to an end, but I was lucky enough to find a great little cottage to rent just over the hill from Prickly Bay. It was owned by Chris Doyle, an ex-pat Englishman who had lived on the island for years. It was a tiny, one room affair, but it was comfortable, and it was cheap.

One day, as I was painting the final coat of light blue on the topsides, I noticed a figure appear from the shadows of the coconut trees. Walking up to the water's edge, she put down her shopping bag and waved to the newly arrived yacht anchored near shore. The girl was moderately tall, but not slender, and moved with an athletic grace. Her skin was nut brown, and so was her long straight hair, except for the ends, which were bleached golden by the Caribbean sun. As she waited for the dinghy to arrive, she turned, and upon seeing me, smiled. It was a beautiful, white flashing smile, and I was smitten, as if by an arrow to the heart. As her dinghy arrived, she coyly turned away, but our eyes met one more time as she climbed in. It wasn't long before I met Dianna and Jeff, her American boyfriend. She was from Rhodesia, and from the first moment I saw her I couldn't get her out of my mind. As I worked on my boat she would come and visit me, sometimes even lending a hand. On occasion she would swim ashore to say hello. As she emerged from the calm waters of the bay, her well-proportioned body barely held back by her bikini, it was all I could do to concentrate on what I was doing as she swayed up the beach to have a chat with me. She was friendly but not flirtatious, genuinely interested and well-intentioned but still happily involved with her partner. I was hopelessly love struck, but knew I didn't have a chance.

I launched *Corsair* in mid-January, 1975, and it was a very exciting event for me. The day before the launch, as I painted on the last of the anti-fouling, my brother Rick suggested I pour some water inside to see if there were any leaks. I poo-pooed the idea...what does a guitarist know about boats, anyway? To placate him I threw a couple of buckets of water into the bilge just the same. It was a good thing I did, because to my surprise a big leak showed up just under the mast step in the garboard seam. I raked the seam out and filled it with Navi-Coat, a magical underwater epoxy filler prevalent in the Caribbean in those days ("Navi-Coat keeps the

Caribbean afloat" was how the saying went), and thanked Rick and my lucky stars we had found the problem before launching the boat. I didn't know it then, but that leak would plague me forever.

The launching was a big party, with friends from all of the cruising boats now in the bay coming ashore to help roll *Corsair* in. Dianna was there, and more than friendly, but I tried to keep my distance. From the moment the boat entered the water it leaked like a sieve, and I spent most of the next couple of days baling her out. My friends all told me not to worry; all wooden boats needed a few days in the water to "take up". One morning, as I emptied yet another bucket of water over the side, a tall, shirtless West Indian I hadn't seen before strolled up the beach and stopped in the shallows in front of me.

"Your boat sure is makin' a lot of water," he shouted, a mischievous grin spread across his face. "You should haul her up and have her properly caulked."

"I just launched her. She just has to take up," I knowingly replied.

"What's she planked with?" he asked.

"I'm not really sure, but people around here tell me it's Greenheart," I said proudly.

"Greenheart! Well man if it's so you never goin' to stop bailin'! Greenheart's so hard it doesn't even know de word 'take-up'!" And with that he continued on down the beach. I later discovered this fellow had just sailed in from Bequia, and his name was Nolly Simmons. What exactly Nolly was doing in Grenada at that time I haven't a clue, and there was no way I could have known it then, but this enigmatic character would later play a huge part in my life and this story. That was still a fair way off in the future, however. I had a leaky boat to deal with, and there was no way I was hauling her out again.

At about this time a friend of mine from California turned up. Nolen Boyer was another teammate of mine from Saddleback, and a good friend of Mark's. He had written earlier saying he wanted to go traveling and sailing. Mark had encouraged him to take the plunge, and I let him know he was welcome. He moved in to the little cottage with me and we hit it off immediately. Nolen had been working construction in California since leaving college, and so he knew how to use tools. He also knew how to party. By day he helped me work on the boat, and at night we raised hell.

Basically, we only had the vaguest of ideas about what we were doing. Much of the deck and the entire cockpit had been torn out when we replaced the ribs, and now we had to rebuild all of it. The Spice Island Marina gave me a little corner alongside the dock where we could work. We also received help and encouragement from many of the yachtsmen passing through, as well as some curious glances. When told we were getting *Corsair* ready to sail to Antigua for Race Week, I'm sure most people thought we were crazy. But nobody was going to dissuade me. After all, I figured, getting to Antigua would be easy. We didn't have to cross any oceans; we only had to sail from island to island. No problem. Nolen and I worked on, oblivious to any criticism, and had a blast doing it. Every night there was a party somewhere, and if not, we would head down to the Red Crab, where Scratch the bartender would pass us as many free beers as he could without getting fired.

11

How Bad Do You Want To Get To Bequia?

"Now I only have three words to say. How bad...do you want to win...the Mission Conference Championship?"
- George Hartman, Head Coach, Saddleback Gauchos

Nolen and I were on the downhill run. Race Week was fast approaching and we still had work to do. As hard as we worked in the day we partied just as hard at night. There was a young sailmaker named Steve Hollis sailing on an old ketch called *Zephyrus*. Stevie was from Bermuda and an expert at hot-wiring cars. Many a night we "borrowed" the mini-moke of the famous author Don Street to go galivanting around the island, visiting as many different rum shops as we could. Don never could figure out why his car was always out of gas.

About this time the Grenada Yacht Club organized an overnight race to Trinidad and back. The course would cover close to two hundred miles, and would take the competitors twenty-four hours to complete. Jeff was keen to enter, and asked me, Nolen, Steve and a couple of others to join him as crew. Dianna hated racing and so would be staying ashore at a friend's empty house. Somehow, I discovered I had something urgent to do, so declined Jeff's invitation to join him. The race started at sunset and Dianna and I stood on the dock and waved the boys off. They were fired up to win the race, but I was fired up for other reasons. As they motored out into the bay and started raising their sails Dianna turned to me and asked, "Now what do we do?" My knees went weak. Visions of fireworks and jackpots and rainbows flashed before my eyes. We didn't waste any time and made the most of our night together, but we both knew there was no future in it. Tomorrow the boys would return and things would go back to normal. Well...almost. I was now hopelessly head-over-heels in love.

Finally, the boat was ready for her maiden sail, when who should turn up but another true Corsair of the high seas - Bob Taylor. I recognized the sloop *Freedom* immediately as it sailed into the bay. The last time I had seen Taylor was when we sailed out of the Seychelles on *Hawcon*. At the time we only assumed he was yet another rugged individualist drifting around on the ocean currents of the world. In the ensuing years I discovered he had a notorious reputation amongst cruising sailors as a balls-out renegade who after sailing away from Hawaii to escape the draft had burned a trail through Oceania, been kicked out of Australia, become persona-non-grata at the Bombay Yacht Club, had to run from the Seychelles for undisclosed reasons and scorched his way through South Africa and Brazil before arriving in the Caribbean. He was an outlaw in every sense of the word, a great guy and a hell-of-a sailor. It was quite fitting, then, that a modern–day pirate should join us for our maiden sail on *Corsair*.

The little blue boat sailed sweetly. We tacked out of the bay and made our way east along the shore, shooting through the reefs into the fiord-like bays on Grenada's south coast. There was only one minor concern...the bilge had to be pumped on a regular basis. This didn't overly concern me, though. "She'll tighten up. She just has to settle herself in," I said to myself.

We returned to our spot on the dock to a rousing welcome. Friends off yachts, workers from the boatyard, even the uniformed Custom and Immigration officials who had given me such a hard time for so long were there to greet us. Dianna was there too, and gave me a discreet hug. She and

Jeff were leaving the following day for Race Week. "We'll catch up with you in Antigua," I said.

"I hope so," she responded.

Taylor was gone, too, disappearing mysteriously in the middle of the night without as much as a word. A day or two later a couple of police officers came sniffing around the boatyard looking for someone of his description; something or other to do with traveler's check fraud. I found out later through the grapevine he was arrested in Panama for being a draft-dodger. His boat was confiscated and he was shipped back to the States where he was convicted and sentenced to a minimum-security facility, where he stayed until President Jimmy Carter gave an amnesty to draft evaders and he was set free.

Nolen and I finally moved aboard the boat. The *Tyree* was small, but at least you could stand up inside her. *Corsair* was tiny, and with sitting headroom only it didn't take much gear to fill her up. It was obvious we could only take the bare necessities. And then there was nothing left to do but go. We shoved off from alongside, waving goodbye to a small crowd of friends. We sailed out of the bay and I watched Lance-Aux-Pines disappear for the last time. Rounding Point Saline, we reached across the Bay of Saint George, finally anchoring for the night in a little spot not far from the village of the boatbuilder George Paris. The boat was still making water, but hey, that's what a bilge pump is for. Right.. ?

Early on a breathless, cloudy morning we got under way, ghosting up the coast past dense tropical forests, black sand beaches and colorful fishing villages. Around noon we cleared away from Grenada's calm lee and headed out into the channel, the island of Carriacou lying a distant twenty miles away and well to windward. Scattered through this notoriously rough passage of water are a number of small islets and cays, among them the infamous Kick-em Jenny, an ominous pinnacle looming mid-channel like an evil sentinel sending dark squalls and confused seas towards any seafarer attempting to pass through its domain. I had crossed this channel several times on *Muiden Maid*, and it was always rough. Through a quirk of nature, a strong counter-current ran almost continually to the east against the prevailing Tradewinds, generating big, lumpy and confused seas which helped give this passage the reputation as the roughest twenty miles in the Caribbean. To get north we had no choice but to sail through it.

The wind was strong and from the northeast, there was a heavy sea running, and we were both anxious to see how the little boat would handle such a test. Gradually we became more confident as *Corsair* showed she could weather the imposing conditions, the only problem being we had to pump the bilge with regularity. Somehow the leak which had been there since day one had not miraculously repaired itself, and so after giving Nolen the tiller I mixed up some Navi-Coat and crawled forward to see if I could stem the flow of water at least a little. Of course, the laws of physics make repairing a leaky boat from the inside whilst underway almost impossible, so my attempt was doomed from the start. What I did do was somehow get some of the epoxy in my eye. I tried washing it out, but to no avail. I was in agony.

The wind continued to blow straight out of the northeast or "right on the nose" in sailing terms, and we were being set miles to leeward of Carriacou. Giving Nolen the tiller again, I went below for a few minutes to give my eye a rest. As I lay there surveying our situation, all logic pointed to turning back. I was half blind and in pain, the conditions were not at all favorable, the boat was leaking, we were miles from land, and my crewmate had virtually no sailing experience. Not to mention we were relying on only my surfboard as a life raft. Grenada, it seemed, had some kind of hold on us and we were struggling to break free from its gravitational pull. But when I envisioned seeing all those same faces again, I became more determined than ever to press on. The thought of never seeing Dianna again might have also played a minor role in my decision-making process, but I wouldn't have wanted to tell Nolen that.

At sunset we tacked on to port towards Carriacou, close to ten miles away. The wind and sea conditions hadn't abated, my eye was running water like a leaky faucet and extremely painful, night was coming on, but the boat was sailing beautifully and we were actually feeling quite positive. My plan was to anchor in Carriacou's well protected Tyrell Bay and take stock from there. But being one-eyed on a pitch-black night I somehow missed the entrance and the next thing I knew we were clearing away from the north end of the island and sailing right into the heart of the reef-strewn Grenadines. It was after midnight, there was no moon, we were dead tired, my eye was streaming, the islands nothing but dark shadows around us and I decided to make for the only anchorage I knew, which was under Petite St. Vincent. From somewhere out of my subconscious I recalled the bearings given to me by a local fisherman ("you does line up de peak of Petite Martinique wit' de saddle of Union Island") that would take us through the narrow passage between the reefs to the safety of the anchorage beyond. Miraculously we found the passage, and were soon gliding through the calm water in the lee of the small island. Rounding up, we lowered our sails, and in the shallows just off the beach dropped anchor. Dead tired, we dove down below and crashed.

The sloshing of water next to my ears shook me from my slumber. The bilge needed pumping and we hadn't been sleeping for an hour. "Bowman, you've created a monster," Nolen chuckled as he pumped the bilge dry. It needed pumping a couple of more times before sunrise as well. It was certainly a problem.

After some sleep my eye felt a little better, but it was still red, swollen and weeping. As we prepared to make a start an open Bequia fishing boat motored slowly past. "You should touch your boat up on the beach and fix that leak," one of the fishermen advised.

"Oh, we'll be okay," I answered confidently. Those experienced seawater men knew what they were talking about, of course. They must have been watching us from their camp under the trees and thought we were crazy. But being young, hard-headed, love-struck and in a hurry, I ignored their sage advice. Bequia was only thirty miles away, and I was determined to get there that night. The thought of catching up with Dianna was still in the forefront of my mind.

Making sail, we dodged out through the reefs and reached past Palm Island, the high peak of Union Island just under us to port. It was a beautiful, sunny morning, the wind had eased off a bit from the previous day, and we were in good spirits as we headed north across the channel towards Mayreau. With the steady easterly Trades and countless reefs and islets protecting the waters from the open Atlantic swell, the Lower Grenadines provide the greatest sailing conditions on earth, and we were making the most of them. Skipping out from the lee of Mayreau, we pushed on towards Cannouan, the next island in the chain. We came under the high hills of the island sometime around two in the afternoon. Charlestown Harbor is a good anchorage, and we could have stopped right there. In fact, we had sailed past numerous perfect anchorages that very day. We could have hung out in the fabulous Tobago Cays and lived off fresh fish, as Cisco and I had done a year earlier. But no, we were going to Bequia and then on to Race Week and neither of us had the slightest inclination to stop. After tacking in close to the northern end of Cannouan, we went about onto starboard and with the bilge pumped dry we put our head north, Bequia laying light blue and faintly visible eighteen miles away - and dead to windward.

Although not as intimidating as Kick-em-Jenny, the passage between Cannouan and Bequia can still be plenty rough. The direction of the wind was still from the northeast, and like the previous day we were being set well to leeward. Around four o'clock we came about on to port and tacked in towards the islet of Petite Cannouan. I knew this tack would be the toughest one; the seas in this area were always irregular and lumpy. If we could weather the next forty-five minutes the rest would be easy. We almost made it. Just as we prepared to tack north a big, square wave came rushing at us, and as it was about to break, I pushed the tiller down, punching the bow up through the lip as the wave went rushing beneath us. We seemed to almost freefall off the back of the monster, crashing into the sea. As we did, I had the feeling something had happened. Nothing tangible that we saw or heard, simply the gut feeling things weren't right. The breeze had strengthened, pressing the little boat hard, so I decided to change to a smaller jib. I gave Nolen the tiller. "Okay, but make it fast. I'm having trouble keeping up with the bilge," he said. He had been pumping almost continually for the past while, and now it was getting worse.

"I'll be as quick as I can, amigo," I replied as I rushed forward to make the sail change. Five minutes later I jumped back into the cockpit and sheeted the new sail home. "There - that's better," I remarked.

Nolen quickly handed me the tiller. "Have a look below!" he exclaimed. And I did. Water was sloshing over the floorboards!

"Jesus! Well get pumping!" I yelled as we lifted over another rip-snorter of a wave.

Nolen pumped without stopping for fifteen minutes solid and then looked at me, his hair wild and eyes filled with worry. "The pump's broken! There's nothing coming out!" He pulled the pump out and we looked at it. It was finished. But at this point it didn't really matter.

"Forget that thing," I said, handing him a bucket from out of the after hatch. "This is a lot quicker anyway."

Nolen jumped below and started handing me full buckets of water, which I dumped overboard with one hand while steering with the other. After several minutes we could see we were keeping up with the flow, but for how long? The radio was playing great music, the wind and seas had moderated a little, and our course was good. It looked like we could lay West Cay, but the westernmost end of Bequia was still a good nine miles away. Once again, I considered our options. The easiest, and safest, thing to do would be to turn back for Cannouan. It would be downwind, putting less pressure on the boat, and we could be there relatively quickly. But then what? A sinking boat in Charlestown Bay? Could we beach the boat safely, and if we did was there anyone there to help us fix this leak from hell? On the other hand, we had sailed through the worst part of the passage, and the conditions were improving. Because Bequia was renowned for its shipwrights, I knew it would be the best place to fix *Corsair* up. All we had to do was get there. Option three - sinking and being adrift on nothing but a surfboard, miles to leeward on the vast Caribbean Sea - never entered into the equation.

We plodded on, and with each bucket we bailed we were a little bit closer. Then Nolen went into his "Stub" routine out of *Moby Dick*. "Aye, bail easy lads, 'til the veins are poppin' outta yer skull, but bail softly, softly, 'til you're gaspin' fer air, 'til your hearts 'bout to burst…but bail softly, bail easy, bail quietly lads."

"Aye," I joined in. "bail easy mates, 'til you're spewin' yer guts, but bail gently, gently 'til you're arms 'r fit to fall off. But easy, softly, gently lads…bail gently."

And the water-logged *Corsair* sailed on.

More than anything else, the one common denominator which bonded the two of us together through all of this adversity was the fact we had played football together at Saddleback College. Our coach was an ex-marine who hailed from east Texas, and our training sessions were hell on earth. The contact was brutal, the sprints were endless, the conditioning torturous. Hardly a day went by when the thought of quitting didn't cross one's mind, but somehow, we stuck it out. And we were a very tough team. Our coach was legendary for making unfathomable statements, like "Padbury, I could take your brain and Boyer's brain an put 'em in a thimble," or "Fletcher, on that play you looked like a flying dead swan!" Say what? His most memorable quote, however, came in his pep-talk before our biggest game of the season. "Now gentlemen, I only got *three* words to say. How bad…do you want to win…the Mission Conference Championship?" It was a serious moment, but we stared at each other with raised eyebrows and used our best self-control to keep from cracking up that night. Looking around you could see each of us counting the words out on our fingers.

And so on that day, as we bailed nonstop to keep from sinking and after asking me for the fiftieth time "how far is it now" only to hear, "not far, not far…we're getting there," Nolen looked at me with a glint in his eye and said in his best Texaneese, "well goddammit Bowman, you faggot fairy flower salesman from Laguna (which is what Coach Hartman used to call me), I only got three words to say - how bad…do you want…to get to Bequia?"

The sun's last rays flickered and died and we were left with a bright half-moon and still two miles to go to West Cay. Nolen, now standing in the cockpit, had been bailing for hours and was starting to flag, but we couldn't change places because he couldn't steer to the switching breeze and every inch gained was precious. We finally cleared the point and entered the outskirts of Admiralty Bay. "We're doing it, Nolen, we're making it. There are the lights of Port Elizabeth! Come on, we're almost there!" I chanted, doing my best to keep his spirits up

"Fuck man...I haven't worked this hard since wind sprints," he gasped.

The boat was sluggish now. The relentless influx of water was getting the better of us. Tack by painstaking tack we pushed ourselves on, but it was a race to see who was going to win the contest - us or the seawater. As we crept towards the outskirts of the harbor, I tried to keep Nolen's lagging spirits up. But he'd been bailing for over twelve hours and used up all his reserves. I too had been using one hand to bail while steering with the other, and didn't have much left to give. Getting to the beach was going to be touch and go. My eye was practically swollen shut, it was dark as hell, and Nolen not only had to bail but also keep a lookout for anchored boats ahead. The winds at the head of the harbor were light and fluky, and the boat was so full of water it was sailing upright. Dodging our way through the anchored yachts, we crawled forward towards the beach at the top of the bay, the only place I knew we could go to save the boat. Fifty yards from shore the water was up to our knees in the cockpit, and Nolen had all but stopped bailing. *Corsair* seemed to settle and I truly thought she was about to go down.

"Come on bro; we can't lose her now! One last sprint...we can do it!" I urged, and both of us put what was left of our energy into one last frantic effort to bail us to shore. Just then a puff of wind filled the sails, driving the wallowing boat forward. As we ghosted those last few yards, I dropped out a stern anchor, and as the bow touched softly onto the sand Nolen jumped ashore with a bowline, tying it a coconut tree.

It wasn't the trip either of us had had envisioned, but somehow, we made it to Bequia.

12
Loren

"Every disappointment leads to success."
- Loren Dewar, Master Shipwright

1975 was a busy year for Bob Dylan. After releasing *Blood on the Tracks*, an album some critics term as his greatest ever, he went on the road again with the Rolling Thunder Revue, a troupe consisting of a huge cast of performers. The tour never turned up in Bequia, but I probably would have related to the "Blood on the Tracks" theme. With *Corsair* stuck on the beach like a stranded pilot whale, Nolen and I were certainly wounded and weary survivors.

Standing in the shallows I noticed a stooped figure making his way towards us holding a kerosene lamp high over his head. "Is everything all right here?" he asked. "Do you need any help?" I immediately recognized the voice behind the lantern. It was my friend Kees Staple (pronounced Case), the enigmatic Dutchman who owned a trimaran he called *Wizard of Is*. Aged somewhere between forty and sixty, he had a wild mop of sandy blond hair and a big, unruly beard. His brown leathery skin was pulled tight over a bony frame, and he walked with an old man's stoop. Nolen and I had met Kees when he sailed into Prickly Bay, and if I were casting a part for the maroon Benn Gunn in *Treasure Island*, he would be the guy. He was extremely sympathetic to our plight, and straight away got stuck into helping us do what we could to secure *Corsair*

for the night. He then took us back to his boat, which he had hauled up high and dry between the coconut trees.

After welcoming us into his comfy den he began to fuss over us like an old woman. The first thing he did was pour us each a strong shot of Mount Gay rum. The backs of Nolen's hands were a bloody mess from where they had been chaffing on the cockpit sides as he emptied those endless buckets of water over the side. The two of us were physical and emotional wrecks. In plain English, we were fucked. Kees bandaged Nolen's hands as good as he could and then rigged up a patch for my weeping eye. Next, he arranged two mattresses for us to stretch out on, which meant there was nowhere for him to sleep. He would hear nothing of our protests; telling us he would keep an eye on the boat. Finally, he prepared a little pipe of hash for us to smoke. "Strictly for medicinal purposes," he said with a smile.

Kees Staple, the Wizard of Is

Kees blew out the lamp, I closed my eyes, and the next thing I was conscious of was someone firmly shaking me out of my coma-like stupor. "Hey, come on guys! Let's get your boat up onto the beach. Come on!"

As I slowly came to, I watched Kees scuttle out into the grey dawn. Nolen and I crawled into the cockpit and couldn't believe what we saw. Assembled around the boat was a crowd of sleepy sailors from the various boats anchored in the harbor. Steve Hollis was there along with the crew of *Zephyrus*; Kenny and Johnny from the Baltic Trader *Jens Juhl* bustled about the boat, shirtless as usual and full of energy; young Bequian Carl Ollivierre had rowed ashore from *My Desire*, the little sloop he was in charge of; along with many others who had been rounded up by Kees to give a hand. We made a start, and although the effort and intentions were all good, we were making little progress. The boat was proving too heavy and hard to move. As the morning sun began to peak up over the top of the hills fishermen and other curious islanders arrived and began to join in. By seven we were only half out of the water and really struggling. Son Mitchell, who I learned later owned a hotel and was the local Member of Parliament, rolled up with his vintage green Land Rover, and that did the trick. With a bridle tied around the boat, and the rest of the crowd putting their backs into it, *Corsair* was finally hauled high and dry onto the Bequia sand.

With the job finished, everyone began to slowly wander off. Kees was last to leave, and I couldn't thank him enough. Nolen and I were left alone with the forlorn *Corsair*, looking every bit worse for wear and tear. Son Mitchell offered to buy us breakfast at his Hotel Frangipani, so Nolen and I made our way slowly down the beach.

So now what? Dianna and Jeff had left the day before, and I knew it was the end of that hopeless dream. Race Week was no longer even a remote possibility. Within a day or two Nolen had befriended a fellow skippering a nice forty-five-foot sloop bound for Antigua who needed crew. I told him to go for it because I had no idea what I would be doing except trying to get *Corsair* seaworthy again. Nolen took off, and I was once again on my own.

What a mess. This was not the rosy scenario I had foreseen in my dreams of the future. Instead of cavalierly sailing through the Caribbean, I was shipwrecked on a strange beach with nothing but the unknown laying somewhere dead ahead. As difficult as it was, I tried to remain positive. I figured the future would take care of itself. It went without saying the alternatives could have been much worse - like the two of us being adrift on a surfboard somewhere miles to leeward of the Grenadines.

I had an inkling there was something special about Bequia from the first time I stepped ashore almost one year earlier when Francisco and I stopped in briefly on our way to the Tobago Cays. Instead of anchoring in the well-protected harbor of Admiralty Bay, Cisco decided to drop the hook off the southside of the island at Paget Farm. It was early afternoon when we paddled our surfboards ashore. At the top of a small bluff we found a bitumen road with a village of brightly painted houses running up the hill behind it. Wandering over to a group of men lounging on the steps of a small shop, we asked directions into town. The proprietor appeared at the doorway. With the pinkish complexion of an Albino and sporting a Panama hat, this well-dressed gentleman squinted at us through dark-rimmed glasses, openly curious as to the unexpected appearance of these two white strangers in his village. "It's a couple of miles up de road to de harbor. If you'd like you can leave your planks here. Dey will be safe wit' me." We shrugged and took the man up on his offer.

We climbed along the potholed road, the small bluff on our right growing into a steep cliff. At the top of the hill we stopped, and with the warm afternoon sun and the cool Tradewind in our face gazed over the countless islands and rocks and cays of the Grenadines as they tumbled south across the sparkling Caribbean. Leaving the road, we followed a well-worn path paralleling the rocky shoreline, descending towards another tidy village tucked into a hollow between the steep hills. At a turn in the track we came across a teenaged boy building a small wooden boat, double-ended as all of the island's craft seemed to be. Looking to be about thirteen -feet long, it was set up in the backyard of a simple turquoise weatherboard house. Holding a hatchet, he glanced up from the piece of wood he was chopping and flashed a smile as we stopped and admired his work, curiosity reflected in his dark brown eyes. Wearing an old pair of khaki shorts and an unbuttoned white cotton shirt, he shyly explained that he was giving his father a hand fitting ribs that day. We continued on, and as we did, I noticed several other similar styled boats in various stages of construction about the village. "What a great spot to build a boat," I thought.

Re-joining the winding road, we pressed on up the hill, stopping at the top and taking in the view before starting down the other side. Admiralty Bay arched out in front of us, a few yachts lying idly at anchor in the well-protected harbor. As we neared the bottom of the hill, we saw several large trading schooners tied to the coconut trees at the mouth of the palm fringed bayside. Near the center of town several men were building a fishing boat of about forty-feet in the shade of a couple of large almond trees growing at the harbor's edge, and we stopped at the side of the road and watched them work. I was fascinated. It is difficult to explain, but as I stood there a feeling came over me, an awareness that I had some sort of connection with this place. It wasn't something tangible, but more like the sensation of a dream one might have had but can't quite remember.

And now, camped out in a sunken boat on the very bayside where a year earlier I had stood intoxicated by the peace and tranquility of the place, I was still ignorant and unaware of the magic which lay in store for me.

In those last desperate minutes of our adventure, I could have beached *Corsair* pretty much anywhere. We could have gone ashore in Lower Bay or Hamilton or Belmont. But we didn't. For some reason I had an idea where we must go, as if drawn like a moth to a flame. We landed in pretty much the perfect spot, parked right across the road from Lincoln Simmons' sail loft. Bluesy, as he was known, was a white West Indian, a descendent of the Scots-Irish indentured servants who were brought to the islands by the British almost two hundred years earlier. Over the first couple of days on the beach I only caught glimpses of him, as if he were silently checking me out. Then one morning I awoke to find a fresh papaya awaiting me on deck. The following day there were mangos. Somehow, I knew it was him who put them there. It was on the third or fourth afternoon when I helped him haul his boat out after returning from fishing that I met him properly. He gave me a fish. And then he advised me that if I wanted to fix my boat properly, I would have to speak to Loren, and he took me to meet him.

Loren Dewar...the Master.

A hundred yards up the beach towards town was where Loren had his "workshop". A couple of old boards nailed between the almond trees formed his workbench. The forty-foot fishing boat that Cisco and I had watched being built a year earlier was still there, waiting for her engines. When we arrived, he was working on a small double-ender. Wearing khaki trousers, a collared shirt with sleeves rolled up, a baseball cap and glasses with a pencil stuck behind his ear, Loren was the epitome of a wooden boatbuilder. Aged around sixty, he was tall and lanky with a nut-brown complexion and a kind and caring disposition. I was also to learn he had a wicked sense of humor. He walked down the beach with me to have a look at *Corsair*. The seam through which half the Caribbean Sea had just passed was about six inches long. After squatting down on his haunches and having a poke around he turned to me with a mischievous grin. "Man...now dat is what I would call a cunt seam. You could try an caulk her with a whole bale of oakum an never stop she from leakin'." He advised the best way to "make she guarantee" was to replace the faulty section of plank, and while we were at it put in some new floor timbers alongside the mast, which would reinforce that area of high stress. I didn't have much choice but to go ahead and get the work done. Loren said he would come sometime in the next few days to see what he could do.

As the church bell from the near-by Anglican church struck seven on a bright Monday morning, Loren arrived with his toolbox of carefully placed, well-oiled tools. The first thing we did was lay the boat over on her side. Loren picked up his hatchet and began to chop out the section of plank that needed replacing. We had been at it for a couple of hours when Bluesy marched over from the sail loft to have a look, typically attired in plaid Bermuda shorts and white T-shirt, dark green sunglasses and a white flat cap. "Stand by your peak an throat Chris boy, we're about to get hit by a squall," Loren muttered as the sailmaker approached.

"You know that boy Mac is a blasted dictator," the sailmaker started in his unique, sing-song sort of way. "How's a man to run he business? De boy just works as he pleases. You know where he is today? He gone down to the Cays with some Yankee fella on a yacht." Looking straight at me he asked, "You think it's right he just comes and goes as he wants without saying a word to anyone?" I wanted to say something but didn't know what. It didn't matter because he carried on regardless. "And then if I say anything the mother takes a turn in me ass. You tell me…how's a man to run a business like that? He's a blasted dictator I tell you!" He then wheeled and was gone, striding back towards his loft.

"Hold on…" Loren said under his breath. "He's not done yet."

As predicted, Bluesy wheeled around and attacked us once more. "I thought you said this boat was planked with greenheart. This here isn't greenheart," he said, picking up a splinter off the ground and putting it to his nose. "This here is silver valley." Picking up another piece he turned it over in his hands, studying it closely. "Yes, man, this is silver valley certain sure. But then, Loren would have told you that." He dropped the chip and was gone.

"What's he saying?" I enquired, picking up a piece and looking at it myself.

Loren took the splinter from me and examined it. "He could be right you know. It sure smells like silver valley, and it isn't the real color of greenheart."

"Is that good or bad," I asked, not knowing if I really wanted to hear the answer.

"Well if it is, you couldn't do any better. I haven't seen any for years - not since Klaus built *Plumbelly* with it. In days gone by schooners used to bring it up from Demerara. There was nothing better to plank a boat with. It's hard and bends well, but the best thing is the worms don't like it at-all. No man, you got a good boat if she's planked in silver valley."

This discovery made me feel a lot better about my boat. It also made me curious about this unknown wood. I stored it away in my memory bank. Even the name sounded mysterious.

Over the next couple of days, as I helped Loren with the repairs to *Corsair*, we attracted many curious onlookers. And as I was to learn, nothing took place on the island without Nolly knowing something about it. Nolly was Bluesy's son, and as much a character as his old man. He was the same fellow who advised me to haul *Corsair* back out just after she was launched in Grenada. Tall and well built, he had copper colored skin, a goatee and an afro style head of hair. Wearing a spotless pair of khaki shorts, rarely a shirt and never any shoes, he patrolled the bayside, and similar to his father had an opinion on almost everything. When he moved, he reminded me of some kind of big cat. He had a great sense of humor, an infectious laugh which showed off a pearly white set of teeth, and eyes that noticed every detail.

Kingsley, the fisherman who down in Grenada had originally encouraged me to take on *Corsair* in the first place, hauled his fishing boat out nearby and was a constant visitor. Carl Ollivierre rowed in often from *My Desire* to have a look and put his two cents worth in. Nolly's younger brother Mac, Bluesy's notorious "dictator", was a kind, warm hearted soul, and was as interested as the rest to see how I was progressing. And naturally Kees and the other yachtsmen were all curious as to the progress I was making. It was as opposite a situation as could be imagined to my lonely existence in that quiet corner of Calabash Beach in Grenada.

Loren handled all this attention with a deft hand, especially Nolly's more pointed comments. To all and sundry, he was "Uncle Loren" or "Mr. Joe" ("Joe" was the West Indian pronunciation of Dewar, his surname). He and Bluesy had a strange relationship, in that they didn't actually speak to each other. Both admired the others skills, but somewhere in the murky past there had been a falling out which neither of them was able to forget. This was just an introduction to me of the politics of living on a small island.

Loren finished his work in a couple of days. I did the rest, and so a few weeks after my near disaster, the *Corsair* was shoved back into the sea. She didn't leak now. Floating just off the beach I was still a bit shell-shocked and battle-weary. I was in no hurry to go anywhere. I had learned the hard way that the sea was not to be taken lightly, and luck can only carry you so far. In my short time on this island of hardened seafarers I began to understand the amount of respect the ocean is due. If my Atlantic experience with Cisco hadn't taught me anything, the latest close call did. The warm hearted reception I had been given by the people of the island was encouraging. Perhaps Bequia would be a good place to spend some time after all.

~ BOOK II ~

THE BOAT

1
Bequia Magic

"I'm buying me a cabin in Colorado. The roof might leak but at least the bitch won't sink."
- Willy Halsey (after a rough sail back from the Tobago Cays)

Corsair was floating a stone's throw from shore and I had made her into a comfortable abode. For the first time in months I was enjoying doing practically nothing. It was now May, the charter season was finished, and with most yachts having sailed for northern climes the harbor was close to deserted. Days started early on the island, and I enjoyed sitting in my small cockpit watching the island slowly come to life. The schooner *Friendship Rose* was the lifeline between Bequia and St. Vincent. The sound of her big Kelvin diesel starting up at a quarter to six when she moved alongside the wharf from her moorings was my alarm clock. Just after first light the main wharf came alive as passengers and cargo arrived for the schooner's daily trip across the eight-mile channel to the "mainland". Across the calm surface of the bay, fishermen would quietly motor in after a night on the water, the occasional sound of a conch shell blowing on the beach signaled "fish in de market". The church bell chimed at seven sharp, it's echo reverberating around the natural amphitheater formed by the surrounding hills. And under the almond trees I would see Loren arrive for work.

After breakfast I would go ashore and wander up the beach, where I would watch Loren build his new boat, giving him a hand where possible. But there was much more than boatbuilding going on at this little yard. From the time Loren struck his first blow until late in the afternoon when he packed his tools away, there was a constant flow of people coming and going. Fishermen and sailors, old schooner captains, whaler men, drunks...even the village priest would stop and spend some time in the cool shade to discuss the island's latest issues. People passing on the nearby road were constantly hailing "Mr. Joe", and would invariably receive a good-humored response. He was always particularly friendly to passing women, who would giggle and joke with the well-mannered shipwright. "Chris boy, in me younger days I used to string 'em up like beads," he would say with a mischievous smile.

Nolly was a regular under the trees. Two years earlier, he and Loren had built a gorgeous little vessel called *The Last Schooner*. Twenty-four feet long, she was an open boat with no decks or cabin. In every other way she was a miniature of the classic schooners Bequia was renowned for. She was moored just off the Frangipani Hotel, floating pretty as a picture with gleaming white topsides and glistening varnish. Nolly had studied architecture in Canada, was intelligent, opinionated, belligerent, provocative, and unpredictable. He patrolled the bayside like a self-appointed harbormaster, and from his vantage point on the hill was always abreast of the shipping movements in the harbor. On a parcel of his family's land on the hillside he was building what would have been the biggest house on the island, a large "A" framed structure which he designed himself.

Bluesy was another constant visitor, termed "the island reporter" by Loren. His nick-name said it all. He loved an audience, and his "debates" were more monologue than discussion, generally presented in a machine-gun like spray which normally left everyone chuckling. The latest island gossip or rumor was his daily fodder. Political news from over the water in St. Vincent was another popular subject. But despite his hard exterior he had a heart of gold. Mac, Kingsley, his brother Yankee and many others joined in the colorful daily conversations. The banter was genial but intelligent, and usually there was some kind of moral or life-lesson attached. It was a great spot to while away the hours.

As pleasant as all of this was, I had no real idea what I was going to do next. And then one day someone mentioned Steven's Yachts in St. Vincent were looking for skippers for the upcoming summer charter season. I jumped aboard *Friendship Rose* and went across to see them and was hired on the spot. The work would not be full time, but the pay was great and more than welcome. I figured there could be worse things to do than sailing the Grenadines and being paid for it.

I finished my first week of charter and when I returned to Bequia had a letter from home awaiting me at the post office. Ray said he had some good news and I should call home. There weren't many phones on the island, but Marie Kingston, a lovely Canadian woman who managed the Frangipani Hotel, allowed me to use theirs. It was always great to talk to my folks; I had probably only spoken to them a half of a dozen times in the three years since I had left home. My dad was full of humorous anecdotes, and my mom was always concerned about my wellbeing. The good news was things were really rolling for Ray. He and my mom wanted to come and visit me in Bequia. As I've said, there was no airport on the island, so they flew into St. Vincent and I was there to greet them. I was excited to meet up with them again, but when my folks got off the plane Ramon was in a foul mood. The trip had taken over two days, and the hardest part was getting from Barbados to St. Vincent because of the unreliability of L.I.A.T, the local airline. Ray was in a red-faced rage when we finally met. "Jesus Christ! It would be easier to fly to the Goddamn moon!" were his first words. There was also another surprise for me. My sister Joan and her two-year-old son Brahm had also come along. It was a real family reunion.

I booked rooms for them at the Mariner's Inn, the same place I had met Jim Shearston of *Shearwater* a year previously. The hotel was owned by a hard drinking Canadian by the name of Dave Corrigan, and he and my dad hit it off famously. This overnight stopover calmed them down and eased them into the spirit of the Caribbean. The trip across the channel the following day, however, brought home the harsher realities of island life. The Grenadines Wharf in Kingstown was absolute chaos as we made our way to *Friendship Rose,* with throngs of people busily loading various cargos on board. Honking trucks and taxis edged their way onto the wharf, and swarms of young kids hustled my folks for a dollar. The beamy, ninety-foot schooner was a traditional cargo vessel in every sense of the word, and on her return to Bequia she carried everything - cases of frozen chicken, live cows, pigs and goats, cartons of beer and soft drinks, bags of potatoes and other provisions, stacks of lumber and sacks of cement besides the one hundred or so passengers and all of their goods. Even hoisting the schooner's heavy flaxen sails was an adventure, with passengers joining the crew on the halyards as they raised the three big working sails. My family looked everything like fish out of water amongst all of this, but the sail was pleasant and exciting and by late afternoon we had come alongside in Port Elizabeth and I had them all comfortably ensconced at the Frangipani Hotel.

It was a fantastic family reunion, and Bequia was an idyllic place to have it. Two-year-old Brahm was up at first light searching the hotel grounds for fallen mangos, and with his platinum hair was a hit with the island women. My father's eccentric presence always demanded attention. Whether at the bar buying my friends drinks or simply having breakfast, Ray loved to play the part of the big-time wheeler-dealer to the hilt. "You better treat me right," he would say to Marie the manager, "because one day I'll be so rich I'm going to buy the whole island." My mother quietly existed in the shadow of all of this, but she was numb to it after all the years and seemed to follow along simply out of habit. Behind her impenetrable sunglasses and constant cigarettes, she was truly a tragic figure. But I was her son, and she was just happy to see me alive and in one piece.

And then an event took place which would have a huge bearing on what was to follow. The fishing boat that Loren and others had been building up under the trees was finally ready for the water. Brother King, the owner of the boat, was from the white local enclave of Mount Pleasant, and his family had built and owned several large schooners in the past. As luck would have it my family and I were privileged to witness a traditional Bequia launching.

On the wall of the Frangipani hung a large photo of the 1936 launching of *Gloria Colita*, the largest schooner ever built on the island. She was one hundred and thirty feet on deck, weighed over three hundred tons, carried three masts, and was built by Reggie Mitchell, Son's father. Standing next to the photo, Son told my dad and me the story. "You know it took over two weeks to launch that vessel! Everyone on the island came to help. She was laid on her side on rollers, and an enormous block and tackle was made fast to a giant anchor set out in the harbor. The vessel was so heavy that the anchor kept dragging ashore, so eventually they made the tackle fast onto the land on the other side of the harbor. Practically every goat and cow on the island was slaughtered over those days just to feed the people working." Only a few years later the *Gloria Colita* was found floating in the Gulf Stream north of Cuba by the US Coast Guard with her sails up but without a soul on board – yet another unsolved mystery of the sea.

The launching of *Kingfisher* wasn't as extravagant as *Gloria Colita's*, but it was a very exciting day. It was like an island holiday, with old sailors, sea captains and fishermen along with uncles and aunties and family members from across the island turning up to lend a hand. Bluesy was there, and so was Loren, a dapperly dressed guest of honor as the head shipwright. Just like in the old schooner days, the boat was laid on her side, block and tackle were hooked onto a large anchor sunk out in the harbor, and when all was ready everyone grabbed onto the line and hauled the boat into the water. Sea shanties were sung as the crowd heaved away. Being a West Indian event there was plenty of shouting and confusion, but the vessel floated off eventually, and then the party started. A mountain of food had been prepared by the women of Brother King's family, and everyone was fed. Brother and his family were all Seventh Day Adventists, however, which meant there was no alcohol. Nolly and Mac and a few others had chipped in to make a rum punch, though, so it wasn't a completely dry event. My parents and I were very impressed, especially my dad. An idea which had been germinating in my mind was about to come into fruition.

It was lunchtime a day or two after the launching, and I was sitting with my folks around a table in the shade as we watched Joan play with her naked little boy in the placid waters of the bay. "So, tell me, Chris," Ramon asked, "what do you really want to do with your life? You've had a wild ride up to this point, but I don't want to see you go off and kill yourself on that crazy boat of yours, and neither does your mom. What's the plan? What are you going to do from here?"

"Since my last little adventure, I've been thinking about that question a lot," I replied. "What I would really like to do is make enough money to build a boat here in Bequia. These guys are incredible boatbuilders, and they are working for six US dollars a day! The wood for the ribs grows right here on the island, and I can get the planking material from Guyana. I think I could build a great boat here, and quite cheaply. And two good things would come of it. I would learn how to build a wooden boat, and I'd have something to show for it in the end."

Ray looked at me seriously across his cup of coffee. "How much do you think it would cost?"

The ball was now rolling. The die had been cast. It was only an idea at that moment, but the outcome would prove to be inevitable.

As I have mentioned, my dad was an ideas man. And he latched on to this one. To him, the thought of building a boat on the beach in Bequia was brilliant. Our conversation was a well-kept secret for about half an hour. Ray, being the promotor that he was, couldn't help himself. I'm more of a "show me don't tell me" kind of a guy, but not my old man. Before I knew it, he was canvasing the idea with Son, and then when Nolly wandered by, Ray cornered him as well. Within an hour, anyone within earshot of the Frangipani had heard about it.

Just before the launching of *Kingfisher*, a couple of hard-partying Americans appeared on the scene. Willy Halsey and Les Anderson had sailed "down island" in tandem on their respective yachts and like most sailors made the Frangipani Bar their first stop. Ramon took an immediate liking to them. Willy was a fun loving, shaggy haired, rum and coke swilling scoundrel with a quick smile and an infectious laugh who just happened to be the grandson of the famous Admiral William Halsey, the WWII war hero who my dad had served under when on an aircraft carrier in the Pacific. He had grown up in upstate New York, but was now living on the Dutch/French island of St. Maarten/St. Martin, where he worked at a marine chandlery his father had set up there. Les Anderson lived in the US Virgin Islands. An ex-navy man, he was a talented artist and craftsman who had built his own beautiful schooner called *Penelope*. When the two of them rolled into the bar they were quickly drawn into the discussion. They were immediately encouraging and thought it was a great idea. Les was an aficionado of the traditional sailing craft of the Americas, which he drew on heavily when he built his own boat. He jumped back into his dinghy and rowed out and retrieved a pile of books from his neat green schooner. Les was full of advice and it wasn't long before we were all huddled around a well-worn copy of Howard Chapelle's *American Small Sailing Craft*, examining everything from Block Island cowhorns and Tancook Whalers to pinky schooners. I quietly listened to all of this advice, but already had a vision in mind. I wanted to build a traditional Bequia schooner of about thirty-five feet. The Frangipani was on fire with excitement.

My head was spinning. Everything was happening so quickly. It didn't take long for Bluesy to hear about it, and once he had hold of it there was no turning back. Naturally, I went to speak about it with Loren. He was immediately interested and said he would give it all some thought. He said we should also discuss this with another shipwright named Crosby, as he was the only man on the island who knew how to read a plan. I agreed, and so it was arranged that we would meet on Sunday with my dad.

Around the hotel this ephemeral wisp of a notion was taking on a life of its own. Son, who not only came from a long line of shipbuilders but was also a member of government, thought it would be an excellent chance to showcase Bequia's boatbuilding talent. Nolly was on board, which was important. Though he had no official title, held no office or represented any popular authority, he still was not someone who you wanted to put offside. Ray had taken control of proceedings and I was riding in his slipstream.

The Sunday meeting rolled around. Ray and I walked up the beach, where we met the neatly attired Loren. Crosby wasn't there yet, but Loren assured us he would be there "jus' now". Leaning against a fishing boat hauled out in the shade, I outlined to Loren what I was thinking about building. We knew, of course, that without anything more substantial than an idea he couldn't tell us how much it would cost, but said that with three men working alongside of me we could surely build such a vessel within a year, and though he couldn't speak for others he would work for twelve BWI (British West Indian Dollars) a day, which equated to six dollars US. He said that should we go ahead, he would ask a shipwright from Paget Farm named Gilbert Hazel to join us. "He's a real hard workin' fellah, and easy to get along with." We chatted and waited for Crosby. Loren told us that several years earlier two white men from the States had built a yacht in Bequia, and Crosby had been hired to work with them.

Eventually this funny little man arrived, and when he did, he was half drunk. He probably had been waylaid in The New York Bar, Baby Lou's rum shop, building up his courage. Short and caramel colored with tufts of black hair growing out of his ears, he wore a tweed flat cap and baggy dungarees. He had an old book of yacht designs carefully preserved in a plastic bag as well as an official looking document which stated he had passed one year of correspondence naval architecture. These he pressed on us in drunken exuberance. Ray didn't know exactly how to take this in, and Loren, being a non-drinking Seventh Day Adventist himself, was obviously embarrassed. After a few more minutes of Crosby's ramblings Loren diplomatically encouraged him to go home and sleep it off. After he left, Loren apologized profusely, and said that despite what we had seen Crosby did know what he was talking about. "He's a good shipwright," Loren assured us. "He's a bit slow working, but you can't beat him when it comes to a plan." We shook hands with Loren and thanked him for coming. Though not impressed with Crosby, his antics hadn't really dampened our enthusiasm.

In the end we worked out the boat would cost around fifteen thousand US dollars to build. I felt I could earn a third of that working for Stevens Yachts, and Ray said he would put up the remaining ten grand, and when back in the States he'd start looking out for all of the gear we would need. My family's stay at the Frangipani sadly came to an end, and they said goodbye to all of the friends they had made. Ray thanked Son and Willy and Les for their encouragement and their help. Nolly and Bluesy came to see us off on the early morning trip across the channel, and as we stepped onto *Friendship Rose* Ray turned to Bluesy and said, "Look after this character for us, will you?" to which Bluesy replied, "We'll keep him out of trouble, don't worry."

As we sailed out into the channel on a blustery morning, I stood by the windward rigging and gazed towards the sunrise and the eastern horizon, out across the ocean that a little over a year earlier I had been battling for survival on, and I couldn't help thinking how much my life had changed since then, and even more so over the last two short weeks. All of a sudden, the weight of responsibility hit home. I was going to be building a boat in Bequia.

2
Hard Work in Paradise

"When you find a coin in de road, somebody dropped it."
  - Bluesy Simmons, Sailmaker

We booked back into the Mariner's Inn for the last night before my folks flew home, and found Dave Corrigan sitting in his usual seat at the bar working on his daily consumption of rum and orange juice. It didn't take Ray long to fill him in on our plans, and Dave was of immediate help. "The first thing you need to build a boat is a keel, and I know exactly where you can find one. A fellow here in St. Vincent started to build a slipway out on the lee side of the island but never finished it and has a whole pile of greenheart 12x12's out there. They've been there a few years, too, so they'd be well-seasoned. I'll give him a call. I'm sure he'd sell one of them to you. And if you're putting a lead ballast keel on your boat there's one sitting just down the beach from here. *Paulina* is never going to be repaired and I'm sure you can get her for a song." So now I had good leads on two of the most difficult pieces of the boat to find.

Later that afternoon Ray and I walked down to where *Paulina* sat propped up on the beach, almost exactly the spot where Leo the water taxi had picked me up a year earlier. Dave had told us she was an old English yacht that had been sailed out to the West Indies by a "mad drunken Englishman" a year or so previously. That man was none other than Michael Bailey, who I had sailed with on *Shearwater*. He had sold her to a couple of local yachtsmen who could never stop the tired old girl from leaking, so they pulled her up on the beach with a bulldozer. She was a classic from the early 1900's; narrow and deep with a plumb stem and long overhanging stern. The bronze rudder cap read *Paulina – 1903*. She was broken and rotten and too far gone to save, but she had a beautiful three-ton lead keel, a solid mast and some good bronze fittings worth saving, so we decided to see what these local guys wanted for her. Again, Dave came to our aid and negotiated a price of a thousand local dollars, which we didn't hesitate to accept.

The following morning, we went to the airport. It was a sad farewell. My mom was pleased I had found such an exciting project to get involved in, but I could see she was still a little nervous as to the outcome. Ramon had total confidence in me to pull it off, and I have to say the most important lesson I ever learned from him was to believe in yourself, and never step back from a challenge no matter how big.

I returned to Bequia and from the moment I stepped ashore could tell things were different. There was a definite buzz in the air. It was a small community and it hadn't taken long for the word to spread. Chris was building a boat. I was twenty-five years old and walking straight into something I knew very little about. I was about to learn many lessons; the first one was that building a boat is a logical process. You start with a keel and from there you take things one step at a time.

Over the next month I was busy with charters. Afterwards I stayed on in St. Vincent to deal with *Paulina,* as well as see to purchasing the greenheart keel. Before my folks departed, Dave Corrigan told me that anytime I needed to come to St. Vincent on business I could stay at the Mariner's Inn for free, a kind gesture I would never forget. In a wooden boat the wood keel forms an integral part of the backbone, structurally the foundation of a sound vessel. And to make this piece there are few woods superior to greenheart. Long, straight, hard and impervious to rot or worm, this wood is so heavy it sinks. Kenneth Adams took me out to his unfinished slipway in Wallalabu Bay, where six forty-foot 12x12's were stored in the water on the edge of a beautiful black sand beach. "Best place to keep 'em's in the water," Ken said. "The saltwater's good for 'em - it not like they're going to float away!"

I purchased one and the next day organized the transport to go and get it, which was truly a West Indian experience.

Early in the morning I rode out with the jovial owner of a large lorry. I was worried how we would get this heavy piece of wood onto his truck, but he told me it wouldn't be a problem. "This piece of wood will weigh over a ton," I said more than once. "How are we going to move it without a crane?"

"I'm tellin' you it will be easy, mon…don' frighten," he laughed. "You'll see."

The man was true to his word. Pulling to a stop in the last village before Wallalabu Bay, he asked for a few dollars to purchase two bottles of strong rum, the local firewater close to 80% pure alcohol. He walked over to a shop where a group of fit young men were loitering around ("on de lime" or "liming" in West Indian parlance), and the next thing I knew there were a dozen strapping guys jumping onto the back of the truck. "Dat's how we do it, mon. Just buy de boys some rum!" And indeed, loading the keel wasn't a problem. It didn't take much more than an hour to get that heavy piece of wood onto the truck. Naturally, we didn't give them the rum until after the job was done! Later that afternoon we backed the truck onto the Grenadines Wharf and tumbled the keel onto the ground. Now all I had to do was get it across eight miles of water and on to the beach in Bequia.

With the keel waiting on the wharf, I next tackled *Paulina*. She might have been old and rotten, but those copper bolts and rivets still had some strength left in them. I had no idea where to start to dismantle her. Dave put me on to a shipwright by the name of John Gregg, a man who worked like a human hurricane. The first thing he did was remove the props and push the boat over so that it came crashing down on its side. And then he tore into it. With only a sledge hammer, crowbar and axe, we dismantled the old *Paulina* in a matter of two days. I stripped away all the bronze fittings I thought useful, and by week's end we had the three-ton lead keel lying on the wharf next to the greenheart. As helpful as the owners of *Friendship Rose* were (they never charged me passage as long as I was building a boat), they couldn't carry those two awkward pieces across the channel. Looking up to the commercial wharf I saw a big steel freighter offloading cargo. I went aboard and met the captain, a young, friendly Dane. As the weekend was coming, he said he would help, and so on Saturday afternoon, when the Grenadines Wharf was clear, he maneuvered his one thousand-ton freighter alongside and used his shipboard derricks to lift the two pieces aboard. I don't remember what I paid him, but I'm sure it went nowhere close to covering the cost of moving such a ship. He did enjoy his weekend in Bequia, however. The keels were craned aboard the island's only dump truck, and so by Monday morning the two pieces lay in the sand in the same spot where *Kingfisher* had been sitting only a few weeks earlier.

Nolly and the keel.

The excitement was building. With a massive piece of greenheart and a three-ton lead keel laying on the beach, everyone could see I was serious. Nolly recommended I hire Crosby, so Loren and I had another meeting with him and he was sober this time. He obviously was respected for his skills, but when he asked for a dollar more than Loren per day I refused. After a bit of to-and-fro, he saw I wasn't budging. In the end he accepted my terms.

The next thing on the agenda was finding the wood for the frames. Bluesy owned a large tract of land on the back side of Mt. Pleasant called Paradise, and said we should go up and take a look. Early one morning I walked up there with Bluesy, Nolly and Crosby. (As good of a shipwright as Loren was, he drew the line at "goin' in de bush"). A narrow dirt road led us to a rugged ravine that ran from the top of a ridge to a rocky little bay called L'Anse la Coite, which could barely be seen far below. The bush was tangled and thick, but it was full of white cedar. Facing east into the Tradewinds, these trees grew with the natural bends needed for a boat. Using a cutlass to chop away the dry, thick undergrowth, we followed Bluesy in. It took a while for me to understand what exactly we were looking for, but soon I started to see the dark shapes looming through the wild saplings of cinnamon wood and cashee vines. Bluesy said we could come and cut what we wanted. "How do we know what shapes to look for?" I asked. "We don't even have a design yet."

"Don't worry 'bout dat, mon," Bluesy replied. "You just cut wood and den use it where it fits. You does need to work quick an' get your wood out before de rainy season starts."

"When de time comes for certain pieces, we'll make molds and go lookin' for dem," added Crosby. "We got plenty of work to do until then." As I had another charter booked for the following week it was agreed that Crosby would organize the start of the timber cutting.

Living on the boat was proving too difficult, so I rented a small house a half a mile up the road from the harbor. It had two bedrooms, a living room, kitchen, bathroom and a fantastic view. And it was cheap.

It was the end of July and the rainy season was quickly approaching. Bluesy was stressing the urgency of getting my wood out of the bush before the heavy rains set in and the dirt roads turned to mud. Crosby had hired two laborers to do the cutting under his supervision. After a couple of weeks away on charter I was anxious to go and see what they had done in my absence. Early one morning I walked up to Paradise. At the edge of the small dirt road running past Bluesy's property lay a large pile of freshly cut cedar, all bends and twists and curves. Pushing into the thick bush I descended down the hill, listening more than looking for my mysterious wood cutters. The terrain was dry and rocky, the forest a tangle of vines and sprouting saplings. I was following a freshly made footpath, and after a few minutes I could hear the faint echo of axes hewing through wood. Moving towards the sound I pushed through the shadowy undergrowth until I came upon two men hard at work dismembering the carcass of a freshly fallen tree.

Upon seeing me they stopped their chopping and waited respectfully for me to introduce myself, after which they shyly gave me their names. Sutherland was a tall, muscular young West Indian with short cropped hair who was obviously uncomfortable meeting this strange white man. There was something different about Nero, however. Shorter than his companion and with a nut-brown complexion, he was of undeterminable age. He possessed a mischievous, flashing smile, a wispy moustache and goatee, and dark bottomless eyes which had an almost oriental appearance. In talking to them, I found they were not from Bequia but St. Vincent, and that Nero had lived on the island for a long time. I later discovered Nero to be a native Carib Indian from Sandy Bay, a village located at the northernmost end of St. Vincent. These people were the last descendants of the few who survived the British genocide which virtually wiped the fierce Caribs from existence back in the 1700's. Most of these survivors interbred with the African slaves brought to the islands by early planters, and only a few pure blood Caribs remained. I'm pretty sure Nero was one of them.

I spent the day with the two wood cutters, mainly "droguein' de wood" up the steep hill to the road. I was to learn quickly this was the worst part of bush work. The pieces all varied in size and shape, from smallish knees and upper branches to massively large limbs and trunks far too heavy for one man to lift and carry. The average piece I carried was between one and two feet in diameter and could weigh up to a hundred pounds. The two men would help lift a piece onto my shoulder, and then I would go non-stop until I reached the road. As the sun rose higher into the morning sky, the bush started to heat up. The humidity was extreme; mosquitos and gnats buzzed around my eyes and ears, prickly vines and bushes tore at my skin, and the bark from the heavy logs chaffed my shoulders raw. It was all I could do to stagger up the hill with my pieces of wood, and I was in awe of how easy Nero made it look as he nimbly darted up the track, half running under the weight of an enormous piece of bent wood. For the bigger pieces, two of us would shoulder a log with the help of the third man, and then strain together to get it up to the slowly growing pile by the side of the road.

I could see that Crosby knew what he was doing when he hired Nero because he was a natural in the bush. I took an immediate liking to this interesting little fellow. Besides being an extremely hard worker, he had a breezy personality with an impish sense of humor. I followed him as he chopped his way through the scrub with his short, pointed cutlass sharpened on both sides. He knew what kind of wood we were looking for, and pointed out trees that had been earmarked for felling because of the decent amount of round wood in them. Not every tree was good, and the majority of them were left alone. That afternoon I walked back to the harbor with the two woodcutters. Weary, hot and covered in scratches, I now had an idea what was in store for me. I couldn't wait to get to the bayside to go for a swim. After a day in the bush, I could see why Loren said he was too old for it. "I've done enough bush work in my time. I'll leave dat to the young bulls like you."

    I was off early the next morning to start another charter for Steven's Yachts. Although I'd made tremendous progress in acquiring materials for my boat, I still didn't know exactly what we were going to build. Up to that point in time it was always going to be a "forty-foot Bequia schooner" (Bluesy had decided if I was going to build something thirty-five feet I might as well make it forty), but there was nothing on paper yet, and no specific design decided upon. Loren, Crosby and I had spent a couple of hours at Nolly's house one afternoon going over different ideas, but I hadn't finalized anything in my head. Surprisingly, my inspiration was about to come from a direction I least expected. And just at the right time.

3
Under the Almond Tree

"When you know what you're doing, half the work's done."
- Loren Dewar

I picked up my charter guests and sailed south for the Grenadines. A typical trip would generally involve picking up two American couples from the base in St. Vincent and sailing them through the islands for a week. There was no hard and fast schedule; I would simply let them dictate the pace and try and show them a good time along the way. On my previous trip south, we had stopped in to Petite Martinique, a picturesque little island where there was usually a boat or two set up on the beach under construction. With no hotels or other amenities, it was well off the traditional charter boat trail. I had taken my guests to a very local rum shop for a bit of home-grown flavor when I fell into conversation with a fellow by the name of Baldwin DeRoche, the builder of a beautiful sloop called *CCC*, which the year before at the Carriacou Regatta had been the first vessel ever to win a race against the legendary *Mermaid of Carriacou*. I told him of my plans to build a boat in Bequia and that I was hoping to get to the upcoming regatta, whereupon the good-natured shipwright invited me to sail with him on *CCC*. When I told my current guests about the two days of racing, they were very keen to go, and so I looked forward to Baldwin's invitation. The Regatta always took place over the first weekend in August when two full days of racing were held. I had been there the year before with my brother on the *Muiden Maid* and we had really enjoyed ourselves. I left Bequia with my guests on Saturday morning, hoping to cover the thirty-five miles to Carriacou in time to see the finish of the first race. The venue for the racing was Hillsborough Bay, an open semi-circular stretch of water with three small islands in the middle of it, and as we cruised past the north point of the island a sea of sails spread out before us. Through the binoculars I could make out the high-peaked gaff mainsails of the large sloops, and it looked to me like *CCC* had worked herself into the lead. We anchored in time to see *CCC* come charging home to win the first race against the *Mermaid*. The crowd ashore was going crazy. After they anchored, I rowed across to congratulate Baldwin. The crew was jubilant and half-drunk already. Baldwin invited me aboard for a drink and reiterated his invitation to sail with them the following day, which I did.

The race was tremendously exciting and left a huge impression on me. When I returned back to Bequia after that charter I was so moved I sat down and wrote an account of the experience, which I later audaciously sent into *Sail* magazine. Months later I was shocked to receive a check in the mail for two hundred dollars in payment for publishing my article. As we headed north and Carriacou fell astern, a vision of my boat appeared before my eyes and all confusion was thrown overboard. I knew what I was going to build…a forty-foot Bequia sloop.

CCC racing in Carriacou, 1975.

I returned once more to Bequia after dropping my charter off only to find a huge row going on. Crosby had decided to assert his authority over Nero, telling the wily Carib he wasn't satisfied with how hard he was working, whereupon Nero got drunk and wanted to carve Crosby up with his cutlass! I had no sooner settled that argument when another skirmish broke out, this time between an old shipwright named Ethelbert King and Crosby. Now Ethelbert, or Uncle Atty as he was called, was of the King clan from Mount Pleasant, and renowned for his hasty manner and wild, uninformed opinions. He spoke at a rapid-fire velocity which for me was almost incomprehensible, and moved at the same pace. It was as if he rushed through life so fast his brain couldn't keep up with his rapid activity. At any rate, Uncle Atty turned up under the tree with his idea of what we should be building, and taking up a stick drew a picture of it in the sand. It was a cartoonish, child-like sketch and it was all I could do to keep a straight face. Crosby, however, laughingly told him it looked like Noah's Ark, and then the quarrelling began. It seemed everyone on the island had an idea what I should be building except me, and the quicker I sorted it out the better.

Les Anderson had recommended two books he felt would be absolutely essential for me to have, and when my dad returned to California, he sent them to me. *Boatbuilding*, and *Yacht Design and Planning* were written in the 1930's by a naval architect by the name of Howard Chappelle, and covered every aspect of wooden boat design and construction. Both had only recently arrived and I spent most nights trying to unravel the verbiage of Chappelle's explanations as I attempted to fathom the complex art of yacht design. Crosby had also loaned me his treasured book on yacht design, and in it I found the lines drawing of a thirty-two-foot sloop by Sam Crocker which I liked the look of. Using Chappelle's guidance and Crocker's design I modeled a forty-footer which I thought was about what I wanted. In my short time on the island I had learned that the Bequia style of boat design was centered on experience and educated eye. Except for Crosby, who actually hailed from St. Vincent, Bequia vessels started with the rudimentary dimensions of length, width and draft. No plan was made, no calculations done; there was no lofting of patterns and shapes, not even a scaled half model would be made - simply old master molds which had been passed down through the generations and years of experience were used to model the new form. I knew I could count on these skills when building my boat, but considered it important to start with a concrete concept on paper. In other words, I wanted to know where we were going before we started. Doing my best, I drew my boat.

Somehow, after all the passing years, I still have those drawings, which I found not long ago folded up neatly in one of my Chappelle books, and when I look at them now, I can only shake my head in wonder that we could have built anything at all from such basic sketches. Because my days were filled with the push to get my wood out of the bush, I could only work on the design at night, and try as I may I could never get my head around Chappelle's style of writing. I had no real grasp of the basic concepts of stations, waterlines, buttocks and diagonals, let alone the technical applications of prismatic coefficient, center of buoyancy, displacement or wetted surface. It was probably lucky I was so ignorant of the fact that yacht design is a science which takes years to learn, let alone master, because if I was, I would probably never have started. So how did I get around these complications? Basically, I attempted to draw the new shape by eye, trying to copy each section of the Crocker design as closely as possible to my desired dimensions. It didn't take me long to sketch something I liked the look of, so I let Loren and Crosby know I was ready to go. Loren basically shrugged his shoulders and told me straight out he knew nothing about a plan. What I needed to do was bring him dimensions and some molds and he could make a start, but don't ask him any technical questions about lofting or design. Crosby too was being elusive, probably because he could see my "design" was nothing more than a crude sketch. I was impatient, however, and wanted to make a start. I didn't want to spend any more time trying to figure out the intricacies of naval architecture.

Frustrated by the apparent indifference shown by Loren, Crosby and others, I took Bluesy's advice and using the sail loft floor started lofting, or drawing my boat to full scale, on my own. After getting the profile down, I went and found Crosby. He was obviously impressed because the next day he was at the sail loft bright and early. It was immediately obvious he knew what he was doing when it came to lofting, and over the next couple of days we drew the boat out to full scale, lofting the center frame and six others. In the end we actually refined my rough idea to a basic but workable shape on the loft floor. We then transferred these shapes on to thin white pine which became our molds. My boat was now defined. A start had been made.

Every morning was a new lesson for me, and it wasn't just boatbuilding I was learning about. I chose Loren to be the head shipwright on the project and unwittingly put Crosby's nose out of joint, for on the Monday when we were to start work, he was nowhere to be seen. Nolly told me not to worry about it - Crosby would come around over time. Loren had organized Gilbert Hazel, a shipwright from Paget Farm (also called Southside) to come and work with us. Short, strong and stocky, he was an extremely hard worker. He was a happy, friendly fellow with an endearing smile and a jovial nature.

All the cedar had been brought down by truck from Paradise and dumped on the bayside, a mountain of twisted and bent shapes which would miraculously someday transform into a boat. Nero had been working his way through the pile, stripping the bark off so the wood could "quail" (cure). Our first job was to square and side each timber. This job entailed selecting a piece of wood from the pile which matched the shape of one of our molds. After marking out the curve on the wood with a piece of chalk, this shape was then chopped square inside and out using an ax. The piece was then turned ninety degrees and the other two edges sided off, leaving a squared baulk of timber conforming to a part of one of the molds. This was stacked onto a growing heap of sided timber and another piece selected. On those first days what completely amazed me was the skill with which Loren and Gilbert could use an ax. They made it look so easy. As they motored through the pile, I did my best to keep up, but in reality, my first priority was to not chop my foot off. Day by day the stack of sided Paradise wood grew and grew, but still there was no sign of Crosby.

The next step of the process was to line the squared baulks out to the finished width of the frames and saw them into slabs. In most places in the world an electric band saw would be used for this, but in Bequia that was an unknown piece of equipment, so sharp handsaws were used instead. This was the time to work the cedar, before it dried out and became hard. It was still extremely tedious, hard labor. Gilbert was amazing at this, ripping through slab after slab of timber, his khaki shirt drenched with perspiration but rarely stopping for even the shortest of breathers. I did my best to help, but there was quite a skill involved in handling the saw. Keeping to the

Loren and Gilbert shape the keel.

lines and not wandering off was the main task, where a whole piece of wood could be unwittingly spoiled. I tried to follow my grandfather's advice to "let the saw do the work - don't force it", but that didn't make it any easier.

In the meantime, Loren began chopping the taper into the 12x12 greenheart keel. For this he used an adze and a roofing square. After setting the keel up level we marked out the taper with a long batten. Loren then began to chop the excess off, stopping right at the edge of the line. By the end of the second week we had achieved a phenomenal amount of work. We had squared up and sawn down a giant pile of timbers and shaped the keel, and received plenty of advice from all and sundry as we did so. I only wondered when Crosby would be joining us.

Loren may have been the master shipwright, but Nolly was my ever-present advisor; his place in the scheme of things was invaluable. Everyone on the island knew Nolly and treated him with a kind of princely respect. He lived in a small house next door to Bluesy while his new house was being built, and I would spend many of my evenings hanging out with him at the White House, as it was called, along with an ever-changing cast of cruising sailors who happened to be passing through at the time.

And then one day the enormity of what I was doing hit me like a ton of bricks. It wasn't as if I was just an anonymous beachcomber re-building a wreck on a remote beach somewhere; here I was right out front, on center stage, two hundred yards from the center of town under the critical eye of the whole island, who if they knew nothing else, knew about boats. When I mentioned this to Nolly one night, he said, "It's like watching a movie, man. That whole scene down there is just like a movie, except you are in it! And no matter how much you spend on this boat it's a pittance compared with what you are learning. You talk about politics, religion, fishing, sex…everything under the sun. And you are right there, on stage the whole time, under the almond tree. It's the greatest university there is, and this is your first semester." Day after day we continued to slab up timber, and slowly the pile grew.

"Chris boy, we are going to need a stem," Loren said to me one day. This important piece of wood would form the bow of the vessel, so one morning Gilbert, Bluesy and I took the seventeen-foot long curved white pine pattern and walked up to Paradise to see if we could find anything suitable. After spending the morning searching through the bush, we returned to the harbor without any luck. We got back under the tree just before lunch, explaining to Loren how we could find nothing big enough to fit the shape. It was at this point when Evelyn Davis, an old sea captain leaning against the workbench who had been quietly listening to our conversation, spoke up.

"What? Need a stem? Why I know a tree down in Ravine that would make a nice stem. Solid wood, man. Solid. You'll get a nice stem down there, certain sure." After lunch Mac Simmons drove Gilbert and I up the steep winding road to Mount Pleasant in his Minnie-moke, where we picked up Evelyn. He came walking down his drive dressed for 'de bush' - baggy shirt and pants, a big straw hat and carrying a cutlass. "I always takes me cutlass into de bush," he said as he climbed into Mac's moke. He directed us down an old dirt track, and as we drove, I had a good look around. This was a part of the island I didn't even know existed. It was like being in Scotland, with its big green meadows and rolling hills. This was where Bequia's clannish white community lived, and it was a revelation to me. Off in the east the dramatic, rugged islands of Baliceaux and Battowia stood like sentinels to windward. What a spot! What a view!

The moke wound down the narrow, rutted trail until Evelyn motioned for us to stop. The three of us followed him onto a shaded footpath leading steeply down the hill into the bush. Armed to the teeth with axe, hatchet, handsaw, cutlass and the long mold, it was like we were on safari in search of big game. On the way down the hill we checked five or six different trees, but all were either twisted or not round enough to suit the mold. When we finally reached the bottom of the hill Evelyn directed us to a large stand of a dozen or so huge trees, any of which could make a good stem. We placed the mold on four or five until we spied just the right one. "I remember seeing these trees as saplings when I was just a

Hunting the stem at Ravine.

boy," Evelyn remarked as we cleared away the scrub around the tree so Gilbert could swing his axe. Chips flew as the sharp axe cut into the base of the tree until finally it sighed and shuddered before crashing to the ground.

"Solid wood, man - solid wood," Evelyn said again as he bent over and checked the inside heart of the tree.

It was decided the tree was far too heavy to drag out of the bush as it was, so Gilbert suggested he find a couple of other shipwrights to help rough shape the stem where it lay. I left it up to him to organize the other fellows. There weren't many cars on the island, but there was a man with an old green Land Rover who operated as a taxi, so at six the following morning he picked the four of us up from under the almond tree. Along with Gilbert and myself there was his cousin

Sinclair and an old shipwright in his late seventies they called Captain Cojo. We threw all of our tools into the back of the Rover and drove up to Mount Pleasant.

Once we reached the piece of wood and got organized, the three shipwrights quickly started to work, each knowing the job at hand so well they hardly had to say a word. By early afternoon they were done, the roughed-out stem resting on blocks amongst the mountain of woodchips. Picking up our gear, we climbed up the hill and walked back into the harbor. Now all I had to do was get the piece of wood out of there.

After discussing the options, it was decided the easiest way to get the still very heavy piece of wood out of this difficult location was to manhandle it down to the beach at Ravine where we could launch it through the surf and then tow it around by boat to Friendship Bay, where a truck could pick it up and take it back to the harbor. The following afternoon after work I accompanied Gilbert as he walked back home to Paget Farm to organize a boat and a couple of fellows to help me get the stem out. As we passed through the village of La Pompe, I spotted Carl Ollivierre, and after explaining to him what I needed he said he could easily get a boat and someone to help us, and so it was arranged that I would meet him the following day.

Next morning, I met Carl at Kenneth Allick's rum shop in La Pompe. He was ready to go and had found a cousin of his named James to give us a hand. I followed this pair of fit young fellows down a footpath to the beach where the fishermen hauled their boats up. Carl had borrowed his uncle's blue and red eighteen-foot double ender which lay at anchor just outside the gently lapping surf. Carl pulled on a fine line made fast to shore and we all clambered in to the stout little boat smelling of coal tar, the traditional coating with which the inside of most Bequia boats were painted. The old six horsepower Johnson outboard fired up with one pull, James hauled up the anchor and we were off, motoring across the short chop of broad Friendship Bay. Rounding the point at Saint Hilary's we bounced out into the wind and waves of the open ocean. Ravine Beach stretched between two rocky points and facing southeast was exposed to the swell, so after anchoring the boat outside the surf-line we jumped overboard and swam ashore.

The crop of trees where the stem lay was several hundred yards from the beach. I had no idea how the three of us would be able to move it from where it was to the surf, but after a few minutes of assessing the situation Carl and James had a plan worked out. Using his cutlass, Carl cut several straight young saplings and trimmed them clean of their branches. After shoving and sliding and levering the stem out onto the open ground, Carl lay the saplings down on the ground in front of it to act as rollers. With two of us pulling the wood with a rope and Carl steering we then launched it over the rollers towards the beach. In what I thought was a surprisingly short amount of time we had the big piece of wood floating through the surf and tied onto the stern of the boat, along with several other small pieces of good wood. James picked up the anchor and we slowly motored back to Friendship, towing our enormous catch behind us. After reaching a part of the bay close to the road, James jogged up the beach, returning with several young fellows in tow. We then picked up the timber and carried it to the road. By late afternoon the roughed-out stem lay in the sand next to my keel in Port Elizabeth.

4

Like the Bones of a **Whale**

*"There is an art to fairing lines that is difficult to describe.
This is true because the sole judge of fairness is the eye;
neither mechanical nor mathematical means will produce
a fair set of lines without this assistance."*
- Howard Chappell

Piece by piece the various components of the boat appeared and lay scattered about the bayside. Having no idea what was coming next I would turn up for work at seven o'clock in the morning and Loren would say, "Well Chris boy, we will need a stern-post now along with a deadwood knee," and so we would discuss sizes and dimensions and make a template if needed and then Nero and I would go off into the bush in search of these various pieces. Sometimes this could take a couple of days, and slowly I started to see how important it was to always have the material on hand so work could progress in a continuous flow without any hold ups. I was learning that it was my job to always keep one step ahead of the shipwrights, which wasn't always easy because they worked so quickly.

The next job was to bolt the lead keel onto the greenheart. With plenty of manpower we managed to shift the three-ton lead keel into its final set-up position. We bored the inch and a quarter holes for the bolts through the greenheart with a hand auger. I bought an old bronze propeller shaft from a fisherman, and after measuring the lengths for the keel bolts, I made a trip to St. Vincent to the Public Works workshop where they cut the threads for the bolts on a lathe. The long greenheart keel was clamped on top of the lead and the two pieces were then bolted together. The next step was to set the boat up. Loren was adamant it was bad luck to set a boat up on a Friday, so we decided to leave it until after the weekend.

For two days I hardly slept, but Monday finally rolled around and it was time. We stood the stem up first, and in typical Bequia fashion there were plenty of people around to give us a hand. The sternpost was done the same way. A string line and plumb bob were then used to make sure everything was true and in line before the holes for the bolts were bored, again using long hand augers. The bolts were measured, cut, threaded and driven home. The backbone of the boat was now bolted together. Next came the center frame, which had been previously made and held together with stretchers. This was put into position, plumbed, leveled and "horned off", which

Raising the stem - me, Nolly, Gilbert, Nero and Bluesy.

Uncle Sim helps us set up the center frame.

checked it for square. As Crosby and Loren and Gilbert went about the business of setting up the boat I watched and learned and held molds and did what I could to help, and I could see there was a technical and precise process going on and these guys knew exactly what they were up to.

Being set up so close to the main road, the emerging shape began to attract a huge amount of attention. Women walking by with their shopping would stop and hail out a comment, which would smilingly be answered by Loren or Gilbert, or more usually Nolly. Old timers would casually stop in the shade and pass judgment. "Chris boy she standin' up like bones of a whale," Uncle Sim said to me one day. In the midst of all of this, on center stage, Nolly held court. There was no subject which wasn't discussed, and never a time when he was at a loss for words or an opinion.

As the other lofted set-up frames found their place, the lines of the boat began to be defined. These frames proved to be mostly fair and accurate except for the forward one, which was far too full under the waterline. Loren's sharp eye picked the flaw up immediately. "What de hell are you building here...de *Wallace Triumph*?" he chuckled. (The *Triumph* was a fat, bulky schooner famous for her cargo-carrying capacity). The frame was whipped out and "rectified". The last stage of the set-up was when the "staffs" (technically "ribbands") were run around the boat. These temporary battens represented the planking and checked everything for fairness. The rest of the frames would then be fit to them. Standing back, I was blown away with my boat's shape. To take a glimmer of an idea, put it on paper, and then see it unfold before my eyes was an incredible experience. Most of the pieces fit together perfectly, and the few inaccuracies were soon fixed. Now with a giant pile of slabs to pick from, the timbering of the vessel could begin.

By the end of October, the shape of the boat was clearly defined. In the Bequia style of boatbuilding, once the

Nolly and Kingsley limin' under de tree.

staffs had been run from stem to stern and the frames deemed fair with "no hollows or sucks", the rest of the framing could begin. This was known as "timberin' de vessel". The spacing of the ribs was decided upon and each man was given a section to "timba". Gilbert took the forward section, Loren amidships and Crosby the stern. The frames were always made in pairs (port and starboard), and there was a distinct method as to how each pair was made. A pattern or template of the chosen frame would be made out of a piece of one-half inch white pine board by carefully fitting it to the staffs. Taking the pattern to the pile of slabs, the search for a piece with the right amount of curve would begin. Once one was found, it was dragged over to the bench and the shape marked out on it from the pattern. It was then roughed out with a hatchet and planed square, after which it was carried to the boat and fit to the staffs. Since we had no jig saw or band saw or power tool of any kind, this shaping would be done with a hatchet and then finished with a spoke shave or block plane. Each frame was made out of two or three pieces bolted together with one-half inch galvanized bolts. It was my job to cut and thread these bolts. I must have made hundreds of the bastards.

It was about this time when Nolly decided he had to build a boat. He had sold *The Last Schooner* to a Frenchman from Martinique, and with all of the excitement going on under the almond tree he couldn't contain himself, so one day another shipwright turned up from the southside of the island. Lincoln

Ollivierre was a small, thin, wiry man who dressed immaculately in khaki shirt and trousers and Panama hat. He arrived and quietly went about his work setting up the keel for a twenty-four-foot double ender which Nolly wanted to install a little Saab diesel in. The yard was now a hive of activity, and Nolly held court perched on his throne of an old cray-pot. Two boats were now being built around him, and he was in his element.

As for me, I had two very big jobs ahead. The first was to get the deck beams cut and slabbed so they could quail, so it was back to the bush. For deck beams we needed straighter, taller trees, and so we went to a different part of the island to cut them. Mr. Gooding, an old sea captain, allowed us to cut the trees on his land in Mt. Pleasant, where because they grew in a hollow away from the wind they were not bent and twisted. To beat the heat we started early, when I would meet Nero on the road outside my house well before first light, and with the long beam mold over our shoulder we would hike up the hill to Mt. Pleasant. The trees we were cutting were big and extremely heavy, but at least the road was below us, so gravity helped us drag and tumble the logs out. Despite this the work was extremely hard, and I was glad when we got the last of the logs down to the boat so they could be sided out and sawn into slabs.

My other major task was to organize the lumber I needed to plank the boat, and after my experience with *Corsair* I was determined to use silver bali (not "valley" as the locals pronounced it). This wood came from the South American country of Guyana, and all of my efforts to procure the wood by phone from Bequia had failed. In the end I had no choice but to go and track this elusive wood down myself. The scuttlebutt under the almond tree didn't fill me with much confidence. Guyana was a hardline communist state ruled by an iron-fisted dictator by the name of Forbes Burnham, and I was told it was an extremely difficult place in which to do business. I also heard that in the years since the British had left social order had broken down, so much so that the capital Georgetown was known more for its "choke and rob" than anything else. I took all of this information with a pinch of salt. I had been to some pretty rough places in my time, so going to Guyana didn't really faze me. When the Baltic trader *Jens Juhl* passed through Bequia on her way to Port-of-Spain to pick up a load of cargo, I took the opportunity and jumped on board. Once in Trinidad, I could then catch a plane onward to Guyana.

5
Land of Many Waters...
and Choke and Rob

"Eternity is putting plumbs in seeds,
And wing-correcting decibles in terns."
- Shiloe Veronica, blind Guyanese poet

Jens Juhl was owned by Kenny Mitchnik, a young American who bought the rugged wooden cargo ship in Copenhagen in the early seventies and brought it out to the West Indies. Unlike most Baltic Traders, which in the 70's became fashionable to convert into charter yachts, the *Juhl* was kept in her original configuration and used to haul cargo. The vessel was ninety feet on deck and twenty-four feet wide, had a large cargo hatch amidships and a varnished wheelhouse aft. Kenny, his English first mate Johnny and crew kept the boat in immaculate condition; the black hull was always well-painted, the varnish sparkled, and you could eat your dinner in the engine room it was so clean. The engine itself was the original slow-revving two-cylinder B&W Alpha diesel, and maintained in perfect order. It was painted white, there was never a spot of grease or grime anywhere, and the brass and copper pipes were kept well-polished. Hauling cargo in the West Indies was a tough way to make a living. The competition for cargos was fierce; the conditions were rough, the hours long and demanding, and the work extremely physical. But Kenny and his crew not only managed to survive in the trade, they had a great time doing it. When they did have a couple of days to kill between trips or had some maintenance to do, they usually stopped in Bequia, where the boat and her crew were liked and respected by the island's people.

We arrived in Port-of Spain at sunrise. The crew of a rough wooden trader from Guyana took our lines as we muscled our way in alongside Queen's Wharf amongst a jumble of vessels of all descriptions hailing from every corner of the Caribbean. The various crews were getting ready for the day's work ahead, and a more motley, rag-tag collection of hardened sea-dogs you could never come across. Barkers and stevedores and hustlers were already busy on the wharf, gearing up for another day of push and shove and heat and humidity and sweat. To Kenny and the crew of the *Juhl* this was just another day at the office. By mid-morning we had cleared customs and immigration and I was on my way to the airport, where I caught the daily flight to Guyana.

"Taxi Skip! You need a taxi?" As I emerged from immigration, I was accosted by a mob of taxi drivers. The plane from Trinidad was almost empty and I was one of the few targets for the hungry drivers. After negotiating a fare, I was off down the pot-holed road. It was an hour's drive through flat, green countryside, and the driver had plenty of time to tell me how hard things were in his country.

"Since Burnham came in things have gotten hard…real hard," he told me. "No one is flying because nobody's got any money. A person is only allowed to leave the country with fifty US dollars, and you have to apply to the government for that. How far are you going to get with fifty US? The government has taken over almost all of the business, there is only one store for people to shop at, and everything's rationed. Anyone who can leave this place is leaving. I'd be leaving too, if I could." My driver continued along this vein all the way into town. It was a story I would hear many times over during my stay in this country.

When my driver asked me where I was going to stay, I'd told him Bill's Guest House, which had been recommended to me by the guys from the *Juhl*. He gave me a sidelong look, but otherwise didn't comment. As we got closer to town, he broached the subject once more. "You said you wanted to stay at Bill's? You sure you don't want to go to the Pegasus? It's the best hotel in town. Or the Park? It might be old but it's still nice." I didn't like it when strangers tried to sway me from my intentions. You could never trust their motives. I said no; just take me to Bill's. He shrugged his shoulders and shook his head as if to say, "Well if that's where this crazy white man wants to go then I'll take him there. Don't say I didn't try..."

As we entered the city, I could see that during the height of the British Empire Georgetown would have been quite a spot. Wide, tree lined avenues meandered past beautifully built two-story white-washed wooden houses with red corrugated iron roofs. But on closer inspection it was evident the houses hadn't been painted for a while, and the iron roofs were rusting. It was a city descending into disrepair. My driver pointed out the Pegasus and the Park Hotels in the forlorn hope I might change my mind. Leaving the center of town, we bumped down a pot-holed road lined with rough-looking, unpainted shacks. Eventually we pulled up in front of Bill's, a plain white concrete building surrounded by a high fence topped with razor wire. The tropical evening was descending quickly as I rang the bell at the gate. I noticed my driver didn't hang around too long after I entered, and I had that sinking feeling that maybe I should have listened to him.

I was met at the gate by Bill and his wife, and they seemed a little perplexed to be receiving me. After observing the local surroundings, I felt confident I wouldn't need a reservation. They ushered me inside and showed me a room. The place was a dive, but for six Guyana dollars a night I couldn't expect much more. It was now dark outside, but since it was still early, I thought I might stroll into town and find something to eat. When I expressed my intentions to my friendly hosts, a cloud of concern immediately transformed their faces.

"Are you sure you want to go out? My wife will cook something up for you if you are hungry," Bill said hopefully.

"No thanks," I answered cheerfully. "I need a bit of exercise anyway. So which way is it into town?"

Bill and his wife exchanged a worried glance before Bill answered. "Well when you go outside turn left and it is a couple of blocks into town. Whatever you do, don't turn right!" He escorted me out the door and down the steps to the chain link fence and unlocked the two padlocks for me. "Ring the bell when you return. We'll be waiting up for you."

I stepped through the gate and out onto the dim, unlit street, hearing the padlocks snap shut behind me. Turning left, I set off towards town. It didn't take me long to see that my lodgings weren't located in the best of neighborhoods. Rundown shanties lined the pock-marked road, with barely an electric light to be seen. Except for the occasional flicker of a kerosene lamp, the only other sign of life was the eerie amber glow of a cigarette emanating from the steps of one of the shadowy stoops. This was not the happy, friendly feeling of an easy Bequia evening. As I walked along the dark road, I could almost feel unseen eyes trained on me. The further I went, the more the hair began to stand up on the back of my neck. I started to think that perhaps I should have taken Bill's advice and stayed in for the night.

After two blocks I could see the bright lights of town ahead. Halfway along the third block I could feel I was being followed. I stopped at the street corner and looked over my shoulder to see two black faces just inches behind me, literally breathing down my neck. Across the street a crowd of people stood in the bright lights of an arcade, and thinking this was nothing more than some sort of intimidation I chose to ignore the close attention. I started to cross the street with my two shadows right behind. As I stepped onto the opposite curb they sprung, the tall one grabbing me around the neck and pulling me up against a wall. The corner was well lit, and as my attacker spun me around, I could tell no one was going to do anything to help me. I was pulled up, and as I was being choked from behind the other short, thick, brute of a black man bored in for my pockets.

What happened next occurred so quickly I didn't even have time to think. Although I was being held around the neck, both my arms were free, and as this guy reached for my pockets, I gave him the hardest right hand I could deliver, landing it just above his eye. As he staggered backwards, I reached around and flung the man behind away from me. At this point I didn't know who else might jump me, so with the adrenaline pumping I ran out into the middle of the street and got into my athletic football position which had been hammered into me over the years, yelling "Come on motherfuckers! Come on!" I was ready to take on all comers, like in one of Coach Hartman's "machinegun" drills.

My attackers looked at me for a moment and then ran off into the crowd. Everyone else seemed to be frozen. All I could see was black faces and white eyes. Eventually I stood straight, turned and shakily made my way back to the guesthouse. Bill's wife ended up cooking me that meal, and first thing the next morning I paid them six bucks for the night and checked into the beautiful colonial Park Hotel. I should have listened to that taxi driver in the first place.

After getting my accommodation settled, I set off for the timber production area. In the indigenous Amerindian language, Guyana translates into "the land of many waters", which proved to be a very apt description. Georgetown is located at the mouth of the Demerara River where it empties into the Caribbean Sea. This is one of the many large rivers originating in the Amazonian hinterland to the south which serve as important arteries connecting the remote inland areas with the ports on the coast, and are used for the transportation of logs and sawn timber, among other things. These many rivers are lined with sawmills, and the timber district of Georgetown was no exception. My first stop was the Guyana Timber Export Board, located in the heart of the district on the banks of the Demerara. This agency was set up by the Burnham government to control the export sales of all timber, and it was essential for me to deal with them. I had been in touch by both mail and phone, and I was told by the managing director that several producers had been contacted and that silver bali logs were currently in Georgetown waiting to be sawn to my instructions.

My arrival at the plush offices of the Timber Board was greeted with much fanfare and ceremony. After being ushered into the office of the general manager, I was taken on a voyage through Guyanese timber production and introduced to the scores of exotic hardwoods that grow there. I was told ninety percent of export production was centered on the two species of purpleheart and greenheart, and the big commercial mills concentrated solely on these timbers. Smaller domestic mills cut the variety of other woods for local consumption, and I was given the name of a man I should contact at one of these mills which had acquired silver bali logs and was waiting to meet me. I left the air-conditioned offices of the Timber Board on a positive note, thinking confidently that I should be able to get my timber sawn in a couple of days and then get out of what seemed to me a hell-hole.

The sultry, thick humidity of the grey, overcast morning hit me in the face as the door of the air-conditioned office closed behind. Heavy, low clouds hung overhead and threatened of imminent rain. As I walked into the heart of the timber district the bitumen road ended, turning into a muddy, rutted track teaming with old Bedford trucks, as well as wooden carts pulled both by hand and donkey, loaded down with sawn wood of all sizes and dimensions. On the water side of the road, large tin sheds housed giant sawmills actively engaged in sawing the huge logs laying in the mud at the brown river's edge. I made my way along bustling Water Street until I found the offices of Toolsie Persaud Ltd.

After being rudely received, I was ushered to various departments until I was finally sent to a bald-headed Indian by the name of Mr. Ahmed, an arrogant man who acted as if he was far too busy to deal with me. He vaguely knew of the request by the Timber Board, but his company had no silver bali logs and didn't know when they would have any. Basically, he was of no help whatsoever. I emerged back out on the street with no idea as to what to do next. As I started back up the road it started to rain. Within minutes it became a torrential downpour. Looking for shelter, I stepped inside the open doorway of a small timber merchant. Thinking I might as well make use of my time, I spoke to one of the workers and was quickly introduced to the proprietor, Mr. Leslie Ishmael. Maybe, I thought, he can help me in my search for the elusive silver bali.

Leslie Ishmael was, like almost anyone I had seen connected with the Guyana timber business, of East Indian descent. He had close-cropped black hair from which emerged an enormous set of ears. A pair of thick, black horn-rimmed glasses sat above a banana-like beak of a nose. To top it all off, the man was a hunchback. When introduced he was humble and gracious, almost fawning over me as a rug trader might in the bazaars of Marrakesh. He led me proudly into his paneled, air-conditioned office and offered me a coffee.

"Now, sir, what can I help you with," he asked with a big-toothed smile from across his polished timber desk.

After I explained what I was looking for, he told me he dealt with all species of local hardwoods and tried to interest me in a variety of different types. Silver bali, he said, wasn't an easy timber to buy. It came mostly from the eastern part of the country. Millers didn't like it because the return from a log was poor, which was why it was scarce. When I persisted, he said he did have an associate who dealt with silver bali. If he didn't have any then he didn't know who would. He picked up the phone, and after a lengthy conversation informed me his friend would be there within the hour, which I spent listening to Leslie's laments about how quickly the country was going downhill, as well as his interests in pornographic movies and magazines, which he described in graphic detail.

As I stood at the office window watching the rain bucket down, the door opened behind me and in walked a well-dressed Indian gentleman with compassionate eyes and an engaging smile. Leslie introduced me to Idris Deen. It transpired that Idris and his brothers owned a sawmill on the Courantyne River in eastern Guyana. He did have some silver bali logs on hand, and should be able to supply the amount I was looking for. It was decided I should meet Idris at his mill at Crabwood Creek in a few days' time. I left Leslie's office in a much better frame of mind, feeling on first impression I could trust Idris' word that he would do what he said he would. As for Leslie, well he was a likeable rogue, but I wouldn't trust him as far as I could spit.

The taxi was an old English Austin, and the chubby Indian drove like a man possessed. The rich, green countryside streaked by as we swerved, honked and careened along the narrow two-lane road, all the while dropping off and picking up passengers as we went. Unpainted wooden houses built up on stilts blurred past. People on bicycles and on foot made their way purposefully up and down the side of the road. We passed women dressed in traditional saris carrying various items on their heads. Large meandering cattle seemed to graze with impunity, crossing the busy highway as they wanted. Several times we were forced to skid to a halt and wait patiently for them to move. After four hours of this insanity we finally reached the ferry terminal at New Amsterdam. I climbed out and paid my five dollars, thankful to still be alive. I watched my driver make a beeline to join scores of other drivers sitting in the shade of a huge shed, drinking shots of local over-proof white cane rum as they waited for the ferry to arrive from the opposite shore.

    I joined a throng of people waiting in the shade of the antiquated terminal. Eventually the ferry came, and we climbed aboard the rusty barge. I was crossing the Berbice River, and it was on that ferry that I felt for the first time the enormity, the weight, the inertia of the mighty South American continent. The wide, muddy waters of this powerful river flowed from unseen sources hundreds and hundreds of miles away. As I stood in the intense heat of the tropical sun, I observed my fellow passengers, a mixture of peoples of both African and Indian descent who seemed to understand and accept their insignificance in the face of this timeless land.

    After landing on the eastern shore, I found the correct taxi that would take me to Crabwood Creek. Off I went, my driver a clone of my last who had obviously attended the same driving academy. I eventually arrived in Skeldon, the last town before Crabwood Creek and the end of the road. There was only one establishment that offered overnight accommodation, so I took a room at the Malvern Tavern. The place turned out not only to be a busy local watering hole, but a brothel as well, and so I spent a hot, breathless night amidst the sounds of mosquitos buzzing around my ears, loud music from the bar and grunts and groans emanating through the thin walls surrounding me.

    I was up at first light and out of the place, deciding to walk the couple of miles to Deen's Sawmill. The road was as straight as a rule and filled with locals walking to work at that early hour. Typical stilt houses paralleled the road to my right; to my left built up on the banks of the Courantyne River were

the high, open sheds of sawmill after sawmill. Finally, I came to a brightly lettered sign which read:
DEEN'S SAWMILL ~ SPECIALIZING in
KABUKALI, CRABWOOD, TATABU, SILVER BALI
etc. etc.

News must have reached the mill ahead of my arrival because as I approached the high sheds I was met by a smiling welcoming party. "You must be Mr. Bowman," the first man said, holding out his hand. "I'm Manjob Deen, Idris' brother. Welcome to Crabwood Creek." I was introduced to his brother Deleep, and a tall silver-haired man with a large handlebar moustache who was the foreman of the yard. His name was Raiyo, and I could not help but notice as he shook my hand that he was missing several fingers on his right hand, an occupational hazard of working in a sawmill, I surmised. Idris was on his way from Georgetown and would be there later in the day, so after dropping my bag in the office I was given a tour of the mill.

The sawmill, like most of the others I had seen in my short time in the country, was set up in an open-sided shed under a galvanized iron roof. From the beginning of my tour to the end, the main theme of discussion was the same: how difficult it was to do business under the Burnham regime. Manjob told me there were fourteen sawmills in Crabwood Creek alone, and yet there was no electricity provided by the government. Each mill used diesel engines to drive their equipment. These engines connected to drive shafts which ran long, flat rubber belts to turn the machines. Amidst young boys endlessly running sawdust-filled wheelbarrows to the river's edge, and trolleys loaded with timber moving helter-skelter between the screeching machinery, these great wobbling belts crisscrossing through the shed had to be contended with.

The front of the mill overlooked the broad Courantyne River; on the opposite shore was Surinam, formally Dutch

Guyana. The river here, being close to the sea, was tidal and that morning the tide was very low. A strong, pungent stench emanated from the boggy banks of the wide, muddy river. Lying in the mud in front of the mill was a giant tangle of logs. Being hardwood, these logs didn't float, so they stayed where they were dropped after being brought downriver by barge from the rainforests of the Amazonian interior. One at a time, each log was strapped to a long cable and winched into the mill, where the process of sawing would begin. Raiyo was in charge of strapping the logs, as well as almost every other operation in the mill. He was a warm, charming Zorba-the-Greek kind of a fellow, and everyone in the mill respected him. He was constantly on the move, sorting out the various problems which seemed to be endlessly presenting themselves. Manjob told me that since foreign currency restrictions were in place, spare parts for their machines were almost impossible to buy, so they had to make the replacements themselves in their own workshop from whatever materials they could find. It was immediately obvious to me these were extremely clever and creative people who were able to ingeniously keep things working in almost impossible circumstances.

    Idris arrived from Georgetown later that afternoon, and after hearing about my unpleasant night at the Malvern, invited me to stay with him and his family at the mill. Idris and his family were Muslims whose ancestors had originally been brought to Guyana from India by the British as indentured servants back in the 1800's. Everyone who worked at the mill was of Indian decent; in fact, from what I had seen, it seemed as if the whole of the eastern end on the country could actually have been part of India itself. I was treated as an honored guest, and during my stay learned not only about the day-to-day workings of the mill but also much about life in this far-off, exotic country hidden away deep in the heart of the tropics.

After a week of waiting the day finally arrived when my silver bali logs would be sawn. It was a beautiful, sunny morning when I went out into the mill with Idris to get started. First Raiyo had to select the logs from the heap lying in the mud in front of the mill. The tide was high, however, and the logs were completely covered by the murky black waters of the Courantyne. This was obviously a common occurrence, and I watched as Raiyo nonchalantly stripped down to his baggy underwear, and after taking a diving mask hanging from a nail on a post in the shed, he gingerly made his way out into the water over the slippery logs, dragging a fine rope attached to the end of the steel winch cable. Once out in chest deep water, he proceeded to do the most amazing thing. After taking a deep breath he would dive under, and then, after resurfacing, would stand and put something in his mouth. After tossing away whatever it was, he would move a few feet and repeat the process. After a few minutes of this I had to ask Idris what was going on. "Oh, he's tasting the bark of the logs," Idris answered with a smile. "Each species has its own taste, and no one is better at telling the difference than Raiyo. At low tide he located your logs…now he just has to find them again." It wasn't long before he found what he was looking for. Pulling the cable out he dove down and made it fast, then with a signal of hands the winch operator began to drag the heavy log out of the water. As this was being done Raiyo moved on to find the next one.

The first operation was to cut the log to length. I wanted the longest lengths possible, which Idris said were thirty-five feet, the maximum a truck could carry on the ferry across the Berbice River. This was a shame, because otherwise I could have had full length planks for my boat. Still, thirty-five feet was excellent. Idris told me earlier that the reason most mills stayed away from silver bali was the return wasn't as good as it was with other timbers. "You see, silver bali trees have a water channel which runs up the center. Sometimes this channel can be so big it can ruin a whole log, so it is very important to cut a good tree from the start. Once it has been felled you have bought it. The best cutters are the Amerindians, the indigenous people who originally inhabited this country. Before cutting, they "sound" the tree by hitting it with a hammer. From this they can tell whether it is a good tree or not."

My logs took a day to saw, and for that day the mill was turned over to me. It was a fantastic experience to be able to walk through the mill with my wood and decide exactly how each piece was to be cut. As each perfect plank worked its way through the various stages of processing, I knew that nowhere could I find better material. It was late afternoon by the time Manjob and I finished tallying my wood, but there it was, stacked neatly and waiting to be shipped to Georgetown. Idris was driving back the next day and I would be accompanying him. In the morning I said farewell to these friendly people and returned to Georgetown, where I still had work to do.

I ended up spending another week in Georgetown arranging payment for the timber as well as shipping. Because the wood was being exported, all payment had to go through the Timber Board at inflated export prices. This meant the government (i.e. Forbes Burnham) would keep the "hard" US dollars and pay Deen Sawmills in Guyana currency at local prices. This hardly seemed an equitable arrangement, but then, who ever said communist dictatorships were fair? This system seemed counterproductive because when Idris needed to order a spare part for one of his machines that came from Germany, for example, he had to apply to the government for US dollars to pay for it. This could take months or even years to process, and then the amount doled out severely reduced or flat out rejected. Idris told me that to replace something as simple as one of their drive belts, the whole family would have to queue up for hours at Guyana Stores, the one government outlet, where the rubber belting was rationed to one meter per person! One belt could be over ten meters long. No wonder they were put together with so many joiners. No wonder the country was falling apart at the seams.

Organizing the shipping was extremely frustrating as well. Because of the country's economic meltdown, fewer and fewer ships were calling into Georgetown. The agent at the Timber Board told me I would be lucky to find one going to St. Vincent, let alone Bequia. He advised me to leave the order with him and he would send it on in due course. I didn't like the sound of this idea, so I set out on my own. By patrolling the wharfs, I was eventually lucky enough to find a small freighter owned and captained by Bill Ollivierre from Petite Martinique, and although his cargo was bound for Barbados, he agreed to take my wood as deck cargo and drop it off in Bequia. This was only because he was sympathetic to my cause. He himself had built and owned wooden schooners in Petit Martinique in the past, and knew how important it was for me. Otherwise there is no telling when my timber would have arrived.

With my business finally concluded, I said goodbye to my good friend Idris, without whom my trip could have proved to be a disaster. It had taken a hell of a lot longer than I thought it would, but as I flew out of Guyana I was extremely satisfied with the result. "It was hard goin'," as they would say in Bequia, "but I got through."

Returning to that small emerald isle floating in a sea of diamonds was the best of feelings after the hot, still, oppressive and seemingly endless days and mosquito buzzing nights in choke-and-rob Guyana. In retrospect, I was lucky to have stumbled on to Idris Deen and accomplish what I had in only three weeks, but it seemed as if I had been gone for a year. I was surely happy to get stuck back into work. Loren was especially warm hearted in his greeting, and being back under the almond trees felt as if I had returned home.

In the time I was away work had progressed smoothly, and by the end of November all the frames were in. The boat was "done timbered" and ready for planking. Bill Ollivierre and his freighter *Kate* amazingly arrived in Bequia only a few days after my return. In a matter of a few hours we had my lumber offloaded and stacked neatly beside the boat. By Christmas we had the top two planks (or "bends") fastened on to each side, had fitted six internal stringers, made and fit all of the deck beams, and put in all of the fore and aft carlings ("scarlin's") that defined the size of the cabin, cockpit and hatches. Nero and I had gone back to the bush and cut thirty little knees which tied the deck beams to the hull. We were flying.

Siver Bali, White Cedar and Greenheart.

6
Oh Life!

"Ah, Davidson…woe to the man whose heart has not learned while young to hope, to love, and to put his faith in Life!"
- Heyst, from *Victory* by Joseph Conrad

"Hoot, hoot, haw, haw, hey! I love life and I live it that way!" This was the happy, exuberant philosophy of a young kid who sailed into Bequia on a rickety twenty-six-foot catamaran called *Tantra*. Reid Stowe had built his Polynesian-style craft at his home in North Carolina and sailed it across the Atlantic to the Azores and on to the West Coast of the Iberian Peninsula. I had heard tell of this wild character from Francisco, who had met him in Spain during his own Herculean single-handed voyage. After sailing down the coast of Africa, Reid re-crossed the Atlantic and sailed up the Amazon, where he was kidnapped and held for ransom by pirates. He and his girlfriend Iris somehow escaped their clutches and got to the coast, where Reid regrouped and went back in alone and in the dead of night grabbed his boat and sailed away to Barbados, then on to Bequia where he hauled *Tantra* out on the beach. (Later he would carve a voluptuous, very well-endowed figurehead which adorned the bow of my boat). To me, Reid epitomized the adventurous spirit of the rugged young sailors who sailed through Bequia at that time. Some were round-the-world sailors; others bought old wooden boats and sailed over from Europe. Many appeared from places like Martha's Vineyard, Maine and other sailing havens along the East Coast, a few even braved the long slog to windward against the Trades to arrive from Panama after sailing down the West Coast from home ports as far away as San Francisco and Seattle. Of course, the bar at the Frangipani Hotel was the place for everyone to meet, where countless stories were told, naturally accompanied with the appropriate amount of rum.

My boat on the beach under those sweet-smelling almond trees was the center of my universe, but what made those days so very special was the life which swirled on around me. Working away in the center of town was a daily adventure. A constantly changing cast of island characters, each of whom had a lifetime of stories to tell, was gradually introduced to me. The old timers were all called "Uncle". Gilbert's father Uncle Sim visited us every day, keeping a learned eye on our progress and though quietly spoken his words of advice were respected and heeded. In his youth Loren had done his apprenticeship with this kind man. Uncle Mellie, Bluesy's brother, was cut from the same sailcloth as his sibling. A veteran schooner captain, he loved to spend time leaning on the workbench telling tales of his days at sea, and with his sardonic whit keep us all laughing.

There were loads of others, each with their own peculiarities and colorful idiosyncrasies, and when woven together created the fabulous fabric of the island. One of my favorites was Uncle George Gooding, who was well into his eighties. He would occasionally come into the harbor from Mount Pleasant, making his way down the road with his curly walking stick in front of him to spend some time in the cool of the afternoon watching us work away. I recall him telling me about the first time he ever tasted cheese. He was a young boy, so his story took place sometime in the early 1900's. It was the day the schooner *Columbia* was launched. "She was a big vessel; well over one hundred feet," he said, "and the men were having a hell-of-a-time launching her. There happened to be a steamboat in the harbor run by a Dutchman, and he tied a cable onto her and pulled her in. There was a big fête on the beach afterwards and the women had cooked up a lot of food. The Dutchman brought in a wheel of cheese, and that was the first time I ever tasted it. You can imagine, hey Chris boy! The smell, the taste. At first, I thought it very strange. I got to like it though," he added with a chuckle.

Gambini was a skinny rake of a man who was forever walking through town with a brown paper bag in his hand containing bottles of his own brew of hot sauce he attempted to sell. He had the look of a man who hadn't eaten in weeks. When you talked to him his blue eyes bulged out of his chocolate-colored face, and although quite an intelligent man in the odd times he was sober, when on the rum could often be seen standing in the middle of the road carrying on a rambling dialogue with the sun, which he would stare at unblinkingly for hours. He claimed to have traveled the world in his youth working with a circus, hence his name, and several times told me tales of his days under the big top.

Old Dells lived in a little shack I passed daily on my way to and from work. He, like Nero, was a Carib Indian who always dressed immaculately and had a distinguished air about him. He would come into town and stand on the road under the stern of the vessel propped on his gnarly walking stick quoting scripture. Sometimes, when he was really on a roll, he could be provoked by Nolly and the others to speak in the Unknown Tongue, which he took very seriously. *"For he that speaketh in an unknown tongue speaketh not unto men, but unto God: for no man understandeth him; how be it in the spirit he speaketh mysteries," - Corinthians 14:2.* Since none of us could understand him maybe he was - who knows?

Uncle Arnie Ollivierre was a boatbuilder from Paget Farm, and according to Nolly one of the most gifted on the island. Arnie had the rugged looks of Anthony Quinn, the largest hands I had ever seen, and when sober a quiet, gentle soul with a devilish sense of humor. "But", as Loren would say, "when de moon hits him, look out!" He could be drunk for a week or more. He would literally stagger along the road insulting anyone or anything that moved. I witnessed him arguing with some inanimate objects (such as trees) as well. He could be heard long before he would be seen, making his way down the road abusing at random any innocent passer-by with the most vulgar language imaginable. Eventually he would reach the stern of the boat, weaving and struggling to keep his balance as he would cuss all and sundry, as well as their mothers and all their relations, before staggering on. In this mood anyone was fair game, and respect given to no one. Sometimes it landed him in jail, but generally Uncle Arnie was all bark and no bite and tolerated for his excesses.

And then there were the regulars who visited the boatyard almost daily, the fishermen like Kingsley, or Prop as he was called, his brother Yankee, the white fellas from Mount Pleasant like Blake, Cutter, Uncle Mackie, Brother King or his father Uncle Teaman, who after an early morning's fishing would stop in under the tree and take turns in 'provoking' Nolly or Bluesy or Loren into getting involved into some sort of entertaining conversation. Every hour of every day, a constant cast of characters were drifting through our boatyard. Many times, they might actually get involved in the work by taking the saw out of my hand and sawing a piece of wood for me.

And the stories! "Hey Chris," Nolly asked one day, "you ever heard the story of Willy King and his new shoes? Willy lived up in Mt. Pleasant and on Sundays used to come down to the harbor in his best clothes to spend the afternoon in town. He'd never owned a pair of shoes until one day he bought a shiny pair in St. Vincent. This Sunday he tied his shoes over his shoulder and ran down the goat track that led to the main road, where he sat down and put his shoes on. After spending the afternoon strolling through the harbor showing them off, he reached the track home and took his shoes off. On the way back up the hill, he kicked a tree root and knocked his big toenail clean off. When he got home, he told his wife, 'it was a good t'ing I didn't have me shoes on, otherwise I would have mashed 'em up!'"

It was a cool, clear, windy January morning. One of those mornings not long after sunrise when the shadows were still long and the harbor continued to sleep, and it seemed to be the most peaceful place in the world. The yachts anchored in the bay swung to the strong gusts whipping down the valley; the water was a deep ice blue, and the swaying palms were all that appeared to be alive as they rustled to the wintery Tradewinds, except for the few of us busily building our boats under the almond tree.

The mood was suddenly broken when a passer-by in a car slowed and shouted, "*Lady Angela* mash up over Bequia Head!" After a moment's discussion, Nolly and I jumped into Mac's Minnie-moke and drove quickly over the pot-holed road up the valley behind town towards the rising sun. After winding down through the shady coconut plantation at Spring we hit the beach, veered left and swung onto a dirt road back up the hill through the bush towards the windward end of the island. At the end of the road we left the car and made our way through the thick scrub until we found ourselves perched on the edge of a cliff overlooking the savage, windswept sea. To our left rose the "Bullet", a jagged sheer pinnacle shooting vertically out of the sea like a whale breeching. Huge surf pounded the razor-like rocks that lined this unfriendly windward shore. The wind screeched into our faces off the open Atlantic Ocean. Two hundred feet below us a desperate scene was still unfolding. There was nothing for us to do but watch as 'those white shipwrights', as Nolly called the breaking waves, went about their destructive business of tearing apart a hundred-foot schooner right before our eyes.

The *Lady Angela* ran passengers and cargo between St. Vincent and the islands of the Grenadines. In her prime she would once have been a proud sailing schooner, but in her last days was nothing more than a hogged, leaky motor vessel with only her fore mast remaining. The after half of her deck was covered by an ugly white deckhouse, giving her the look, as Nolly once pointed out, of "a weary pilgrim bound for Jerusalem carrying his coffin on his back." Morris Tannis was the captain that day on the *Angela,* a man whose nickname "Captain Hog" said all you needed to know about him. On that windy January morning he was bound to St. Vincent from the exclusive island of Mustique, which lies roughly seven miles south-east of Bequia. On board were over one hundred passengers, most of them workers and their families going home for a break after tending to the rich and famous over Christmas. Bequia lies directly between the two islands, and the shortest distance would be to take a north-easterly course and sail to windward of Bequia to reach St. Vincent. On this day the wind was blowing thirty-five knots, with a heavy sea running. A more prudent captain would have chosen the far safer but longer route of passing to leeward of Bequia. Not Captain Hog. He set his course over Bequia Head, and pointed the bow of his battered, smoke-spewing "weary pilgrim" towards one of the roughest patches of water in the Grenadines.

First the gaff broke and the tattered canvas foresail ripped immediately to shreds. Morris pushed on, pounding into the heavy seas which broke over the bulwarks and swept the deck. Nearing the rocky windward point of the island, he was leaving no room for error, passing only a couple of hundred meters clear of the reefs and jagged rocks. Then, just as the broken schooner approached the dreaded Bullet, the engine stopped running. Some say he ran out of fuel; others that she just broke down because of poor maintenance. At any rate, the vessel was only minutes from destruction as she was swept towards the awaiting rocks. The crew let go the anchor and somehow it held, pulling her head to wind. The *Angela's* stern swung only meters from annihilation as huge waves broke over her bow. Aboard there would have been sheer panic and pandemonium. Somehow, the tattered old anchor line held. As chaos and panic reigned on deck, the ship's boat, which was being towed astern, was brought up alongside. Immediately the mate Patterson and eight of the crew jumped into the boat to save themselves. A desperate father begged them to take his baby girl, and just as he was handing her to them the anchor line broke and the big blue schooner fell away to starboard, immediately capsizing the skiff, with the father just able to cling on to his child.

It was nothing but Benevolent Providence which saved those people that day. As the ship was driven ashore, she landed broadside on to a low, rocky ledge, and with each violent roll of the vessel scores of passengers leaped ashore, as if jumping onto a wharf. Most stepped ashore with their belongings intact. Some didn't even get wet! As for the mate Patterson, he and his greedy shipmates drowned and were the only casualties.

As the survivors gingerly wound their way up the cliff, Nolly and I sat and watched those "angry white shipwrights" do their business. It didn't take long. In less than an hour there was nothing left but floating driftwood and debris. A few days later a fishing sloop from Southside was commissioned by the government to see if they could find any of the bodies of the drowned crew. They returned to the harbor with seven corpses, and we watched from under the tree as the bloated bodies were hoisted by the neck, leg or arm and unceremoniously slung onto the wharf from the end of the boat's gaff. Being from St. Vincent meant there was no respect shown by that Southside crew for the dead. As for Captain Hog, he continued on as if nothing happened. Not much more than a week later he broke down while skippering the *Whistler*, another swine of a vessel, and was adrift for hours to leeward of Bequia before a passenger finally got the engine started again.

Nero and I went back to the site of the wreck not long afterwards to see if we could salvage the mast. We made our way down to the rocky shore and found the spar washed up on a small beach. It was snapped in half. The broken mast wasn't all we found. Sticking out of the sand like a grotesque piece of driftwood was the black forearm and hand of Patterson, the only unaccounted-for crewman. When we arrived back at the harbor, I reported our find to the police. The following day they sent two police officers out to the remote beach with Coolie, the half lunatic town drunk, who was given the job to destroy the body with a jug of acid. Apparently, the officers didn't actually accompany Coolie to the beach, because when he rejoined them, he said he destroyed two bodies and demanded to be paid double! He might have been crazy, but he wasn't stupid.

The Money Tree.

The boat continued to quickly come together. With the hull planking completed, we began to work from the inside of the boat. Getting on deck was interesting. In true Bequia style, we made the most of what was on hand - in this case an ancient, gnarled tamarind tree the locals called the Money Tree. It grew by the side of the road, just at the stern of the vessel. And it grew in such a way as to make a perfect stairway to the deck. We never had to build a ladder; the Money Tree was all we needed.

By the end of April, the cabin sides and hatches were made, and a month later the decks were laid and we were caulking the hull. Ray had been shopping and found a marine hardware store in San Diego going out of business and shipped down several crates of fittings, sailcloth, and tools. We reached the end of June and the main part of the construction was finished. It was good timing, because I had run out of money. As much as it hurt, I had no choice but to pay Gilbert and Loren off and continue working on alone. This situation was always something which I knew to be inevitable. In the boom and bust cycle which permeated the Life of Ray, the downward trending of the cash flow graph was never far around the corner. From my point of view the number one priority was to get the boat in the water and get her sailing…by hook or by crook. If I had to sleep on bare floorboards it would be okay, as long as I had sails on her. For this I needed blocks and wire and rope and shackles and all the other bits and pieces which make up the rigging. None of this was available locally, but I heard the duty-free islands of St. Maarten and St. Barths three hundred miles to the north had chandleries which sold what I needed. A friend of mine was leaving to sail north to St. Maarten and offered me a ride, so I called my old man to find out how things were going and see whether he could come up with enough cash to see me through.

"Look, when this deal goes in a couple of weeks, I'm going to have enough money to build a fleet of boats!" he yelled down the phone line.

"Yeah, but if I sail up north to get this gear, will you be able to get me the money to pay for it?"

"Don't worry about it. You go ahead and sail up there and call me when you're ready. I'll transfer down what you need - no problem," he said with total authority. With those positive words of assurance, I threw some things in my knapsack, grabbed the last of my cash, and sailed north.

St. Maarten was wild! Once I caught up with my old friend Willy Halsey, I was hooked straight into the local party scene.

This Dutch/French island was a far different place to Bequia. A popular holiday destination for tourists from the States, the island was saturated with big high-rise hotels, casinos, pricy restaurants and trendy bars. I hadn't seen anywhere like it since the Canary Islands, and though it was fun for a day or two, it wasn't really what I was there for. The Heineken beers and rum were cheap, but I still had to pay for them. I phoned home collect and was told that money was on the way. And so I waited. And phoned home. And waited. And despite all the promises, nothing turned up. The big chandlery Willy worked for had all I needed, but I had no money to pay for anything.

While I was waiting, I decided to take a trip over to the nearby French island of St. Barths. What I found was a very quiet, sleepy island that reminded me a lot of Bequia. Just off the main wharf was a small marine store, and it didn't take me long to meet the owner. Lou-Lou Magras was a bright young local, and we hit it off straight away. He wore a Ché Guevara-style beret and khaki work clothes, had a wispy red beard and a jovial disposition. He quickly took an interest in my project and showed me to his Aladdin's Cave of a warehouse, which was littered with rolls of schooner style rigging wire, anchor chain, wooden blocks and other work-boat type equipment.

I got straight to the point. I told Lou-Lou I had run low on cash and wanted to get my boat sailing. If he were willing to credit me for what I needed, I would pay him at my first opportunity. Lou-Lou smiled, accepted my offer and we went straight to work putting together what I needed. He had lots of traditional old-time gear that modern yachtsmen weren't interested in, so he could work out a great deal for me. Then we shook hands, and that was that.

Of course, it was one thing to get my hands on all of this gear, but how was I going to get it back down island? The *Fidelity B.* and Captain Ellis Bethel from Petite Martinique solved this dilemma. The big sloop was alongside the Gustavia wharf loading tax-free rum, whiskey and cigarettes to smuggle back to the Grenadines. The rough-and-ready Captain remembered me from my time sailing aboard the *CCC* at the Carriacou Regatta, and so agreed to help out and carry the stuff south and drop in Bequia for me.

The money never did materialize, but I still returned to Bequia with another mission accomplished. Somehow, I kept moving ahead. It wasn't the first time Ray hadn't become the World's Richest Man, and it wouldn't be the last. I didn't let it get me down. I'd learned to roll with the punches. I was confident everything would work out in the end, and I knew he was doing his best. One thing was for certain…I wasn't going to be left stranded on the beach with an unfinished boat. The thought never even entered my mind.

It was early on a Sunday morning. The rainy season had arrived and I stood at the doorway of my little house and gazed over the cornfields across the road, watching a rain squall march down the bay towards the western horizon. A young boy timidly came up the steps and handed me a folded piece of paper before scampering off again. In neat, perfectly formed handwriting it said:

Dear Mr. Chris,

Come see me. I have some crutches for you.

Sincerely,

W. Bynoe

Paget Farm

I read the cryptic note once again. It could only mean one thing. The *Fidelity B.* must have reached. I quickly put on a shirt, closed the door and jogged down the steps to the road, where I turned left, stepping out on the three-mile walk to Southside. "Walter Bynoe," I thought. He was the same guy who looked after our surfboards when me and Cisco first visited Bequia. "Amazing how seemingly random events can dovetail together given time."

I entered Walter's small dry good's shop. The pungent smell of salt fish permeated the building. There wasn't a whole lot on offer - tins of sardines, corned beef, packets of crackers, that sort of thing. And rum, naturally. "Hello Crutch!" Walter smiled from behind the counter. I had no idea what he meant, but I had noted he obviously enjoyed the sound of that word. "I have some crutches here that someone left for you." Walter was one peculiar individual. His alabaster skin was heavily blotched by the tropical sun. He wore black, horn-rimmed glasses, and a white panama hat sat jauntily atop his kinky red hair. A portly man, he was neatly attired in khaki drill, and when he talked his head laid back and swayed from side to side as a mischievous glint emanated from his squinty pink eyes. He was a highly respected man of the village, and he was on my side. "Your crutches are safe here with me. Our friend from south dropped them in last night. I'll organize a taxi for tonight to bring them up for you." And true to his word, there was a knock on my door in the early hours of the morning, when all my gear was quietly shifted in and stored safely in my spare room. Looking over it all the only thing missing was a gallon of Woolsey's White Yacht Enamel. "Freight", was all Nolly said when I mentioned it to him.

I now had everything I needed to finish my boat. I was just lacking one minor ingredient to keep the wheels in motion…cash. I was between a rock and a hard place. My dad and I had made a deal. I was committed, exposed, out on a limb, and didn't have a lot of options. There was no telling when Ray might come through again. Steven's Yachts had enough skippers, and I didn't have any other options for work. Somehow, I had to get the boat in the water and sailing. Waiting for money on a hope and a promise would not be enough.

The answer to my dilemma presented itself in the way of an old friend. Dave Davis owned a beautiful Aberking & Rasmussen yawl named *Muki*, which he chartered through the islands every winter. I had known him since my Grenada days. I was working on the boat one day when he passed by and offered to buy me lunch. We went to the Admiralty Cove and sat down to conch roti's. Dave asked me how things were going. I told him things were fine, but I just needed a last bit of cash to get me over the final hurdle.

"How much do you need?" he asked.

"A thousand U.S. would do it, I think," I answered.

Dave quietly ate his roti. "I'll loan you the money," he said. "I'll be returning next season, and you can pay me back then."

I was blown away. I could now get my boat off the beach and into the water, where she belonged.

The locals had a saying I used to hear almost daily. It was a sort of exclamation, quietly exhaled under the breath. "Oh Life!" That was it. Short and sweet, those two words said it all.

7
Onward and Upward

*"Ohhhhhhh...the pump's give out
and the galley's overboard,
it's time for us to leave her!"*
- Traditional sea chantey sung on launching day.

Slowly but surely, I was collecting the myriad of materials I needed to finish the boat. What I didn't have was a mast. In the old days, Canadian and American schooners sailing south to the West Indies with cargos of salt fish would also load Douglass fir trees as deck cargo, which could be on-sold to local boatbuilders to make masts and spars, helping to fuel the island's schooner-building boom after WWII. Those days were long gone, however, and I wasn't going to find an appropriately sized piece of wood just lying around. Or would I? In the far corner of the harbor the bones of the forlorn hulk of the schooner *Gardenia* lay half submerged in the shallows where she had reached her ignominious end. Up on blocks next to our little boatyard was her old foremast, which now belonged to the owners of the *Friendship Rose*. It was fourteen inches in diameter and over sixty feet long. It had acted as a giant park bench for passers-by for years, and had been there so long it was hardly noticed. I asked Loren about it, and he dismissed it as being rotten, but I persisted and spoke to Kelvin and Henry from the *Rose* about it. They agreed to sell it to me for three hundred local dollars on the condition that I only paid for it if it proved to be sound, so with Gilbert and Loren back on board we started to work on it. Loren sucked his teeth and frowned, as he did when things weren't right, and said we were only "throwin' good money after bad", but I persisted.

Spar making is a skill in its own right, and I wouldn't have had a clue where to start. I watched and learned with keen interest as Loren and Gilbert went about their business. We decided my mast would be eight inches in diameter and fifty feet long. Using a string line, one side was marked out and chopped down plumb with an adze. "Good wood so far Chris-boy," Gilbert smiled. "She looks solid." Loren wasn't saying anything yet.

After making the first side perfectly flat, we ran a centerline and laid out the new spar's dimensions, including taper and length. The mast was then chopped square. The rot, which had made the old mast look so bad, was only on the outside and was cut cleanly away. When the spar was planed square, Loren turned to me and shook his head. "You know Kingsley is right. Your name should be Christopher Goodluck in truth!" The mast was then formed into eight and then sixteen sides before finally being planed round. I now had a mast, and it was as good a piece of Douglas fir as you would ever want to see.

Lincoln Ollivierre, who was working on Nolly's boat, recommended a cousin of his to help me with my rigging. Sippy Ollivierre was a tough, hardworking fisherman from La Pompe who had served as mate for years on the big family schooner *Turtle Dove*. He a was short and wiry man, red in complexion, and his eyes were the aquamarine blue of the Tobago Cays. Sippy always wore an old green fedora and checked flannel shirt with the sleeves rolled up. The harsh sun had taken its toll on his skin over the years; it was splotchy and burned and his lips were covered with what looked like permanent blisters. But he knew his rigging. He proved to be a hard worker. And he could talk! The galvanized rigging wire I acquired from Lou-Lou was strung up between the trees where it was greased, wormed, parceled and served with tarred marlin twine. And as Sippy worked, he carried on a constant monologue. "I don't like too much a land work, mon. Too boring. Land work's too much a hog-shit work, mon. But seawater? You can gi' me any kind a seawater work and I'll take it. No, there's nothin' better than seawater work." Sippy finished off the rigging by neatly sewing canvas over the tightly served marlin, which he then painted with a mixture of white lead and linseed oil.

"Guarantee riggin', mon. This here will see out de life of de vessel and more. This ain't no hogshit riggin', mon…" is how he put it when he was done.

From the time I first began to discuss the idea of building a boat in Bequia, I had heard stories of the legendary Klaus and his boat *Plumbelly*. He was a German architect who had arrived in Bequia sometime in the early sixties. After spending a year or two on the island, he decided to build a boat and sail it around the world, and so in 1964 got Loren to help him build her. Modeled after the local Bequia double-enders, she was stout and strong and planked with silver bali. The boat was only twenty-six feet long, and though extremely seaworthy still a very small craft for such an undertaking. During those last months of the construction of my boat, Klaus returned to Bequia after seven years to complete his circumnavigation, much to the excitement of the whole island. He and I became good friends, and evenly matched chess opponents. When it came time to make my sails, he joined Bluesy and me in the sail loft to help design and cut them.

Captain Neils Thomson was an eccentric American who owned the Friendship Bay Hotel on the south side of the island. He had commanded square riggers for years in the Pacific before he made his millions with a king crab processing plant he built on one of the desolate Aleutian Islands in the North Pacific. He loved ships and the sea, and always owned several large sailing craft. One of them was a lovely Baltic Trader named *Lilly*, which he had decided to finally let go of. I had made a last-minute dash to Grenada to buy my anti-fouling paint, sailing down with Kees aboard his trimaran *Wizard of Is*. While purchasing my paint, I noticed *Lilly* on the slipway. Outside at the dockyard bar I ran into Sid, the cockney son-in-law of Captain Thomson, who I knew looked after the boat.

Sid was sitting at a table covered with beer bottles with a few other log-haired guys I wasn't familiar with. They seemed to be having a jolly good time. "Must be the new owners," I thought. Sid saw me and shouted out for me to join them for a beer. We ended up having a few. A fellow named Neil had just bought the boat, and he seemed to be a really good guy. There was something about him that struck a chord, but I couldn't quite place it. The afternoon wore on, and when we were on our last beer the realization finally hit me. I knew who the new owner was. It was Neil Young.

A week or so later *Lilly* sailed into Bequia. It was a quiet Sunday afternoon, and Sid brought Neil ashore to check my boat out. We climbed up the Money Tree and went down below and had a bit of a yarn. "It's like being in the belly of a whale," Neil said as we sat on the bare ribs amongst the shavings. That night Neil brought his guitar ashore and played for us all, jamming with a local guy named Flazzo, who was a wonderful musician in his own right. My mind rolled back a few years to a night at a little club in Huntington Beach called the Golden Bear, where I saw Neil, dressed in his American Indian jacket, cranking with Buffalo Springfield. Who would have ever guessed I'd be drinking beers with him in a bar in Bequia ten years later?

We dug out under the boat and leveled the sand off so she could run easily into the water. We built a wooden cradle beneath her which sat atop rollers and ways. By mid-

November she was very close to being ready to launch. Amongst the long list of last-minute details was the job of coming up with a name. This is not as easy as it sounds. I had lots of ideas, but none of them stuck. Then one night at a party at the "Church" a girl named Patty, who was crewing aboard *Jens Juhl,* mentioned a name. And I knew that was it.

Just Now. Built by hand and eye.

For months people in the road would hail Loren as they passed. "Hey Mr. Joe! When are all-you goin' to launch dat vessel?" to which he would always reply, "Jus' now...we'll be launching her jus' now." In island terms, that could mean anytime. It could be next week, or it could be next year. So that was it. I would call her *Just Now*. But in Bequia tradition I couldn't tell anyone else except the Godmother of the vessel, whose job it was to make the ship's flag with her name on it. The flag would then be unfurled on launching day for the first time, when everyone would learn her name. For this job I asked Bluesy's wife Mary. She said she would happily make the flag, but as for doing the christening I would have to ask someone else.

Naturally, my parents would have to be there. If I were going to announce a date, I needed to know that I would be ready. Boxing Day sounded like a good day to launch a boat, so that would be it. Any day was okay with Loren as long as it wasn't on a Friday. This would give me about a month to be ready. As the day approached, a tall, bearded black fellow wearing a white hard hat wandered past the boat singing sea shanties. He was called simply "Big", and Loren told me whenever he turned up it was time for a launching. The countdown was on.

From my experience with *Corsair*, I knew that having everything totally organized for launch day was absolutely essential. For several months leading up to the big day the old timers under the tree were advising me to get my launching anchor out so that she could "set". Stories of schooners being stuck on the beach for days because their anchor "came home" was not what I had in mind, so weeks earlier Nolly and I had pulled up "Satan", a massive fisherman's anchor that belonged to Macdonald Davis, and dropped it well out into the harbor and marked it with a buoy. The block and tackle that would pull the boat in would be attached to this anchor.

My family all arrived a couple of days before Christmas and moved in to the Frangipani. The boat was ready… now all we had to do was get her in the water.

Launching day and I was up at first light. I was wired, like my body was plugged into 240 volts. My nerve endings were tingling. I stopped into Bluesy's house and collected the ship's flag from Mama Simmons. As I stepped back out on to the main road a rainsquall drifted overhead. "It's a shower of blessing, Chris-boy," Mary called out. "The rain won't stay," she continued. "It's just a passing shower. But it's always a good sign. Don't frighten! You'll be right!"

I walked down the hill and around the corner, where I stopped and took a long look. A feeling of sadness passed over me. This was the last time I would be making this walk to find my boat waiting for me on the bayside. I walked on and stood next to the Money Tree, remembering all the hard work and good times, and thought that it was a shame it all had to end.

This feeling passed quickly because from that moment on people began to arrive from every direction. Nolly began organizing the hauling line. I had borrowed a huge set of block and tackle from the guys on *Friendship Rose,* and this had to be put into a boat and then run out to the anchor. In the meantime, Bluesy was setting up the check line, which led astern of the boat and looped around the Money Tree. This was to control the speed of the boat as she rolled across the sand towards the water.

Sippy turned up with a crew of fishermen from La Pompe. They got stuck into rigging a bridle around the boat to tie the hauling line onto. Kenny and Johnny and the crew from *Jens Juhl* touched ashore and hauled up their little sailing dinghy *Panama*. Other yachtsmen began arriving and were milling around the boat. A man I had never seen before appeared like a hurricane, and with no questions asked took my anchor chain and began strapping down the boat to the cradle. There was no discussing the point with him. It just had to be done. "Who the hell is that?" I asked Noel Bevin, an elderly English sailor. "That's Henry Wakelam. He's off that big steel three master out there. Bit of a living legend, actually. Old friend of Bernard Moitessier, the famous French single-hander." What he was doing made sense, so I let him get on with it, but I couldn't have stopped him even if I wanted to!

There was so much going on that I couldn't stand still for a second. A colorful garland of flowers had been put together by some of the girls, and it was being tied under the bowsprit. Kingsley's wife Delores and some other women from Mt. Pleasant had cooked up pots of food to feed everyone after the boat went in, and were setting up on the work bench. Someone came with a message from Father Adams asking if I would be ready for him to bless the boat at nine, and I said yes. The rum punch and cold beers were set up, and Harold, the bartender from the Frangipani, put himself in charge of doling out the drinks after she floated. Loren was there, silently observing, but with concern written all over his face. Crosby turned up, prancing around proud as a bantam rooster, having obviously been into Baby Lou's rum shop on the way for a couple of early whiskeys. Nero was there, and Big, and Evelyn Davis who got me the stem, and Klaus and Uncle Sim, and Mac Simmons, and Kees the Wizard, and Son Mitchell, and Walter Bynoe and most all the people I knew on the island, and a lot that I didn't.

My mom, dad, and brother Rick, along with my sister's little boy Brahm walked up the beach together from the Frangipani. Although Mary had made the flag, my sister Joan was going to christen the boat. At nine o'clock the Anglican priest Father Adams, dressed in his robes with bible in hand, arrived to bless the boat. First, he read a passage from the bible and then circumnavigated the vessel, sprinkling it with holy water. When he was done, I went to the stern and made a small speech thanking all and sundry who had helped put this fabulous boat together. The ships banner was unfurled and then I screwed the name board on the stern and everyone cheered. *Just Now* the name board said, and underneath it *Bequia*. Then we went forward and Joan smashed the

Launching Day on the Bequia bayside.

Champagne over the bow. We were ready to launch! By now there were hundreds of people milling about the boat, and to be honest, it was all a bit chaotic.

Kenny, Nolly, Bluesy and I got together and worked out how we were going to do this. The key was to go gradually and carefully, and not let the crowd get carried away. We decided Kenny would be in charge of the hauling line, with Bluesy on the check line. When Kenny said stop, we had to stop. A crowd of people jostled to get a hand hold on the inch-and-a-half manila rope. There were islanders and yachtsmen, laughing and joking next to each other, stretching from the water's edge past the starboard side of the boat all the way up to the road. The order to take up the slack was given, and everyone slowly started to haul together until the tension came onto the boat, at which point Kenny raised his hand and held them up. The rope was stretched tight as a piano string. Sippy and his crew held the turn on the check line. Everything was looked over, and then Bluesy gave Kenny the nod. The team started pulling again, the check line was eased. The tension increased until finally with a start and a low rumble the boat moved! A loud cheer went up in the air as Kenny threw his arm up to stop and the check line was snatched tight. The rollers and cradle were looked over again, everything was deemed to be okay, and the boat was pulled another couple of meters. And so it went. As the end of the cradle came off a roller everything was stopped, at which point the roller was 'overhauled', or carried to the front, and when in position the boat was moved again. Slowly she moved down the beach until the cradle and rollers reached the water's edge.

From here things got tricky. This is where the experience of the men at the end of the rollers really came into play. They were called "watermen", and they came from all parts of the island. Their job was to keep the rollers moving in the murky, stirred up shallows. It was quite a dangerous job, but they just jumped in and knew what to do. The cradle entered the water, the rollers and ways were overhauled, and she went on. The keel touched the water. The watermen were up to their armpits in the sea, and had to duck under to keep the rollers moving. Kenny and Bluesy huddled together for a discussion. The word was given to pull hard and "let she run".

December 26, 1976 – Just Now floats out onto the calm waters of Admiralty Bay.

The check line was let go, Kenny gave the order and the crowd ran with the hauling line. *Just Now* rumbled and bounced over the rollers and shot out into the bay and floated. The crowd threw their arms into the air and cheered. She was made fast to a mooring, and young kids swam out and climbed aboard and then jumped off.

"Any water? Any water?" Loren yelled to one of the kids aboard. He ducked below, then came back on deck and signaled no. "Well done!" Loren exclaimed to me, happy and relieved. Gilbert had a smile from ear to ear. People shook my hand and slapped me on the back. There were tears in my eyes. After a year and a half of hard work, *Just Now* was floating! Ray, my mom and I found each other and shared a big hug. They were all smiles. Harold opened the bar, and the party started.

Thinking about it now, the whole thing really was quite an accomplishment. For a man who didn't have a "real" job and a kid who had no skills, we'd done okay.

The smoke cleared. The party ended. The holidays passed and my family went home. I worked away to get the boat rigged, as well as getting a basic interior together. Going for my first sail was as emotional to me as the launching. The boat looked great on the water, but how would she perform? "Only a rock can't sail," Gilbert Hazell once said to me. I was hoping she would do a little better than that. Loren, Kingsley, Sippy and a few others made up my crew that day, and *Just Now* turned out to be everything I had hoped she would be. Solid, stable and well balanced; she glided through the water and was a delight to steer. The month of April rolled around, and almost two years to the day after my serendipitous crash landing on the sands of Port Elizabeth. I was once again bound north for Antigua Race Week. Not on a tiny, leaky death trap this time, but on an immaculately built, sweet sailing Bequia gaff sloop.

Sailing home after winning the PSV Regatta

The summer months came along, the Trades swung to the southeast, and the harbor emptied of cruising yachts. After spending a bit of time exploring the islands up north, I had returned to Bequia, passing my days working on the boat and playing chess with Klaus at the Frangipani. Most evenings I wandered up to Nolly's house, where we spent a lot of time dreaming over the beautiful lines of the famous Grand Bank's schooners catalogued in Howard Chappelle's great book *American Fishing Schooners,* which was another of the books Ray had given me. Looking at the photos of those old schooners under construction led us to imagine the Bequia waterfront in its hey-day and on how great it would be to build something like that. I got to know the book by heart. My favorite of the one hundred and thirty-seven designs cataloged by Chapelle was the schooner *Stranger,* designed by the notable Bostonian Naval Architect B.B. Crowninshield way back in 1903.

Amidst the October doldrums in the heart of the rainy season I made up my mind. After being away for close to six years, I was going home. I had five hundred dollars left in my pocket, which was just enough to buy a round-trip ticket to California. I knew if I didn't go then, the money would eventually be spent on the boat, and there was no telling when another chance might come again.

I touched my dinghy ashore early on a clear, calm Bequia morning just in front of the spot where we built *Just Now*. Nolly was there to help haul the boat up. We walked together up the beach towards the waiting *Friendship Rose*. At the edge of the concrete wharf we stopped and shook hands. "Have a great trip and don't worry about your boat," he said. "I'll keep an eye on her for you."

I thanked him and set off down the wharf. Walking backwards I yelled, "Hey, when I come back, we'll be building an eighty-foot schooner!" He smiled and waved. I turned and made my way through the busy crowd and climbed aboard the waiting vessel.

8
0/00

"Scientists have calculated that the chances of something so patently absurd actually existing are millions to one. But magicians have calculated that million-to-one chances crop up nine times out of ten."
- Terry Pratchett

It was ten o'clock at night when I stepped into the arrival lounge at San Diego Airport to meet my smiling dad. My mother wasn't feeling well, he said, and that's why she wasn't there to meet me. We walked across the rain-swept parking lot to the car, climbed in and found our way onto the San Diego Freeway heading north. As the car drove through the rain, and I listened to my dad laugh and joke, I looked out the streaky window at the red taillights and wondered what was going to happen next. I had three dollars in my pocket and a return ticket to the West Indies. And that was it. Only time would tell.

My parents were living an hour north of San Diego in a condo on the beach in Oceanside, right next to the marina. Walking in and seeing a lot of my mom's old antiques filled me with joy. After a wild six years it felt fantastic to be home again. Jean, however, wasn't doing too well. She had just had a breast removed because of cancer and was on chemotherapy. When she saw me, her dark brown eyes filled with tears of joy, but I could tell that deep down she was in a lot of pain. Buoyed by Ray's limitless optimism, as always, they both felt she was on the road to recovery. But my heart sank at seeing her as she was.

Ray's business seemed to be doing well. Because of the Arab oil crises, there was a lot of interest again in the idea of making oil out of coal. Ray had found some investors and he was back to driving his favorite, and probably the world's biggest car, a Lincoln Continental. He once told me as he pumped fuel at the gas station, "This baby uses so much gas that if I don't turn off the ignition she'll never fill up." He also pointed out a bumper sticker he had made up. NUKE THE GAY WHALES! it said. Obviously, Ray didn't mind causing a stir.

My first few days at home I was spoiled rotten. I was not only well fed, there were football games on TV and the fridge was well stocked with cold beer. After a couple of days of relaxation, I began to track down some of my old friends. Mark, who I had last seen as I sailed out of Pythagorean, was making a living working construction. He was living with his girlfriend Patty not far up the coast at Dana Point, just beyond the pearly white domes of the San Onofre Nuclear Power station. Nolen wasn't far away either, ensconced at a motel in Capistrano Beach and pouring concrete. I spent a rowdy weekend hanging out with those guys, sharing tales about what had happened to us since our last meetings.

One person I really wanted to locate was Ben Burkhalter, my old buddy from my Malibu days who came to Hawaii with us in the summer of '69. Over the years of my travels we had totally lost contact with each other. Somehow Ray tracked down his parents, who were living in a small town in Oregon. (Once at a dinner party in the fifties Ray claimed he could call anyone in the world, and won a bet when he actually called Khrushchev). They told us Ben was living in LA, working as a designer for some home builders there. I gave him a call. He was surprised to hear from me after so long and decided to drive down and spend the weekend with us in Oceanside so we could catch up.

Over the next couple of days we traded stories, and I learned that Ben was working for a company called Gilbert and Chang, who were on a roll building houses and doing renovations for rock stars and other celebrities around LA. His present project was doing the design work for a house they were building for Bob Dylan in Malibu, which sounded very interesting. I then gave him the condensed version of my adventures, finishing up with the building of *Just Now* on the beach in Bequia. As I showed him the photos and described how the boat was built by "hand and eye" on the beach with no power tools, his ears pricked up. "You know, one of the guys I'm working for could be really interested in your story. For as long as I've known him, he has told me his dream was to build a wooden sailboat. If I can borrow some of your photos, I'll show them to him when I get back to work tomorrow. You never know what could happen."

Monday morning and I was sitting with a cup of coffee reading the sports page when the phone rang. It was Ben. "I've shown the photos to Bob Gilbert, and he's blown away. He wants to know how much it cost to build your boat." The conversation had started. They called back another three or four times, asking questions. "Do you think you could build a one hundred and twenty-five-foot schooner in Bequia?"

"Sure," I answered. "No problem."

Late in the afternoon, Ben rang one more time. "Look," he said. "Gilbert wants to know if you can come up to LA for a meeting tomorrow. He'll take the whole morning off if you can make it." I checked my diary. Luckily, I had no other pressing engagements, so agreed to drive up and meet with these guys at their Sherman Oaks office. The only problem was after not having driven for so long I wasn't game enough to take on the LA freeway system quite yet, so my brother Rick offered to chauffer me up there.

Early on a foggy October morning, we turned onto the San Diego Freeway, heading north. I was still suffering culture shock. The cars, the concrete, the smog, the hustle, the intensity of entering the megalithic Babylonian monstrosity that is LA was a far cry from the tranquility of life in the West Indies. After three hours of insane freeway driving, we pulled up in front of the offices of Gilbert and Chang. I had no idea what to expect, but from the moment Rick and I passed through the front door it was high energy, it was full on, and it was rock and roll. The office was redwood paneled; the secretary was young, good-looking, wore bell-bottomed jeans and lots of turquoise. Concert posters hung haphazardly from the walls. An underground FM station played the Eagles *Hotel California*. Ben came out to meet us and ushered us into a hallway where we were introduced to Gilbert and Chang.

Bob Gilbert was thickset, stocky and around five foot seven inches tall; he wore a black tee shirt, faded jeans and construction boots. His long brown hair was tied back in a ponytail and he sported a bushy, David Crosby-like moustache. His partner Dave Chang was of similar proportions but of Korean extraction with a round, pockmarked face and unreadable almond eyes. His hands were stuffed into the pockets of an old high school letterman's jacket; he said little but expressed a heavy "don't fuck with me" attitude.

After a brief introduction, Chang left and the four of us stepped into Gilbert's office, closing the door behind. Picking up the phone, he told his secretary to hold all his calls as he motioned for us to have a seat. The conversation began with Gilbert telling us how he had lived through most of the sixties on a commune in Big Sur, and then spent the early 70's working as a metal sculptor before joining up with his present partner to create one-off houses. What he didn't mention was what my dad had told me - that his old man was Sam Gilbert, the construction magnate, who had built half the freeways around LA and was the Godfather of the ten-time NCAA champion UCLA basketball team. Gilbert went on and explained how his company was renowned for their quality woodwork, and that he always had a fascination with wooden boats. He told us he owned a classic wooden Dragon which he kept to the highest of standards, and since acquiring it had dreamed of building a big wooden boat. My story had stirred his imagination and he wanted to hear it from the beginning.

And so I told him. As the day wore on, Gilbert was full of questions. How much would a one hundred- and twenty-five-foot schooner cost to build? I had no idea, really, but I was twenty-six years old, bulletproof and chock full of confidence. By late afternoon it became apparent there was plenty more to talk about, and so it was decided I would stay in LA for another day or two. Ben had a spare bed at his place in Venice Beach, and so I thanked Rick and he took off for home. Little did I know that those couple of days would turn into three weeks, and that I would have to borrow money from Ben to buy a change of clothes and feed myself!

From the start, Gilbert was mesmerized by the prospect of building a schooner in Bequia. We began talking about a one hundred and twenty-five-foot schooner. This is a big vessel. Ships this size had been built back in Bequia's boatbuilding zenith, but in my ignorance, I had no idea how difficult and expensive such an undertaking would be in a well-equipped boatyard, let alone on a beach on a forgotten island in the far-off Caribbean. First off, I related to him the proud history of schooner building on the island, and how there was still a highly skilled workforce there capable of building such a vessel. I was adamant from the beginning, however, that whatever the size it would have to be of the type they were familiar with building, and that it needed to be a schooner with inside ballast so it could be launched off the beach in the traditional manner. So, what kind of schooner would this be?

More detail was required. We needed to come up with a tangible concept from which to start a discussion.

Ben made space in his office for me, and I went to work. The first thing I did was go out and buy the book Les Anderson had first shown me, the same book we had spent so many nights looking through up the hill at Nolly's house: *The American Fishing Schooners 1825-1935*, by Howard Chapelle. I explained to Gilbert that this book was the key. I told him how in the 1930's, naval architect Chapelle had meticulously taken off the lines of as many builders' half-models of Grand Banks schooners as he could find. He saw that these fabulous vessels were on the verge of extinction, and so he catalogued these designs and placed his collection in the Smithsonian Institute, where he later became curator of maritime history. He also went aboard the last of the remaining vessels of that once-proud fleet and made sketches of their unique construction and rigging details, which he included in his book. The reason I felt this book was so important was there was an obvious connection between the New England schooners and their West Indian cousins. In the first few decades of the twentieth century during the northern winter months, many 'Banks schooners were employed sailing south to the islands carrying cargos of salt fish and lumber, returning before the fishing season with holds full of salt - or Barbados rum. Their designs and details were copied by the island boatbuilders and evolved into the West Indian trading schooner. This book gave us a great place from which to begin.

It didn't take us long to discard fanciful dreams and get down to a realistic concept. "Well, Christopher, which boat would you build?" Gilbert asked me as he leafed through Chapelle's book. I turned straight to page 248 and showed him my favorite - the schooner *Stranger*, designed by the famous Bostonian naval architect B.B. Crowninshield. "This is a smaller schooner than most of the others in this book. She's only eighty-five feet long, and I think it would be a more practical size to build," I said. Gilbert liked her looks. Les Anderson had told me copies of Chapelle's drawings could still be procured from the Smithsonian Museum, so I called them up and ordered the full-scale set of lines, which cost the extravagant amount of three dollars. As we waited, I began to make up a materials list for such a sized schooner. The drawings arrived a few days later, so we now had something concrete to work from.

Like I said, the offices of Gilbert and Chang were high energy, and just spending time there was an eye-opener for me. Talk about life in the fast lane! Long-haired hippie cabinetmakers, cowboy contractors and Mexican concreters were constantly drifting through the place; joints were being smoked and coke was being snorted. Houses were being done for high profile movie, rock and sports stars, the biggest of which was Bob Dylan's house in Malibu. And there I was in the midst of all this, starry-eyed and flying by the seat of my pants.

After a couple of days, I had worked out a rough price for building the *Stranger*. Gilbert looked at it and thought it was too expensive, and asked if I couldn't just scale it down a bit. "Sure," I said. "I'll scale it down to sixty-five feet...no problem." I started working out a price for a smaller version.

Gilbert was also keen to see a conceptual portrayal of the proposed "dream ship", so Ben set me up with a drafting board and tools and I began a drawing using the Smithsonian plans as a model. Except for the few sketches I had done for *Just Now*, the last time I had done anything like this was in an architectural drafting class in high school. Ed Bowen must have taught me well, because it all started to come back to me. As the days went by the vessel started to materialize on paper, the costing began to solidify, and magic started to happen.

One week drifted into two. Living with Ben was a trip. He was a real city boy, and loved LA. He had done a degree in art, and was a very talented painter, but after graduation found it hard to make a living as an artist. Somehow, Ben had found a job with Gilbert and Chang, and once his talent had been recognized became their in-house designer. He lived a bohemian existence, renting a rundown apartment in the beaten-up seaside town of Venice Beach. We ate our dinners at old-time diners. Our breakfast was usually a coffee and Danish-to-go from the cafe around the corner, which we'd have in the car as we battled the freeway traffic on our early morning drive over the hill into "the Valley" to work. Doing Dylan's house in Malibu was by far the biggest project Ben had ever done, but because he wasn't a qualified architect, he felt he would never make any real money unless he went back to school and got a degree. Ben's ultimate goal was to set himself up in his own architectural business, which after several years of long days and night school he successfully accomplished.

I finished the conceptual drawing and we printed off a few copies. Gilbert was stoked. He had a plan in mind, and he told me about it. He wanted to approach Dylan and see if he was interested in going in partners with him in the proposed boat. In the meantime, what I had to do was get the numbers right. Gilbert came back from Malibu one day and said he had given Bob a copy of my drawing, which he had apparently shown an interest in. It seemed like things were still moving in the right direction.

I called Nolly in Bequia and told him what had been going on. I explained where I was and what had transpired and how excited everyone was but there was nothing concrete as yet. I told him I wouldn't even think of doing this project without asking him to be my partner, and he accepted. "I don't think you need to say anything to anyone just yet," I said. "Let's keep our fingers crossed and hope I can pull this thing off."

After two and a half weeks we had the parameters of a design and I had a price which I thought we could build it for.

I insisted that as part of the deal we would buy some basic power tools, which would stay on the island afterwards. I obviously didn't have any kind of professional experience in this kind of thing, but I was optimistic, confident, and hell-bent on making the deal happen. I told Gilbert we could build his schooner in a year, and that it would cost one hundred and twenty-five thousand dollars.

The third week came to an end and I was ready to head back to Oceanside. "You go home and have a good think about the whole thing, and I'll kick it around with my people," Gilbert told me that Friday. "I'll call you next weekend and we'll take it from there." Rick picked me up and I rode south with a lot to consider.

When we reached home, Ray was beside himself with excitement, especially when Bob Dylan's name was mentioned. Once away from the LA environment, however, I began to have second thoughts. I didn't know if I really wanted to take on the responsibility and pressure. Behind all of the smoke and hippy-style rhetoric, these guys were heavy dudes. The spotlight would be on me to perform. Just cruising around on my boat in the Caribbean started to look very good to me, although the fact that I was dead broke did put a proviso on that dream. When I expressed these thoughts to Ray, he couldn't believe it. "What? Are you crazy? Don't you realize what this would mean to you? You're building a boat for Bob Dylan, for Christ's sake! It could set you up for life!"

"Yeah, but it's a lot of responsibility. I don't know if I really want to get locked into something like this. It's really a hard decision to make. And Dylan hasn't committed to anything yet," I said.

"Let me tell you something - these opportunities don't come rolling down the turnpike every day, you know. You might think they do, but this is a once-in-a-lifetime deal. If you turn this down, what are you going to do? And just think what it would do for the island. You can do it. I know you can."

The week ticked by and I tossed and turned. I walked on the beach and sat by the stormy ocean. I went out and stayed for a couple of days with my sister Joan and her two kids. Rick was living there growing an organic garden and playing his guitar. Eventually Sunday night came around. I had made my decision. There were butterflies in my stomach when the phone call finally came.

"So, Christopher, have you decided what you want to do?" Gilbert asked.

"Yes - I've thought long and hard about it. I'm ready to go if you are," I answered.

"Great to hear! I'm in, and so is Dylan. Let's go for it, brother!" And that was it. Gilbert had organized a meeting at his lawyer's office for the following morning where we would sign an agreement he had drawn up. I put the phone down and my parents congratulated me. I didn't really know what to feel. I was nervous and excited and apprehensive all at the same time.

Early the following morning I was once again northbound on the San Diego freeway, this time heading for the expensive commercial district in downtown LA. I had by now gotten over my nervousness behind the wheel and was driving my mom's car. Eventually I found the skyscraper I was looking for, and as I got in the elevator and sped towards the thirty-second floor, I had to pinch myself. "Am I really here? This has to be a dream! It was only a few weeks ago I was walking through San Diego Airport with three bucks in my pocket and no idea of the future, and now here I am travelling at warp speed in this modernistic elevator to sign up an agreement to build a boat for among others Bob Dylan. What are the odds?"

Sitting in the reception room I gazed at the wall of leather-bound, gilt-edged law volumes and wondered what they would be worth, let alone the rental of the office space. Yes…this was definitely the Big League, and here I was just a young wandering vagabond of a sailor wondering what turn of fate could have ever brought me to that spot in the first place. And then it was time. I stood, took a deep breath, and followed the secretary into the lion's den.

Through big wooden doors I entered a glass-lined room of light. The desperate battleground known as the City of Angels spread out through the plate glass windows below us for as far as the eye could see. Gilbert stood to meet me, his long hair hanging in a braided pigtail halfway down his back. He obviously didn't dress for the occasion. The lawyer was younger than I expected, with well-groomed sandy hair and wearing a snappy cream-colored suit. We exchanged pleasantries, and then got down to business.

"Listen Chris," the lawyer began, "Robert here has indicated to me that he wants to proceed in this boatbuilding project with you, and instructed me to keep your agreement as simple as possible. Now, he has received this advice from his father's attorneys which you may want to have a quick look at." The lawyer passed a stapled document across the varnished walnut table. At the top was the letterhead of an impressive-sounding legal firm. The document outlined four pages of reasons why Bob Gilbert should not be building this boat. What if this happens? What if that happens? Four pages of things that neither Gilbert nor I had even thought about. I flipped through the pages and then placed the document back on the table.

"In the normal course of day to day business we probably would have drawn up a contract which would have incorporated many of these considerations," he continued. "Robert, however, wants to enter into this agreement on the basis of trust, and so working on this advice I have drawn up the following agreement. Have a look at it and see what you think." He then passed across the desk another document, this time with his own firm's letterhead.

The proposed agreement was only a half of a page long. It simply stated that Chris Bowman and Nolly Simmons agreed to build the *Stranger*, a schooner of sixty-five feet, for Bob Gilbert and Bob Dylan on the island of Bequia in the West Indies. The cost would be no more than one hundred and twenty-five thousand dollars, and the time of construction would be one year. We were to build the hull and rig it with masts and sails and install an engine. And that was it. No fancy legalese. Straightforward and to the point.

"Any problems?" the lawyer asked.

"Looks fine to me," I replied.

I was handed a gold pen from the impressive holder in front of me and I signed my name on the allotted line. Gilbert, who up until then had been as silent and smiling as the Cheshire cat, signed it and then standing offered his hand to me. We shook heartily. "Christopher," he said to me, "in my business I have signed a hell-of-a-lot of contracts, and I have found that no matter what you sign it all comes down to a man's word. And Dylan's the same. You either do what you say you will do, or you don't. I have built his house on a handshake, and now you are building us a boat on one."

With smiles all around we shook the lawyer's hand and Bob and I took our leave. My head was still in the clouds. I continued to have the feeling all of this wasn't real, this couldn't be me, it was actually a movie and I was somewhere on the outside just watching. I followed Gilbert to his blue Volvo station wagon. "Jump in," he said. "We've got to go and meet up with Bob. He's got to sign this thing too."

My mind was reeling. What? We're actually going to meet Bob Dylan? This really does have to be a dream.

As we parked on the street in front of an unremarkable building somewhere in the seedy maze that is the real city of Hollywood, Gilbert explained that Dylan was in the middle of finishing a movie he was making called *Renaldo and Clara*. He had been making it for a while and was frustrated that he couldn't get it finished, so he might not be in the best of moods. We entered into a makeshift site office and stood at a desk cluttered with papers. Moments later Bob came through the door wearing a broad cream hat. A brown leather jacket was draped casually over his shoulders. He looked older than I thought he would. His face showed no expression, but his eyes squinted slightly as he carefully looked me over. When we shook, his hand gripped mine only slightly, as if I alone was making all of the effort. The guitarist G.E. Smith, who once played in Dylan's band, describes this handshake perfectly: "Bob doesn't shake hands real hard, you know. He's one of those guys who just hands you the dead fish." Gilbert asked him how he was doing and he only mumbled a reply. Fidgety and seemingly nervous, Bob wasn't in the mood for small talk. The agreement was produced, he signed all three copies, and then put the pen down and we all shook hands once more. There was an awkward silence, and then Dylan shrugged his shoulders and arched his eyebrows as if to ask, "Is that it?" After taking another glance at me he turned and absentmindedly walked from the room. I watched him pause at the doorway for a moment hands on hips, then disappear from sight.

We drove back to my car. Parking alongside, Gilbert reached into the glovebox, pulled out a brown paper bag and tossed it on my lap. "There is five grand there, Christopher. This is just like a drug deal where the only thing that counts is trust. So away we go. We're off on an adventure."

Gilbert wheeled out of the parking lot and I slowly headed home. Once I reached the freeway, I started to come to grips with it all. A cold determination came over me. What I had to do was take the first step. Somehow, through an amazing turn of events, Nolly and I really were going to build a schooner in Bequia, just as I had jokingly predicted.

9
The Schooner "Stranger"

*"We didn't really know what we were doing, even in the Beatles.
We just went on our gut feeling, and that is all you can do in life."*
- George Harrison

Sitting here years later, knowing what I know now, I shake my head in wonderment and disbelief that this whole story transpired as it did. There was no design. I had a three-dollar print of the lines drawing of a boat we weren't even going to build. There was no boatyard, and the agreement we had was hardly a rock-solid contract containing building and payment schedules, specifications or penalties. There were no detailed construction plans to build to, there were no material lists or table of offsets, there were no stability calculations, no sail plan. In fact, there wasn't even a designer. What I did have was an undying faith the people of a small Caribbean island knew what they were doing when it came to building a schooner. "What you don't know won't hurt you," is how the saying goes, and in my youthful ignorance I had full confidence that we could pull it off. Not having a set of detailed drawings didn't faze me in the slightest…mainly because I didn't know any better. I'd already built a beautiful boat without plans. This one was just a little bigger, that's all. And there had never been a schooner built on the island to a set of plans anyway, and that was what we were going to do - build a Bequia schooner.

The first thing I did upon reaching home was to call Nolly and tell him the deal was signed up and we were actually starting. He said he would begin to organize things from that end. Ben, who was the key link in the chain of these remarkable events, was glad to see the whole thing come to fruition. My old buddy Mark was stoked to hear I had pulled the deal off and expressed a huge interest in coming down to Bequia at some point to help work on the boat. In fact, it was Mark who drove me up to the heart of industrial LA in his classic `54 Chevy pick-up truck to collect my first purchase for the project: a dozen long lengths of three-quarter inch silicon bronze rod with nuts and washers with which to make the bolts for the schooner's backbone. Ray was over the moon to see everything come together (he immediately began telling anyone within earshot his son was building a boat for Bob Dylan), as well as were the rest of my family.

The next thing I knew I was winging my way back to Bequia with a pocketful of cash and a schooner to build. It was mid-November 1977, and as I looked out that airplane window, I knew the next year was going to be a busy one.

The moment I climbed aboard the *Friendship Rose* alongside the Grenadines Wharf in Kingstown I could feel the vibe. It was certainly a different feeling than when I left a couple of months previously. And from the time I stepped ashore in Bequia I could tell the news had already spread like wildfire. "Chris and Nolly goin' build a vessel!" would have been heard from Hamilton to Paget Farm. The last schooner of note to have been built on the island was the *Friendship Rose*, and that was back in the mid-sixties. There would have been few on the island who could have hummed one of his tunes, but they all would have now heard the name Bob Dylan.

I reached my dinghy under the almond trees and the boys there met me with enthusiasm. Nolly greeted me with his customary big smile, and after a quick stop aboard *Just Now* I came straight back ashore. The first thing on the agenda was to find a spot to build the boat. Loren's workshop under the trees wouldn't work for this one…half of the boat would have been set up on the main road. Nolly suggested we go and talk to Son Mitchell. We walked down the beach to the Frangipani Hotel.

Son was very excited to hear about my adventures in the jungles of LA. The three of us sat down at a table near the water's edge and I related my tale. Son's smile flashed through his Castro-like beard, and his cheery eyes danced in merriment. With three generations of boatbuilding heritage running through his veins he would like nothing more than to see the ribs of a big schooner set up once more on the Bequia foreshore. We got up and walked a couple of hundred meters along the water's edge to a stretch of land where a grove of tall coconut trees stood.

"This is a parcel of my land which you are more than welcome to use. Several schooners were built in this place. My grandfather, Old Harry Mitchell, set up quite a few here, and I remember as a young boy back in the thirties seeing my father Reggie build *Water Pearl* right here where we are standing. It's an ideal spot except for one thing," Son said as we stood on the worn footpath running through the tall grass between the trees. "There is no road into the place, and that wicked aunt of mine next door would never let you use hers." Our eyes all turned towards the big white house which stood on a rise just below the main road. This was the abode of the infamous Doctor Lee.

Doctor Lee was one of Harry Mitchell's four legitimate children, and was therefore Son's aunt. She had been educated in the States and was actually a qualified doctor of some kind, but she was an extremely bitter, fire-breathing woman who was constantly at war with Son and other members of her family. Harry also had several "outside" children, and Nolly's mother Mary happened to be one. Doctor Lee's feud with her half-sister was renowned across the island, and they were famous for the insults they traded whenever they met on the road. Unfortunately, she owned the parcel of land which lay between us and the Frangipani. It had road access, but she would never let us use it.

"If our only choice is to float everything in, well then that's what we must do," I said with a shrug. "Otherwise this spot is perfect." We struck a deal then and there. Son would rent us the land for a nominal fee, and we would build the schooner in this quiet, out-of-the-way spot under the swaying coconut trees.

Nolly and I rowed out to *Just Now* to discuss how we would go about getting started. I had a strong vision as to how we should proceed, and automatically assumed Nolly would be on my wavelength. Unfortunately, we never really were on the same page. I had just returned from rock and roll LA and was fully amped and raring to go, whereas Nolly had his own way of going about business. With more experience, perhaps I would have been able to stand back and be more objective. We were partners, after all. Unfortunately, I was attacking this project like a bull at a gate and failed to see the warning signs, even at that early stage.

Nolly was a very complex, mysterious character to begin with. The island people said there was a lot of his grandfather in him. Loren would suck his teeth and say, "Noll-ee! Man, he is Old Harry self." In his younger days, Nolly had gone away to study architecture in Toronto, but returned with an unflattering view of the outside world, and he rarely left the island after that. There was a bit of aristocrat in him, and on the island, he had assumed a self-appointed position of power which few locals were game enough to challenge. He put unfathomable importance on the most trivial of matters, would hold grudges forever, and could shun a person for something he didn't even know he'd done. Nolly expected everyone in the world to live up to his self-imposed ethical standards, and woe be it to the poor person who transgressed his undisclosed rules. He could be a good friend, but no one could be a worse enemy. To keep Nolly onside took a bit of work. Unfortunately, at that time I wasn't too concerned with hurting someone's feelings. All I wanted to do was get a boat built.

A list was started. The spot which would become known as "The Boatyard" would have to be cleared. Shipwrights had to be hired. Timbers needed to be cut. I knew where to find a keel, so that would have to be organized. Planking would have to be ordered. And there was one other minor issue to be dealt with. It might be helpful to know what it was exactly we were building. In LA I had assumed the lines of Crowninshield's eighty-five-foot *Stranger* could simply be scaled down by twenty percent, so I started, using a pair of proportional dividers Ben had given me. It didn't take me long to figure out the dimensions of the new boat weren't working out using this method. I quickly came to the sobering conclusion that simply scaling down the drawing wasn't an option.

In the meantime, we started to organize a work crew. Nero was hired straight away and put to work clearing the site with his faithful cutlass. Unfortunately, Loren had gone to live with his daughter in Brooklyn (his vision of the Land of Milk and Honey), but the rest of the boys from under the almond tree were around. Crosby was taken on, along with Gilbert Hazel and Lincoln Ollivierre. The other shipwright to join our team was Herbert Ollivierre, Lincoln's brother. Even though we didn't have a definitive design, we still could go ahead cutting timbers.

Once again I found myself in the cool of the 'fore day morning leaning against Loren's workbench under the almond trees getting set to venture off into the bush. Paradise had done her duty supplying the timbers for *Just Now;* this time we were off to another remote spot called Park Gutter, near the northeast tip of the island. There were five of us who set out that first morning: Nero, Crosby, Herbert Ollivierre (henceforth known as Uncle Herbie or more simply Herbie-coo), Nolly and myself. It would take us over an hour to walk out there. So off we went, through the streets of the waking Port Elizabeth, over the hill past the rustling coconut plantation at Spring to the windward coast. We watched the sun rise as we followed a dusty track which ran parallel to the reef and rock-strewn eastern shore where the *Lady Angela* wrecked until the road ended, when we turned inland. Following a trickling streambed carved into the rocky hillside, we entered a small valley, or "gutter" as the locals called it, thick with yam vines and cinnamon, which Nero had to chop away with his cutlass. It was also chock-full of some of the biggest cedar trees I had ever seen, trees soaring into the canopy loaded with round wood. "Man, you can close yo' eyes an cut wood," I can hear Herbie saying. With Crosby, Nolly and Uncle Herbie doing the spotting, Nero and I began cutting. Before leaving the States, I had bought a chainsaw, which helped speed up the process. The trees were growing in a large estate owned by an absentee Englishman, and we made a deal with its manager to pay twenty dollars a tree. We certainly got our money's worth.

For the next couple of weeks, it would simply be Crosby, Nero, Herbie, and myself who made the morning walk to Park Gutter. Those days in the bush were tough, but rewarding. One day at lunchtime Nero told us the Story of Lord Devine. (Note of explanation:

Nero – Lord Devine of the bush.

208

from pre-war days until the mid-sixties many men from the islands ventured to the oil refineries of Curacao in search of employment and the Yankee Dollar.) "Man...when I come back from Curacao," (Nero never went there), "me pockets was filled wit' monee. Every day was a clean suit of de best khaki I wearin'. At de rum shop it was pure Johnny Walker me drinkin' - no strong rum at-all – an' me always had a pretty girl on each side huggin' me up. I did wear de best o' Panama hats, and me wore it at an angle just so. An' cigarettes? One pull, an' me tro' away de balance. Dey did call me Lord Devine. An' now? Me pickin' up bumps (old cigarette butts). Dey does call me Fowl..."

After a couple of weeks of cutting wood we had a good set of timber scattered through the bush. Now we had to get it out. Some strong bodied laborers were needed, and Nero knew the place to find them. Just off the road leading out of town was Paul's Rum Shop, Nero's home away from home (come to think of it, I don't think Nero even had a place he called home). Each morning we would pick up an ever-changing crew of workers who Nero had organized from the previous night's drinking session. These men generally hailed from St. Vincent, and had come to Bequia looking for work, crashing on the floor at Paul's shop after drinking away most of their day's meager wages knocking back 'nibs' of the white rocket fuel known as Strong Rum. The work wasn't easy. Much of the wood was massively heavy and awkward to shift. Luckily, we had gravity on our side as we "only" had to roll and slide and tumble and pry the wood down the hill, stacking it up alongside the narrow track we called a road. Our most successful method was to tie a rope onto a log and run down the hill as far as we could with it. "Son-a-Gun" Davis somehow got his dump truck up there and hauled ten loads of timber back down to the bayside, dumping it on the beach in precisely the spot where *Corsair* had been hauled up. Piece by piece we launched the timbers into the water and tied them together into rafts, which Nero herded along the shore to the boatyard where they were hauled up over the rocks and thrown on top of an ever-increasing pile.

As soon as the first set of timbers arrived in the boatyard, Lincoln, Gilbert, and Herbie set about chopping them out so they could quail. With axe and adz, the boys had the chips flying. What we needed now was a definitive design and a set of molds to work to. Crosby and I were set to begin to work up a design on the loft floor, as we had done with *Just Now,* but Nolly began to voice his concern about the speed

Ollivierre brothers Lincoln (l) and Herbert (r), and The Boatyard in full swing (below).

with which we were proceeding. The tip of a wedge began to be driven between us, and it would affect our off and on relationship all the way to the end.

Around this time, the crew of *Jens Juhl* was spending a lot of time hanging out in Bequia, and more specifically with Nolly up at the "Church". Kenny, Johnny and company were intelligent, practical, and energetic people, and they were giving Nolly plenty of advice. Their point, and it was a valid one, was that we should have a properly engineered, well-proven design to work to. Something by one of the great naval architects like John Alden or L. Francis Herreshoff. When you get a set of plans from someone like them, you receive sheets and sheets of specifications and drawings. No detail is overlooked, and no room is left for doubt. Good idea in theory, I responded, but I wasn't about to be dissuaded. It was easy to say "just go find a design", but neither Nolly nor anyone else understood the pressure I was under to perform. We had only a year to build this vessel, and it could take weeks, or even months to find a design which would fit our criteria. Besides, it wasn't part of the deal to begin with. The facts were simple - we were committed to building a Bequia schooner based on the *Stranger*, and it had to be done within a year. It had been a conscious decision in LA not to build a yacht. Finally, I had full confidence the Bequia shipwrights could build the boat in the traditional manner…that is, without a detailed plan. I couldn't explain it any other way except that I knew we could pull it off. There was just something inside me that told me so. Not very logical, I know, but I couldn't see it happening any other way.

These disparate views caused a major rift between Nolly and me. He stopped coming to the boatyard, ignoring my advances to smooth over the waters. The longer this standoff existed, the worse it got. Decisions had to be made, and with no one to talk to I went ahead and made them, at which point I heard through the grapevine that Nolly was upset because I wasn't consulting with him. It was the perfect definition of a vicious circle. I have to admit my stubborn hard-headedness didn't help the situation, but as Ken Kesey would say, "You are either on the bus or off the bus", and in those days Nolly hadn't made up his mind.

Despite the distractions and contradictory advice floating around the place, I simply bored ahead - just as Nolen and I did in the *Corsair*. I rented a meeting hall that had a wooden floor big enough to loft the boat on, and Crosby and I started to put some lines down. I had worked out some rudimentary measurements such as length, beam and draft, and then using the three-dollar Smithsonian photocopy as a guide we started to deduce stations, heights, deck shape, sheer profile, waterlines, buttocks and finally sections. While developing the sheer and stem shapes we found that by stretching the length we had a more pleasing line to the eye, so in the end the vessel finished at sixty-eight feet, eight inches, instead of sixty-five feet. In other words, we were basically drawing the new boat to full scale on the lofting floor. This was where Crosby was at his best. He, above all the others, had the knack of visualizing something that wasn't there. Within a week we had started to make molds. It wasn't very scientific, but I was fully confident that it would work.

Nolly and Kenny still felt I was rushing headlong for disaster. To be truthful, most people with any conventional idea of boatbuilding would have thought so, too. There was a Danish boatbuilder anchored in the harbor, and they dragged me to a meeting with him at the Frangipani. I liked Hans and I respected him, but he reiterated what the others were saying - that is, I was going about it totally the wrong way. What is the boat's displacement? What about prismatic coefficient? Where are your centers of gravity, buoyancy, and lateral resistance? What about stability and ballast ratio? Sail areas, center of effort and other calculations? Construction plans and scantling sizes? I listened to them, and when they were done, told them that logically they were correct. I had no answers to these technical questions. However, it was my decision to continue to proceed as we were. My argument was that well over one hundred schooners much larger than ours had been built in the past without the aid of any of this science, and they had turned out all right. I stood my ground. By hook or by crook we were building this vessel the Bequia way, and that was the end of it.

Crosby and I finished making the white pine molds from the lines we had put down on the floor. From these patterns we could now piece together the long, raking stem, as well as the seven frames we would need to set up the vessel. I knew from previous experience that this was where the laser-sharp eyes of the other shipwrights would come into play. Before we could do that, however, we needed a keel. I knew where a stack of forty-foot long greenheart twelve-by-twelves was, and so I set off for St. Vincent to purchase a couple of them.

Once again, I made the trip out to Wallalabu Bay in a truck to pick up the two pieces of wood that I had purchased. After loading them in an identical fashion as we did for *Just Now*, we returned to Kingstown and dumped them on the Grenadines Wharf. I now had to figure out a way to get them back to Bequia. The *Rose* couldn't carry them, and there were no small freighters in port this time. I noticed a big, black, strange-looking three masted vessel anchored not far from the wharf. I had seen this curious looking craft before, but had no idea about her crew. I stood at the end of the jetty waving my arms and hailing; finally, I attracted someone's attention. A dinghy was soon motoring ashore. The man who climbed out of the fiberglass dinghy and up onto the wharf was over six feet tall and was wearing nothing but a greasy pair of shorts. A curly head of thick, grey hair showed the only hint of his age; his sinewy nut-brown frame didn't reveal an ounce of fat. I recognized him. Where had I met him before? Then I remembered...it was the guy who strapped *Just Now* down to her cradle with my anchor chain on the morning of her launching.

His sea-blue eyes searched my face, asking "What do you want?" I introduced myself. He remembered me from the launching, saying his name was Henry. I told him I needed to get these two pieces of wood over to Bequia and asked if he wanted to make a few dollars. He walked over and examined them, thought about it for a few minutes, then said, "I'll do it for two hundred dollars."

"You've got a deal," I replied, and we shook on it. "When can we do it? I'll give you a hand."

"Tomorrow morning. And don't worry. My son and I can handle it. We'll float them out to my ship."

"Are you sure you don't want to bring your ship alongside?" I asked nervously. "This harbor is really deep, and greenheart doesn't float."

"Don't worry. Your wood is safe. Just leave it to me."

"Do you want me to at least round up some locals to help launch them into the water?" I asked perplexedly.

"No, my son and I will move them," he steadfastly insisted. He jumped back into his dinghy and motored back aboard.

I was on the wharf the following morning as Henry and his son brought their dinghy ashore towing eight empty forty-four-gallon fuel drums. Jumping up onto the wharf the master and his young apprentice sprang into action. As grimy as a couple of chimney sweeps, they went about their business as if they moved one-ton pieces of wood around every day of the week. First, they used a crowbar to lift one end off the ground, and then they placed a small piece of pipe underneath as a roller. They did the same at the other end. After hauling the drums up onto the dock, they strapped four onto each piece of wood. Getting behind, we then launched each piece off the wharf into the harbor. After an enormous splash, each floated peacefully alongside, whereupon they simply towed them out to their boat. Once alongside, they used an amazing lifting device called a Terfor, which was similar to a chain block but used wire instead of chain. With two of these made fast to the rigging on each side of the boat, they simply hauled the heavy greenheart out of the water, strapping them alongside. Once everything was made shipshape, they motored off for Bequia. I stood on the dock dumbfounded. I had just witnessed a man and a twelve-year-old boy move two tons of wood in a little over an hour.

When I arrived back in Bequia that afternoon the greenheart keels were already delivered, lying in the shallows in front of the boatyard. It took our whole crew plus a few passers-by to haul just one of them out of the water. "Who was that mystery man?" I had to ask myself. I had just seen the legendary Henry Wakelam in action. I didn't know it then, but this was the same man who was written about by the famous French single-handed sailor Bernard Moitessier, the man who would ask himself in sticky situations, "What would Henry do now?"

With the keel on the spot, it was time to go into the bush again. Park Gutter had provided a good set of timber but we hadn't found wood for a stem or a sternpost knee, generally the two most difficult pieces of wood to find. Nero and I spent several days searching the bush before locating a couple of huge trees near the overgrown ruins of an ancient house in a valley behind the Spring Plantation. Herbie called it "a Frenchman's house." There was a well and signs of other dwellings, and I imagined it to have been a manor-house built by one of the early French planters who settled the island back in the 1700's. The trees we cut were too big for us to get out of the bush as they were, so Lincoln, Herbie, and Gilbert came in with Nero and me to rough side them so we could manhandle them out.

When it came time to "drogue de timba's out" we got some unexpected help from an old friend. John Smith was a well know character who had been sailing through the islands for years. A year or so earlier he had purchased the legendary *Mermaid of Carriacou* from the famous Carriacou boatbuilder Zepheryn McLaren, and now he was anchored in Bequia with his Bermudian mate Scotty. John had at that time what he might term a "temporary liquidity dilemma", so when I offered the two of them jobs at the local laborer's rate of five Eastern Caribbean dollars a day, which is what I paid Nero, they grudgingly accepted. John was a lively character, and his booming laugh could be heard echoing across the water as those two desperados rowed ashore to the boatyard in the murky pre-dawn light. "Whatever you do Scotty, don't eat the ship's cat...har, har, har!" was one of John's sayings at the time.

Christmas came and went, and as we sprinted into the year of 1978 things were coming together quickly. Curved pieces of cedar. in various stages of squaring, siding, sawing and stacking, could be seen scattered around the boatyard amidst a carpet of woodchips. The long, "Gloucester style" stem had been shaped and scarfed and bolted together. Crosby was busy molding the seven "set-up" frames. The keel, sternpost and deadwood were "gotten out". All of this work, may I remind you, was being done strictly with hand tools. Electricity was still a long way away.

By the end of February, we were ready to set the vessel up. Bob Gilbert let me know he would be coming to check on progress in mid-March and I was desperate to get the boat set up by then. The keel and deadwood were bolted together and blocked up at the correct declivity; the stem and sternpost were then carefully lined up and bolted into position. Once the backbone was locked together the set-up frames were put into place. When we ran the staffs around the boat, we could see that not all of the frames were perfect, but these were soon easily rectified. By the time Gilbert arrived the vessel would be set up, and at least he would have something to see.

In a matter of a few short days the shape of the new boat magically appeared before our eyes. Crosby and I had pulled it off. Everything fit into place, and the shape and proportions of the new vessel all looked fantastic. We were always going to get some criticism. Some said the stem was too long, others that she could have had more beam, or that the sternpost had too much rake. But I was extremely happy with what we had come up with. B.B. Crowninshield would more than likely have given us his nod of approval. Even Nolly reluctantly agreed that she looked good.

The new vessel "showin' off she lines..."

10
Where Are You Tonight, Mr. D?

"Is this the boat being built for Bobby Darin?"
- Question from passing tourist.

1977 and 1978 were not easy years for Bob Dylan, as far as I can tell. With earlier 70's albums *Blood on the Tracks* and *Desire* hitting critical acclaim, along with his successful carnival-like Rolling Thunder Review tour, Bob was once again at the top of his game. Just when he seemed to be on a roll once more, his personal life took another tumble when in June of '77 he and his wife Sara were divorced. He finally finished the editing of his much-anticipated film *Renaldo and Clara,* and it was released in early '78. The film was basically about the Rolling Thunder tour of '75, but it was done in a French noir style with Bob wearing masks and white face paint amidst a confusing conglomeration of characters. With a running time of close to four hours, it was oblique and misunderstood. Panned by critics, the film was pulled from circulation and wouldn't see the light of day again for many years.

In the spring, Dylan released his first album of new material in two years with *Street Legal*, recorded in his own Rundown Studios in Santa Monica. Though the album did well in England, it didn't reach the dizzying heights of his previous two records in the USA. He then left on a world tour, seemingly in search of a new sound with a band which included an R&B horn section and back-up singers, yet again sailing into uncharted waters. I don't know if he thought much about what we were doing down in the Caribbean. But we knew. Everyone in Bequia knew, and word was spreading fast throughout the islands. According to public perception, we were building a boat for Bob Dylan.

With the advent of the boat being set up, Nolly and I seemed to smooth over our differences. There was no denying we were partners, and if there was to be any profit to be made at the end of this venture, we were to split it fifty-fifty. Seeing Nolly down in the yard again was a great relief to me, as it was one thing less I had to worry about. We weren't back to the heady days of yore up under the almond trees, but at least we were getting along.

    I had come down with a bit of dengue fever, so asked my friend Chris Crawford to sail over and pick Bob Gilbert up on *Just Now*. When they arrived in Bequia I was happy to see that Ben had come along as well. Although it was a lightning trip just to check on progress, I was looking forward to them both getting a feeling for the magic being created in that peaceful coconut grove. Unfortunately, neither of them became fully attuned to the Bequia wavelength. It was obvious they were well out of their high-powered manic LA comfort zone. To be fair, they were only there for a few days, but Gilbert continued to make it clear to me that as soon as the boat was fit to sail, he planned to get it back home to Marina Del Rey, where his carpenters could fit out the interior. "There's no way I could afford to come all the way down here just to go for a sail," he said. He also informed us that he had purchased an engine while passing through Miami, and that he stayed true to his word and bought the woodworking machinery I demanded be part of the deal. I sailed them back to St. Vincent to catch their flight home. Gilbert seemed reasonably happy, but left me with some sobering parting words. "Nine months to go, Christopher…nine months to go." I wasn't fazed, but in reality, I should have been. We had a lot to do.

With the set-up frames made right and the staffs run, the shape of the vessel was locked in to place. Each shipwright now took a section and began to fit timbers to the staffs. From the start it became apparent that I couldn't do my work and continue to live aboard my boat, so I rented a little house halfway up the hill on the road to Mount Pleasant, where I spent the time after work doing accounts and planning for the future. Obtaining the planking was a top priority, but it had been ordered in early December and my friend Idris Deen assured me he would have the logs at his yard sometime in April.

Another pressing issue was the rig. Masts, booms, gaffs and bowsprit would be needed, and for these we couldn't just walk up to the bush and cut them, or order them from nearby Guyana. Once again, Kenny and *Jens Juhl* became obliquely involved. Back in the days when he first purchased his Baltic Trader in Copenhagen, Kenny had become friends with a Danish engineer by the name of Burt Henriksen. By chance, Burt came to visit Kenny while his vessel was in Bequia, when he fell in love with the place and decided to relocate to the island and set up an engineering workshop. One day while visiting the boatyard, it came up in conversation that Burt had a good connection in Denmark for obtaining spar timber. And so began the saga of the masts.

To tell this story I need to go back a little bit in history to the 1600's when Denmark had developed a strong navy to fight for control over trade routes in the Baltic Sea. King Christian IV was a far-sighted fellow as he understood that for Denmark to maintain their naval strength, they needed a reliable source of good timber for masts and spars. He therefor sent off an expedition to Canada which returned with saplings of the best spar making timber there is - Douglas fir. The king ordered a forest planted for the sole purpose of supplying trees for masts for the Danish navy. Three hundred years later the forest still stood, and it continued to be managed by the navy. Every year a handful of trees were culled to make room for others to grow, and these trees were generally sold to make masts and spars. As luck would have it, Burt knew the chief forestry officer of this old forest, and when he returned to Denmark ordered six trees (four of which I planned to sell locally to help cover costs), along with smaller pieces of material for the other spars.

Another aspect which made this arrangement so good was with the advent of containerization in Europe, the small coasting freighters which used to ply their trade between the myriad of European ports were quickly being made redundant and going out of business. Many were laid up in Copenhagen, where a steady market was found selling these ships to West Indian owners for use in the inter-island cargo trade, ironically replacing traditional wooden schooners and sloops. When these ships were delivered across the Atlantic, they were always on the lookout for cargos to carry. Because Burt was also well connected with the Copenhagen shipping industry, he felt sure we would have no problem finding a ship to deliver these trees the five thousand-odd miles, straight to Bequia.

With the hull shape now settled and plenty of timber on hand to finish framing the vessel, it was time for me to go back down to Guyana and push Idris to saw the planking. I wouldn't be going alone this time; I would be accompanied by a young American named Robert Luke, or more simply Deadly. He and his girlfriend Sandy had been sailing as crew on *Jens Juhl* for a couple of years, and they decided to build a boat in Bequia. When Deadly heard I was going to Guyana for silver bali, he asked if he could accompany me. The two of us flew out for Trinidad and then on to the dreaded Georgetown. I was glad to have Robert with me. From my past experience I knew there was safety in numbers.

Seeing Idris again was like meeting up with an old friend. On our first morning with him he took us around to say hello to Leslie Ishmael, who, true to form, asked us if we had brought him any porno mags. That night Idris took us out to eat. We had brought him a bottle of Black Label Scotch, and after dinner the three of us put a serious dent in it. Later in the evening he took us for a drive in his Merc, and as we cruised down one of Georgetown's main streets, he spotted an acquaintance and pulled quickly over. Idris ushered us along the sidewalk to meet his friend, who then invited us up to his office for coffee. It turned out this man was a sitting member of Parliament, on the front bench of the opposition, and the leading representative of Indian Muslims, who made up a large proportion of the Guyanese population. According to Idris, the politics of the country hadn't changed since my last visit. Forbes Burnham was still ruthlessly in charge, and his links to Cuba and the Soviet Union had only strengthened. The country was now virtually a socialist police state and operated as a parliamentary democracy in name only. The United States and the CIA were blamed almost daily in the government-controlled press as the main contributors of the country's economic woes. Idris had always been outspoken in his criticism of Burnham, and as we sat down, I was feeling a little nervous when we were informed his friend was a high-ranking government representative. It only got worse when Idris decided to play one of his impish tricks on us.

"Haji, I'd like to introduce you to my two young American friends," I heard him saying. "This is Robert and Chris, and you had better be good to them because they both work for the CIA."

My heart jumped up in my throat. What?!!! Deadly and I both broke our stunned silence at the same instant as we hurriedly tried to explain to our honorable host that we were simply just a couple of boatbuilders trying to buy some wood. Idris thought it was a great joke, however, and was laughing about it for days.

Nothing had changed at the Deen Sawmill at Crabwood Creek since the last time I had been there. We received a friendly welcome from everyone at the mill, including the mustachioed, three-fingered Raiyo. We were told that everything was ready for the mill to begin cutting our wood. Two rooms had been prepared for us in Idris' home, and we were treated as honored guests. First thing in the morning our logs were hauled from out of the muddy banks of the Courantyne River, and the milling process began. Halfway through the morning Deadly and I were out in the mill with Idris and Raiyo. Diesel engines were screaming, the giant rubber drive belts were wobbling about in every direction, saws were buzzing, boards were flying off the various machines, and sawdust was being carted out by the barrowful to the banks of the river by pre-teen Indian boys. In the midst of our conversation, Deadly fell to his knees with a grunt of anguished pain. Blood was streaming from the palm of his hand. We got him to his feet and rushed him into the house. It was as if he had been hit from a bullet out of a gun. Raiyo and Idris knew fairly quickly what had happened. A drive belt had broken, and a piece of metal from one of the heavy staples which joined the belts together had let go and flown across the mill, burying itself deeply in Deadly's hand like a piece of shrapnel. Idris pulled out a rudimentary medical kit and 'operated' on the wounded hand, which was quite a painful procedure – something like pulling out a bullet. There wasn't much choice, as the nearest clinic was a two-hour drive away. Deadly was alright, although the hand took a long time to heal. It could have been worse. That flying staple could have hit him in the head, when his nickname would have proved to be very appropriate indeed!

Our logs were milled and the planks were stacked and tallied. Unfortunately, Idris could only supply about half of my order, but he had more logs coming. This meant I would be making another trip to this rough and tumble country…something I didn't really look forward to. Our wood was trucked off to Georgetown, and as luck would have it there was a ship loading cargo for St. Lucia and the captain agreed to take our wood as deck cargo and drop it in Bequia for us on his way past.

Our lumber arrived in Bequia and after floating it all down to the boatyard we didn't skip a beat before starting to put it on the vessel. Sheer clamps and stringers went in first, then the massive grown cedar deck beams began to be fit. I wasn't back very long when it was time to return to Guyana. Back at Crabwood Creek, I felt almost like a local. Raiyo, who had five wives himself, said he could find me a nice Indian girl to make my visits more comfortable, but I politely refused. The last set of lumber was finally shipped off for Georgetown, where I had to spend an agonizing two weeks to find a ship.

As I was doing my rounds to the various shipping agents, I met another saw miller who specialized in aromatic red cedar, which he shipped to Cuba for the manufacture of cigar boxes. Bernard Mathews was a very friendly fellow, and when I showed interest in buying some red cedar, he took me to his colonial Georgetown home, which like most houses in Guyana was built off the ground on stumps. Underneath was stacked some of the most beautiful boards I'd ever seen. Without hesitation I bought a stack of it. Bernard's mill was located in the remote northwest of the country, and when he discovered I had time on my hands waiting for shipment, he invited me to fly up there with him in his private plane. "You might find it interesting," he told me. "Some countrymen of yours have set up a commune not far from my mill. They seem to be some sort of religious cult. They are a curious bunch and mainly keep to themselves, but they have done some good work for the community. The name of the place is Jonestown."

I seriously considered his offer, but declined in the end. Who knows...I might have dropped in to pay them a visit and never returned. It was only a few months later when the mass suicide at Jonestown created international headlines.

I returned from the second, and last, torturous trip to Guyana just in time to greet Mark, his girlfriend Patty, and Ben, who arrived from California keen to work on the boat. They were accompanied by Ray. My old man loved Bequia, holding court at the Frangipani where he told his stories and bought rounds of drinks for visiting sailors, even though he had given up drinking himself. Free spirited and happy-go-lucky, Pat and Mark slotted straight in to the rhythm of island life. Ben, however, never really adapted to the island pace. I think he was really a city boy at heart. He eventually headed home with Ray after a couple of weeks, but Mark and Patty stayed on and soon became an integral part of the project, injecting their fun-loving California spirit into the mix.

The power tools and engine which Gilbert had purchased in Miami finally arrived. Whilst in Guyana, I had bought a stack of simple construction timber (Kabukali) which we used to build a shed to cover our tools. It also gave us a nice undercover work space where we could get out of the rain and sun. We set the power tools up, but it took a frustrating six months to get our electricity run from the main road. The man in charge of electricity in Bequia wanted me to play his game and "peep in his hand" – in other words bribe him - but I declined, and he refused to flip the switch. I used to tell visitors it wasn't really a workshop, but a power tool museum.

With all of our lumber now on site we could begin to put planks on. Teams were formed and they began to go on like clockwork. Crosby and I worked out the width and length of each plank, then carefully went through our stack of boards before choosing a piece and shaping it. The strakes were always made in pairs, so when we made one for the port side, we would make an exact copy for the starboard side. A few months earlier we had taken on a young fellow by the name of Rennison as an apprentice, and he teamed up with Herbie. Before a finished plank was hung the frames had to be "dubbed off", or faired. These two did this job, skirting the boat on our makeshift scaffolding using a fairing baton and adz to make the frames fair. Gilbert and Linkie then followed, fitting and "hanging" the planks. Finally, the last team made up of Mark and Lanceford, Gilbert's cousin, fastened the planks off and punched the galvanized spike nails home. The system worked perfectly. As with most things we did on that schooner, it happened without fuss or fanfare. As one team finished its job the next one stepped in behind to do theirs, and so we proceeded smoothly around the boat.

In early October we fastened on the last plank and shared a bottle of rum to celebrate. It was less than a year since that fateful weekend when Ben came to visit me in Oceanside, and in that time, I felt we had performed a minor miracle. There was still much to do, but we had made a great start.

Looking ahead, I could see there was a myriad of materials we would need in the near future so we could finish off the boat, and there was only one place to find them, so I flew to the States. Nolly would keep the show rolling while I was gone. I landed in Miami, the gateway to the Caribbean. I rented a car and spent a couple of days canvasing the many marine hardware suppliers before I finally found what I was looking for. John Phillips worked for a large marine store and immediately became fascinated with our project. I told him what I needed was one man in Miami who I could call and count on to find whatever item we might need and get it to me, and he agreed to be that man. We ended up working together for years and became quite close friends.

With my shopping done in Miami, I was asked to fly to California and report in. Gilbert wanted to set up a meeting with Bob so they could have a progress report. Next on my list were the mast fittings and various deck hardware needed to get the vessel sailing. Since you don't just buy these very specific items off the shelf, I knew they would have to be custom made. For that we would need drawings. While I waited in Oceanside with my parents for this meeting to take place, I set up a drafting board and using the many sketches Chapelle provides in his American Schooner book as a guide sat down and went to work. Before leaving Bequia I had discussed the spar sizes with Crosby and the other shipwrights, and using their rule of thumb calculations along with Chapelle's invaluable sketches from *The American Fishing Schooners*, I worked out the dimensions for all of these fittings. Now while I waited, I made the engineering drawings. Once again, those high school drafting classes came in handy.

After a week and a half, the call finally came. We would meet at Dylan's house in Malibu. I borrowed my sister's car and set off for a place I knew very well - Point Dume in Malibu. The Santa Monica freeway ended and I wheeled onto Pacific Coast Highway, the enigmatic flat top of the Point clearly visible through the cool winter haze twenty-five miles to the north. Pulling over, I picked up a hitchhiker who said he was going to Zuma Beach. "I can drop you pretty close," I said.

After a while we turned off at the Point and I headed down Dume Drive. "Doesn't Bob Dylan live around here somewhere?" the hitchhiker asked.

"Yeah...I think I've heard something about that," I said.

"I used to live right there," I said, nodding with my head towards the tree-shrouded house on the corner. "This is the first time I've been back in years. The place sure has built up a lot since I lived here."

I dropped the kid off at Zuma Beach, then backtracked and followed my instructions. I found the obscure dirt driveway which ended at a guardhouse. The gate guard, I had learned, was a Dume local who had the same surname as a kid I'd gone to junior high with. I checked in, and then asked, "You aren't any relation to Tom, are you?"

"Yeah," came the curt reply. "I'm his brother."

"How's he going these days," I asked politely.

"He's dead," was his grumpy reply. "He died in a car accident."

"Sorry to hear that," I said.

He shrugged his shoulders as he motioned me through. "He was off his face on PCP." I drove down the winding drive and parked. As I stepped out of the car, I shook my head in disbelief. I had been here before. This was where Rick Murray's old house once stood, where I had heard the Byrds sing "Chimes of Freedom" for the first time, and although everything else was new, the old red barn-like garage was still the same. In fact, the backboard and hoop where Rick and I played one-on-one was still there. And here I was, fifteen years later, going to meet Bob Dylan and his cohorts to discuss the boat I was building for them in the far-off Caribbean. Hmm...

The three of them were waiting for me by the swimming pool. Huge granite rocks and boulders jumbled on top of each other surrounding what looked like an alpine swimming hole. They were sitting at a table in the cool Malibu sun; Chang on one side of Bob and Gilbert on the other. Three sets of Ray-Bans were boring down on me. I felt like a subject of the crown meekly approaching an audience with the King. "Maybe I should kneel," I thought.

"So how are things going on the boat, Christopher," chief minister Gilbert inquired.

"Great! We're flying along. We just finished planking before I left, and Nolly is keeping things together while I'm gone. I just completed all the drawings for the mast fittings. I have them here if you want to see them." I proudly placed them on the table but no one moved to pick them up. "I've found a great old foundry in Nova Scotia who can make these fittings," I continued brightly.

After a long silence Dave Chang spoke up. "How are you on time?" he asked. There wasn't a lot of humor emanating from the other side of the table.

"Well I'm not quite sure when we'll be launching, but we aren't far off," I answered optimistically.

"So, when do you think the boat will be ready to sail back to California?" Gilbert asked.

"We're not bringing the boat back here are we?" Dylan inquired, speaking for the first time. "What do we want to bring it here for?"

"Um, well I just kinda thought that was a given," Gilbert replied. "I've even organized a slip for the boat in Marina Del Rey, which wasn't easy."

Bob didn't say anything more, but I could tell there was a split in the ranks. The meeting went on for another half hour or so. Then Dylan yawned, and that was the end of it. I picked up my unseen plans. Gilbert walked me to my car. "Just remember our agreement, Christopher," he said. "You'd better crack the whip and get a move on. We're cutting you a little slack, but we don't want to see any problems pop up in the future, do we amigo?"

I took one last look around; at the house with its spires and stained glass and wrought iron, and at the garage where the ghosts of two kids were playing basketball. I slowly wound my way off the Point, turned right on to Pacific Coast Highway and made the three-and-a-half-hour drive back to Oceanside. Returning the car to my sister, I walked into the house to drop off the keys. On the wall in the kitchen was the album cover of *Street Legal*. Bob was standing in a doorway looking off to his left. Pinned up next to it was a copy of the drawing I had done in Ben's office a year earlier. In my sister's kitchen, Bob Dylan was looking at the boat.

11
Unlikely Shipmates

"There'll be no killin' tonight, Jim lad, 'til I gives the word!"
- Long John Silver

I arrived back in Bequia to find turmoil in the boatyard. Nolly had fired Crosby. The reason he gave was that he was working too slowly. Crosby came to see me to ask for his job back. I could see the man was shattered. But what could I do? I was in a terrible position. To rehire him and go against Nolly would cause a war. And Nolly wouldn't reconsider. I had to tell him I couldn't change the decision. It broke my heart.

Somewhere someone had told me about the Lunenburg Foundry and Engineering Company in Lunenburg, Nova Scotia. I had written them a letter to enquire about the equipment they made; I also needed to know if they were capable of making all of our other fittings. I received a courteous reply from Mr. Lloyd Conrad, General Manager, who sent me a catalogue of products they produced. Worm drive steering gears, cast iron and bronze ship's wheels, hawse pipes, anchor windlasses, deck pumps, boom buffers, skylight hinges, all of the old-time schooner gear. This place was the answer to my prayers. Mr. Conrad also informed me that although his firm couldn't make my mast fittings, there was a blacksmith in town that could. I immediately sent him a copy of my drawings.

Burt Henriksen wrote from Copenhagen to tell me the six trees I ordered had been cut and were lying on the ground in the king's forest for the winter. He said it was an exceptionally cold winter, which was excellent for them. He also sent me a bill; the trees cost three hundred US dollars each. Not bad.

John Phillips was turning out to be a great contact in Miami. While in California I had visited Howe and Bainbridge, the renowned manufacturers of sailcloth, in Newport Beach. There I had ordered the rolls of Dacron sailcloth Bluesy would use to make the schooner's sails, and they were on their way to John in Miami, who would then forward them on to me. Everything seemed to be coming together nicely.

All around the boatyard, various pieces of the boat were being shaped and fit unto place; the deck beams had been dropped in and the hanging and lodging knees fastened off. The covering boards were screwed down; the top timbers, which supported the bulwarks, had been bolted into position. Loren had returned from the States, and we immediately hired him, which was a big boost to team moral. Our power tools were now in operation, and just in time too, as they really sped up the work. Mark took over the shop and was really helpful in teaching the other shipwrights how to use these tools. They were very apprehensive at first, but quickly caught on when they saw the work the tools could do. Lincoln and Gilbert hollowed out the two enormous pieces of silver bali I had milled specifically for the rudder case, and then bolted them together. Knightheads, horn timbers, keelson and mast steps had all been fitted. The heavy greenheart rudder was under construction. And the amazing thing was it all went on without much discussion. As with anything in life, there is always more than one way to accomplish a task. When a decision had to be made, I would listen to the various alternatives, make a choice, and the boys would just get on with it.

Life in the house with Pat and Mark was a blast. I had finally someone to relate to and confide with. They brought with them the latest music and a high energy California spirit. Mark was a true craftsman and Patty was happy and positive and kept us well-fed. All in all, I couldn't have asked for things to be better. The Mount Pleasant cottage proved to be too small for the three of us, so I rented another place in the perfect position - right next to the boatyard. It also happened to be located directly behind the Green Boley Bar and Restaurant, one of the best beach bars on the island, which was perhaps at times just a little too handy. There were some mornings when it was tough to make our seven o'clock start, even though we only had to jump over the wall to get to work.

One Sunday morning I was awoken from my sleep-in by a young boy knocking on our door. "Mr. Chris, dere's a white man 'board yo vessel who says he wants to see you," he said shyly before scampering off.

    I sleepily got dressed and wandered over to the yard. Sitting amidships atop one of the deck beams I found a well-groomed yachtsman whose face seemed somehow familiar to me. "So, you're the guy building this fine vessel," he said in an accent faintly tinted with a refined southern drawl. "I hear it's for Bob Dylan."

    "Well, sort of. He's actually got another California guy as a partner."

    "Interesting. But how did this whole thing come about, anyway? There has to be a story behind it all."

    "There is, but it's a long one," I replied.

    "Well you sure are doing a fine job. It's very impressive. My name's Boz. I sailed in last night with some friends. Maybe you'd like to join us for lunch at the Frangipani and tell us some of that story."

    And that is how I met Boz Scaggs. I'd heard his music on the radio during my many hours of freeway driving at various times while back in the States, which was really popular at the time. But there was another image I had seen somewhere which I couldn't quite put my finger on. After busting my brains, I remembered where I'd seen his face before…from an album when he was part of the Steve Miller Band back in the 60's. It was one of my favorite records at the time. The name of the album was *Sailor*.

I did go to lunch with Boz and his sailing companions, and afterwards asked if he would like to come to a party that night and jam with some local musicians, which he graciously accepted. I spent the rest of the day getting the party organized with Nolly. The "Church" was packed that night. Boz' rendition of "Harbor Lights" was especially memorable. Later, I spent a day with him in Hollywood on one of my trips back to the States, which is a whole other story in itself. We actually had a conversation about building an Alden schooner in Bequia, but nothing ever came of it.

In February of 1979, I decided to go to Nova Scotia to meet the people at Lunenburg Foundry and discuss in person exactly what gear we needed. With shipping distances of over three thousand miles, I wanted to make sure we got things right the first time. I planned to return via Miami; sort things out with John Phillips and then air freight whatever gear I had collected to duty-free St. Maarten, where I could pick it up myself. So off I sailed on *Just Now*, and for crew I took Justin and Bamu, two guys I knew to be excellent sailors from Paget Farm. We sailed for St. Barths, where I decided to leave the boat in the well-protected inner harbor of Gustavia under the watchful eye of Lou-Lou Magras. And with Justin and Bamu aboard I knew she would be in good hands.

Early February probably isn't the ideal time to visit Nova Scotia. I landed in Halifax in sub-zero temperatures. My simple Caribbean wardrobe hardly equipped me for this kind of weather, but I figured I could somehow cope with it for a couple of days. I rented a car and drove to Lunenburg, the home of the famous schooner *Bluenose*. At the Foundry I met up with Lloyd Conrad, and he took the rest of the day off to show me around the town, which was steeped in maritime history. In her day, Lunenburg was the center of the Canadian salt cod industry. Hundreds of schooners had been built there to combat the perilous waters of the North Atlantic as they worked the rich fishing grounds of the Grand Banks. A few of the original businesses built around this industry were still in existence, and the Lunenburg Foundry was one of them.

Lloyd took me aboard the *Bluenose II*, which was laid up for the winter. This magnificent vessel was built in the sixties as a tribute to the original schooner that had been the pride of Canada in the 1920's and 30's, when she defeated everything Yankee shipbuilders could produce to retain the International Fisherman's Trophy. This two-masted schooner was one hundred and forty feet on deck, carried a twenty-six-foot beam with a draft of sixteen feet. The main boom was ninety feet long! Lloyd proudly showed me all of the bronze and cast-iron fittings the Foundry had made for this special ship.

Our next stop was the Thomas Walters and Son blacksmiths shop, makers of ship's hardware since 1893. My order was well under way. Many of the mast bands and bails and irons were already made. We went back to the foundry and I had a search through the hundreds of patterns stored there for something the correct size for our hawse pipes. It was a shot in the dark, but I miraculously found a perfect set of patterns, which could then be used to make bronze castings. I ordered a worm drive steering gear, windlass, deck pump, hinges and other equipment. The plan was for Lloyd to pack up and send all this gear to Miami, where John would collect everything and air freight it on to St. Maarten. That night Lloyd and I had dinner at the beautiful little inn he had booked for me to stay at. Not surprisingly, I had codfish. Lloyd Conrad was a great guy, someone from the old school who still espoused the honest values of a quickly-fleeting era. I was glad to have made the effort to come to Lunenburg in person. I was learning that putting a face to a name could prove to be invaluable.

Once back in Miami, I phoned Gilbert and suggested he fly over and meet me and decide how far he wanted us to go with the interior of the boat. I figured it was a good chance for him to buy any fittings he thought he might need and ship them off with the rest of the gear we were collecting. "No, Christopher, I think it would be better if you fly out here to the coast," he said. This didn't make any sense to me. I had no reason to go to LA. He didn't sound happy; I detected a note in his voice I hadn't heard before. I began to wonder what was really going on.

The minute I entered the office of Gilbert and Chang I could feel the vibe. Things had changed. This time it wasn't such a friendly place. Ben wasn't working there anymore for a start, so I had lost my main ally. And from the moment I sat down in Gilbert's office, I knew someone had gotten to him. His wife, his partner, his old man, all three…it only took me a second to see he had buckled under pressure. "The boat is a long way from being finished, isn't it, Christopher," he said, leaning back in his chair. Dave Chang sat cross-armed in his letterman jacket; his face locked into a stone-cold glare.

"It's not that far away. She's planked, the decks are going on, the wood for the mast is cut, the gear for the…"

"Man - I don't want to hear any more of that shit!" Chang interjected, as subtle as a sledgehammer. "You haven't done what you said you were going to do! It's been over a year, you've spent a hundred grand, and you're not even close to being finished!"

"Yeah, well I can't argue with that," I replied, trying to remain calm. "But it is a big boat, and considering the logistics I think we're doing really well. It's a great project, it's the biggest thing that has happened on the island for a long time, and in the end, you are going to have a fantastic boat."

"Fuck this airy-fairy Disneyland shit! The point is: when are we going to get our fucking boat? And how much more is it going to fucking cost? That's all we want to know!" Chang was getting into gear now, getting into character.

I looked at the two of them and shrugged. "Look, all I can say is I'm doing my best. There is no money being wasted. It'll cost what it costs and will be finished when it's finished. Hopefully this year."

"That's not good enough, bro," Chang said.

"Take it easy…take it easy," Gilbert chimed in. "We know you're trying your best." The old good cop bad cop routine. If I'd have been a little more experienced, I would have spotted it. "Have you brought the books?"

I passed my ledger for the past year over to him. I wasn't worried. Every cent was accounted for.

"Listen, we'll have a good look at this and then get back to you," Gilbert said.

I left the office feeling like I'd been kicked in the guts. "What's going to happen now? How am I going to get out of this one?" I wondered.

When I got home, I called Ben, who was now back at school studying for his degree in architecture. "Yeah, well after a while I could see that Gilbert was going to have his problems," Ben said. "First of all, his wife was on his case big time. She hated the idea from the beginning. And Chang couldn't ever see the point. He hates boats. But I think his biggest hassle is with Dylan. Gilbert wants the boat here in California so he can impress his friends with it, and I think that's the last thing Dylan wants. As far as I know, he wants to leave it down in the Caribbean."

Time dragged on. Then I got the call. Gilbert wanted to see me at his lawyer's office in the Valley. I called Ben for advice. "You don't want to be going to that meeting by yourself, Chris," Ben warned. "I'll meet you there."

It was dark when I pulled up to the office. This wasn't the fancy high-rise tinted glass sitting-on-top-of-the-world kind of a scenario as before, but rather a low-profile, mean, non-descript, invisible sort of a place. The type of place where interrogations were done, where dirty tricks and dark schemes were cooked up. I had a bad feeling about this; a choke and rob kind of a feeling. Ben was waiting for me in his little Honda. "Whatever you do, don't sign anything," he said.

"Don't worry. My dad told me the same thing," I replied as we walked in.

We were ushered into a dark room with a long table and bright lamps. There were three or four of them, and they had their shirt-sleeves rolled up. They were ready to go to work, to get a result, and from the start it wasn't pretty.

"What the hell is he doing here?" Gilbert asked as we filed in.

"Ben's here in an advisory capacity," I answered.

Evil glances were shot in his direction as Ben slouched down at the end of the table where he almost disappeared, becoming nearly invisible in the peripheral darkness. But he listened to every word said. They might have forgotten about him, but I was damn glad Ben was there.

There were few pleasantries expressed before they went to work on me like hardnosed detectives hell-bent on obtaining a confession. Gilbert just sat in the shadows, letting his henchmen do the dirty work. They hit me hard, letting me know in no uncertain terms how I had failed to deliver my end of the bargain. My moral character was called into question. How I could have ever signed such a deal when I must have known from the start that I wouldn't be able to deliver? All I could say was that I was doing my best and that in the end they were going to get a great boat.

"If you're so confident, then why don't you just buy us out?" Gilbert finally chimed in.

"Er...ah, yeah, well I haven't really ever thought about it. I already have a boat. Plus, that was never the deal in the first place. What's the matter, Bob? Don't you trust me anymore? Is there a problem with the accounting? What's going on here, anyway? Are you accusing me of something?" I asked. I was perplexed.

One of the lawyers jumped in, his honey-coated voice trying to ease the tension. "Hold on, hold on! We're all friends here. We're not accusing you of anything. What we are here to do is solve a problem. Circumstances have changed, and all we want to do is work things out so that everyone is happy," he said.

"Look, there are no problems with the books, Christopher," Gilbert said. "My wife went over them with a fine-toothed comb, and she says they seem to be in order. The problem is, you said you could build it for a certain price and now you are saying you'll need more money. We've put our share in. Where's the rest supposed to come from? We're all on the same side here. What we really want to do is try and work out a way to get the boat finished, because we know it is very important to you."

This seemed to be a cue, because now they all began to work on my conscience. We know you don't want to let your island down and neither do we, they said. We just want everyone walking from the room tonight to be winners. We just want all parties to be happy. And so on.

"What we have done is taken it upon ourselves to draw up this agreement, in which you take over the responsibility of finishing the boat. It looks long, but really it is a very simple contract," one of them said, sliding a multi-page document in front of me. "Take your time and look it over. You'll see it's a good deal."

I leafed through the pages. It looked like nothing more than legal gobbledygook to me. Through all of the haze, through the hokum and fancy footwork I now began to see what they were up to. They wanted to turn the tables. They wanted to get their clients off the hook, and hang me up on a bigger one. In essence, the contract said I would be borrowing the money that had already gone into the boat from Gilbert and his partners. I would then own the boat, but Gilbert et al would have a lien on it until repaid. My dad would go guarantor of the loan. There would be interest. It would be amortized. I didn't even know what amorized meant! I finished reading and looked up. They leaned over the table, pens in hand. "So, you see - it's a good solution for all concerned. Just sign here and here and here."

I looked at Ben. He was shaking his head in the shadows. We were on the same wavelength. "Look," I said as I stood. "I'll have to have a good look at this. I'll need to speak to some people. I'll get back to you, Robert." And with that I picked up the document and Ben and I left.

It was a sticky situation. Things were beginning to spin out of control. It was getting ugly, and that was the last thing I wanted to happen. I was fully conscious of the fact that the terms of our agreement weren't being met, but what could I do? All I knew was the boat had to be finished. Ben came to the rescue yet again. He knew of a lawyer who gave legal advice *pro bono*. Once again, I drove up to LA. It was a cramped, cluttered office in somewhere like Encino. The lawyer wore a crumpled suit and looked weary after a long day at the office, but he was a nice guy and listened attentively to my story. When I finished, he asked to see the original agreement. After reading the brief, half-page document, he asked where St. Vincent was and under what jurisdiction did it fall. I told him it was an independent country which operated under British law.

"Do you own any property in the State of California?" was his next question.

"No," I answered.

"Well, I don't see that you have any legal problem here at all. In the first place, I would hardly call this a bullet-proof contract, but even so I've seen contracts signed in California which can't be upheld in Arizona, let alone in a foreign nation operating under a different law altogether. They can't sue you here since you don't own property in this state. In reality, they could have been sending this money down to you on your Caribbean island and you could have been doing what you want with it. The only court which would have any jurisdiction over this dispute at all would be in St. Vincent, and since you tell me you've signed nothing down there, I would say they don't have a leg to stand on. Bottom line - you have nothing to worry about."

Taillights reflected through my windscreen as I drove back home to Oceanside. It was a relief to know I was okay legally. Gilbert's motives also became quite clear. He'd lost his nerve; he wanted out but still was searching for an angle where he somehow could make money on the deal. But what about Dylan? Did he know what was going on? Gilbert said he was representing Bob's interests, but was he really? Beyond all of this bullshit was the boat itself. It simply had to be finished. There was no way I was going to let Bequia down. And I was not going to leave the boat to rot on the beach, standing as a monument to my own failure. I went back home and sweated on it. I walked around the nearby marina. Grey storm clouds blew in off the Pacific. I needed to find an honorable solution, one without acrimony. What would Henry Wakelam do? What would Long John Silver do? What would Bobby Fischer do? There had to be an answer to this problem, and somehow, I had to find it.

Great ideas often come to me in the middle of the night. I awoke one morning and a semblance of a plan, a germ of a solution began to solidify before my eyes. I worked on it and developed it and kicked it around in my mind. I talked it over with my dad. He thought it was an excellent idea and encouraged me to go for it. Finally, after a couple of days, I took a deep breath and called Bob Gilbert and presented my plan to him. Basically, the deal was this: I trade *Just Now* to Gilbert for his share of the unfinished schooner. He puts some cash on top so I can pay Nolly his original builder's commission. I then sail *Just Now* up to Miami, where Gilbert can put it on a truck and have it delivered to LA. I even found a trucking company in South Florida and worked out the cost for him. Now for the key to the trade - Dylan and I become fifty-fifty partners. He puts up enough money to get the boat into the water and sailing, and I match it with my two years of labor on the boat. Once the boat was up and running, I would start chartering to cover expenses. Gilbert gets his boat on the West Coast where he wants it, and Dylan gets his in the Caribbean. I lose my beloved *Just Now* but embark on another adventure. The schooner gets completed and hopefully everyone is happy.

Gilbert liked the plan and said he would put it to Dylan. A day or two later he called back and said that he agreed. A meeting was set up between all concerned at Bob's studio in Santa Monica. The night before I tossed and turned, hardly sleeping a wink. Was this really what I wanted to do? Did I really want to give up *Just Now*? In the end, I could see there was really no other choice. It was another huge step for me. "Sometimes Bowman, you just have to grab the bull by the horns," is how Ben simply put it.

It was a beautiful, fresh, California day when I pulled up in front of the nondescript building in Santa Monica. Ben was waiting for me in his beat-up Honda. It was because of him that this whole thing started, and I felt he should be there in the end. A big, friendly fellow unlocked the front door and led us up a set of stairs to a boardroom with a long, varnished table and chairs. Sunshine poured through the open windows. Bob Gilbert was there, along with Dave Chang. We all shook hands. Gilbert was all smiles. Chang didn't say much as he watched me through his steely eyes. After a few minutes Dylan came in. He was dressed casually in a blue checked flannel shirt and faded jeans, and seemed a lot more at ease than the previous two times we had met.

We all sat down and the meeting started. Gilbert opened proceedings. "As we all know, we have come to a point in this project where Dave and I don't feel we can continue," he said. "Christopher here, however, has worked out a way for it all to keep going, and we are happy to go along with him." At this point Gilbert handed the meeting over to me and I once again went over my solution to our impasse. Gilbert asked Bob what he thought of the idea. "As long as everyone is happy then it's alright with me," he said. "We can't just leave that boat down there on the beach half-finished."

With the decision made, we worked out the details. And that was about it. Gilbert wrote down all the particulars on a piece of paper. Bob took it out and came back with a couple more copies, which we all signed. "Well I guess we are partners now," I said to Bob with a shy shrug and a smile as we shook hands.

"Yeah…I guess we are. Hang on a minute and I'll get you my numbers."

We all walked out of the boardroom smiling. As we did, a voice from behind whispered into my ear, "You don't have to worry about it if you don't keep your end of the deal…you won't even feel it when the ice pick is stuck into the back of your head." I didn't even have to turn around to see who said it.

"Yeah, and peace and love to you too, bro," I thought as I walked out into the sunshine and down the steps. "It's been a pleasure to have known you."

12
Ain't Nothin' Goin' Stop Us Now

"You are greater than you think. You need to live your natural spontaneous greatness; not think it! Go forth with relaxed awareness and trust that this is so."
- Leopold Soham

St. Barths was a universe away from the mean streets of LA. With a few days to kill before the shipment arrived in St. Maarten, I took a deep breath and enjoyed a few well-deserved rums at Le Select. Bamu and Justin had made friends with some local guys who went over and shot a couple of goats on the rocky Isle de Fourche and then barbequed them on the beach on my first night back, which eased me back into the West Indian pace of life. The boat was in tip-top shape. The guys had the varnish work sparkling. Bob Marley's *Babylon By Bus* rocked out of the tape deck from first light until last lap. "Man, you goin' bore a hole in dat tape if you don' slow down," Justin said to Bamu one day. I should have thought to buy some more music while in the States, but somehow it slipped my mind. The guys probably wouldn't have played anything else anyway. After a few days back on the boat I started to get my balance back.

I received a message from Paul Marshall at Island Water World that my shipment had arrived in St. Maarten, so we said goodbye to our friends in St. Barths and sailed over and collected it. All the gear from Lunenburg was there, as well as the sailcloth from California, fastenings and hardware from Miami, paint and varnish... *Just Now* looked like a floating marine chandlery. We even had a load of beautiful Brazilian mahogany boards I had purchased in St. Barths stacked on deck which I wanted to use to make up the capping rails. Now all we had to do was sail all this stuff three hundred miles back down to Bequia and smuggle it in under the cover of darkness so I could dodge paying duty on all of it. Just another typical week of life in the Caribbean.

Back in Bequia the boys hadn't skipped a beat. All the arm wrestling and ugly stateside machinations didn't mean much to them. Every day, at seven o'clock sharp, they struck their first blow. At four o'clock they knocked off, packed up their tools, and made their way home. And Friday afternoon they got paid. Before I left the States, I'd made sure I'd gotten in touch with Bob's office in New York and made myself known to them, and from that day onward there was never a problem as far as money was concerned.

As we rolled into summer, the work progressed smoothly. Every day on the boat was a joy and a pleasure. Our spirits were high, we all got along, and the teamwork was outstanding. I did have one pressing commitment which I needed to get over and done with. I had to get *Just Now* to Florida, and with the hurricane season fast approaching I had to make a move. I got a crew together and we sailed north. The voyage was fairly uneventful, except to say what a pleasure it was to be sailing in the open sea on such a fine vessel. After ten days we arrived at Nassau, Bahamas, where we met up with Gilbert and another one of his lawyer friends and made the transfer of ownership. From Nassau we had an absolutely cracking sail across the Great Bahama Banks to Fort Lauderdale, where I said goodbye to my boat and Gilbert for the last time. Who would have ever thought back in those days around the bar at the Frangipani with Ray and Willy and Les when *Just Now* was only a dream that it would all have come down to this?

With all of the loose ends tidied up it was time to make the final push towards launching. I received a call from Burt in Copenhagen, and he informed me the trees had been loaded onto a freighter being delivered to the West Indies. I asked him to make sure the bill of lading (official freight bill) was made out for Bequia, and he assured me this would be no problem. We fit the engine beds and drilled the hole for the stern tube and propeller shaft. The decks, deck house, cargo hatch, skylight, wheel box and foredeck scuttle were all finished off, built basically in the traditional manner Chapelle documented in the back of his American schooner book. The caulking of the hull and decks started, and for this I hired three more fellows to help push the job along. Cap'n Cojo, Ethelbert King and Uncle Esau for the most part had made a living throughout their life as caulkers. They joined Lincoln, Gilbert, Lauren, Herbie, and Lanceford in hammering cotton into the seams of the new schooner. It is a very unique sound when a wooden caulking mallet strikes a caulking iron, and to hear eight of them going at the same time was very special. It would have been something which was commonplace in Bequia's historical past, but as we moved towards the 1980's it would probably be the last time this special sound would ring through the harbor in such profusion.

In retrospect, those last few months of the 70's as we worked towards the launching were the most enchanted of a magical era. We were surfing a golden wave, locked in and hooting. As George Harris, the fun-loving Canadian skipper of the funky red Norwegian fiord-ferry-turned-charter boat *Tor Helge* would later say, "Man, we were peaking!" Life was exciting from the instant you opened your eyes in the morning until the moment you closed them at night. Bequia had evolved from that sleepy little dot on the chart Francisco and I encountered six years earlier to a lively sailor's haven. Anchored in the harbor was an ever-changing mix of characters who each had their own interesting story to tell. Old war-horses and young adventurers, round-the world legends and green novices, all mixed together with the friendly, open and welcoming seafarers of the island to produce a rare time when everyone contributed to what Bob Marley would have described as Positive Vibrations. And of course, this high energy stew was perfectly flavored with just the right amount of reggae music, rum and sprinkling of ganga.

It was some time around September, in the height of the rainy season, when I received a phone call from the captain of the ship bringing the mast wood from Denmark. "Hello, this is Captain Wellman," the northern European voice said. "I am here in Barbados with your logs. What do you want me to do with them?"

"What do you mean?" I asked. "The wood was supposed to be delivered here to Bequia."

"No, the bill of lading shows the freight has only been paid as far as Barbados. Do you have an agent here who can arrange the trans-shipment of this cargo? These are very big logs and will not be easy to handle."

Landing the logs in Barbados would be a disaster! To trans-ship them to another freighter would cost an absolute fortune. Barbados was only ninety miles away. The ship had just traveled close to five thousand miles to get there, and the logs were still aboard. Surely the captain would see reason and deliver the wood those last few miles to its ultimate destination.

"Look, you've got the cargo aboard already. Can't you simply deliver it here to Bequia?" I asked.

There was a long pause at his end of the phone. "Yes, I suppose I could deliver it to you there in Bequia. I will do it for two thousand US dollars. Cash, to be paid before I start up my crane."

"What?" I shouted into the phone. "Two thousand bucks? The freight all the way from Copenhagen was two grand! Now you want to charge me two thousand just to bring it ninety miles? That's outrageous!"

"Take it or leave it. This is the deal. Otherwise I will simply discharge it here in Barbados. You just tell me what you want me to do. And I will need to know now."

This was nothing less than out and out piracy. I instantly knew I was dealing with someone who knew the Caribbean well. Landing the wood in Barbados and handling it there would cost far more than what he was asking. I had no choice but to agree to his terms, and he knew it. The devious, wily old bastard had me over a barrel (or log), and that was all there was to it.

"Alright," I said. "When can you be here?"

"I can leave today and be there by mid-day tomorrow. And you agree to my terms, cash to be paid before I discharge the logs?"

"Yes, I agree to your terms, Captain."

The following day the little coaster rounded the point and motored into the bay, right on time. Nolly had heard of this Captain Wellman. He was a professional delivery skipper who obviously knew the ropes and had cleverly made sure the original bill of lading was written to Barbados instead of Bequia. I went aboard and had a few words to the old scoundrel. He wouldn't budge from the arrangement, so I handed him the cash and after counting it twice he fired up the ship's derrick.

Nolly came alongside in *Romanuks*, and we started slinging the massive trees over the side into the water. Nolly then towed each tree to the boatyard with his little double ender. And trees they were! Except for all the limbs having been removed, they came just as they had grown in old King Christian's forest - bark and all. There were six of them, and they were massive lumps of timber, each seventy feet long with a diameter of three feet at the butt. There were also smaller pieces with which to make the bowsprit, gaffs and booms. After rounding up a crowd of friends, we strapped a block and tackle to a coconut tree, and with rollers underneath hauled each tree up into the yard next to the boat. It had been raining all day and we were soaked and muddy and once we had the last of them out of the water it seemed like a good idea on a Sunday afternoon to adjourn next door to our friend Liston's Boley Bar and celebrate with a few rums.

We were into the home stretch now - we could just feel it. A couple more guys were taken on to help with the sanding and painting. With most of the heavy work done we were concentrating on the details. Everything was moving towards its inevitable conclusion, but it wasn't until a grey, rainy afternoon in October that launching the boat had become anything more than an obscure, distant concept to me. The rain was tumbling down, cascading off our tin shed roof like a waterfall. As we waited for the squall to pass, Uncle Linkie turned to me and asked in his very serious way, "So Chris, who are you going to get to help we launch de vessel?"

I wasn't prepared for the question. Launching had hardly entered into my calculations. "I haven't thought about it much, to tell you the truth," I answered. "I just thought we would be cutting her down and launching her ourselves. Why? Do you know somebody who might be able to help?"

"Launching a big vessel like dis isn't easy. You must know what you is doing," he said in his cryptic sort of way. "If it was me, I'd be axin' someone who done it before. Why don't you see if Uncle Athneal will gi' we a hand?"

I was taken aback. Ask Athneal Ollivierre? I had never met the man but only heard tale of this Herculean harpooner and his legendary battles with the giant humpback whale in the last of the island's whaleboats. It would never have occurred to me to ask him to help launch the boat. "Do you think he would be interested?" I queried skeptically.

The rain had stopped and Linkie was going back to work. "Why don't you go ax him an' see," was his offhanded remark as he climbed up the ladder towards the boat's deck. Later in the day I passed the idea by Loren, who also thought it was a good idea, so that same afternoon I joined Linkie, Gilbert and Herbie in their daily trip home to Southside. Reaching the main road, we climbed into the back of Bill's dollar-a-drop Toyota truck, cramming ourselves in alongside a full load of passengers. Lincoln and Herbie jumped out at the village of La Pompe, leaving the smiling Gilbert and I to ride on towards Paget Farm. As we left the village Bill stopped the van and Gilbert pointed out Athneal's house.

Crossing the road, I anxiously stood and called out from the legendary harpooner's gate. The person who came to meet me was tall and lanky, his silver-grey hair and moustache contrasting with his pale blue eyes and almond skin. I knew the face from a photo in an article about the Bequia whalers I had seen in National Geographic magazine. I was nervous as I introduced myself, not knowing what to expect, but I was immediately put at ease by the man's welcoming smile and warm handshake.

"As you probably know, I'm building the schooner up in the harbor and we're getting pretty close to launching. Uncle Linkie suggested I come see you and find out if you would be interested in helping us get her in the water." Athneal motioned me in and led me across his tidy courtyard, the odd whale bone catching my attention out of the corner of my eye. I followed him through some Dutch doors into the lower story of his house, which was built in traditional Bequia style with the kitchen and eating area downstairs and the main living area above. Inside this cool and shady room, he showed me his pride and joy- a mural painted across one wall by a visiting American of him harpooning a whale. Looking around the room reminded me more of a whaling museum than a kitchen, and he spent a lot of time explaining to me the uses and names of the various paraphernalia. Athneal made me feel right at home, and acted as if he had known me for years. We sat down at the small kitchen table, where he explained that his wife was not feeling well and he was cooking up a "fish broff" for her. After a while we got down to business.

"You know, I have launched a number of vessels in my time. Some big ones too." He went on to describe his experiences of launching a variety of schooners throughout the Grenadines. "As far as I'm concerned, there is only one way to do it. I don' mind helpin' all-you out, but if I do, we'll be doin' it my way." Athneal sat casually at the table, but his eyes were locked on to mine, and I knew this was no time to waver.

"You just tell me what you need, and I'll make sure it happens," I replied. "I've never launched anything like this before, so I'll go along with whatever you think is right." Athneal walked me to the front gate. "I'll be up sometime in the mornin' to have a look," he said.

Stepping out on the main road I waved goodbye. After a few paces I stopped and gazed over the Grenadine Islands as they swept away to the southeast. Just then Taxi Bill came careening around the corner in his red truck on his way back to the harbor, slowing just enough for me to run and hop into the back.

Athneal turned up in the boatyard the following day around mid-morning, and was greeted by all the boys in a very friendly fashion. We walked around the boat and he had a good look. I had told him I had borrowed "Satan", Macdonald Davis' huge fisherman's anchor, and several months earlier we had dropped it in line with the vessel on the other side of the reef so that she could set. He didn't say much. After a few minutes he turned and faced me with his arms crossed. "You've got a lot to do here to get ready. I'll be up here first thing Monday morning and we'll get started," he said. After a few more jovial shouts to the fellows up on deck he was off, striding up the track towards the main road and home. I wanted to ask him how much he wanted to be paid a day, but never got the chance.

Athneal was in the yard bright and early on Monday morning. Straight away he had me on my toes. The first thing he wanted done was for us to dig a channel from under the vessel to the water – in effect making a slipway for the rollers to run on. This was quite a job, as a lot of sand, soil and rocks had to be moved away. I put a team of Nero and two laborers onto it, with Athneal cracking the whip. A couple of days later Athneal asked, "Where are your rollers?"

"I have eight telephone poles, but they're still up on the beach in the harbor," I said.

"Well dey aren't doing us any good up there, are they? I want dem here by de end of de week," he ordered. And so it went. It didn't matter to him that I was still trying to get the boat finished. It was his job to get the vessel safely into the water, and that was what he was going to do. Slowly but surely the ground beneath the schooner became more and more like a slipway, and as we entered the month of November, we knew the launching wouldn't be too far away.

As most of the exterior woodwork had been completed, we started making the spars. October-November is the hottest, most humid time of the year in the Grenadines, so using simple bush poles and palm fronds we set up a sun shade over the mast-making area. The two best-looking trees were manhandled into working position and centerlines laid out. Using a combination of chainsaw, ax and adz the trees were quickly made into square twelve-inch beams, each well over sixty feet long. The mastheads and hounds were then marked out and chopped down to the dimensions of the mast bands forged by the Lunenburg blacksmiths. Once all of these sizes were developed, the masts were then made into eight, sixteen, and thirty-two sides before finally being shaped round.

Sippy Ollivierre came up from La Pompe to start the rigging work. There was a lot of rigging to do, so from time to time a number of old salts would come by to give Sippy a hand. Uncle Bartley, a schooner man and fisherman from La Pompe, would turn up occasionally, taking nips of strong rum as he worked. Macdonald Davis from Mount Pleasant lent a hand; even a sober Arnie Ollivierre, the shipwright notorious for his drunken sprees, spent time working on the rigging.

It took a couple of weeks for Athneal's slipway to be completed. After shoveling out and leveling the sand into an even slope to the water, he placed heavy planks or 'ways' under the boat, running them parallel to the keel. The eight big rollers were then positioned under the boat, crossing the ways. When the time was right, we would lay the vessel down on one side so that her bilge rested on the rollers. In preparation for this some sacrificial boards were nailed on to the boat where she would touch so that the planking wouldn't be damaged. This was known as "cutting de vessel down", and it sounded like a very tricky exercise to me. Traditionally this was done in the days leading up to the launching by replacing the shores (which held the boat upright) on one side with freshly cut green ones. A shipwright would then be stationed at the base of each shore with a sharp ax, and on a signal they each would simultaneously chop the same amount off the bottom of the new shore. Slowly, cut by cut, the vessel would lean over to one side, until finally she would be lying on the rollers. This sounded scary to me. The timing would have to be perfect. If anything went wrong, we would have forty tons of schooner crashing down onto its bilge. On his first day at the boatyard Athneal quickly dispelled any fears I might have had. "Cutting down? Man, we ain't doin' it dat old-time hogshit way." He had a far more simple and safe solution. We would use sandbags, which would be stacked up under one side of the boat. The shores which held up the boat on that side would then be removed and the vessel pushed over the couple of inches until she touched them. The sandbags would then simply be cut and the sand dragged out by hand, whereupon the boat would be slowly laid down on to the rollers. It was a simple idea. So simple it was pure genius.

13
Bull-foot Sauce

"Once a ship's been christen'd, so let her be I says. So it was with the 'Cassandra' that brought us all home safe from Malabar, when England, the great Cap'n England, took the 'Viceroy of the Indies'. And so it was with the 'Walrus', Flint's old ship, that I seen run a-muck with blood and fit to sink with gold."
- Long John Silver

A buzz was going on around the island. There would be a launching soon. My life was like a stereo and someone was cranking up the volume. We had guys everywhere applying finishing touches, and I had my afterburners on to keep up with it all. Paint and varnish were going on, the rudder and steering gear had been fitted, and the windlass, deck pump and hawse pipes were all bolted into place. One by one the fiddley little details were being ticked off the list. What the vessel required now was a name. This is never an easy task. What I needed was some inspiration. I took a deep breath and decided to call my partner.

Bob was a few days in to his latest tour in San Francisco when I reached him. Not only was this the first time I had ever phoned him, it was the first time we had spoken since our Santa Monica meeting a few months earlier. I have to admit I was a little nervous. He sounded tired, like he had just woken up, even though it would have been early afternoon his time. We hardly knew each other; there was little room for small talk.

"Hey Bob, how's it going."

"Okay, I guess. Just on the road, you know. How's the boat?"

"Yeah good. Really good. Just getting her ready to launch."

"Oh yeah? When's that going to be?"

"We don't have an exact date yet, but sometime next month. Any chance of you being here?"

"Naw. I'm pretty booked up." Long silence.

"That's too bad," I said. "Anyhow, the reason I called is we don't have a name for her yet, and I wondered if you had any ideas. The original name was *Stranger*, but that doesn't do much for me."

After a bit he said, "How about *Queen Ann?*" Another long pause. "Or *Resurrection?*"

Now there was silence at my end. "Yeah...well those are a couple of ideas to think about. We don't have to decide now; we've still got some time. Is it okay if I call you back in a few days and see if we have come up with any alternatives?"

"Yeah, just call me back. I don't know where I'll be, but you know how to reach me." We said goodbye and hung up.

To be truthful, I was a little disappointed. I figured Bob could have come up with something a little more romantic. But really, what could I expect? I had put him on the spot. He'd never been to the island; he'd never seen the boat. To him it must have been something happening far away, on the periphery of his experience. The last thing on his mind was coming up with the name for a boat he'd never seen.

I had no idea about it then but know now he was just a week into his controversial Gospel Tour and had other things to think about. I knew nothing of his latest release, *Slow Train Coming*, or the great stir he had caused by giving the impression that he was "born again". In that light, *Resurrection* made some sense. But I was in Bequia, a universe away from the bright lights of a rock and roll tour. I could only go with what I knew.

If nothing else, our conversation made me think more seriously about the name. For my part, I really wanted to stick to tradition. Maybe the name of an old Bequia schooner might be right. *Mandalay* sounded nice, and *Water Lily* had a ring to it, but the one which kept coming back to me was *Water Pearl*, which was the name of Reggie Mitchell's original schooner built on the same spot forty years previously. I continued to roll others over in my mind, but in the end *Water Pearl* was it. I decided to call Bob again. This time he was in Arizona, and the conversation went pretty much as before.

"Yeah, so anyway Bob I've come up with a name. How does *Water Pearl* sound?" I asked. I then told him a bit of the history behind the name. "What do you think?"

"I don't know," he replied. "I still like *Resurrection*."

"Well if you think about it, *Water Pearl* is sort of a resurrection," I tried. It was a battle of wills, and it ended in a stalemate.

I changed tack. "I've decided on Sunday, December 9th for the launch. Any chance you can take some time off and make it?"

"No, like I said I'm pretty tied up. Let me know how it all goes."

We hung up. I sat and stared at the phone, figuring I was no better off than before. "Stuff it," I said to myself. "I'm building this thing. I'm pulling rank. The name is *Water Pearl*. He'll learn to live with it." And he did. *Resurrection* was never mentioned again.

In Bequia tradition I had to think of a godmother for the boat. Only she would know the name before the launch, she would make the flag bearing the vessel's name, and she would christen her. Mark's girlfriend Patty was my automatic choice. In a way she had been involved from the very beginning; I had met her on that first fateful trip back to California even before my weekend with Ben, and she had been blessing the project with her happy, positive aura for well over a year. When I asked her, she gleefully accepted.

It was getting to be very exciting. The word was put out as to when the launching would be, and I knew it would spread like wildfire across the Caribbean through the sailors' grapevine. I let my parents know. Ray said he wouldn't miss it for the world, but the cancer was hitting my mom very hard and he doubted she could make it. "Big", the shanty-man, turned up, walking past the vessel singing his sea shanties, which gave official notice the launching was on. The first spar to be made was the bowsprit. We rigged a block and tackle off a coconut tree and manhandled it into place. The slipway was finished, and the rollers and ways were placed under the boat. It was all systems go except for one thing - Nolly.

Our relationship had been rocky since the project began, but once I became a partner, things only got worse. "It takes two to tango" as the saying goes, and I'm sure my one-eyed approach had a lot to do with it, but it bothered me that Nolly chose to stay away from the boatyard in those last few exciting weeks. After all, he had been there since the beginning and had always kept things running when I was away, but as a partnership, things never really worked out. Even though my role had changed, I always reaffirmed to Nolly he would get paid his commission once the boat was launched. Now he was playing his "disappearing Nolly" trick, and trying to make things right with him was like grasping at shadows. Rumor had it he was going to stop the launching because he hadn't been paid. I had his money, but wasn't going to give it to him until after the boat floated. It was difficult to tell him this since he was going out of his way to avoid me. This issue with Nolly only added to the pressure. It was just another thing I had to think about. "Don't worry 'bout him, man," Loren advised. "You got more than enough 'tings on your mind. He'll come around…don't frighten. When dis vessel goes in de water Nolly won't be able to stay away." I tried to follow his sage advice, but it wasn't easy. I didn't have much choice but to call his bluff.

Launching a boat is a nerve-wracking enterprise. There will be a lot of eyes on you, and it is important everything goes smoothly. As the appointed time drew near, the list of things to do only seemed to get longer. Through all of this Athneal proved to be a true champion. From the time I asked him to help, he never missed a day. The launch had become his responsibility, and he was going to make sure that the vessel rolled in without a hitch and nothing was left until the last minute. Of course, I wanted to make sure this launching would be one to remember, in keeping with all of the old Bequia traditions. I made sure there would be plenty of drink on hand. I had organized the Comets, a great local reggae band, to supply the music. I knew that food should be provided, but was at a loss as to what to prepare. So, I asked Athneal.

"Well, mon, it is a schooner you launchin', so you must do it right," he said. "The real old-time way would be to slaughter a bull-cow."

"A cow?" I queried. "I thought a couple of goats maybe, but a cow? Where the hell would I find a cow to buy?"

The question was passed on to the shipwrights and a great discussion ensued. Finally, it was suggested I check with Uncle Mellie, Bluesy's brother. "He does generally raise a cow or two," Loren said. After work one day I walked up to Mount Pleasant to see him. It was late afternoon when I reached his place. I found him sitting in the cool of his shady front porch. "Come aboard, Chris-boy, and get out of de heat. Dat afternoon sun does have a bite to it," he said, speaking in the tone of a man who had known me all his life. Uncle Mellie was an old schooner man, and had lived most of his life sailing the waters of the Caribbean hauling cargo. Now he spent his time tending to his garden and raising a few animals. I listened to him complain about growing old, his troubling arthritis and the cost of living, amongst other things, before we got down to business.

"You know we're getting ready to launch our schooner, and the boys in the boatyard advised me to come and see you. I'm looking for a bull-cow to buy, and they said you might just be the man."

For the longest of moments the old sea captain stared at me from under his tattered Panama, as if assessing me. "Yes, as a matter of fact I do have a cow I can sell you…a fine young bull." Painfully pulling himself to his feet, he led me in his rolling gait out into his back paddock, where we found the animal grazing.

Animal husbandry has never been one of my strong suits. One cow looked pretty much the same to me as another. "Looks good to me," I said, trying to sound knowledgeable. We struck a bargain, and Mellie said he would find someone to bring the bull down to the harbor in the next day or two. Uncle Athneal had told me it was important for the animal to graze around the boatyard. "He must spend some time getting to know de vessel," he said.

The final countdown was on, and Athneal was in full command. Every day more people turned up to help. Mackie Simmons from Lower Bay, (no relation to Nolly) volunteered to take on the job of supplying the sandbags, and so along with my Australian girlfriend Vanessa and her close mate Lynnie spent several days rowing back and forth to Princess Margret's Beach, bringing back half-a-dozen sandbags at a time to stack up under the bilge of the boat. Mark set himself up on a scaffold and carved the intricate oak leaf scrolls around the hawse pipes, which were then painted gold. Sippy and Bartley rigged the heavy bridle around the vessel to which the hauling tackle would be attached. A wire cable making up the check line was also rigged, running aft of the boat where it was made fast to a coconut tree. Gilbert's sister Molly, who provided me with my daily lunch, offered to organize the cooking for launch day, so two big "coppers" were brought up from La Pompe and set up in the back yard of my house underneath a broad shade tree. These big round pots would have come to the island in the old whaling days where they were used for boiling down whale blubber to oil. One copper would be used for cooking the beef stew, the other used for rice. Several bags of potatoes and other root vegetables were bought at the markets in St. Vincent, which the cooks, along with their daughters and other helpers, would later peel and prepare.

The bar was to be set up in the shade of the work shed, with the band just behind. Harold, the head barman at the Frangipani, agreed to be in charge of the bar, and I asked Frankie Ollivierre and Donovan from Southside to give him a hand. Athneal's Rules stated there would be no drinking or music until after the vessel floated, but once she did there would be a rush for the bar and we needed some hard-nosed characters to deal with the mob. Later the food would be served, and the system for that had to be set up as well. Although I had a vague idea what to prepare for, Athneal knew far more. "When it comes to freeness, Chris-boy, well look out...dese people does turn beast," he warned.

Uncle Mellie sent the cow down from Mount Pleasant, and he spent the last week or so contentedly munching on the grass growing under the coconut trees in the boatyard. The time would come for him to play his part, but I doubt if he suspected exactly what role that might be.

Athneal was determined no detail would be overlooked and everything would have been organized well in advance. "By eleven o'clock when most people turnin' up to see launching me want she floatin' already!" were his often-said words. There would be no last-minute rush or panic, and with the amount of people set to be there it was critical there wouldn't be. Early in the morning the day before launching Athneal arrived with Fiji, Ferdie and the rest of his Southside whale boat crew. These fellows were like the royal guard, and were there to make sure their captain's orders were carried out exactly. Bluesy turned up, and a crew was organized to assist him with the check line. This was a critical job, because if the vessel wasn't stopped on time and over-ran her rollers it could take hours or even days to get her back on them again. As with *Just Now*, slow and steady was the order of the day.

Finishing touches: Mark carves the oakleaf scroll.

I once again borrowed the launching tackle from the owners of the *Friendship Rose*, and this was run out and secured by divers to "Satan". Every connection was checked and rechecked by Athneal, Sippy and the rest of the crew. It was obvious these men all knew what they were doing. This wasn't the first time a schooner was launched in Bequia.

By mid-morning Athneal was happy. From his point of view everything was ready. There was, however, one more important job to do. The cow had to be slaughtered, butchered and prepared for cooking. Since his arrival he had been carefully shifted to all parts of the yard so he could view the vessel from every angle. Now, unfortunately, his time had come. Athneal gave Bartley the order.

Bartley led the animal up to a coconut tree and tied him up close so that his head was butting the tree. He then took his long rigger's knife out of its sheath and using the palm of his hand drove it into the soft base of the beast's skull. I was expecting (and hoping) for the cow to drop dead immediately. It didn't. The poor thing let out a huge bellow of pain and began to struggle against his tether. Bartley was obviously flustered. Aiming another plunge of the knife would be extremely difficult. Everyone in the yard stopped what they were doing, freezing in their tracks. All eyes were on Bartley and the bellowing bull.

In a flash Athneal sprang into action. This was the man who had famously jumped up onto a humpback whales back and "killed her stone dead with one lance straight to de heart." At that moment he was standing under the stern of the vessel alongside Herbie and a couple of others. At the first hint of the bull's discomfort Athneal grabbed the hatchet out of Herbie's hand and crossed the twenty meters to the struggling cow in what looked to be three strides. Bartley jumped clean out of the way. After raising the hatchet high over his head, he paused for a millisecond, taking aim. Then, using the blunt end of the hatchet, he bashed it into the top of the bull's skull. And in that instant the animal's legs buckled and he collapsed stone dead to the ground without as much as a quiver. Walking back to the boat he handed Herbie his hatchet. "I hate to see any animal suffer," he said.

Nero and Bartley got stuck into butchering the animal. The meat was then taken over to Molly and her helpers, who were getting the fires started under the big black coppers. Later in the afternoon the women brought over bowls of a yellow looking soup. Athneal handed me one.

"What's this?" I asked as I tasted my first spoonful.

Molly cookin' up de souse.

"Bull-foot souse. It's special...just for the builders. Sweet, isn't it?" I forced down a few more spoonful's of the thick, gelatinous soup. I felt like I had to support the tradition, but I think it needed an acquired taste. Uncle Mackie's son "Neighbor", who had been working with us for the previous couple of months, climbed a coconut tree and dropped down some green water-nuts. I cracked open a bottle of Johnny Walker and we all had a drink. We were ready.

The building crew pose the day before launching.

14
Another Launching

"Of all the living creatures upon land and sea, it is ships alone that cannot be taken in by barren pretenses... that will not put up with bad art from their masters."
- Joseph Conrad

In the pre-dawn darkness people began to arrive at the house, and I was up waiting for them. Molly and her helpers were the first to turn up. After getting the fires started underneath the coppers they came into my kitchen, where Molly bustled about jovially giving orders as the women set about preparing the mountain of food for the day's festivities. Athneal and his crew of whaler-men turned up next, their voices drifting down the hill ahead of them as they made their way along the narrow track from the main road past the house to the waiting vessel. My girlfriend Vanessa came out of the bedroom half asleep and gave me a big hug. "Good luck," she said as I went out the door. "I pray that all goes well."

Following my daily routine, I jumped over the low stone wall. In the first light of that cool, clear December morning I stopped, pausing for a brief moment to gaze for one last time at the brightly painted schooner waiting in the shadows of the coconut trees, her bow pointing steadfastly out towards the sea. After a last long look, I hurried on to join the quickly growing gang of men busily getting all in readiness.

Athneal stood like a general beneath the schooner's stern, his khaki fisherman's cap shining like a beacon in the growing light. Nothing escaped his keen eye as the last details were finished off. There would be no messing about on this day. Athneal was resolved to get his job over and done with as quickly as possible. Bluesy strode into the yard in his blue golf shirt and plaid shorts. He and Sippy would control the check line, and they made sure everything was set to run clear. The heavy hauling line was neatly run out. The day before the vessel was dressed with an assortment of flags and bunting borrowed from the various yachts out at anchor, and now Patty arrived with a huge bouquet of colorful flowers which Mark tied beneath the glittering bowsprit. The crowd was growing by the minute, and Athneal was anxious to get started.

"Okay, let's get dis vessel down on her side," Athneal ordered, and everyone sprang into action. The shores on the port side were knocked out and with one push the crowd shoved her over the few inches, where she softly settled onto the stack of well-placed sandbags. Bartley began to slash the bags open with his knife while we dropped down on hands and knees to haul the sand out. The vessel slowly lowered, and within a few short minutes her bilge was resting gently onto the rollers. The sun hadn't broken over the hilltops yet and the schooner was already on her side.

At seven o'clock sharp the priest arrived to bless the boat. Father McGonagall was the Catholic priest on the island, and quite a character. He hailed from Nova Scotia and had grown up listening to the tales of that island's famous fishing schooners. He was known to be partial to the odd nip of whiskey and had a delightful sense of humor. The father delivered a fine, seafaring type of blessing, which he finished off with the words, "And now I christen this ship *Water Pearl*." With these last words I released the name flag, where it fluttered from its makeshift flagpole on deck. I studied the faces of the crowd standing below. One face which stood out was that of Walter Bynoe. I watched as recognition of the name sunk in. A broad smile spread across his face, and then he raised his arms and started to cheer. The name passed through the crowd like a floating, murmuring whisper, until they too slowly joined in the chorus. As I climbed down the ladder, I was congratulated by all for choosing a good Bequia name, especially Son Mitchell, who had a smile from ear to ear. He pumped my hand profusely, expressing his appreciation that I would name the new vessel after one of his father's schooners.

I prepare the champers while Nolen and others look on.

We walked around to the bow and got the bottle of champagne ready for Patty to smash over the bob stay iron, and as I did, I noticed one particular smiling face in the crowd. It was Nolen, who had only hours before sailed in from Antigua. We hugged and had a laugh and he said, "This is a bit of a step up from the *Corsair*. It seems like every time we see each other you've got some kind of a boat on the beach!" Athneal's voice behind me broke up the reverie. "Come on Chris - let's get dis vessel in de water." Like I said, he was a man on a mission. Patty performed her job perfectly, smashing the champagne bottle to smithereens to yet another rousing cheer. The crowd was growing

Patty Perkins smashes it!

Serious locals show their concern.

quickly. Underneath the vessel a who's who of Bequia shipwrights, freighter captains, fishermen and sailors milled about, intently examining the details of how the boat was rigged for launching. There was no joking or levity now, we were coming to the serious part of the operation. For my part, it was as if I was floating in a dream. Faces in the crowd blurred past as I went from one thing to the next. Locals mixed with yachtsmen, old friends with unknowns. I glimpsed my dad taking photos; I saw the faces of my brother and sister. It seemed like everyone I had ever met in my years in the Caribbean was there, but I moved as if in slow motion in my own world, in my own bubble. Snatches of conversations drifted past; anticipation, curiosity and excitement filled the air. It felt like the whole of the island's population was there, drifting about under those coconut trees. Much to my relief I spotted the smiling face of Nolly, who moved through the crowd as if nothing had ever transpired between us. But I couldn't stop, I couldn't dally. Athneal was on the move. Things were about to happen.

The hauling line was stretched out and people squeezed in, jamming themselves together to get a handhold on the line. At each end of the eight rollers Athneal assigned an experienced waterman to keep the rollers moving so they didn't twist crossways. Athneal's mammoth "Kangaroo" jack had been placed under the after end of the keel and would be used to 'start' the vessel enough to get her moving. The check line crew took up the slack, and Bluesy stationed himself so he could see Athneal. I stood up and shouted for the crowd to be silent. "Athneal is the only man for us to listen to now!" I said. "When he says haul you haul, but when he says stop its critical you all stop!"

The order was given to start to take up the slack. There must have been a hundred people hauling on that line. Probably even more. The rope stretched and stretched until the tackle was bar-tight. Fiji started pumping the jack handle. More people grabbed on to the end of the rope. Still it stretched, continuing to tighten under the immense strain. Three men put their weight on the long jack handle. The hauling line was now only taking up a few inches at a time but still all were urged to put more effort into it. Something had to give. The tension was incredible. And then with a sudden lurch she jumped! With a low groan and a rumble like a hollow drum, *Water Pearl* bounced over the rollers towards the water!

Athneal let her roll only for a moment before throwing his arms up. "Check her up!" he shouted.

"Stop hauling!" I yelled.

Bluesy and Sippy held their turns on the check line and the wire grew as taught as a violin string as it cut into the base of the coconut tree. Slowly the vessel eased to a stop. A silent pause followed, and then the cheers exploded. The vessel had moved! Her forty-odd tons of deadweight had shifted! West Indians are an excitable lot, and with that first movement the place erupted. There was noise, chaos, and confusion. To the crew on the hauling line it was party time, but we still had a long way to go. A lid had to be put on all this enthusiasm, and that would not be easy. Athneal made a tour around the boat making sure all was in order, talking to the roller men, to the cooler heads, to his lieutenant Fiji and others. He strode back to have a word to Bluesy and his crew. The heavy rollers which were left behind were overhauled and brought around to the bow of the boat. Gradually the excitement abated.

Nearing the danger zone. Note the amount of people on the hauling line.

I stood back and surveyed the scene. I observed people from all parts of the island standing shoulder to shoulder with cruising sailors, everyone hell-bent on lending a hand. Many of the people I hardly knew. There were groups of old-timers in their khaki trousers and straw hats studying proceedings from a distance. Athneal nodded to me and everyone got ready to haul again. More people pushed in to get a hand on the line. Locals next to strangers. Black next to white. The order was given and the line grew tight. The throng of people strained and pulled until once again she rumbled over the rollers and Athneal's arms were thrown in the air and the check line held fast and she snatched to a halt, the bow of the boat coming to a rest just at the water's edge. The rollers from astern were overhauled, this time being paced into the murky shallows of the bay. The next bit would be the tricky part. The watermen got ready at the ends of their rollers. Athneal gave the order to haul, and with the sound of a falling tree the boat bumped and groaned and entered the water, wetting her skin for the first time. Again, she was held up and the same procedures repeated. The crowd had filled in the slipway behind the boat, and I could see Athneal beginning to lose his cool. I understood now why he wanted to launch early in the morning, before all and sundry turned up.

Athneal pulled me aside to have a word. He felt it was time to remove the check line. "It's time fo' we to let her run," he said. Bluesy and Sippy released the check line, and word was spread along the hauling line. "This is it," we told them. "Pull for your lives and don't stop 'til she floats."

"Let she go!"

"Run wit' de line!"

The order was given and the crowd began to pull. The vessel started to move once more, and this time with some speed. "Let her go!" Athneal shouted. "Let her run! Don't stop! Run wit de line!" And so they turned and ran with it and with a sound of rolling thunder the boat boomed over the last of the rollers and slowly became upright and then, with one last shudder, she freed herself from the grip of land and glided out into the bay. *Water Pearl* was floating!

The cheering turned to a roar. I made my way to Athneal and shook his hand. We stood at the water's edge. People slapped me on the back. A bunch of local kids had made their way aboard and were dancing, arms in the air. Athneal called to a young boy to row us out in his little double-ender. As we climbed aboard the Comets began to play. The bar was now open. The party had begun. Although she was floating well out of the water because she had no ballast, *Water Pearl* sat perfectly...neither bow up or down. Her bilges were as dry as chips. A dinghy with an outboard towed us to our temporary mooring, where Athneal made sure she was well secured. When he finished making the mooring line fast to the Sampson post he examined the rope one more time, just to make sure. "Well," he said, turning to me, "my job is done. Now why don't we go ashore and have a drink."

"She floatin' like a gull on de watah!"

By the time we got ashore the party was in full swing. Loren, Linkie and Gilbert met us at the water's edge to find out if she was making any water, and I told them she was fine. As we walked up the slipway my dad congratulated me, along with Son Mitchell. Nolly was there and we shook hands. I saw Vanessa standing with some friends and I walked over and we had a big hug. "You don't know how glad I am that things went well," she said.

"I'm glad for you too," I laughed. "I think you were more worried than me."

Athneal called out to me. "Come Chris, we must get some food before it's gone!" And the party went on. Everyone got a heaping plate of food and plenty to drink. The old boys from Southside sat in groups drinking strong rum just as they liked it…straight with just a chase of water. The shipwrights all got drunk, except for Loren, being a strict Adventist. Athneal and I had our drink, and then he was gone. He wasn't much for parties, he said. Eventually the bar ran dry, the music stopped, and everyone slowly drifted off. By sunset the boatyard was empty, except for me and Mark. We didn't say much as we sat quietly on some keel blocks, slowly passing a bottle of Mount Gay rum back and forth between us. The yard looked so different now: so strange, so empty. But there she floated, sitting as light and as sweet as a gull on the water.

It took a few days for me to come down. Vanessa and I could finally spend time with my family. Needless to say, Ray was as proud as punch. My brother Rick had brought along his guitar, and one night he and his friend Eric Henderson put on a classical guitar concert at the Frangipani. A couple of days later that circus flew back to California. Nolen sailed north and the harbor slowly emptied. The island gradually returned to normal. We towed the vessel up to the mouth of the harbor and tied her to some coconut trees just in front of where we built *Just Now*.

When the smoke cleared, I walked over to La Pompe to see Athneal. When he first agreed to help us launch the vessel, I naturally asked him how much he wanted to be paid but he simply said that we could talk about it later. Several other times I had broached the subject with him, only to be told to wait until after the launching. Now I wanted to sort out our business. I found him on the hillside behind his house moving his goat. We walked back to the house and sat down at his simple kitchen table and chatted. Eventually when I got around to asking him how much he wanted for his work he simply said, "Don't worry about it, man. Maybe one day you can do me a favor." I was taken aback. For over six weeks he had spent every working day in the boatyard

Athneal Ollivierre.

supervising our preparations. Surely, he would take something for all his effort and time. He wouldn't hear of it, and there would be no further discussion. End of story.

15
Ready to Rock and Roll

"Nothing comes before it's time."
- West Indian Proverb

It took us another six months to get *Water Pearl* ready for her maiden voyage. Using up the balance of wood I bought in Guyana, we built an interior, which was basic but functional and well-finished. I had no idea what type of work we would be doing with the boat, but knew we would be doing some sort of charter work. I sold the engine Gilbert had bought in Miami as it was not really suitable for a heavy schooner like *Water Pearl*, and with the money bought an English slow turning, heavy-duty Gardner six-cylinder diesel. With the help of Bert Henriksen, who now had a workshop in Bequia, we installed the engine. The masts and other spars were ready to be stepped, but first we had to ballast the vessel. I calculated we would need approximately twenty tons of weight to get her down to her lines, and over the time of construction I had been accumulating various pieces of iron and lead. What I had collected was barely a quarter of what we would need; the balance would have to be made up of stones. For this, I was to learn, you just couldn't use just any old rocks that were lying around the place, but a special stone from a special place.

About six miles to windward of Bequia lay two large, uninhabited islands. Battowia, the northernmost of the pair, is a rocky, high, sheer-sided isle, while her sister Baliceaux is low and flat. This is where the British exiled the last of St. Vincent's Carib population whom they hadn't ethnically cleansed after settling the island in the early 1700's. Plenty of these Indians died on Baliceaux before the last of the survivors were herded up and shipped off to Honduras, where even today they are still called "Black Caribs". I heard several stories from Bequia fishermen who spent time camping on the island that the place was haunted, and bones were regularly uncovered every time a storm hit. The stone from there was ideal for ballast, however, because it was dense and heavy, and the smooth, round shapes made it perfect for handling. So, a trip was planned for 'picking' ballast, and to do this I hired Collie Ollivierre and his cargo sloop *Zulia O*.

Early one Saturday morning we motored out of the harbor. Vanessa joined me, Collie, and his crew of Southside buccaneers for the trip out to the island. An hour or so later we anchored in a small, well protected bay. Joslin, Collie's first mate, pulled up alongside the big double-ender we had towed over, and five of us jumped in, blond-haired Vanessa standing out like a lighthouse beacon on a dark and stormy night alongside this boatload of rough West Indian pirates. After touching the boat up on a spit of sand, the crew jumped ashore and spread out. They obviously knew what they were looking for. "You wants dem just de size you can grab wit' one hand. Any bigger an' dey is too hard to handle," Joslin explained. So off we went along the shore, carefully picking up stones and carrying them back to stack inside the ship's boat. Vanessa obviously had missed the tutorial on ballast picking, because the next thing we noticed was her staggering down the beach with a giant boulder hugged tightly to her chest. "Look what I found while you boys were off collecting pebbles," is what the look in her eyes seemed to say. We couldn't help but have a silent giggle. "You got a strong woman there, Chris," Joslin said with a snaggle-toothed smile.

The ship's boat was loaded to the gunnels, and with all of us perched like shags on a rock we rowed out to the high-prowed blue sloop. After forming a line, the rocks were quickly passed aboard and dropped down into the cargo hold, the smooth granite stones making a sharp cracking sound as they struck the growing pile. A dozen or so trips ashore like this were made and the *Zulia O* was floating well below her waterline. Early on a bottle of strong rum was produced, and so we were all in good spirits that afternoon when we steamed back into the harbor and tied up alongside *Water Pearl*, where a human chain was once again formed and the ballast passed aboard and stowed deep in the schooner's bilges.

With the ballast in we could step the masts, which were now varnished and painted. Sippy had all the rigging ready to go, so one day when Captain Raul King brought his freighter *Lirico* into the harbor to spend a few days at home, he agreed to help us step the masts. Bert Henriksen had finished the engine installation; we had previously taken the vessel for a test run around the harbor. So, with everything prepared we motored *Water Pearl* alongside the big steel cargo boat, and after getting a crowd of people together to help we launched the masts into the water and towed them out alongside. After 'dressing' the masts with the rigging, each one was slung and hoisted high into the air with *Lirico's* derrick and then lowered carefully into place. Following prescribed seafaring tradition, I placed a West Indian penny under the foot of the fore mast, but under the main spar I put a gold sovereign.

With the masts and rigging sorted out, the booms and gaffs could now be put in position and the running rigging pulled through the blocks. Bluesy came aboard one evening and we measured for all the sails. Marv Berning from the yacht *Impunity*, who I had known since Grenada, was also a sailmaker. He took our measurements and then did all the technical calculations for building the proper shape into the sails. When all was ready, he, Bluesy and I took the rolls of sailcloth out to the tennis courts in Spring to cut the sails, as it was the only flat area big enough to lay them out. Visiting

Bluesy in his sail loft was always an enjoyable experience. Mac still worked with him, along with a young apprentice named Alec, and as much as everyone liked Bluesy, he would have been a difficult man to work for. There was always someone who had done something to stir his ire - his landlord Father Adams, the Government in St. Vincent, a local shopkeeper or neighbor, Mac, Nolly, Alec, even his wife Mary - any or all of them were fair game for one of Bluesy's harangues. "Blasted Mary!" he hit me with one day as I walked into the loft. "She say she done with de world. Done with de world? Dat's alright for she, but what about de man? A man has got he nature, eh Chris? A man has got to live, isn't it?" What else could I do but agree.

On board, the accommodation fit-out was coming rapidly to a finish. Mark played a huge part with all of the ship's joinery, especially at this stage when his creativity, talent and know-how with the power tools blended so fantastically well with the great woodworking skills of Loren, Gilbert and Linkie. After two and a half years of construction, I could finally see the end of the job was near.

It didn't take long for Bluesy to finish the sails. As each one was completed, I would carry it aboard, bend it on and hoist it aloft. I would then jump into the dinghy and pull myself the few feet in to shore, where I would walk down the beach and stand with Bluesy and analyze the cut and set of each sail. As the late afternoon breeze rustled through the coconut trees, gently filling the hoisted sail, we would stand on the white sand at the water's edge and admire our handiwork. Mainsail, topsail, foresail, staysail, jib, flying jib and fisherman's staysail were all fit and examined in this way, until finally there was nothing else to do but go for a sail.

This was the third time I would be taking a new boat out for her maiden sail, and each time it was equally exciting. A day was chosen for this big event, and all of the people who had worked on the boat were invited to come along for the maiden voyage. It was quite a crowd. The shipwrights were there; Loren and Gilbert and Lanceford and Herbie and Uncle Linkie and even wild old Ethelbert King the caulker came along. Sippy the rigger came aboard with Uncle Athneal, as well as Johnny Ollivierre and Justin Providence and Neighbor, who were the guys who painted the boat. Rennison the apprentice shyly joined us, as well as Nero the bushman who had been there from the beginning. Bluesy wouldn't let me talk him into coming though, and Nolly simply didn't turn up. Bert Henriksen became the chief engineer, and of course Mark was on board along with Patty and Vanessa.

It was a beautiful day in April when we slipped our mooring lines and motored out beyond the last anchored yacht in the bay, where we headed up into the wind and hoisted our sails. Everyone jumped in to get a hand on the halyards as the sails were slowly raised. I spun the cast bronze Lunenburg Foundry wheel, the bow fell off, the sheets were eased, and we glided out of the harbor. We ran down and gybed around West Cay and reached south, past Isle d' Quatre and Rameau, where Nolen and I almost sunk. We pressed on towards Cannouan and the distant Lower Grenadines. She handled like a dream.

I turned the wheel over to Athneal and went forward. There were smiles everywhere I turned. Johnny had climbed up the foremast ratlines to the trestle trees where he stood alongside the masthead, so I climbed up to the main masthead. From fifty feet above decks the view was sensational as the schooner creamed along, carving an ivory swath through the indigo Caribbean Sea. To the east a string of islands stretched across the windward horizon, below me the sails billowed and filled with the steady breeze, the peak halyard stretching and easing as we lifted over each gentle wave. Eventually it was time to turn back, so we tacked ship and headed back north. After rounding West Cay, we went hard on to the wind and beat into the harbor until we finally fired up the engine, dropped and furled the sails, and motored back to our spot just off the beach.

The day had gone perfectly. Everything worked just as it should. There would be many small details to iron out, but that would happen over time. For all intents and purposes, the boat was finished.

Rigged and ready to rock and roll.

~ BOOK III ~

A GUY NAMED BOB

1
Vanessa

"You two should make children and sell them."
- Bob Gilbert

There had been plenty of girls in my life...sometimes for a night or two, sometimes for longer, but there was never anything which evolved to what could be called a serious relationship. Eventually we would say our goodbyes, they would sail away, and I'd be alone again. I first met Vanessa at the Carriacou Regatta in 1978. She and a friend were sitting at the bar at the Mermaid Hotel, and seeing two attractive Australian girls on their own naturally drew my attention. I soon discovered they had sailed there from Grenada with an eccentric Englishman, which was their first sailing experience. I had met quite a few Australian girls over the years, and had found them to be a lot of fun. I can recall our bar-side banter on that particular day to be light-hearted and entertaining. I was also amused to discover that the two girls had been living in Chris Doyle's little cottage near Prickly Bay, the same house Nolen and I had shared a few years earlier. I couldn't see it then, but we were already connected.

    A while later Vanessa and her friend Teeny turned up in Bequia, where I caught up with them once more alongside the bar at the Frangipani. Again, my conversations with Vanessa were friendly but completely platonic. They were simply two fun-loving Aussies on a spree in the West Indies having escaped from a working life in London. We were both going in different directions, and our occasional conversations were as far as it went. Then one day I heard Vanessa had fallen and broken her arm while climbing Mount Soufriere, St. Vincent's towering volcano, and had to return to London. And life rolled on.

Living on this far-away isle was an exhilarating experience for a person so enamored with the ocean. Every aspect of life in Bequia was somehow connected to the sea. The schooner *Friendship Rose* was the lifeline to the island. Her daily runs across the channel to St. Vincent kept the island supplied with everything from fresh produce to frozen chicken, soft drinks and beer. Most of the men either worked offshore as professional seamen, or were fishermen or boatbuilders. Even the islander's sport was centered around the sea. Impromptu boat races were held between the fishermen of every village, the biggest of which was the annual Whitsun Regatta. This race attracted thirty or more spritely double-enders and would be enthusiastically followed by most of the island's population. The morning of the race the beach in front of the Frangipani would be lined with the flapping sails of these colorful craft, crewed by an equally eccentric cast of characters. In the harbor, a small fleet of thirteen-footers had developed into a highly competitive class, and on most afternoons at least a couple of these beautiful little boats could be seen darting between the anchored yachts as they raced around the bay. I had acquired one of these boats. Uncle Herbie had built it several years earlier, and when I bought her from him, I asked if she had a name. He chuckled and muttered "Rocking Chair". I loved the name, I loved the boat, and sailed her every chance I had.

One Sunday afternoon I was out sailing around the harbor in *Rocking Chair*. Feeling a bit thirsty I ghosted in and touched her up on the beach in front of the Frangipani. Sitting at the bar was none other than Vanessa, who I hadn't seen in over a year. This time she was accompanied by another Aussie traveling companion, who she introduced to me as Lynnie. They had just stepped off the *Friendship Rose*, and after taking a room at a small backstreet guesthouse in town had made their way to the Frangi and were enjoying their first of Harold's seriously strong rum punches when I sailed in. "Bloody hell, I'll be legless if I have another one. This thing's gone straight to me head!" Lynnie laughed when I bought them a second.

"I think that's the whole idea," I replied. After a while we finished our drinks and with the flapping mainsail of *Rocking Chair* calling out to us, I invited the two girls to join me in a twilight sail, which they cautiously accepted.

"I don't know…we have no idea what we're doing," Vanessa said.

"Don't worry. Its dead easy," I assured them. And so off we went. That was the first time Vanessa and I ever sailed together. The next time was a week later. Several thirteen-footers were rigged up on the beach in front of the Money Tree for our Sunday harbor race. Wayne Gooding was there with *Cream Skin*; visiting yachtsman Gordon Baxter was keen to go with his boat *Eclipse* (built by Uncle Linkie), Aussie vagabond and artist extraordinaire Peter Carr had rigged up *New Talent* and local modelmaker Lawson Sargent had brought his boat over from Hamilton. I was there with *Rocking Chair*, but was on the lookout for a "jib hand" to crew with me. The boats and their shaking sails had attracted a small crowd, and standing amongst the onlookers in the shade of the almond trees was Vanessa. I wandered up and asked her if she wanted to come along with me.

"Are you sure? I wouldn't have a clue what to do," she said.

"Hey, it's no big deal," I responded. "We're just going out for a casual Sunday sail. It's just for the fun of it."

"Go on Ness," Lynnie smiled. "You'll enjoy it."

"Well okay, as long as you don't mind sailing with a complete novice."

"Really, it's nothing serious. We're just going around some marks here in the harbor. I'll tell you what to do. I'm sure you'll be a fast learner. It's easy." Vanessa nervously climbed in, and when all was ready someone shouted "Go!" and we all pushed off from the beach, dodging between the anchored yachts as we ran out into the open reaches of Admiralty Bay. The course was a simple one, taking us around the harbor before finishing on the beach at Lower Bay in front of the beach-bar De Reef. The first boat to hit the sand was declared the winner. I wasn't expecting to even be near the front, and told Vanessa so. I could see, however, that she was very keen and picked everything up quickly. It was a perfect day for a sail with a sweet breeze blowing, and as we rounded the leeward marker, we sat in second place, just on the stern of my long-time rival *Cream Skin,* skippered by wily local sailor Wayne Gooding. Vanessa jumped up on the rail as we set off to windward, handling the jib like a pro.

"Now when we tack," I said, "you have to let go of the sheet, and as we shift across the boat you have to pull it in on the other side - understand?" She nodded seriously.

"Okay, here we go. Ready about...tacking! Let go the sheet!" We went about and came out of the tack perfectly. "Well done! Excellent! You're a natural," I said. We sailed on, splitting tacks with Wayne, and slowly leaving the others astern. At the top mark we went around just behind Wayne. One more lap to go, then a reach off for the reef. "Hey we're doing pretty well here you know, Vanessa," I said as we ran down the harbor. "One more lap and anything can happen." I don't know if she heard me, she was so intent on trimming. Just then we picked up a gust which pushed us past Wayne, and now we were in the lead. All of a sudden, I started to get serious. We were in with a chance to win! A good mark rounding was crucial. Patiently I went through all of the steps which Vanessa would have to do. She licked her lips and nodded attentively. We gybed and rounded the mark perfectly. "Great rounding! Are you sure you haven't done this before?" Vanessa only half-smiled, obviously too nervous to say anything.

The last mark was the *Dayton*, a rust-stained hulking steel dredge, and as we tacked our way towards it, Wayne tried all his tricks to get past us. He went about and we covered, classically staying between him and the next mark. One more tack and we would be there. "If we get around that mark first, we'll have this race in the bag," I said. "There's no way he can catch us on the reach to the finish." Wayne went about in a last-ditch effort to try and get through us, but I didn't fall for the bait and carried on to the lay line. "Okay, one more and we've got this." Vanessa nodded her curly blond head. "Let's make this a good one. Ready about…" And with that Vanessa anxiously let go of the jib sheet and quickly pulled in the opposite one. She executed the move perfectly. The only problem was she was about five seconds too early. I hadn't said "tacking" yet, hadn't put the helm down. It was if we had slammed on the brakes. With the wind now coming from the wrong side of the jib, we stopped dead in our tracks. Wayne scooted past us as we struggled to get going again. I was now starting to get excited as I saw the race slip through our fingers. We rounded the *Dayton* astern of Wayne, and on the run down to Lower Bay in the time- honored tradition of racing skippers everywhere I exploded, reminding Vanessa on more than one occasion how close we were to victory, and how from just one simple mistake at the end we threw away the race. A colorful assortment of expletives filled the air as Vanessa stared resolutely ahead.

We sailed up on to the beach, and a few of the Sunday crowd came down to help us haul up. Wayne came over with a big smile, and we congratulated each other on a good race. By now I had shrugged it off and gotten over it. "Great race

Vanessa, you did well," I said. "How about a cerveza?" She half smiled and nodded and I walked up to the crowded bar and bought a couple of cold Carib beers. When I returned to the dinghy, I couldn't see Vanessa anywhere. Finally, I spotted her out in the water with Lynnie. As I waded out to them, I could see that as much as she tried not to show it, she was quite upset. "What's wrong?" I innocently inquired.

She didn't reply, only shaking her head. "Come on - what is it?"

Finally, she answered. "I'm sorry. I didn't mean to lose the race for you," she exclaimed. "I told you I didn't know what I was doing. I'm just upset because no one ever has spoken to me like that before."

I was surprised. "What did I say?" I thought to myself. Coming from my family, I thought I was quite restrained. Finally, I smiled and gave her a friendly hug. "Hey - don't worry about it!" I laughed. "That's ancient history. You did great! Fantastic! It was my fault anyway for not being clear. Come on, have your beer and relax. I just got over-excited; I didn't mean anything personal. If I hurt your feelings, then I sincerely apologize."

This was my first lesson in what was to become a thirty-year education at the University of Vanessa. Somehow, she overcame that tough start to stay with me all of these years. And from her point of view, I'm sure it hasn't been easy.

Vanessa and I began to see each other. She and Lynnie had rented a house across the street from the Seventh Day Adventist church, which was right next door to Loren's house. The girl's house became known as the Australian Embassy because of the turnover of single Aussie girls staying there. I soon discovered Vanessa was a nurse, as was Lynnie. The two girls had trained together in Fremantle, Western Australia before finding their way to London, where they worked and shared a house together with a mob of other nurses from

Down Under. With money in their pockets, several of these nurses followed Vanessa out to the West Indies, looking for fun. Naturally, good-looking single women attracted considerable attention from the local male population. When news got out that fresh arrivals were expected, guys were known to make their way down to meet the *Friendship Rose* and surreptitiously check out the new talent as they stepped ashore.

There were many things which attracted me to Vanessa beyond her good looks and spunky gap between her teeth. There was an inner beauty which emanated from the depths of her soul. She truly cared about others, and never had a bad word to say about anyone. Having trained from the age of seventeen in the autocratic Australian nursing system, she had learned to be self-reliant and independent. She was headstrong and adventurous, an example being her journey through Africa when she hitch-hiked single-handed from Cape Town to Cairo, a trip which took her in 1976 through two brutal civil wars - one in Mozambique and another in Ethiopia - where only her innocence and good luck saved her from what could have been very ugly complications. Although born in England, she had spent the first ten years of her life growing up in the British East African colony of Tanganyika, where her father ran the government Public Works department in the remote highland district of Arusha. In 1962, she and her family emigrated to Australia when Uhuru put an end to their idyllic colonial existence.

After a while Vanessa left the Embassy in Bequia and moved in with me, but told me from the start she and Lynnie had applied for nursing positions in the Central American country of Belize, and when their contracts came through, they would be off. Eventually those jobs did materialize, and it took all of my persuasive powers to convince her to stay on. After living together for close to a year I took the next step and asked Vanessa to marry me. Luckily for me she accepted.

On November 1st, 1980 we were wed in the gardens of the Frangipani Hotel and Vanessa became an integral part of Webster's "connected series of events" I talked about at the beginning of this story. For the next eight years we would share a seafaring existence living aboard *Water Pearl*. Sometimes we would enjoy blissful, fair wind sailing; at other times we would have to batten down the hatches and hove to, but no matter the conditions Vanessa would always be there, solid and strong.

Vanessa and I tie the knot at the Frangipani. Ray asked me which bakery sold me my suit.

2
Bob on Board: An Introduction

A song will lift
As the mainsail shifts
And the boat drifts on to the shoreline
And the sun will respect
Every face on the deck
The hour that the ship comes in

Then the sands will roll
Out a carpet of gold
For your weary toes to be a-touchin'
And the ship's wise men
Will remind you once again
That the whole wide world is watchin'
- Bob Dylan, "When the Ship Comes In"

The shipwrights had packed up their tools and gone home. The sails were bent on and anxious to be hoisted. It was time to get the vessel working. It was May, 1980, and the charter season had flown north for the summer. I had to try something, so we started out doing the ferry run to St. Vincent alongside of the *Friendship Rose*. On our first trip we were joined by our local Parliamentary Representative Son Mitchell, along with a few other passengers. It was a beautiful morning out in the channel as we hauled off to leeward of the *Rose*. The crew of Johnny Ollivierre, Justin Providence and Neighbor Davis trimmed the sails, and once we were on course, I gave Son the wheel. He was all smiles. We reached Kingstown harbor where we tied up alongside the Grenadines Wharf, and that afternoon did the return trip with a few more passengers and a bit of cargo. At a charge of five local dollars per person we didn't make much money, but it was a start.

Over the summer months we stayed on the run, and although it was only a break-even proposition at best, it at least kept the boat busy, and we learned how to sail her. Once we were asked by the Government to do the mail run to the Lower Grenadines, when the regular mailboat broke down. This two-day trip entailed carrying over one hundred passengers and their belongings, a hold full of freight as well as the government mail south to the islands. Starting in St. Vincent, we sailed south, landing at Bequia, Cannouan, and Mayreau before finishing at Union Island. The deck was covered with people, and it was a constant fight to keep the passengers from venturing below as our accommodation seemed very enticing to many of them. Johnny's brother Andrew came along as purser, and it was good that he did because these people knew all the tricks to keep from paying. But you would have to get up very early in the morning to out-fox Andrew Ollivierre. That night at Union Island he was up in the hills in a taxi until well after midnight chasing down freight money from people who jumped off without paying. The trip back north was a miserable one as it rained almost the entire way, and the ninety-something people were soaked to the skin as they had nowhere to hide. No one complained, however, and they took it in their stride. It was all part and parcel of living in the Grenadines, I suppose.

It didn't take me long to figure out that I had to get myself somehow linked into the much more lucrative tourist charter trade if I was going to make any money. And it was about time I got my partner down for a sail.

It took a couple of phone calls and a bit of persuasion, but finally Bob Dylan flew into Barbados and I went over to meet him. Over the years we had only met a couple of times, and there were always extenuating circumstances. I have to admit I didn't know what to expect as I waited for him outside of the airport customs. I presumed he would arrive with some sort of an entourage of managers and muscle, but was quite surprised to see him wander out through the doors alone. Our flight to St. Vincent wasn't until the next day, so we took a taxi to a hotel I had booked out amidst the sugarcane plantations on the windward coast. The Crane Beach Hotel was a classic; a converted plantation manor house situated on a cliff overlooking the Atlantic Ocean. Seven years earlier you might have been able to see a tiny blue rudderless yacht limp off that wide, windswept ocean from the very spot. It didn't take long for Bob to loosen up, and after dinner we went to the bar where we shared a few jokes and downed several rums. I felt encouraged. It was if we had known each other for years. We were on the same wavelength, and after only a few minutes we both were completely at ease. Over the years I have seen many sides of Bob Dylan, some of which could be quite weird and uncomfortable, but that night at the Crane Beach it was as if a door was opened and I was allowed access to the best one.

 The next day we flew to St. Vincent and met the boat anchored at Young Island. I should have gotten Leo to take us aboard in his water taxi just for old time's sake, but called out and Carl Ollivierre rowed ashore and picked us up instead. Bob climbed gingerly up the boarding ladder and as I passed his small leather bag on deck, I commented on how lightly he was traveling. "Well you told me just to bring swimming trunks and a tee-shirt," he replied. And that was just about all he brought.

 Vanessa met Bob as he came aboard, along with Carl's cousin Frankie, who I had taken aboard as our third crew member. They were all given a mumbled greeting. Once on board, Bob's demeanor changed drastically. The friendly, good-humored person I had been with the last twenty-four hours was gone, to be replaced by a mysterious, withdrawn individual. I was to learn this was a common response of his when meeting strangers. Vanessa was a little perplexed but I told her to give it some time and he would come around.

It was a wet and squally day as we sailed across the channel to Bequia; by far the heaviest weather we had encountered with the boat so far, but *Water Pearl* stood up perfectly. Perhaps Bob sensed the anxious, uncertain feeling amongst the crew because by the time we picked up our mooring in the harbor his attitude had changed completely. Soon he and Vanessa were getting along admirably, and I could see he had warmed considerably to Carl and Frankie.

One of the first things noticed by the crew was that Bob hadn't brought a guitar. The next morning Frankie turned up with one he had borrowed from a friend. It was a cheap, beaten up old thing that was missing a string, but that didn't matter to Bob. Over the next week we sailed to Mustique, the isle of the rich and famous, as well as many of the smaller surrounding islands. Bob wasn't much for sightseeing, and was not too impressed with Mustique. He enjoyed jumping overboard for a swim, napping in the sun, and playing the guitar. He would sit on the edge of his bunk in his swim trunks, drinking coffee and happily plucking away at that funky five string guitar for hours on end. One day I asked Bob if he played chess, and he did. I hauled out the chess board and we found we were on about the same level. Over the years Bob and I would play countless games, and I'm sure in the end our scores would have been fairly equal.

On one of his first nights in Bequia I thought it might be fun for Bob to spend an evening ashore with one of the crew. I heard there was a Kung Fu movie playing at the local cinema that night, and so Carl took him along to see it. The movie house was an old weatherboard structure lined with wooden benches. There was no such thing as satellite TV, the internet or even video players in those days, so the movies, the rum shop or the church were about it as far as night-time entertainment was concerned. I knew Bob would be in for an experience. Vanessa and I went to see the original King Kong one time. The place was packed, and watching the audience was more fun than watching the movie. They reacted to the movie as if it were real life, the crowd excitedly calling out warnings and advice to the actors. "Oh God...oh God! Look out girl he comin'...de gorilla comin'!" they would shout, as if the characters on the flickering black and white film could actually hear them. Naturally Bob came back to the boat all smiles.

A few nights later I went ashore with him as there was something he wanted to check out. On his previous night-time excursion with Carl he had noticed a Pentecostal church, and this evening he asked if we could go and find it. In the dark and sleepy backstreets of Port Elizabeth the simple wooden building glowed like a truck stop in the night-time desert. Fluorescent lights had the place brightly lit, and a sermon was in full swing. The Pentecostals were renowned for the exuberance of their congregation and the fiery orations delivered from the pulpit, and this night was no exception. For a while we remained outside in the dark, lurking in the shadows and listening. Occasionally Bob cautiously peeked through a window. Eventually we went inside and sat down on a backrow pew, where we were cordially welcomed by the preacher. I'm not much on religion, but I found this raw and boisterous experience quite entertaining. This was Christianity with an Afro-Caribbean beat. We sat and listened for fifteen minutes or so and then Bob made a move to go. As we walked back to the boat he didn't say much, but the next day I overheard him asking Carl and Frankie quite a few questions about this unique branch of island religion.

Bequia is a small place and it didn't take long for all of the ex-pats and sailors living on the island to hear that Bob was around, and naturally everyone wanted to get a glimpse of him or even get a chance to say hello. Bob was a very private and reclusive kind of a guy, and dealt with his fame in a far different way than say Neil Young or Boz Scaggs. You wouldn't stumble across Bob relaxing in a chair at the Frangipani reading *Finnegan's Wake*, for instance. He was, however, interested in the stories of the characters who made Bequia such a colorful place, and I did my best to spice up his visits by quietly introducing him to some of these individuals.

One evening I got Bob into the dinghy and we rowed over to the *Mermaid of Carriacou* and paid a visit to John Smith, where we were thoroughly entertained by John's riotous sense of humor and singular take on human existence. On another occasion I dropped him off with Klaus aboard his tiny double ender *Plumbelly*. Bob was fascinated by the story of this German architect who had taken four years to sail this small little boat singlehandedly around the world. I recall it was a Sunday, when the local tradition was to spend the afternoon down at De Reef in Lower Bay enjoying a swim, a few drinks and maybe a spot of lunch. On this particular day the rumor had spread that the crew of *Water Pearl* would be coming, and there was quite a crowd curious to get a look at, and maybe meet, this legendary artist. I figured it might be a little awkward for him to be the focus of so much attention, so on our way to the beach I pulled our dinghy alongside *Plumbelly*, dropped Bob off with Klaus, and continued on our way. All eyes were on us as we touched our dinghy ashore in front of the popular bar, and I could almost see the collective sigh of disappointment when it was seen Bob wasn't there. Everyone went back to enjoying their drinks and didn't notice when Klaus and Bob sailed up, squeezed together in *Plumbelly's* tiny dinghy. The two of them walked up and were soon lost in the crowd, and it took quite some time before people were aware Bob was even there.

After ten days on board Bob flew back to New York, and even after such a short time he looked a far more relaxed person than when he arrived. From my point of view his first visit had gone well. There were a few uncomfortable moments, to be sure, but I was happy that he finally made it down to check out the boat and get a feel for island life. We were all pretty sure that he enjoyed himself, and when he left, he said he would be back as soon as he could find the time.

3
Clara, Bamu, Kingsley and Infidels

It was the schooner Hesperus,
That sailed the wintry sea;
And the skipper had taken his little daughter,
To bear him company.
Blue were her eyes as the fairy-flax,
Her cheeks like the dawn of day,
And her bosom white as the hawthorn buds,
That ope in the month of May.
- Henry Wadsworth Longfellow, "The Wreck of the Hesperus"
(as recited by Kingsley King)

On the third of December, 1981, Vanessa gave birth to our first child, who we named Clara Jean. It was a hell-of-a delivery, and a story on its own. Vanessa was in labor for nearly forty-eight hours, where she was misdiagnosed and mismanaged and finally operated on in the nick of time at a point when both patients were going into shock and on the verge of death. The birth took place at a private clinic in St. Vincent where the doctor was forced to perform an emergency vertical caesarean procedure, the likes of which modern

Clara's first sail at three days.

physicians might only read about in books. The Fates were smiling on the three of us that morning, however, and both girls recovered and were sailing back to Bequia within a couple of days. We now had another crew member for the mighty *Water Pearl*.

We were still renting the house next to the boatyard, and this is where Clara was to spend the first part of her new life. She and Vanessa were only given a couple of months to adjust, though, because in February we were back aboard the boat and sailing north, this time bound for the St. Barths Regatta.

Now that Vanessa was otherwise occupied, it was time we found someone else to do the cooking aboard the boat. I had put the feelers out and contacted a few agents in the States who booked us some charters for the 1982 season, and so it was important to nail down a steady crew. Cyril Stowe, known to everyone as Bamu, along with Justin Providence, had sailed with me on *Just Now* on my trip north to St. Barths, and we had always gotten along well. He was a big, happy-go-lucky fellow from Southside, and like many of the professional seafarers from Bequia, made his living working aboard commercial ships. His particular trade was ship's cook. Bamu was not only a good sailor; he was an excellent cook and had no fear of going into the galley no matter how rough the conditions. He had recently left a big freighter which sank off the Dominican Republic in Hurricane David, and when he asked me for a job, I took him on straight away. What we now needed was a deck hand.

One of the local characters on the Bequia waterfront while I was building *Just Now* was Kingsley King. He had a fantastic sense of humor and friendly disposition, and whenever he went fishing, I could always count on him saving me a fish. He had been away from the island for over two years working as an able-bodied seaman for the Liberian registered company National Bulk. Sailors from Bequia had a great reputation with this company for being reliable and hard-working, and many a house had been built on the island by men who had worked for "Bulk". I had known Kingsley, also known as Prop, since my days in Grenada, and so when I found out he was looking for work I didn't hesitate in taking him on. Over the next couple of years Bamu and Kingsley would become a part of the boat, and their personalities and character would become intertwined with the spirit of *Water Pearl*.

In 1979 Les Anderson, together with Lulu Magras, Paul Johnson, and a few other traditional cruising sailors - most likely over a few beers at Le Select - came up with the idea of holding a race for gaff rigged boats in St. Barths. This idea morphed into the St. Barths Regatta. Les drew up and printed a classic poster which was spread around the Caribbean, and the original Regatta, held over three days in February, was a resounding success. This weekend in February grew bigger each year, attracting boats and sailors with traditional and classic yachts who had become disenchanted with the modernization of Antigua Race Week. I had never been able to make it to one, but in '82 I was determined to get there. To add to the occasion, I came up with a fairly offbeat idea, and I wrote to Lulu to see what he thought. Would the boys in St. Barths be interested if I brought a reggae band to the party? The Comets were a great party band, and they were keen to go if I could pull it off. Lulu wrote back and said yes, by all means bring them. He would find accommodation for them, and pass the hat around so they could be paid. And so as crazy as it sounds, we took the Comets along.

It was quite a crowd who sailed north that year; a nine-man reggae band with horn section and all, Kingsley, Bamu and Carl Ollivierre, along with myself, Vanessa, Lynnie and three-month-old Clara Jean. What a crew! I'm sure Vanessa's recollections of this trip would be slightly different from my own, as it couldn't have been easy for her to be a normal mother and take care of a three-month-old babe under such trying conditions. The trip to St. Barths covered a distance of over three hundred miles and took close to forty hours, and there wasn't much privacy, especially with that many men on board. Rarely was this passage smooth sailing either; there were times it was very rough indeed.

We arrived in Gustavia to find the small inner harbor filled with classic boats. There were big schooners and fine elegant yawls, legendary sloops and heavy, Nordic ketches. There were gaffers of every description, manned by a who's-who of Caribbean renegades. The sailing was great, but the quayside partying each night was epic, the normally sleepy streets of the port filled with music and gayety and late-night revelry. The Comets played and played and only stopped when their amps were unplugged, which was a good thing because we all had to front up early the following morning ready to race.

The first race was held in uncommonly light winds, which were not really suited to a heavy gaff schooner like our own. Sometime in the afternoon Kingsley got busy. He began tying matchsticks together to form little crosses, which he proceeded to attach to the rigging with sail twine.

"Hey Prop, what are you up to?" I asked when my curiosity got the better of me.

"I is puttin' in a call to San Antonee. He's the man above in charge of the wind department. Hopefully he isn't too busy relaxin' and he'll send we some wind," he said with a knowing smile. The wind didn't come that day, and it took us until sunset to ghost across the finish line. The next morning, however, it was blowing a gale.

"Hey Prop - you must adjust dat recipe, you hear?" chided Bamu. "Your order was way too hot!"

"Man, you boys ask for wind, and now you get it you're complaining'? You must make up your mind what you want," he bantered back with his trademark scowl.

The regatta finished with a bang. *Water Pearl* collected a few prizes; one for sailing closest to the rocks on the first day, and then Spirit of the Regatta for bringing the Comets to play. Clara even won a prize for being the youngest crew member. The presentations ended and the Comets started up, and there was dancing in the streets until the wee hours of the morning. We didn't know it then, but that would be the last of the legendary St. Barth Regattas. We relaxed for a couple of days and let our heads clear before sailing on to St. Maarten, where the Comets left the boat. Not long after Bob flew in.

I took a taxi out to St. Maarten's Juliana Airport to meet the flight from New York. It was just a small terminal back then, and from your seat at the air-conditioned bar you could sit and watch the passengers disembark and walk across the tarmac to the arrival hall. The flight landed, and I watched as it unloaded. I anxiously scrutinized each arrival as they made their way down the boarding ladder. There was no sign of Bob. The plane was close to empty and I began to think that he may have changed his mind and not come at all, when I saw him emerge at the top of the steps. With his curly mop of hair, trademark dark glasses, black leather jacket, white tee-shirt, black jeans, motorcycle boots, and carrying a guitar it didn't take Sherlock Holmes to figure out who it was. This was not your typical American tourist on a one-week junket to the Caribbean. I went down and met him as he came through immigration, and it was like meeting up with an old friend as we greeted each other. He obviously attracted some attention with the arriving New Yorkers, but he knew exactly how to deal with their pushy advances. I supposed he'd probably had a bit of practice over the years.

A taxi dropped us off in Phillipsburg. It was a Sunday, many of the shops were closed, and the normally tourist-filled town was quiet. There was a hamburger joint next to the little jetty where Kingsley was to pick us up in the dinghy. Out across the shimmering bay the silhouette of *Water Pearl* swung in the soft breeze. It was a beautiful afternoon, there was no one around, and so we sat down at one of the empty tables enjoying the peace and quiet. "Do you want to hear something I wrote?" Bob asked, reaching absentmindedly into one of his pockets and pulling out a folded piece of paper.

"Sure," I answered. I mean, what else would I say? He proceeded to recite a poem he called "Clean-Cut Kid" about a young boy whose life was ruined by war. He went on to read one or two more, which if I remember correctly were "Sundown on the Union", and "License to Kill". To say I was honored would be an understatement. As the years passed, I was never to experience the likes of this again. We would talk about many things, but when it came to his music Bob kept his cards close to his chest.

Once on board, Bob changed straight into his bathing suit and jumped overboard for a swim. He was right at home. "What was it like having Bob Dylan aboard?" someone might ask. To tell the truth, he was probably the easiest, least demanding person we ever had on the boat. Quiet and unassuming, he simply took things as they came. He already knew Carl from his previous trip, and he immediately felt comfortable with Kingsley and Bamu. *Another Side of Bob Dylan* was the name of his fourth album, and as I was to learn later this title was very appropriate because the more I began to know him, the more I came to understand how complicated a person he was. Most people, me included, are fairly one dimensional. What you see is what you get. Not Bob. I would later discover he had more sides than an icosikaitrigon (which, if you didn't know, is a polygon with twenty-three sides). But for us on the schooner *Water Pearl*, Bob just became one of the crew. Whatever we did, wherever we went was usually just fine with him.

Bob headed straight for his bunk next to the galley. He had come aboard for two weeks this time, and so he settled himself in to his old spot. My plan was to sail south and show him as many islands as we could between St. Maarten and Bequia. Our first stop would be St. Barths. It was late in the afternoon and as we motored along the rugged southern shoreline, we passed a small house built on a bluff overlooking the sea, on top of which stood a strange, pyramid-like structure. "Thought collector," Bob said offhandedly as he stood next to me at the wheel.

"A what?" I asked.

"That pyramid thing up on top of the hill. It's a thought collector."

I didn't quite know how to respond. "Apparently the Rockefellers own this whole end of the island," I eventually said.

"That might explain it," he muttered as he walked forward and ducked down below deck to his bunk, as if to dodge the magnetic pull of the Rockefellerian contraption. He didn't want any pyramid collecting his thoughts, I reasoned. We sailed the following day for Nevis. Bob seemed disinterested in St. Barths. Perhaps the thought collector put him off - who knows?

At sea little Clara Jean became Bob's shipmate, her cot being wedged in place between his bunk and the main table, which was the safest spot on the boat for her. He used to spend inordinate amounts of time sitting on the edge of his bunk, arms on his knees, staring at her, as if studying her every movement. Sailing past the windward coast of St. Kitts we headed for the high peak of her sister island Nevis, where after anchoring we went ashore and had a good look around. As luck would have it, we ended up at a fun little beach bar where a live reggae band was playing. We had a swim, drank a few rum punches, watched the sunset and then made our way back to the boat, where Bamu had prepared a nice Sunday roast.

We sailed south the following morning, on a course which took us to leeward of the high, volcanic peak of Montserrat towards the distant island of Guadeloupe. Generally, this was an enjoyable stretch of water to sail across, but on this day, it was a very rough, uncomfortable passage. It was grey and squally and the wind was in the south-east, which is exactly the direction we wanted to go. It was not a good day to go down below, unless it was to be in your bunk. It wasn't easy for Vanessa to take care of a three-month child as we motor-sailed into those large seas; the boat pounding, lurching, rocking, lifting and dropping over the relentless waves as saltwater spray exploded over the bows. On days like these it was hard to even think of food, and not even Bamu, with his famous cast iron stomach, was interested to venture into the galley. This wasn't good enough for Kingsley, however, because when he was hungry, he needed to be fed, as we soon found out. It must have been a sugar thing, because when lunch time rolled around and no food appeared, he exploded. Unfortunately, we hadn't been able to find any bread to buy the day before, but still we had plenty of food on board. Prop demanded Bamu go below and cook him something, but he just laughed and shook his head. This was the last straw. "Man, dis here is a fucking starvation boat!" he stormed. "A man can't work without food! Dis is a starvation boat I tellin' you!" He continued on this vain for several minutes.

"Man...if you so hungry why don' you just go take care of yourself?" Bamu short temperedly suggested. This only made matters worse. Eventually I went down and brought up some sardines and crackers, which calmed him down. From that time onward, however, we made sure that Kingsley had his food on time, which kept him tame as a kitten. Eventually, we found shelter for the night under the high mountains of Guadeloupe, and after a solid breakfast of johnnycakes and salted herring or "bull-jowl", as Bamu called it, we set sail across the channel for the neighboring island of Dominica.

Just off the northwest corner of Dominica is the town of Portsmouth, where there is a nice anchorage. It is a picturesque bay overlooked by lush green mountains which jumble right down to the black sand beaches skirting the shoreline. I had stopped there several times before and had always found it to be a pleasant place to anchor for a day or two. As I said, Bob rarely made any demands of me or the crew, but as we motored in to Portsmouth that afternoon he came up to me at the wheel and said, "Hey Chris, we shouldn't stop here. We should keep going."

I was taken aback. "What? Why not," I asked.

"Bad feelings. I get bad feelings from this place," he answered.

I didn't really see the point. The next decent anchorage was Fort de France in Martinique, and that was one hundred miles and a good twelve hours away. "I think we'll be okay. I've anchored here before and never had a problem. I think its best we stay here for the night." We proceeded in and dropped the hook.

Dominica was one of the poorest islands in the Eastern Caribbean, and the people there struggled to find a way to make a dollar. In those days young locals would row their small double-ender's miles out to sea trying to latch on to an entering yacht and sell them anything they could. They were incredibly skillful in getting in one's way, and very tenacious in their salesmanship. "Hey Skip, you need mangos? Bananas? Limes? Just ask me Skip…I can get you anything!" they would shout from alongside. We managed to avoid the initial blockade, but one kid was very persistent and chased us until we anchored. "Okay Skip, I can see you doesn't want to buy nothing," he said as he hung on to our boarding ladder, "but what about a trip up de river? I'll take you fo' de jungle cruise for five dollars. Dat is cheap, Skip. How 'bout it?" The Indian

River runs down from the inland mountains and empties into Prince Rupert Bay just south of Portsmouth and is one of the main attractions for day trips for visiting yachtsmen. It isn't the Belgian Congo, but it's a bit of fun. I had done the trip before, so I thought Bob might like to have a look. He was keen, so he and Carl jumped into the colorfully painted boat with the young Rasta and disappeared up the river. A couple of hours later the two of them returned and Bob said he'd had a great time.

Later, just before sunset, Vanessa, Clara, Bob and I went ashore to have a shower. Just off the black sand beach under the coconut trees amidst the thick green foliage stood an ancient stone bathhouse which I presume had been built by the British sometime in the dim colonial past. Cool, clear fresh spring water ran out from its ancient steel pipes, and we each took a turn standing under the cold water in our bathing suits showering ourselves. An attractive British woman from the only other yacht anchored in the bay joined us in our reverie, oblivious of the fact she was in essence having a shower with Bob Dylan. I silently noted how Bob slowly relaxed and joked playfully with the woman, which made me feel good that he could lower his guard and enjoy a simple experience which comes naturally to most other people. It also made me think of one of his most famous lines – "Even the President of the United States sometimes has to stand naked…"

The next morning, we watched as our neighbors picked up their anchor. As they turned to leave the boat slowed and coasted past our starboard side. "Did you hear what happened ashore last night?" the helmsman called across, standing next to the girl from the shower.

"No," I answered from the rail.

"Some local guy went berserk and chopped a couple of people up with a machete. We're getting the hell out of here!" And with that they waved goodbye and headed out of the bay.

I continued to stand at the rigging, thinking about my partner's reticence to anchor there in the first place. Was it just a coincidence? Or did he actually feel a vibe that no one else did?

"Oh well," I shrugged. "We didn't get carved up by any madman at least." But we did leave for Martinique not long afterwards.

Leaving Portsmouth, Dominica, the day after Bob's premonition.

Sailing south across the Martinique Channel on a beautiful full moon night, I stood in the hatchway and watched a rainsquall make up to windward. The gentle southeast Trades whispered over the silver-topped waves, the only sound being the creak of the gear aloft and the swoosh of seawater as it rolled away to leeward. Prop had given Bob the wheel and was sitting on the lazarette hatch next to the wheel box, keeping an eye. I handed out a couple of rain jackets as I moved aft to the mainsheet and watched as the black cloud obscured the moon and quickly pressed down upon us. The wind rose, the boat heeled and I eased out some sheet. Then the rain hit us, but it didn't last long, and we watched the moon reappear and the squall stampede off to leeward. "Ah boy, now dat is what you call a moonlight squall, Bob," I heard Kingsley almost sing. "Dat is a sweet shower of blessing."

In the early hours of the morning we reached into the lee of Martinique's towering Mount Pele, the wind dropped to nothing and we motored south, finally anchoring under the battlements of the Napoleonic Fort St. Louis at the edge of the island's biggest city. After a bit of sleep and a good breakfast we all went ashore, where I cleared in through customs and immigration. Fort de France was a large, cosmopolitan city and a marked contrast from the surrounding British islands. The Creole women of the city were famous for their elegant style, and because the island was a department of France it was like being in any French city. It was here I learned for the first time of Bob's penchant for shopping. He took his time, and after a couple of hours of strolling through the colorful streets and casually purchasing a variety of curiosities and mementos, we met up with Vanessa and the crew and ventured down one of the New Orleans-like side streets to one of my favorite bistros, where we enjoyed a spicy Creole lunch with a bottle or two of "vin du table". The following morning, we sailed south for Bequia.

We finished the trip by sailing down to the Lower Grenadines. Vanessa stepped ashore and settled back into our house with Clara in Bequia. We had been gone a month, and I'm sure Vanessa thought she was in heaven her first night alone at the house. For his part, Bob had taken to living our communal West Indian lifestyle without any dramas at all, completely content to sit at his bunk while at anchor and work on little riffs on his guitar. Occasionally he would play one of the tapes he had brought with him on the stereo. Hank Williams and Mickey and Sylvia were a couple that come to mind. He couldn't get away from listening to his fair share of Bob Marley and other reggae, which Bamu and Carl liked to pump through the stereo. He also was playing the new Dire Straits album a fair bit. He told me he was thinking of having Mark Knoffler produce his next album. He said he recently had spent a day with Frank Zappa, who he also had been considering as a producer. That would have made for an interesting combination.

Anchored alone in the Tobago Cays, tucked in behind Horseshoe Reef, the Tradewinds blowing across the wide blue Atlantic all the way from Africa, crystal clear water and reefs alive with colorful fish and coral - this was the experience Bob had to end his trip. With Kingsley and I diving up the fresh fish, lobster and conch, and Bamu cooking up his tasty dishes, we sent him back to the "real world" a far healthier person than when he arrived. When it was time to go, we sailed back to St. Vincent and chartered a private plane to take Bob to the international airport in St. Lucia. I joined him for the flight and thoroughly enjoyed this unique way to see the islands. I left Bob to go back to his life in New York while I returned to mine on the boat.

Later that year Bob returned to the boat for another couple of weeks. While we were in St. Barths, he became acquainted with a French girl by the name of Nicole. She was a lively character, an artist who was born and raised on the nearby island of Guadeloupe. She was into a new-fangled form of film work called video, and Bob was interested in it, so he asked her to join us on board for a couple of days. We had a bit of fun playing around with her camera, and still have the tape of Bob playing Happy Birthday to Clara as we celebrated her second birthday, which is a good memory. A month or so later Bob and I watched the Washington Redskins beat the Miami Dolphins in the 1983 Super Bowl. We were anchored in Gustavia and there was this funky local bar high up on the hill called the Santa Fe which had satellite TV and was showing the game. Bob and I walked up there and sat at the bar with a few locals, drank rum and watched John Riggins play the game of his life. There weren't many times that I saw when Bob was able to go out and be just another guy sitting at the bar watching a football game, but that day was one of them.

Over the next few years Bob would make many more trips down to the Caribbean. Most would go smoothly. There was one which was a little awkward; he decided to make a spur of the moment visit to St. Maarten with his three sons on the same day we were picking up eight charter guests for a week. This would prove to be a very awkward double-booking. Instead of the alternative of staying in a hotel, Bob decided to bring his boys along for the ride. The charter guests were not impressed. I spent a difficult week torn between giving them a good time and looking after Bob. On the last night around the dinner table the guests formed into a sort of vigilante committee hell-bent on a lynching. They set about informing me all of the things which did not meet their expectations. Bob was up on deck, listening through the skylight. Eventually he could take it no longer and came below to my defense to vigorously put the people in their places, which was something I was most appreciative of and will never forget.

There were other experiences we had together which still stand out in my mind. One was when we bought a cassette of local reggae musician Bankie Banks in a bayside curio shop in Anguilla. After listening to it a few times on board Bob expressed an interest in meeting this guy, so I went ashore to find him. Eventually I tracked him down and he came aboard the boat with his guitar and spent a few hours with us. Later that evening we went to his place where he had a small studio set up. Bob messed about with a little melody on Bankie's keyboard and then asked Bamu and me if we wanted to do some backing vocals, which we shyly declined. Bankie then went out and found a couple of girls to do them instead. I always regretted not taking up Bob's offer - who knows, I might have missed my true calling. Then there was the time I ran into Jimmy Buffet at Le Select and invited him out to the boat to meet Bob. Bamu cooked up one of his tasty lunches and we spent the afternoon sitting around the table drinking red wine and telling tales.

Countless volumes of expert analysis have been written over the years concerning the music of Bob Dylan. I am sure every song he has ever written has been cut apart, dissected, analyzed and interpreted as to their influences and meaning. The only person who has never voiced an opinion concerning all of this is Bob himself. He just makes them and puts them out there and let the chips fall where they may. In my view... and what do I know - I'm just a boatbuilder...Dylan's songs are compilations of visionary images of almost dreamlike quality which rarely contain one simple story or truth. Many of these images are not so much chosen for their allegorical importance but more for a certain sound or cadence. The word visions he creates are a montage of bits and pieces of everyday life which he is a master in collecting, remixing and then artistically putting to music. In other words, each one of his songs could rarely be attributed to one particular experience or interpreted in only one way. Saying all of this, I do feel that of all of Bob's albums, *Infidels* comes closest to reflecting his collective Caribbean experiences. From the crazy sailors he met on different boats ("Jokerman"), the reggae music played aboard daily ("I and I" and choosing Sly and Robbie as his rhythm section), to the island story of a corrupted priest ("Man of Peace"), I would like to think that a little bit of his time aboard rubbed off and showed up in his music.

4
The Sound of a Butterfly's Heartbeat

*"Almost only counts in horseshoes, hand grenades,
slow dancing and thermo-nuclear war."*
- Anonymous

The days came and went. We kept busy and somehow survived. It was April of 1983 and I had picked up a couple of weeks of charter out of Antigua. My daughter was sixteen months old and it tore at my heartstrings to leave her and Vanessa on the shoreline as I rowed out to the boat in the early morning with my crew, but "dooty is dooty, to be sure," is how Long John Silver would put it. I watched my two girls standing at the water's edge in front of the Boley Bar waving until they disappeared from view as we rounded the point.

The two weeks of charter went smoothly until the morning the guests left, when I received a message that there was an emergency at home and I should call Bequia immediately. Rushing ashore, I found a phone and returned the call to our friend Hilary Sanders, who had somehow located me.

"Chris, Vanessa is in hospital and is seriously ill," Hilary told me in her matter of fact English accent. "She is at Cyrus' clinic in St. Vincent. Clara is being well looked after, but I think you should get here as soon as possible."

I next called the clinic and spoke to Dr. Cyril Cyrus. He explained that Vanessa had experienced a ruptured ectopic pregnancy and had been in a life-threatening condition when she presented herself to him. He had performed an emergency procedure immediately, but she had lost a lot of blood through internal hemorrhaging. The operation had been successful, but she was now in a very weak but stable condition. He advised me not to worry about flying back because my presence there would make no difference for the next forty-eight hours. I told him I would be there as quickly as I could.

    I got back aboard and told the boys to make ready to sail immediately. An hour later we were motoring out through the heads of Falmouth Harbor. We put everything up and on a grey, ugly day pushed the vessel south. Thirty-eight hours later we picked up our mooring in Bequia and I made a bee-line ashore to check on Clara. Fortuitously, Vanessa had offered a young English backpacker by the name of Janine a bed in our spare room a couple of days before she took ill, and she along with Rita and Lyston, our wonderful neighbors, had everything well in hand. Satisfied all was well with Clara, I went to St. Vincent first thing the following morning on *Friendship Rose*.

    The shades were drawn, but I could see Vanessa smile as I peeked inside her room. A young French girl by the name of Catherine stood as I came in, and I could feel how weak Vanessa was the moment I took her hand. "How is Clara?" was the first thing she asked, and I could see her relax when I told her she was fine. She was too weary to tell me what had happened, but later I heard the full story.

    I had no idea what an ectopic pregnancy was. After a basic anatomy lesson from Dr. Cyrus, I understood the severity of Vanessa's case. Basically, what happens when a woman ovulates is that her eggs pass through her two tiny fallopian tubes on their way to her uterus. It is quite rare, but if an over-exuberant sperm somehow makes his way inside and impregnates an egg in the tube you have got big trouble, because the egg will start growing and if it is not surgically removed in time the tube will rupture, causing massive internal bleeding and ultimately death. This is what happened to Vanessa. Over a couple of days, she began to experience intense abdominal pain, and it wouldn't go away. Since there was no doctor on Bequia, she left Clara with Janine for the day and went to see a doctor in St. Vincent. For some reason she went to the public hospital instead of to Cyrus' private clinic. After a quick examination she was told there was nothing to worry about, given a couple of aspirin and sent on her way. Against her better judgement she got back aboard the *Friendship Rose* that afternoon and returned home.

Around six o'clock that evening there was an explosion in Vanessa's abdomen. "It felt like a hand grenade had gone off inside me," is how she later explained it. Drenched in sweat, she was in excruciating pain and probably going into shock. Janine had gone out partying for the night, so not even being able to stand Vanessa rolled out of bed onto the floor and crawled to the phone and called her friend Judy Simmons at the nearby pizzeria for help. She was very busy at the time but sent an English girl by the name of Jackie to help instead. She wasn't in too good a shape herself after drinking for most of the afternoon, so after she got Vanessa back into bed she crashed out in the spare room.

The night was endless. Vanessa sat propped up in bed; she couldn't lie down because of the pain. Internally hemorrhaging, in the early stages of shock, dehydrated, and with no one to help her, she was basically on her own. Clara awoke and started crying and Vanessa simply had to leave her because she couldn't move. Somehow, she made it through the night, willing herself not to pass out. She didn't know what exactly was wrong, but knew she would die if she didn't get to St. Vincent and see Dr. Cyrus.

Morning finally came. *Friendship Rose* left at six-fifteen sharp, and Vanessa simply knew she had to get there. With her hair matted in sweat and her body wracked with pain, she got herself up, and after grabbing her toothbrush she began her journey to the wharf. She reluctantly left Clara in her crib, but knew sooner or later Jackie would wake or Janine would be home and she would be taken care of. The distance was less than a kilometer, but between the house and the Frangipani were three four-foot-high stone walls she had to climb over. Every step was agony. Somehow, she got over the walls, and as she reached the beach on the other side of the hotel, she met Janine returning home after her night out. Hunched over and unable to speak, Janine half carried Vanessa around the bayside and pushing through the hustle and bustle on the wharf got her onto the schooner.

"I'll come with you," Janine said. But Vanessa, hardly able to speak, could only utter the word Clara. "Okay…okay…don't worry. I'll look after her," the English girl responded. Then, just as the boat pulled away from the wharf Vanessa heard the loud voice of a West Indian woman.

"Oh God! Oh God! It's Vanessa!" And as she looked up the big arms of our neighbor Rita pulled her into her large bosom. "What is wrong girl? You looks terrible!"

As many times as Vanessa would have crossed that channel on the *Rose*, this would have undoubtedly been the worst. If it wasn't for Rita, she may not have made it. Legend has it that she called for the captain and told him in no uncertain terms to "turn up de engine and make haste!" Eventually the old schooner tied up alongside the Grenadines Wharf, and in the midst of all the chaos Rita barged her way through the crowd, put her in a taxi and sent her off full speed to Dr Cyrus' clinic. Once there, Vanessa approached the receptionist, who asked if she had an appointment. When she said she didn't she was told to sit down and wait her turn. Barely conscious, Vanessa did what she was told. She at least knew she was there, and would not leave until she was seen.

While she waited, Vanessa was approached by the doctor's English wife, who remembered her from Clara's birth and could see from her appearance she was not at all well. She immediately helped Vanessa in to see Dr. Cyrus, who sat at his desk and by his brisk manner showed that this person without an appointment had upset him. He could not tolerate queue-jumpers. His manner changed abruptly upon looking up and seeing the distressed woman sitting across from him. Hair plastered to her skull with perspiration, face ashen white through loss of blood and twisted with pain, he knew immediately she was in serious trouble.

"Tell me what is wrong," he urged.

"A…hand…grenade…has…gone…off…inside…of …me," she forced herself to say.

"Where does it hurt?" he queried. Vanessa touched her shoulders and then her stomach. Her blood-filled abdominal cavity was putting tremendous upward pressure on her diaphragm, so she could hardly do more than sit rigidly at attention. Cyrus instantaneously diagnosed her from the chair. He turned and told his wife to prepare the operating theatre immediately and to cancel the rest of his appointments. "Do you know anyone with O positive blood?" he asked as he stood. Barely conscious, Vanessa could only utter Judy Simmons' name. The doctor then laid her down on his examination bed. "What I am about to do will be extremely painful, but I must examine you." And as he did so Vanessa passed out.

The call went out to Bequia, and as Dr Cyrus began to prepare Vanessa for her emergency operation Judy Simmons frantically put the word out around the island. She found two donors. First, she organized William Gooding to rush Tiara Thomson across to St. Vincent in his speed boat. The second donor was a young French chef named Catherine Pitzele, who was working in St. Vincent. Miraculously, the two women reached the clinic in not much more than an hour, where they each gave a pint of blood. Cyrus could now begin his operation.

The main danger to Vanessa was the horrific amount of blood she had lost in over fifteen hours of hemorrhaging. It had to be replaced and two pints would not be enough.

Since there was no blood bank on St. Vincent, Dr Cyrus resorted to a drastic solution that in all probability would result in Vanessa's death. He would perform what is called an auto-transfusion, which simply means he drew blood from his patient's cavity and infused it back into her system. The chances were a blood clot would form in her blood stream, and when it reached her heart she would die. It was a huge risk, but he had no other option.

All of this was nothing more than a foggy nightmare to Vanessa. Eventually she came to in a room in the clinic with Catherine still by her side. Moments later Dr Cyrus came to see her. Sitting on the side of her bed he explained what had happened and what he had done. He then said, "I was forced to give you an auto-transfusion, and there is no telling if there is a blood clot in your system or not. The chances are high that there is, but there is nothing I can do to remove it. Now you are conscious I would advise you to prepare anything you might need for that eventuality."

After he left, Vanessa, still under the effects of morphine, groggily wrote a letter to her daughter Clara, telling her how much she loved her and that she would be with her always. She sealed the letter, handing it to Catherine to deliver to her daughter, just in case.

For two days Catherine hardly left her side. Vanessa faded in and out of consciousness, but every time she awoke the diminutive French girl was still there. Eventually I turned up, when she was well on the mend. I asked Dr Cyrus about the blood clot. He said her chances were getting better every day, but in theory one could be shaken loose almost any time. Needless to say, the next couple of days were nervous one's indeed.

A day or two after my arrival Vanessa was allowed to return to Bequia. Janine and Clara met us on the wharf. Vanessa broke down and cried as she hugged her little girl. She had truthfully felt like she would never see her again. It took a long time for her to recover, but the dreaded blood clot never eventuated. Against all the odds, Vanessa's indomitable spirit prevailed yet again.

Later that summer, in the heart of the hurricane season, I received a phone call from Ray. He told me sadly that my mother didn't have much more time to live. After having fought so hard for so long, the cancer had eventually won the battle. Vanessa told me not to hesitate, and so I rushed off to St. Vincent, flew to Barbados and caught the first flight I could for the States.

My dad was waiting for me as I exited the plane. "I know it's been a while, but the last time we spoke you told me mom was doing much better. What happened?" I asked as we climbed into Ray's Lincoln.

We drove north from San Diego and my dad filled me in. Like most things concerning my old man, he had an off-beat tale to tell.

As I have mentioned, Ray had a gift for meeting people. Somewhere along the line he had come across a mysterious old man who said he was an herbalist and had found a cure for cancer. At that time my mother was quite sick and was undergoing chemotherapy. Ray was always open to anything, so encouraged the fellow to tell him more. The old man explained he had spent his life learning how to refine herbs down to their basic essences. These plants in their purest forms can contain powerful properties. After years of experimentation, he had developed a tea he brewed from a certain combination of these potent essences. If taken regularly, he claimed his tea would restore a cancer patient's white blood cell count to near normal, which in turn helped the body fight cancer. He then gave Ray a bottle which would last a month. He told him to call him when he needed more. He also told my dad not to tell the doctors my mom was taking the tea, but within a short period of time he predicted she would show signs of recovery. This is exactly what happened. It wasn't long before Jean was out of bed and visiting her beloved bridge club once again. The man would appear exactly on time and give my mom a new bottle of tea, and for this would never accept a cent. Naturally, Ray thought this was the greatest discovery since Penicillin, and told the old herbalist he was going to raise enough money to build a clinic for him in Mexico. Jean went off the chemo and was well on the road to full recovery when tragedy struck. The fellow was off on one of his secretive sojourns into the Arizona desert when he died in a car accident. He had always been extremely protective of his special tea, and had never told anyone how he made it, not even his son. The formula for his cancer-curing tea was lost forever. From the time her tea ran out my mom went downhill rapidly. Ray ended his story by telling me he felt Jean had only a few days left, at best.

    I reached the apartment in Oceanside and immediately rushed to my mom's side. There wasn't much left of her disease-racked body, but she smiled a relaxed smile when she opened her eyes to see me there. The doctors had prescribed a heavy-duty morphine-based syrup which she said helped ease the pain, but I could see she was still suffering greatly. After a while I left her to rest and went downstairs to sit with my dad. We talked and talked. Around midnight, Ray went upstairs to check on her. A few minutes later he came slowly down the stairs. He had tears in his eyes. "She's gone," is all he said.

    We hugged, and cried, and sat up until dawn remembering my mom. I didn't want to say it, but she had lived a tough life. Her existence with Ray had never been easy. My sister's wild machinations would have taken their toll. And I'm sure my crazy adventures didn't help her, either. She had led a life of hopeful expectation, empty promise, nervous anticipation and worry. Yet she remained loyal through thick and thin. Ray used to say, when asked how things were going,

"Oh, it's just another day charging at those God-damned windmills!" Well, if he was Don Quixote, then she was his Sancho Panza. She followed him everywhere, and never stopped believing, right to the very end.

Despite the trials and tribulations he put my mother through, my dad loved Jean greatly and would have done anything for her. As long as it fit into his personal vision, of course. Yet she faithfully accepted what life dished out, sacrificing her own existence for the good of her husband and her kids.

Looking back on it I realize my mom and I never really spent much time together. It was like I never really had a chance to know her. My most cherished memory, however, was when she and Ray came to visit me in Bequia for the first time. Nolly was taking care of a nice forty-foot yacht for a Swedish guy. He let me use it to take my family down to the Cays. As we sailed south, Ray, Joan and her little son Brahm all became seasick and went below to sleep. My mom stayed on deck with me all the way. I gave her the helm and she loved it, steering away to her hearts content. We didn't talk about much, but we didn't have to. Just being together, just the two of us, was enough. It only lasted a couple of hours, but those few moments were priceless.

5
Up North

*"You have no right to own a yacht,
if you have to ask how much it costs."*
- J.P. Morgan

A sixty-eight-foot schooner is a big vessel. It needs a lot of paint and varnish to keep her up to scratch. Maintenance, as on any yacht, is never-ending, and rare is the day when you find a crew who works for free. Anything with the word "marine" written on it is going to cost you double. Yes, I had a good partner who was fairly well cashed up, but a deal is a deal, it was fifty-fifty, and I had to somehow keep up my end of the bargain. And at the end of the year it would be nice to have done a little better than simply break even. The only way I could see the term charter business working was to have a good agent working for the boat where the tourists came from, be it the States or Europe or Canada, someone committed to filling your season out. This was the weak link in our chain. We had done okay during our first couple of years doing weekly charters, but I was anxious to do better. It was frustrating to me because this end of the business was out of my control. We could give a group of guests the best time ever, but we had to get them on board first. So, I came up with another idea. In a boat race if you are behind it's not always best to simply follow the leader. Sometimes it's better to go off in an opposite direction to find a lifting breeze or a favorable current. The West Indians call this "breaking up de tack." This is what I decided to do.

From my many trips over the years to the duty-free island of St. Maarten I had seen the rapid growth in the tourism industry there. New hotels and casinos were under construction across the island and planeloads of tourists were landing every day. People on holiday were always looking for something different to do, and day chartering was becoming very popular. I had some good contacts there, so I decided to give it a go. Bamu and Kingsley were happy to come along, so Vanessa and I let the house go, packed all of our belongings aboard *Water Pearl*, and in early October sailed north to seek our fortune.

Paul Marshall had lived and worked on the Dutch side of St. Maarten for a number of years. He came from upstate New York and was a childhood friend of Willy Halsey. Willy's dad Bob was quite an eccentric entrepreneur. He landed in St. Maarten sometime in the sixties with the idea of living the Caribbean dream (he pledged to never wear shoes again, and I have to admit I never saw him with any on) while taking advantage of the island's *laissez-faire* business climate to make some serious money. His first business was a Florida-style marine hardware store called Island Water World. Willy, Paul and several other young home-town friends were recruited by Bob to come and run the chandlery. Willy never showed much interest, but Paul was a natural, and a few years later when Bob sold the business, he became general manager. He was a good guy for me to know. With Paul's island connections, *Water Pearl* was soon set up in the quaint French-side port of Marigot, ready to do day charters.

After a few false starts we discovered the deserted islands and reefs of Prickly Pear Cays to be the perfect destination for our day trips. This unspoiled spot, located to the northwest of the neighboring British island of Anguilla, was a two-hour sail away. Surrounded by a pristine coral reef, it had a small protected anchorage off a pink sand beach which we could just maneuver ourselves into. And the best part about it was on most days we would have the place all to ourselves. So, we had the boat, we had the charter license and we had the ultimate place to go. Now all we needed to do was to get people on board. This was the tricky bit.

Our first season was tough. Even though we had the perfect package, it still wasn't easy to break into this highly competitive business. There was plenty of backstabbing, under the table payoffs, sleight of hand, and ugliness involved in getting a load of day trippers aboard. At one point a highly aggressive South African captain was rumored to have even taken a pot-shot at a competitor with a crossbow. This wasn't my scene. I was more willing to sit back and let the cream naturally rise to the top. And eventually it did.

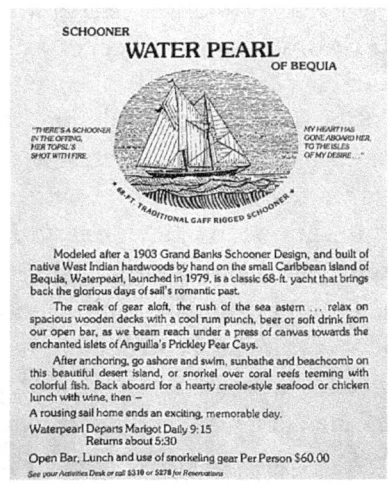

Our charter brochure.

As with most new business ventures, it took us awhile to find our feet. Our first season we tried a few different marketing ideas before finally working out the right combination. We soon learned we couldn't wait for the girls who sat at the big hotels' activities desks to put people on our boat; they were all paid off by one or the other Dutch-side charter boats. What we had to do was go directly to the tourists themselves - and we found the ideal person to do it. Jill was the girlfriend of a friend of Paul's. She was slim, attractive, and a natural salesperson. She told me once that she loved the challenge of making a sale, and she refused to take no for an answer. Jill had no problem approaching total strangers on the crowded beaches in her little bikini handing out our colorful brochures, and with her gift of the gab would generally take a deposit and confirm a booking. We charged sixty dollars US per person, of which Jill took ten. It was a good deal for her and us. Our numbers began to skyrocket; instead of going out with five people, we were loading up to thirty a day.

Our guests definitely got their money's worth. Our day would start at seven when the girls and I would jump in the dinghy and motor ashore. Vanessa and Clara would head off to the local French bakery for an armload of fresh baguettes, while I would take our jalopy of a jeep to the wholesale fish market for the day's purchase of fresh snapper fillets. In the meantime, Bamu and Kingsley would get the boat ready. At nine o'clock we would meet our day's guests on the quay and ferry them out to the boat, whose mainsail was hoisted and ready to go. After delivering my daily captain's speech, we would motor out of the bay as the crew, in true *Friendship Rose* style, enlisted the guests to help hoist the rest of the sails. The steady breeze filled the sails, we eased the sheets and soon we would be reaching off towards the west end of Anguilla. The tap of the rum punch barrel would now be opened, and would stay that way for the rest of the day. Rounding the point, we headed out across a stretch of reef-protected waters towards Prickly Pear Cays. These were ideal conditions for picture-perfect sailing.

Kingsley pilots us through the reef.

On most days, dolphins would play in our bow waves, and many times we sailed through pods of migrating humpback whales. Bamu, Kingsley and Vanessa were great with the guests, but the star of the show was little blond-headed Clara. Everyone simply fell in love with her, and she had no problem playing up to her audience.

After entering through the narrow passage between the islets and anchoring inside the reef, we worked like a well-oiled machine. The guests who didn't want to snorkel were taken ashore to the crescent-shaped beach where they could paddle in the calm, crystal-clear lagoon. Kingsley and I would then get the others organized with gear and take them snorkeling, where after dropping them off to windward the current and wind would carry them over the colorful coral reefs straight back to the boat. In the meantime, Vanessa would be busy making salads while Bamu would prepare a Creole-style lunch of curry chicken, fried snapper in garlic sauce served with black-eyed peas and rice. Once back aboard, our guests were given their hearty lunch, washed down with a glass or two of crisp French Sauvignon Blanc. St. Maarten was duty-free and alcohol was dirt cheap, so we simply ran an open bar. Coca-Cola was more expensive than Heineken beer, and the fruit juice used to make the punch cost more than the Puerto Rican rum (I used to pay twelve dollars a case!). By three o'clock we were hoisting the anchor, and after a pleasant sail back we would be picking up the mooring in Marigot sometime after five, when we would ferry our happily windblown, sunburned and generally inebriated guests ashore. The clean-up and preparations for the next day's trip would then begin. It was

Come on Dad! I'm ready. Let's go!

at this time, after the last of the guests had departed, when the next set of visitors began to arrive. With cold beers in the cooler, a tub full of rum punch and usually lots of food left over from lunch, *Water Pearl* was a natural venue for friends off surrounding cruising boats looking for a party. Many times, this would lead on to further carryings-on ashore. And the next day we would be up bright and early, ready to repeat the whole routine again. Life was full-on, but we were young and full of energy. Somehow, we handled it.

Occasionally, we would do a private charter for the luxury five-star hotel La Samana, whose manager Lynn was an old friend from the Les Anderson/Willy Halsey days back in Bequia. This classy hotel had an international reputation as a discreet hideaway for the rich and famous, and we became the preferred charter boat in the event any of their guests wanted to go sailing for the day. Over the next few years we took out many high-profile personalities, from rock stars to actors to industrialists and politicians who soon lost their defensive edge and relaxed to the casual rhythms of the boat. Over the years we took out Darryl Hannah, Jackson Browne, Mary Tyler-Moore, Ted Kennedy and family, Ivan Lendl, Mic Jones from Foreigner, Jan Winner from Rolling Stone Magazine, and Calvin Kline, amongst many others.

St. Maarten became our home away from home; the business went from strength to strength, and slowly we began to actually make some money. Our life was fun and exciting. We were living aboard a classic gaff-rigged schooner, sailing

Bamu lands a big one.

about the Caribbean with a loyal and dependable crew, had an incredible partner and were gradually making improvements to the boat. How could things be better? At least that was my point of view. Vanessa, however, saw all of this in a slightly different light.

For a start, Vanessa held a life-long fear of the water, going back to a time in her childhood when she nearly drowned, so sailing never held much of an attraction to her. Like most women, Vanessa appreciated her own personal space. She liked to have things arranged in her own way, but every time we went for a sail everything was thrown about and all of that changed. Even though *Water Pearl* was a big boat, it was still a small living space. Sharing it with two grown West Indian men, no matter how good-natured, wasn't easy for her. Add to that twenty-something tourists thundering through our home every day, and you can understand how Vanessa could only dream for the day when she had a little place of her own ashore. "Just give me four walls and a spot where I can plant a garden...I don't care where it is!" At the time I struggled to understand this. To me, we were living the ultimate dream.

In the summer of 1985, we sailed back to Bequia to do a much-needed refit. Because of the amount of work we would be doing, we rented a little house over the hill in the village of La Pompe. This simple turquoise weatherboard cottage was perched on a grassy bluff overlooking the islands and cays of the Lower Grenadines. It was a beautiful little spot, and I hadn't seen Vanessa anywhere near as happy as she was for those couple of months that summer. I tried to see the long-term attraction from her point of view, but couldn't understand why anyone could choose being anchored to one spot over living aboard a beautiful schooner you could sail to anywhere in the world you felt like going. Life is fluid, and time and circumstance can change a person's point of view.

Eventually I would learn this lesson. Back then, however, I couldn't really see her point.

I had two projects to work through that summer. The first was to bolt a lead keel onto the outside of the boat. This would help us get rid of half of our inside ballast, as well as making the vessel more stable. Once again, fate stepped in to lend a hand. The previous year the tail-end of a hurricane had passed over Bequia. It didn't do much damage, but it did drive a rotting old champion of a schooner ashore, where she quickly broke up. This schooner happened to be the famous *Pilgrim*, designed by John Alden and built in Maine in the 1930's. This big vessel was renowned for a couple of reasons: first for her well-publicized circumnavigation in the 30's, and secondly for being the schooner in the TV hit series *Adventures in Paradise*, where she was renamed *Tiki*. We happened to be in Bequia when she wrecked, and I bought the lead keel from her Canadian owner when he sold everything off. The two most amazing facts about this operation were that firstly the keel had been torn off and was buried in the sand directly in front of the Bequia Slip, a small slipway which was run by an ex-pat American. This made it remarkably easy to salvage. Secondly, we discovered once we had the keel on land it was exactly the width (twelve inches) needed to bolt straight on to *Water Pearl*. It was amazing. It was if it had been made to order. The only problem was it was too long, so we simply cut off a chunk and re-cast it into ingots, which we replaced those handy stones with. It was quite a job, and it took a couple of weeks, but when we were finished and the anti-fouling went on the lead keel "looked like she grew there".

The rest of the summer I spent back in the boatyard working alongside Loren. For a time after the launching I tried to keep the business in the boatyard going while getting *Water Pearl* up and running, but found it too difficult. Both were full time jobs. I had no choice but to dedicate myself to the boat. But the tools and the shed were there, and I did what I could to keep Loren in work. For a few years he was kept busy building his classic thirteen-foot double-enders, which I helped him ship to customers all over the world. He sent several to the States; we shipped a couple to Europe. He even built one for a fellow in the Yukon Territories in northern Canada. Because of our expanding business in St. Maarten, I needed a bigger dinghy to ferry our guests back and forth. Our original tender, which Loren had built and we called *Pearly Queen*, was a fantastic boat but simply too small. I would build my new boat using modern materials and techniques for lightness and strength (called cold molding), and would actually use one of Kingsley's old fishing boats for a mold. It was great being back in the boatyard again, and for those couple of months it was almost like old times.

One afternoon while working on our new dinghy I received a surprise visit by none other than that roving enigma of the high seas - Bob Taylor. He was sailing a new boat he had bought in New Zealand, had a Kiwi girlfriend and had cleaned up his act significantly since the last time we had met, which was when he joined Nolen and me for the maiden voyage of *Corsair* in Grenada. He was still living the life of a cruising nomad, and was on his way through the Caribbean to the Pacific. He had heard I might be in Bequia and had stopped in with the hopes of catching up with me. That night Bob and his partner met up with Vanessa, Clara and I at Mac's Pizzeria, where we shared stories and more than a few drinks. This third meeting between Taylor and me might have only been consigned to a footnote of my personal history, except for his fortuitous last appearance a few weeks later, which as you will see came at a crucial time when through improbable circumstance everything happened to be on the line.

The big excitement that summer was a visit to the island by Her Royal Highness, the Queen of England. She and her husband Prince Phillip were touring the Caribbean on the

Royal Yacht *Britannia*, and decided to include Bequia on their itinerary. Son Mitchell was now Prime Minister of St. Vincent and the Grenadines, and so to give the royal couple something to do had organized an afternoon tea party in the gardens of the Frangipani. Because we were close by, he thought a 'walkabout' through the boatyard might be of interest, especially to Phillip, who was known for his love of yachts and boats. So, we tried to fill the yard with as many small boats of different description as we could. We also had security people turn up weeks ahead of arrival to assess the situation. One thing they made us do was cut down all the coconuts out of the trees, just in case one might fall and hit Her Royal Highness on the noggin.

After sailing out with all the other yachts to escort *Britannia* into the harbor, we watched as the Royal Barge brought their majesties ashore. I was in a hurry because I had to get down to the boatyard and change before they arrived. The streets were lined with schoolchildren dressed in white waving little British flags, and the rest of the island's population was out wearing their Sunday best. The couple were met as they stepped onto the dock by the Prime Minister, and after ceremoniously planting a tree they climbed into a motorcade and were driven slowly to the Frangipani. At the same time, I was hustling down the shoreline with my change of clothes in a plastic bag. As I jumped over the final wall into the boatyard a security man emerged from the bushes and stopped me. "Where are you going and what's in the bag," he demanded. I explained my mission to him, saying I had to hurry so I could change ahead of their arrival. Eventually he let me pass. I got to the workshop to meet a nervous Loren, who pointed out I had better hurry because the royal entourage were just about there. I ducked behind the bandsaw to change, and just as I zipped up the fly to my white cricket trousers, they came around the work bench. A minute earlier and I really would have been caught with my pants down.

CJ, the PM and the Queen.

The Queen walked into the yard clutching her white purse, just as any normal elderly Englishwoman would. The Prince was attired in an immaculate dark blue suit, and Loren and I were introduced by the Right Honorable Prime Minister. A crowd of expats stood off in the wings, watching and taking photos. Just then I heard the exclamation "Clara!" I looked up to see my four-year-old daughter running towards us, excited to meet a real queen (although slightly disappointed she wasn't wearing her crown). Clara stayed at Her Majesties side for the rest of her short tour, and a short one it was as the Queen didn't really show much interest in boats. She quickly made her way back to the Frangipani, but Prince Phillip stayed on, asking many questions and telling us a few anecdotes of his own. He also had quite a long chat with Vanessa, who Son introduced as the island's Australian Ambassador. He lingered for at least a half an hour in the yard, tailed by several smiling, well-tailored secretaries, keen to discuss the story behind each of the boats we had on display. He was even interested in a pile of old rusty chain-blocks we had acquired. I got the feeling he'd had his fill of garden tea parties.

"...and these chain blocks?"

6
Getting By With a Little Help from My Friends

*"June too soon,
July keep an eye,
August a must,
September remember,
October all over."*
- West Indian ditty concerning hurricane season

It was a cool, rainy morning in early November when we arrived back in Marigot for another charter season. Kingsley had decided to remain in Bequia, but Bamu had stayed on. I was in a hurry. A few days earlier Bob had contacted me. He was a bit vague about it all, but from what I could understand, his record company was putting on an event for him and he asked if I would fly up and attend this soirée with him. It would be tight, I told him, but I felt we could get the boat to St. Maarten in time for me to catch one of the daily flights to New York. After a forty-three-hour passage we motored into the glassy harbor just after sunrise and picked up our mooring which we had laid down the year before. Later that morning I went ashore and was able to book a seat on a flight to JFK for the following day.

Standing on the Marigot quay the next morning I gave my two girls a big hug. "Hold the fort," I remember saying as I climbed into the taxi. Little did I know how close to the mark those words would prove to be. A few hours later I was stepping out of a cab in front of the Gramercy Park Hotel. For some reason, as I walked towards the doors of the historic old hotel, I decided to stop and buy a hot dog from a street vendor. New York hot dogs are famous; I'd heard about them since I was a kid but had never tried one. What a time to experiment.

Once I'd settled into my room, I called Bob's office and they told me I should catch a cab to the swanky hotel in which he was staying. "This should be interesting," I thought to myself as I made my way across mid-town Manhattan. Things were different this time. I was meeting up with Bob Dylan in his world, and I didn't really know what to expect. Bob greeted me with a smile and a hug. His suite faced out onto leafy Central Park, which was erupting with the sunset colors of autumn. The room was spacious and tasteful and full of antique furniture, the walls adorned with beautiful paintings. From outside on the curb to the tiniest detail in the bathroom the place was reeking of expense, but I quickly had the feeling that it was just another hotel room to Bob, just another place where he dropped his bag and hung his hat. He offered me a coffee, we sat down, I filled him in on the latest with the boat and we shared a few jokes and had a laugh. Then I asked him what was happening that night and we got down to details.

"Oh yeah...well tonight is just one of those things I've gotta do. My record company is putting on a reception for me at the Met (Metropolitan Museum of Modern Art) for selling thirty-five million records, and I thought you might like to come along. It's kind of like a cocktail party. We'll stand around talking to some people for a while, and then we're going to Maxim's for dinner," he said with a sigh, like he was standing in the hot sun holding a shovel after being ordered to dig a mile-long ditch. He laughed and told me my job would be quite easy. All I had to do was get out of the limo and walk in with him. It was arranged as to what time the car would pick me up, and then he said he had to make a few calls and our meeting was done.

I walked out into the brisk autumn afternoon and headed down busy Central Park South, hands shoved deep into my pockets, my mind lost in thought. Doormen in top hats and fancy long coats hailed cabs for fur-clad ladies while the flags of many nations waved gently on their long flagstaffs overhead. It was like I had been transported to another planet, and I wondered what the hell I was doing there.

The limo weaved comfortably through the dark Manhattan streets, and we sat silently in the back. Bob looked out the window with casual interest, every now and then turning his head as if he'd seen something unusual. My role had been explained to me, and it didn't sound very difficult. Once we had run the gauntlet of paparazzi and reporters and made it into the sanctuary of the reception we would separate, but when it was time a few of us would leave together and go for dinner at the world-famous Maxim's. Food wasn't really on my mind, however. Since arriving back at my hotel my stomach hadn't been feeling the best, and as we edged closer to the Met it wasn't getting any better. There was an ominous feeling churning in my bowels. I hoped somehow it would pass.

And then we were there, and our door opened and we were out onto a red carpet, camera's flashing, voices calling out things like "Just a word, Bob!" It was happening just as I imagined, like something I'd seen on TV. But we didn't stop, continuing past people holding glass doors open for us as we were whisked into the brightly lit reception and a glitzy throng of anticipation and attention, and then a breaking wave of applause. As we slipped into this glamorous crowd, in the instant before reaching the outstretched hands of smiling record company executives, Bob gave me a glance that said, "Catch you later." He was then swallowed up by the adulating throng. As all heads turned to catch a glimpse of the legend, I was met by the smiling face of Peter, one of Bob's accountants and the only person I knew in the place.

"Well done, Chris! Well done!" he said to me as he continued to smile and pump my hand. I didn't really know what it was I had done so well, so I just shrugged and let it pass. Then he stopped a waiter and we each grabbed a drink. As we chatted, I glanced through the crowd. It was definitely the who's who of chic New York society. Billy Joel was there with a glittering Christie Brinkley. I noted Yoko Ono in the crowd. Peter took me by the arm and introduced me to the man in black himself, Roy Orbison. He was standing politely off to one side and we chatted briefly. I have no recollection of what we spoke about, but I'm sure we struggled a bit to find common ground. What a scene it was.

I, however, had other things on my mind. I recognized the feeling and knew what the inevitable outcome would be. I could read the future, and I knew I was on a train that was heading for a wreck. Just as in the mountains of Yugoslavia or on that heaving ferry to Crete, I knew the feeling only too well. Gastro. Montezuma's Revenge. Bali Belly. Food poisoning. No matter what you wanted to call it, I knew there was about to be a volcanic eruption, and it wouldn't be pretty. As I stood there talking to Roy the beads of sweat began to spring out of my forehead. The conversation and noise and laughter faded into the background. All I knew was I had to get out of there, and fast. The last thing I wanted was to be stuck in the toilet next to Billy Joel having it come out at both ends. That just wasn't done.

I politely took Peter to one side. "Listen Pete…I'm really not feeling very well. I need to go back to the hotel, and I have to go now."

"Bob won't be happy," he said. "Are you sure you can't hang on a bit? Maybe it will pass."

"No way," I answered. "As much as I would love to stay, there is no possible way that I can. Tell Bob I'm sorry, but I need a cab, and I need it now."

Peter walked me out to the street and hailed a taxi, and it was all I could do to hold things together long enough to make it to my room. It was touch and go as I slammed my door and ran to the bathroom, grabbing a wastepaper basket as I crashed onto the bog and exploded. Afterwards the cold shakes took over, and even after a steaming hot shower and with every blanket I could find on top of me I chattered and shook. And as I faded in and out of consciousness all I could think about was that friggin' New York hotdog.

The next morning Bob called and asked how I was doing. I told him I was a little better, then apologized for not making it to the dinner. He told me I didn't miss anything. The conversation was short and to the point. He said we'd catch up next time he was on the boat. I was starting to understand that Bob didn't dwell much on what happened yesterday.

I was in bed for the rest of the day, when I wasn't in the loo that is, and although I still wasn't feeling the best, I caught a flight back to St. Maarten the next morning. It wasn't until I was on the plane that I found out there had been some excitement on the island while I was away, and my girls were in the thick of it.

My plane would have hardly left the ground on its way to New York when the first reports of the tropical depression were circulating the local St. Maarten airwaves. In those years before mobile phones, the VHF radio was the main form of communication for yachts in the Caribbean, and as the day passed it would have been running hot.

The anchorage at Marigot Bay is average on the best of days. Although protected from the easterly Trades, it is completely open to any sort of weather from the north. It is not a deep bay, so even in good weather it can attract an uncomfortable rolling side-swell. Our charter mooring was solid and well-set, and in about as good of a spot as you could find in that open roadstead. It was located at the head of the bay, about one hundred meters to leeward of the concrete commercial wharf to give us good access to the quay where we picked up our guests. It was not the spot you would choose if you were sheltering from a tropical depression of near hurricane force, where the wind will at some point travel through every point of the compass. The old saying goes "October all over"; it is rare indeed to have a tropical storm in November, but that year there just happened to be one more left, and Vanessa, Clara and Bamu would have to face it on their own.

As I jetted north, enjoying my gin and tonics, the weather in St. Maarten was slowly beginning to change. The day had started out crystal clear, hot and humid. The sea was possessed by a flat, oily calm; there wasn't a breath of wind. As the day progressed, high, wispy 'mare's tails' began to appear in the translucent sky, an ominous portent of bad weather. Reports of an approaching low-pressure system would have begun to filter through, but they didn't cause much concern. Everyone would have been thinking November month to be far too late in the season for a hurricane.

The next day the weather had changed completely. On the same morning I was lying in my Gramercy Park bed in the throes of hotdog lament, low grey clouds scudded overhead and the wind, although still in the east, was packing a punch. Aboard *Water Pearl*, the crew were in the process of going ashore. Bamu, Vanessa and Clara climbed down the boarding ladder and jumped into our bobbing ship's boat *Pearly Queen*, and with little blond-headed Clara standing in the bows holding on to the painter they motored ashore. After finishing their morning's shopping, they returned to the quay a couple of hours later to find things in the harbor had deteriorated dramatically. The wind had backed around to the north and a large, choppy swell was rolling into the bay. The numerous anchored yachts had swung on their moorings and were now facing into the rising wind and waves. *Water Pearl*, which had been positioned to windward of all, now found herself hanging precariously close to a large motor yacht tied alongside the rugged commercial wharf. Bamu drove the bow of Loren's seaworthy dinghy into the choppy waves and brought her alongside the rolling grey schooner. Vanessa picked her time and jumped onto the boarding ladder with the painter and made it fast. *Pearly Queen* tugged at her bowline, slamming into the boarding ladder as Bamu fended off, waiting for the chance to pass up Clara, who was sitting well-behaved on the bow seat. Then, as the schooner took a big roll to starboard, Bamu swept up Clara and passed her into the outstretched arms of Vanessa. As she scurried aft to the safety of the main companionway, Bamu handed up the groceries before jumping aboard himself and tying the dinghy astern.

By mid-day the situation had worsened. The wind was now blowing at forty knots straight into the bay. The swell was rolling in over the shallow bottom, and the bow of *Water Pearl*, rising and plunging into the growing waves, was tugging fiercely at her mooring line. Most worrying, however, was how close her stern was to the wharf and the one hundred-foot motor vessel, coincidentally named *Vanessa*, tied alongside. In the captain's cabin aft the VHF radio was alive with chatter. Vanessa sat on deck near the hatch listening to the radio, her mouth dry and her palms sweaty as she anxiously watched for any sign of the anchor dragging, which would without doubt spell disaster. *Water Pearl* would simply smash apart on the big rocks of the breakwater in front of the wharf. Just then she was summoned to the radio.

"*Water Pearl, Water Pearl, Water Pearl*, this is the motor vessel *Vanessa*." They switched to the appropriate channel.

"We need to move our vessel from alongside and you are in our way," the captain said.

"Our captain is not here," Vanessa frantically replied, "and I have only one crewman aboard. There is no way we can shift on our own."

The captain of the *MV Vanessa* was not impressed. His wooden ex WWII minesweeper was getting smashed alongside the wharf, and it was imperative he move. Vanessa didn't know what to do. Just then Paul Marshall called. He had been monitoring the transmissions and said he would help, but not for several hours because he was busy securing vessels around Island Water World. She thanked him and hung up the mic. What could she do? There was no way she and Bamu could move the sixty-ton schooner on their own in those conditions. As the wind howled overhead, she sat on the deck with her back against the cabin, and looking into the grey sky overhead she began to cry in desperation. Just then she felt Clara's little hand on her shoulder. She turned and looked into her daughter's bright blue eyes. "Don't worry, Mummy," she said. "I have just spoken to God and He says that things are going to be all right."

"Oh, bless you child," Vanessa cried, hugging her little girl.

A voice on the radio was now calling *Water Pearl* again. The captain of *Vanessa* was adamant; his vessel had to be moved. And Vanessa was just as desperate. She alone was powerless to shift the boat. As the weather continued to deteriorate this conversation was repeated several more times. This was an emergency and something had to be done to overcome the impasse.

And then at the height of the storm another voice came over the radio calling *Water Pearl*. It was the voice of Bob Taylor. "I'm anchored here in Marigot and have been listening to all of this," he said. "You guys sound like you're in a bit of a bind. I've talked to a friend on another boat and we are going to come over and give you a hand. Hang in there and we'll be over as soon as we can."

Not long after Taylor came alongside in his rubber zodiac with his girlfriend and another cruising yachtsman to help. They climbed aboard, tying their dinghy astern. Bob took charge immediately. First, they started up the engine. "Listen, this shouldn't be too difficult. All we have to do is drop your mooring line off and then you just have to punch us out of here."

"What do you mean 'you'?" Vanessa worriedly asked. "Aren't you going to take the helm?"

"No, I'll do what I can to help, but you will have to be the one at the wheel."

Vanessa almost fainted. It was one thing to steer the boat in the open sea to a prescribed compass course, but to maneuver her off a lee shore into the teeth of a hurricane through a crowded anchorage was a far different thing. Clara's little face peered out from the cabin doorway as Vanessa put the six-cylinder Gardner into gear, taking the strain off the mooring line as the bow lifted into the heaving seas. Taylor gave the signal, Bamu tossed away the mooring line, and immediately the bow began to blow away to leeward. They were headed straight for a little French fiberglass boat. "Give her the gun and pass under her stern!" Taylor yelled as he rushed back to the helm. Vanessa put the throttle down and did as she was told, just missing their rubber dinghy tied astern. "Now head up and get the hell outta here!" he commanded.

Somehow Vanessa drove the big schooner out of the anchorage, weaving her way between the anchored yachts as Clara stood at the hatchway watching, her tattered Raggedy Ann doll keeping her company. Up forward, Bamu and the others rigged up the massive three hundred-pound hurricane anchor strapped down on the foredeck. Using a piece of fine line, the anchor was lashed to the end of the staysail halyard.

"You aren't going to put that down, are you?" Vanessa yelled into the howling wind. "Chris will freak out! We'll never be able to get it up!"

"What do you think you have it for?" Taylor laughed. "Once you have this sucker down you won't be going anywhere."

Once well clear to windward of all the other yachts, Taylor told Vanesa to slow down. Even at this distance from shore the water was still quite shallow, and so the anchor holding would not be a problem. The anchor was hoisted into the air with the halyard and shoved over the side, and with the engine now in neutral Bamu cut the lashing with his knife. The anchor crashed into the water and the chain rattled out of the hawse pipe. The fierce wind blew the vessel backwards until Bamu held tight on the brake of the windlass and her head snatched into the wind and seas. "That's it. Shut her down. You guys are rock solid. It might be a bit bumpy, but you can sleep well tonight," Taylor stated.

And with that Bob Taylor and friends jumped into their dinghy and sped back to look after their own boats. The storm raged the rest of the day and well into the night. By first light it had blown itself out. Once that heavy anchor was down the boat was safe, but I have a feeling Vanessa still didn't sleep too well that night. The following day I arrived on the dock in Marigot. The weather was back to its normal brilliance. Fluffy white clouds floated in a deep blue sky. Way off in the distance I could just spot the silhouette of *Water Pearl*'s two masts. I watched as Vanessa drove *Pearly Queen* towards the quay, a blond-headed ragamuffin waving from the bows. The dinghy came alongside and as I gave the two girls a kiss Clara blurted out, "Don't be angry with Mum, Dad. She put the big anchor down, but Bamu says it's okay."

"No Clara, I'm not upset. You girls have done an incredible job!"

"And Bamu!" Clara said.

Of Bob Taylor I never heard another word. I never even had the chance to thank him. After helping Vanessa move the boat, he must have left to find a safer anchorage himself. From time to time through the years I've wondered whatever happened to him. Maybe one day someone will write a book about this amazing character, and I will find out.

7
A Voyage to the Antipodes

"The man who wants to lead the orchestra must turn his back on the crowd."
- Captain James Cook

Early in January of 1986 I received a call from Bob. He was about to embark on a tour of New Zealand, Australia and Japan with Tom Petty and the Heartbreakers, he said, and wondered if I wanted to come along. "Sounds interesting, but what would I be doing?" I asked.

"Oh, I don't know…we'll think of something. Call it security," was his answer.

As I drove our jeep back to Marigot I was torn as to what to do. I'd love to go along, but we couldn't afford to shut the business down for six weeks in the heart of the charter season, especially now that we were on a roll. And what would Vanessa think? I couldn't just leave her and Clara in St. Maarten while I'm off gallivanting around the world. Still, it was an enticing offer.

Sitting in one of the local Marigot quayside cafes I told Vanessa about the offer. Her response was astonishing. "I think it's a fantastic offer! There's no way you can turn down an opportunity like this," she said, without a hint of bitterness or jealousy in her voice. "But what can we do to keep the boat going?"

"Well I've been thinking about that one," I replied. "What we need is someone dependable to skipper the boat. What do you think about Mackie Simmons? He has a commercial ticket and if he's up for it he would be perfect."

Vanessa agreed. Our old friend from Bequia would be ideal. I gave him a call and he agreed to my offer straight away. So, I called Bob and informed him I was good to go, and after a few runs with Mackie to show him the ropes I was off to LA to join Bob Dylan on a tour of Down Under.

Landing at LAX I had no idea what to expect. I took a taxi to a hotel where the various members of the crew were congregating. Bob's office had told me a room would be waiting for me, and once I was there, I should check in with Gary Shafner, the tour manager. I dropped my bag on the floor and called Gary's room. He said he needed my passport straight away because I needed to get a visa for Australia. I walked down the hall where I found the door to Gary's room ajar, and he was on the phone as I went in. The room looked as if the maid hadn't been in there for a week. The bed was unmade, there were leather bags and travel trunks scattered about the floor, a tray from the morning's half-eaten breakfast rested on a bedside table next to an ashtray overflowing with dead butts. The desk at which he stood was cluttered with various scraps of paper with scribbled messages on them. Gary wasn't a tall man, his brown hair was slicked straight back, he had dark rings around his eyes and his pudgy complexion looked as if it hadn't seen sunlight for a long time. He wore a grey suede jacket over a black tee-shirt, faded jeans and shiny pointed boots. Gary Shafner was rock and roll all the way.

After hanging up the phone he was on the move, striding around the room like an absent-minded Groucho Marx. He greeted me as if he'd known me for years. Taking up my passport along with of a stack of others, he put on some shades, dropped a packet of Camels into a jacket pocket, and after rooting around on his desk for the room key we were off. "Your flight to New Zealand leaves at nine-fifteen tonight," he said as we walked swiftly down the hall. "You'll find Micky

Hayes on your rooming list. Give him a call and he'll tell you the pick-up time for your bags. He'll also have your passport. Bob is travelling a bit later, so we'll see you in New Zealand." The elevator door closed and I wandered back to my room, still not much wiser as to what exactly was going on.

I looked up Mickey Hayes and gave him a call. His voice was bright and cheery, and he said pick-up time for bags was six o'clock. I hung up, sat back and wondered what to do next. There wasn't much choice but to wait, something I learned to get used to. I would be doing plenty of it over the next few weeks.

The flight to Auckland would take twelve hours. Everything in LA had gone like clockwork. Bags. Transport. Boarding pass. Passport. I just followed the prompts. Now we were jetting into the black night, and I was still in the dark. Bob was nowhere to be seen. I had no idea who was who, or what I was doing, or why I was there. "Just go along for the ride," I kept telling myself.

I turned away from the window. The seat next to me was empty, but there was someone on the isle. I generally keep to myself on airplanes, but this was a very long flight, so somewhere over the vast Pacific I struck up a conversation with the young fellow sitting there. Once we found out we both were on the tour things loosened up considerably. My neighbor shook my hand and introduced himself as Stan Lynch.

"Nice to meet you. And what's your part in all of this?" I innocently asked.

"Oh…I'm the drummer with the Heartbreakers," he replied with a coy smile. Stan proved to be a hell-of-a nice guy, with no airs or graces. He wasn't really what I expected a rock and roll drummer to be like, but then a lot of things that transpired on the tour didn't fit into my preconceived notions.

It was early morning when we arrived in Auckland, and after a wait we boarded a connecting flight to Wellington.

There was quite a crowd of us now, and although everyone's roles weren't clear to me yet I at least began to see who my travelling companions were going to be. It also didn't take me long to see how well we were all looked after. Everything was taken care of. As I walked into the lobby of our plush hotel overlooking Wellington's white-capped bay, Micky Hayes handed me my key along with an envelope containing a list of the room numbers of the rest of our group, some with real names, and some, I noted with a smile, more creative. Like Johnny Yuma. A few minutes after finding my room there was a knock on the door and my bag was delivered. In LA Gary gave me the "True Confessions Tour" book, which contained a day to day description of travel, hotels, gigs and days off. The first show would be at an outdoor venue in Wellington in two days' time. Once again, I could see I would have a lot of spare time on my hands.

Over the next couple of days, I met the other members of the Heartbreakers - Mike Campbell, Howie Epstein and Benmont Tench. All of them seemed to be down-to-earth young guys as excited as I was to be on tour with Bob. Several times over coffee or dinner the name Stevie came up in their conversation. In my ignorance I had no idea who this person might be. That night at an impromptu get-together at the hotel bar it became clear when Tom Petty made his first appearance alongside the diminutive, blond haired Fleetwood Mac star Stevie Nicks.

The morning of the show rolled around and I hadn't seen Bob yet, but I'd heard he had turned up sometime the day before. I got a message from Gary to call Bob at one o'clock. I did, and he asked me to be at his room at three, when we would leave for the gig for a sound check before the show. He greeted me at the door of his room and it was a warm welcome. I hadn't seen him since my disastrous trip to New York, and as he absentmindedly wandered about his room getting organized, we had a laugh over my experience that night in November. Gary met us as we strolled through the lobby, where I immediately felt the eyes of everyone in the room upon us. It wouldn't be the last time. The Heartbreakers were all standing casually together in one corner, and upon seeing them Bob wandered over to say hello. Just then Tom Petty stepped out of the lift with Stevie and we headed for the front doors and our transport waiting just outside. Everyone wore shades and moved with a sort of aloof authority. Bob, Gary and I climbed into the front car and were off, with the others following close behind.

The venue was at a fairground, and as we drove in, we were directed by security to the back-stage area where we made our way to the dressing rooms. This whole scene was a totally new experience for me, Bob hadn't given me a whole lot of direction, and I was running at full speed trying to keep up while acting like everything was under control. Back-stage was a jumble of heavy electrical cables and humming black boxes. A mob of people in black tee-shirts moved busily about, consumed with one task or another, hardly taking notice of us as we passed. I had no idea who was who in this circus swirling about me, but I had no doubt who the ringmaster was and figured I'd just keep close and the rest would take care of itself.

With Bob settled in his dressing room, I wandered off to have a look around. There was so much going on, and my "Access All Areas" laminate was a passport to anywhere I wanted to go. I rambled out on stage and watched the various technicians make their final adjustments to the lighting and sound and everything else that makes a rock and roll concert happen. It was immediately obvious that these boys were pros and had done it all many times before. I also detected through the odd overheard word or conversation there was a ripple of doubt circulating amongst the ranks. What I had picked up in my short time in the fold was that Dylan had come on this tour without a band of his own, and Petty and the Heartbreakers would be backing him up. I learned this connection had been made at a Farm Aid concert a couple of months earlier. Prior to the tour there had been a few rehearsals in LA, where the band had done a crash course in the Bob Dylan songbook in which they had to become familiar with literally hundreds of songs. There had been no hints forthcoming as to which of these songs would be played on the night, and so no one, from the band to the crew, knew what to expect. One thing was for certain, though. Everyone knew who the captain of the ship was, and they were all in awe of the man. It was he alone who dictated the course, and even his pilots were kept in the dark as to where they were bound.

A little later the band meandered out on stage to do their sound check. I could tell straight away this was a tight unit, which was no surprise since they all had been playing together since high school. After tuning up and jamming on a few pieces they ripped into a great version of Howlin' Wolf's "Little Red Rooster". In the meantime, Bob was drifting aimlessly around the stage, picking up a few guitars before finally choosing one. After a bit of discussion and one or two false starts they played "Emotionally Yours". Another couple of numbers were gone through before he put the guitar down, had one more look around the stage and then wandered off, with me attempting to look casual as I tried to keep up with him.

With the sound check finished and Bob safely back in his dressing room, I found catering and joined the various members of the crew in a meal. Returning to the dressing rooms I encountered a cluster of guys standing in the hallway. The group included Gary Shafner and production manager Al Santos, Petty's main man Richard Fernandez, along with a couple of others. As I walked past, Richard left the group and held me up. "Hey Chris, I wonder if you could do us a favor," he said in a low, conspiratorial tone. "Up to now Bob hasn't given anyone a set list, so nobody knows what we're playing tonight. Frank, who is doing the lighting, and Alan the sound engineer, even Tom and the band...everyone is a little bit anxious. Do you think you can see if you can get a set list from Bob for us?"

I didn't really know what a set list was, but I could guess. "Sure," I shrugged. "I'll see what I can do." I gave a light knock on Bob's door and went in, where I found him sitting on a sofa plucking his guitar. He gave me that blank look guitar players give when they see you but are actually lost in their own world. "Sorry to bother you but something has come up," I said, trying to act as off-the-cuff as I could.

He played on a bit more, then put the guitar down and stood up, scratching his curly hair, which was his habit. "Yeah, what's that?" he asked, crossing his arms as he leaned against his dressing table.

"Oh, it's just there are some guys outside who are wondering if you've done a set list yet," I stated.

A mischievous sort of grin brushed across his face. "What do they want a set list for?" he half-heartedly joked.

"What do I know?" I shrugged. "Maybe the guys want to have some kind of idea which songs they are going to play before they step out in front of forty thousand people. It's

Not the exact one, but a great set list nevertheless.

348

just a guess, though," I quipped.

I walked over to the table and poured myself a shot of Jack Daniels. When I turned around Bob was jotting down his list on a blank sheet of paper with a marking pen. "Here," he said, handing the sheet to me with a look as if to say, "I don't know what they need this for, but here it is anyway."

The door had hardly closed behind me when Richard snatched the sheet out of my hand. Rushing into the production office he gave it to Al Santos, who quickly pushed it into the photocopier. Within minutes there were copies of the set list flying all around the place, and there was a collective sigh of relief from all concerned. I was only too glad to help. It was also my first lesson from the Bob Dylan Guide to Life on the Road, and I could see I had a lot to learn.

The show in Wellington came off alright, even though once it started Bob pretty much forgot about the set list. As I stood in the wings of the stage behind Davy Bryson and his giant mixing board, I watched the byplay on stage. Bob had the band and the rest of the crew on their toes, that's for sure. Between songs the lights would go dim and at some point, Bob would start strumming some chords. As the stage brightened the eyes of the Heartbreakers and the four elegantly clad back-up singers would be glued to Bob's left hand, waiting for a clue as to what song he was going to play. It was a real test for them, and to their credit they pulled it off. Benmont Tench, the keyboardist, told me later, "Man, that first show I was freaking out. Over time I got used to it, but that first night all I could do was watch Bob and hope I got the song right. Do you have any idea how many songs he's written? And we had to know them all!"

The reviews the next day were very harsh, but in my view the forty thousand "punters" (as promoter Michael Chugg called them) seemed to have enjoyed the show. When I pointed this out to Bob during the short flight to Auckland the next day, he shrugged it off. "Don't worry about the papers. Those so-called experts are always looking for something to write about. That's why they're called critics. They're paid to criticize. I've been going through my whole life with bad reviews. This isn't the first and won't be the last." And that was it; like water off a duck's back.

After one show in Auckland the tour moved on to Australia, where we had concerts scheduled in all major cities. As time went on, I slowly figured out my position in the scheme of things. Officially I didn't really have a job description. In Australia the promoters provided a professional security person (or "minder" as he was called) for Bob, who had done lots of tours and knew the ropes, but Bob didn't know the guy and kept him at arm's length. I quickly learned that Bob was an extremely private person who kept himself isolated from the other players in the carnival which was swirling around him. From his lofty position he kept everyone guessing, revealing things on "a need to know basis only". This was a different Bob than the one I had come to know sailing around the blue waters of the Caribbean. It was a good thing for me to see, but it didn't change things much between us. I wasn't really on the payroll (although I did get fifty bucks a day *per diem*). I came from another world, an alternative reality. I was just his partner along for the ride, and from that position I could at least call a spade a spade, which I suppose I often did. Maybe that is what I was there for…who knows?

In Sydney before a show Bob asked me if I had brought along a chess set. I told him I had the pieces but needed to get a board. "That's okay…just set 'em up. We can play without a board," he said with a playful grin. I shrugged my shoulders and set them up on a travelling trunk.

"Is that knight on a black or a white square?" I asked after a couple of moves. Bob looked up.

"Use your imagination," he said.

We both laughed. "I'm not sure if this is going to work. Tomorrow I think I'll go out and buy a board." Once I got the board, we started our own little tournament. In the down time between shows there was plenty of time for chess, so we usually had a game on the go. And there was plenty of down time. Many years later I read a quote from Charlie Watts, the drummer of the Rolling Stones, who said he figured he had spent over thirty-five years of his life simply waiting around - either in the studio or on tour - for something to happen. I was learning very quickly that life on the road wasn't all that it was cracked up to be. The pace was mind-numbingly slow. I tried to get out and see things, but at the end of the day everyone was there for only one reason, and that was to get the band on the stage and put on a good show. And even though I was playing only a minuscule part, this included me.

Stevie Nicks joins the boys on stage in Sydney for "Heaven's Door".

From my point of view the shows were excellent. Between Petty and his band, and the Queens of Rhythm (Bob's four gospel-like backup singers), there was a lot of variety, and a lot of energy. Every night the set was different. Sometimes things clicked beautifully, and sometimes they didn't. On a couple of nights in Sydney Stevie Nicks joined in, but this was abruptly stopped by the Australian musician's union when it was discovered she didn't have a working visa. As we moved across the country, we crossed paths with Dire Straits, who were touring Australia at the same time. We went to two of their shows, where Bob joined them for the encore. The contrast between the two was striking. Their set list followed the same order every night, the performances were smoothly produced, with a lot of smoke and other special effects, and each song sounded as if you were listening to the original straight off the album, a stark contrast to Dylan's shows which were edgy and raw with a lot more improvisation. He may have been criticized for it, but he never allowed public opinion to influence his music. As far as I could see, Bob played what he wanted to play, and the punters could take it or leave it...it was up to them.

In Sydney we stayed at the Sebel Townhouse, an old hotel located in the center of the city's notorious King's Cross, home of live strip shows and brothels and drug addicts and pretty much everything else you could imagine. Although she was a little rough around the edges and had seen better days, the Sebel was a classic. Oak paneled, with emerald green carpets, it was as comfortable as your grandfather's favorite armchair. If you were on a rock and roll tour you wouldn't have wanted to stay anywhere else. On one of our days off we were invited to attend an afternoon matinee of the Tennessee Williams play *Sweet Bird of Youth* starring Lauren Bacall and Jack Thomson. The play was as hot and sultry and intense as the hours before a Florida hurricane. The cast was also staying at the Sebel, and one night after a show the hotel staff closed off the restaurant where Bob and I joined Ms. Bacall and Mr. Thomson, drinking grasshoppers into the early hours of the morning listening to stories of Humphry Bogart and his boats and life in an era long gone.

The show rolled on to Melbourne, where it rained solidly for six days. By this time the novelty of being on tour began to wear a bit thin. Standing at the hotel window watching the rain teem down on the gloomy street, I missed my girls and my boat and my real life. "Oh well," I sighed to myself, "things could be worse, I suppose. I could be adrift in the middle of the Atlantic without a rudder."

We moved on to Adelaide and then to sunny, windblown Perth, which reminded me of the Southern California of my youth. It was here that I met up with Vanessa's parents and her brothers. It was also in Perth where a photographer from a West Australian newspaper took a photo of Bob and I playing chess. Struggling to figure out just who exactly I might be, they pulled a name out of a hat and called me Carl Wilson of Beach Boys fame. I guess they figured I had to be "somebody". I mean, Bob Dylan wouldn't ang out with just some random guy from Laguna, would he

Bob had me scratching my head...mate in two?

The Australian leg of the True Confessions Tour finished in Brisbane, and from there would be moving on to Japan. I had been gone for over a month and figured it was long enough, and so on the day Bob and Co. left for Tokyo, I flew back to

the West Indies. The flight to LA was interesting. Stevie Nicks and her personal assistant were also on the flight. Two professional wrestlers were too – Andre the Giant and Big John Stud. We all met in the V.I.P. departure lounge, but when we boarded the plane scattered to our seats; me to economy and Stevie to first class. A few minutes into the flight Stevie's assistant found me and said that Stevie wanted to see me. Apparently Big John was becoming a bit too friendly, so she asked if I could ride shotgun and fend of his unwanted advances. I couldn't see me being much of a match against this massive pro wrestler, but I went along anyway, and ended up keeping Stevie company for the rest of the flight. I'm sure the guy was really nervous when he saw me coming.

8
Red Rocks, the Ghost of James Dean, and More Tales of Ray

"Remember: Life is short, break the rules (they were made to be broken). Forgive quickly, kiss slowly. Love truly, laugh uncontrollably. And never regret anything that makes you smile. The clouds are lined with silver and the glass is half full (though the answers won't be found at the bottom). Don't sweat the small stuff, you are who you are meant to be. Dance as if no one's watching, love as if it's all you know, dream as if you'll live forever, live as if you'll die today."
- James Dean, Actor

Back home in the Caribbean, I stepped off the plane and fell straight back into the swing of things. The boat had been busy. Mackie had worked out great as skipper while I was gone, Bamu had kept our guests happy and well fed, and Vanessa had done an incredible job in keeping everything running smoothly. But my biggest welcome came from Clara, who was the happiest crew member of all.

The charter season rolled on and we worked the boat hard until the end of June, and when things started to taper off, I decided to park her up in St. Maarten's Simson Bai Lagoon for the hurricane season. Around this time, I gave Bob a call in New York, where he was in the middle of the North American leg of his True Confessions Tour with the Heartbreakers. I said I had some ideas for a refit of the interior to discuss with him, and so he told me to fly up to New York and we could talk about it. I arrived on the day of a show being played over in New Jersey. He wasn't in the mood to discuss business, so after the show he asked me to ride along on the bus with them to the next venue near Boston, where the band had a lay day. Bob and I went out for a walk and found a bar where we downed a few beers, but he still wasn't ready to talk about the boat. It was at this point I needed to know what was going on because my bag was still in my hotel room back in New York and I'd been wearing the same clothes for three days. He was in no rush, so he asked me to stay on for the last couple of weeks and finish the tour. I said I had to get back to Vanessa and Clara, at which point he invited them to come along as well. So, I flew back to New York to wait for the girls, and then we caught up with the tour in Colorado.

Red Rocks is a natural amphitheater located outside of Denver and is said to have been a sacred meeting place for Native American Indians. As a venue for a rock concert it is spectacular, and it was quite fitting that Vanessa and Clara's first show was at this special place.

Sunset at Red Rocks.

This tour was all done by bus, and so from Denver we rolled through the Rocky Mountains to Portland, then north for a couple of shows in Tacoma and Vancouver. All of this was very exciting and proving to be a great experience for the girls. Clara fitted right in, and became sort of a mascot for the band and crew. She loved to help Micky Hayes push his daily travel memos under band member's doors, many times adding a drawing or a joke of her own, which kept things lighthearted.

A subject of behind-the scenes interest that summer was the release of Bob's latest album *Knocked Out Loaded*. Critics didn't receive this record very well, but "what else is new?" is something Bob would have said. I have to admit it has never been one of my personal favorites, but there was a bit of trivial history written onto the inner sleeve-cover concerning the crew of the schooner *Water Pearl*. On one side inscribed over a high contrast photo of Madeline Quebec, who was one of the back-up singers in the Queens of Rhythm, is a long list of one hundred and twenty-one people under the heading "special thanks to". There are a lot of big names on this list: Harry Dean Stanton, Frank Zappa, Sam Shepard, David Geffen, Jackson Browne, Tom Petty and all of the Heartbreakers, Randy Newman, Eric, George, Martin Sheen, Jesse Ed Davis, Mark Knofler, Bill Graham, Chrissie Hynde, Ronnie Wood, Ruben Blades, Michael Mann, Eliot Roberts, Iron Mike, Bill Walton, Lou Reed, Stevie Wonder, Sly and Robbie, Richie Havens, Dave Stewart, Jack Nicholson, and Clydie King, just to name a few. Bob's managers and personal assistants are mentioned, as are different restaurants, guitar shops, promotors, bands and producers. There is even recognition given to "Girl Shaped Just Like a Frog". Into this mix we were all surprised to find "Bamu Kingsley", Vanessa, Clara, Nicole (the French videographer from St. Barths) and Chris Bowman written in to various parts of the list - not a big deal, but something to look back on and say "well yes, I really was there."

From Vancouver we had two days to hightail it down the Pacific coast for a show at the Inglewood Forum in LA. Eventually the True Confessions Tour pulled into Babylon, the sprawling, smoky, concrete monster also known as the City of Angels. It was a different scene backstage there, with all sorts of people I didn't know swanning about, acting important. Clingers and glitzy grabbers and coke-snorting business types, who in their blown-up image of self-importance after somehow scamming a backstage pass looked sidelong at me and Vanessa as if to say, "Who are you and what are you doing here?" Vanessa was particularly amusing to observe in these situations, innocently chatting in the hospitality room to social climbing wives of so-called big wigs: taking everything at face value and smiling politely, unimpressed by reputations and self-promotion. Clara was a little gem, well-behaved and patient, in stark contrast to the brats that turned up with their high-flying parents. She just looked on silently and observed their antics as they carried on like monsters and demanded attention.

For the last two shows we drove back north again. After playing at Bill Graham's new Shoreline Amphitheatre near San Francisco, where my job was to keep John Lee Hooker company for the night (it was a tough job, but someone had to do it), we headed for Paso Robles for the final gig, performed at the California Mid-State Fair.

CJ and TP backstage at the Shoreline.

As the caravan snaked along highway 101, our bus took a detour, leaving the others to carry on. It was a bleak, overcast day as we headed east along the little used State Route 46. I had no idea where we were going but knew at some point all would be revealed. After a while we passed through the tiny town of Cholame, where I read a lonely billboard proclaiming the town's claim to fame. A few miles later we came to the desolate, windswept crossroads where on September 30, 1955 the enigmatic young actor James Dean crashed his speeding sports car and died. Tommy pulled our bus over and Bob got out. I figured I would leave him to it. This wasn't the time or place for idle chit-chat or mundane questions. Bob stood facing the bitter breeze, hands shoved deep into his pockets, peering through his dark shades and perhaps visualizing the speeding Porche Spyder approaching from far in the distance in the last seconds before smashing into the old farm truck which ran the stop sign, tragically ending the iconic actor's life. I sat and gazed out the window as Bob listened to the whispers of that lonely wind. After a while he climbed back aboard, Tommy closed the doors and we drove off without anything being said, only the words of Hendrix' "The Wind Cried Mary" drifting through my head.

Bob's primary security person on this tour was an ex-Texas cop who dressed like Roy Orbison. Except when going to and from a show, Bob had little to do with him. Outside of the gigs I spent most of my down-time hanging around waiting to join Bob for a late-night walk or other impromptu excursion, but during this time I discovered a prankster side to Mr. Dylan I hadn't seen before. To my consternation, it actually seemed as though he was testing me out, like he was deliberately trying to catch me napping. He would get in the wrong car, or leave through the wrong door, or duck into a shop when I wasn't looking. But it was at the last show in Paso Robles when he really had me sweating. Bob decided he wanted to take a pre-show ramble. After leading me under the stage, we navigated ourselves through a minefield of high-voltage cables before exiting through a security gate into the shoulder-to-shoulder mob of punters milling about in front of the stage waiting for the concert to begin. At first no one took notice of who it was who had emerged into their midst, but as soon as a few people twigged, a murmur began to grow, and heads started to turn. The crowd started to close in and I had no idea what I would do if things got ugly, but that was the least of my problems as it was all I could do just to stay at Bob's side. His walk-about stuck to no fixed course and lacked any semblance of direction. It seemed like he was deliberately trying to ditch me. At one point I took my eye off him for the briefest of moments, and when I looked back, he was gone. Panic gripped me, but I tried to remain cool. Gazing around the tightly packed crowd I finally spotted his curly head bobbing up, and calmly as I could I caught up with him.

"Nice try," I said as I pulled up alongside. I only received the quickest of acknowledging glances out of the corner of his eye, but I'm sure I also detected a faint shadow of a smile. Luckily the crowd was well-behaved, but I was extremely relieved to re-enter the sanctity of our backstage world.

And then the tour ended. The last show was played, and everyone scattered with the wind. We hung around for a day or two and let the smoke clear. We said goodbye to all of the people who had become like family to us. It hadn't been two weeks since we joined the tour, but it seemed like we had been there a lot longer. Vanessa and Clara thanked Bob for allowing them to experience the whole thing, and he seemed genuinely pleased that they had enjoyed themselves. We were staying in a hotel in Santa Monica. Since we were so close to home, I thought we should spend a few days with my dad in Oceanside, so he drove up in his maroon Lincoln and picked us up. And that is where the fairy tale ended.

We hit the ground like skydivers whose shoots hadn't opened. While on tour we were simply floating in the slipstream, where everything was taken care of and no thought was ever given as to where we were going or what was happening next. It was like living inside a magic bubble with the outside world swirling harmlessly around us, a cocoon where we were safe and warm and nothing could touch us. The moment we stepped outside of the hotel and into Ray's Lincoln, however, was like being doused with a bucket of cold water. The bubble melted away, vaporizing and vanishing into thin air, and next thing we knew we were riding south with Ray at the helm and entering into his reality, which was about as far away from where we had just been as you can get.

It had been a couple of years since we had visited my dad, and things had only gotten weirder. My sister Joan was still living with him along with her brood of kids. Brahm and Aurio, her two oldest boys, were fourteen and twelve and going to high school. Zach was from a different father and was five, and then there was little baby Mara, who had a different father again. Everyone was living in the same small condo just off the beach in Oceanside, whose owner had leased it to Ray for shares in Energy Dynamics - the latest incarnation of his coal deal. It was from here the "Ayatollah Bowmani" ran his business empire.

As crazy as it was, home was home, family was everything, and Ray did his best to take care of us all. He loved two things - cooking, and spoiling his grandkids. His fridge was always well-stocked with the best ice cream or strawberry shortcake, and "enough" was not a word found in his vocabulary. In between rounds of wheeling and dealing over the phone, he would be cooking prime rib or baking bread or changing Mara's diaper or getting the boys off to school, while at the same time trying to deal with my wild booze and drug-addled sister, who would routinely disappear for weeks at a time leaving my old man holding the bag. When she was home Joan could be as sweet as the frosting on a wedding cake; at other times transposing into a foul-mouthed, cranked-up banshee. Luckily Ray had stopped drinking alcohol several years earlier, but he did consume high-octane coffee all day, which couldn't have done much for his blood pressure.

There was always an energy that permeated my dad's life, a sort of electric current of uncertainty. Despite his confident assurances, you never knew what was around the corner. What for some would be once-in-a-lifetime experiences were everyday events for him. One day my brother and I returned home from surfing, and as we dropped our boards onto the upstairs veranda, I heard a terrible commotion erupting from below. I bounded down the stairs to find the front door of the apartment wide open. In the corner of the kitchen a uniformed cop had Ray shoved up against the fridge trying to get handcuffs onto him. As the two wrestled about I thought he was going to have a heart attack. His face was as red as a beetroot. "Get the hell out of my house you Nazi son-of-a-bitch!" he was yelling at the top of his lungs. "You can't come in here you fascist cocksucker! I know my rights! Vanessa, call my lawyer! I'm gonna sue your ass off! Get the hell outta here you jack-booted bastard!" And so on. There was a relentless flood of verbal abuse being hurled at the man, and even though the situation was quite serious, you almost had to laugh.

After pausing long enough to get my bearings, I weighed into the fray. Forcing myself between the struggling pair I held off the officer while I tried to calm down my old man, which wasn't easy because he continued to hurl insults at the cop. In the meantime, Vanessa had no idea what to do, having never experienced anything like this before in her life. Eventually, I found out the officer was a Marshall trying to serve a warrant for unpaid parking tickets. He had been trying to catch up with Ray for months, but always found himself one step behind. Until this day, when Ray opened the door and inadvertently bumped into the officer in the hall. Ray tried to retreat, but the cop was not going to let this chance slip and put his foot in the door, before forcing his way into the apartment. For my part, I could understand his frustration - he was just a guy trying to do his job. But bailing my old man up and cuffing him in his kitchen was a little bit over the top.

After a few minutes of relative calm, I asked the officer how I could resolve the situation. "Simple," he said, "just pay the fine." I agreed, but Ray continued to abuse the man, claiming he was going to sue him for every cent he had, even as we walked down the hall. I followed him downtown and paid off the couple of hundred dollars. The person who was hardest hit by this episode, however, was Vanessa, who talked about it for days. "I simply had no idea what to do," she would say, shaking her head in a kind of shell-shocked awe.

Vanessa has always been fascinated by my oddball family life. It was as different from her colonial English upbringing as ice cream is to ball bearings. My sister only added fuel to an already raging fire. Once she asked my dad to borrow his car to go buy some diapers for baby Mara. Against his better judgement, he gave her the keys. He didn't hear from Joan for two weeks, and when she finally did stagger home, the car was nowhere to be seen. "Where's my god-damned car?" Ray demanded.

"I sold it!" Joan yelled back defiantly. More than likely she traded it for coke.

Ray called the cops and had her arrested. "I thought a few days in the slammer might sort her out," he said, but to no avail. She only came out of county jail meaner and feistier than when she went in.

Beyond all the insanity surrounding him, Ray really was a good man at heart. He was selfless and would never turn his back on his family. He had a strong personality, with an unbending view of the world, and for that reason I was glad to live as far away from him as I could and take him only in small doses. There were many things my dad did in his life I didn't agree with, but you had to love the old rascal despite his crazy ways. He did more for me than most fathers do for their sons, things which I will be forever grateful. And despite all of his ups and downs two things were constant: you never left his place without a few good meals under your belt, and you always had some outrageous stories to tell.

9
Snoopy Island

"Where the fuck are we?"
- Banaca
(Parrot aboard the *Mermaid of Carriacou*)

We jetted back into St. Maarten and found all was well aboard *Water Pearl*. After all the planes and hotels and airports and freeways it was a pleasure to climb out of the dinghy up the boarding ladder and feel those trusty silver bali deck planks under our bare feet again. Clara was thrilled to be home and excited to see Bamu and tell him all about her recent adventures. And for his part he was as solid as a rock, and was as much a part of the boat as one of the masts. He sat and listened to Clara with as much patience as an old uncle would, a pearly white smile flashing from ear to ear as the busy little girl chatted away before running down below to say hello to her dolls and other playthings.

    Life was swirling around us and we were caught up in the current, being dragged along at a rate of knots. Once we were back on board we were straight back into painting and varnishing and getting the boat back up to scratch after a hectic season of chartering. It was also time for us to haul out and anti-foul the bottom, and the closest place for us to do that was English Harbor in Antigua. So early one morning we motored out under the drawbridge at Simpson Bai and cruised over to St. Barths, where we planned to spend a couple of days before sailing on to Antigua. Things were changing in St. Barths. It wasn't really the "quiet little fishing village" it used to be. Because it was officially a department of France, French citizens were moving there and opening business. Locals were being bought out and marginalized. It was becoming a trendy, expensive St. Tropez kind of a place catering for the rich and famous. You couldn't just sail in and wander into Le Select anymore; there were now official forms to fill out and procedures to follow. Cruise ships were even beginning to anchor there, bringing their hordes of tourists onto the once quiet streets of Gustavia. Modern times were creeping into one of the last unspoilt hideaways of the Caribbean.

Party time at Isle de Fourchu.

One evening at Le Select some friends and I organized a party aboard the boat over at Isle de Fourchu for the following day. "Nothing serious" as the boys would say in Barths. It turned out to be epic. I'm not sure how many people turned up, but Bamu cooked enough chicken and rice to easily feed everyone. Once at anchor, the boats began to arrive, the Champagne flowed and the party started. It even was attended, among others, by Mr. Jimmy Buffett, St. Barth's Honorary Muse.

Not a bad way to spend an afternoon in St. Barths.

The boat was hauled out in Antigua and all went well, except we spent a lot of money. After all of those good charter seasons we didn't have a lot to show for it, but what else was new? It was a boat. Bob flew in to join us for the sail back to St. Maarten. At the end of the tour in the States we had finally been able to discuss the work I proposed to do on the boat. I'd had enough of day chartering. Regulations on the island had changed and unreasonable taxes were being levied on charter boats. Our beach girl Jill had moved on to bigger and better things; she was now selling time share at a new resort. And with more boats fighting for business, the competition was fiercer than ever. I decided to take a break and do some work on the boat. The original interior we had put together in Bequia after the launching had served us well, but it was very basic and needed an upgrade. We had no shower down below, and we had very little privacy. On our sail back through St. Barths to St. Maarten Bob and I discussed the changes, and came up with a plan. The idea was to park the boat up in the calm lagoon and do the work there. St. Maarten was duty free, so materials were cheap and easy to get. To assist with the refit, I asked Mark Padbury to come down. He agreed, and said he could bring a fellow woodworker by the name of Keith London to help speed the work along.

 Before we started, however, the girls and I flew back to Australia for Christmas. Vanessa and Clara hadn't been home for years and the America's Cup was in full flight in Fremantle, so it was a good time to be there. We parked the boat up in the lagoon tied to the deserted little sand spit everyone called Snoopy Island, and leaving Bamu in charge we took off for a few weeks with the plan to start the refit early in the New Year. It was a joyful reunion for Vanessa. Despite the years of living apart she had a very close-knit and loving family, and during this trip I began to fully appreciate what a sacrifice it was for her to be living so far away from home. And although I had visited Western Australia while on the Dylan tour, this trip gave me time to take a better look around. I loved the place. It reminded me of my early days in California. "I could live here," I thought. Little did I know.

In February of '87 I flew back alone to St. Maarten to start work on the boat. I hadn't been back for more than a day or two when I received a call from my old man back in California. "I'm up to my armpits in alligators back here and I need some help," he told me. "Your sister has been gone for months, I've now got five kids to take care of, and I'm trying to save the world from acid rain for Christ's sake!"

"Five kids?" I asked incredulously. "You mean Joan has had another one?"

"Yeah...a boy. Joan couldn't think of a name so I've called him Noah."

I laughed. My sister had kept her original married name of Moore. "So, it's Noah Moore?"

"That's right. Noah Moore!"

Ray asked me if I could take the two older boys for a while. Their father was still in "Club Fed" for doing some illicit business with some nasty Colombians, their mother had gone off the rails, and for the last four years the two boys had been shunted between various family members. When I was asked to help out, I really couldn't say no. Brahm and Aurio were basically good kids, but they had been given a shaky upbringing and I knew they would be a handful. I decided not to tell my wife straight away. When Vanessa returned it would be a big surprise, but I figured I'd cross that bridge when I came to it. I felt it was better for her to enjoy the last couple of weeks of her holiday without any added worries.

Mark and Keith turned up along with their girlfriends Stella and Grace, and I found a couple of yachts for them to live on. Brahm and Aurio arrived a few days later. At the ages of fourteen and eleven, it was immediately obvious that keeping them in line wouldn't be easy. They had spent half of their lives living in Hawaii, where they had learned to be hot surfers, but they had also developed cocky attitudes, lacked discipline, and like most brothers fought like cats and dogs. They had never been taught how to work, either, so this was a good chance for them to learn something. Because of all of the work to be done on the vessel, I rented a small apartment ashore. At least when the girls returned, we would have somewhere clean and comfortable to live. I also bought a clapped-out pick-up truck for transport, so in the end we were well set-up.

A couple of weeks after we started work Vanessa and Clara arrived back from Perth. It was with some trepidation that I drove to the airport to pick them up. There was no easy way to tell your wife she had suddenly adopted two teen-aged boys. Needless to say, she didn't greet my 'surprise' with great elation. Those months when we worked on the boat were not an easy time for her, but Vanessa took up the challenge as well as could have ever been expected. "If a child hasn't learned the difference between right and wrong by the time they're six, they'll never learn," is what my dad used to say, and from my experience I would have to agree with him. We did our best to try and teach them some basic values, but it was a mammoth task, and one which we knew would be fruitless, because once they returned home there would be nothing to stop them from returning to their old bad habits.

Working with Mark and Keith was a blast. It was full-on high energy from start to finish, when the stereo would be cranked and the woodchips would fly, the work day usually ending when we would adjourn to the after deck with a bottle of rum and watch the sun go down. A year or two earlier Mark had suffered a personal tragedy when his longtime girlfriend Patty, the godmother of the boat, had died in a freak accident while the two of them were living in Italy. In time he rebounded, but everyone who had ever known Pat was shattered by the news.

The work went ahead at an incredible pace and the interior was transformed into an even more comfortable living space. We built in a hot water shower, installed refrigeration, a new generator, and larger water tanks. I had discovered a cool surfing spot on the northwest corner of the island, so on our days off we would zip across the lagoon in *Number One*, the new dinghy I had built in Bequia, cruising up the island's west coast past the village of Grand Case. Outside the break we would anchor the boat and surf until our arms fell off. These safaris were a welcome distraction from our hard work, and we all enjoyed them, especially the two boys.

A couple of months passed, and then we were done. Sadly, we said goodbye to Mark and Keith and their girlfriends, and Bamu flew home for a holiday. There were still a lot of details to finish off, but it was a great relief to get out of that tiny apartment and back to our life aboard the boat again. Because we were out of the day-to-day grind of chartering, we could actually begin to live the semblance of an orderly family life. The boys began to respond to a lot of love and a bit of discipline and kept themselves busy taking the dinghy to the reefs outside to dive up lobsters while keeping our ice box well stocked with nice little red snappers, which Brahm had a real talent in catching.

For Clara, life at Snoopy Island was like being in Never-Never Land. Along the sandy bayside were moored close to twenty round-the-world cruising boats who found the calm waters of that snug little anchorage a perfect respite from the rigors of their sailing lives. Most of these yachts were sailed by young families with children for whom the brilliant white sand and sparkling azure sea became their neighborhood street. Clara belonged to a whole gang of nut-brown white-headed sea nymphs who spent their days combing the beach collecting shells, building sandcastles and roaming the island searching for pirate treasure clad in nothing but their little bikini bottoms. They would spend hours climbing the ratlines of *Water Pearl's* rigging and jumping into the placid sea. For them our big grey schooner with long bowsprit and tall wooden masts was as close to a pirate ship as could ever be, and it became the gang's headquarters. And what a tribe they were! South Africans, Kiwis, French and English...they were living a life most kids only dream of. And with Brahm and Aurio they even had their own Lost Boys. Unfortunately, nothing lasts forever. As the days passed, one by one the kids would sail way, and what was left of the gang would stand on our stern deck, sadly waving goodbye to their friends.

The Snoopy Island gang anxiously await a visit from Santa.

The months drifted by. We kept a little bit of cash coming in by doing a few trips a month for Hotel La Samana, which paid well and were easy to do. We also did a few day sails with Snoopy Island friends, which were also a lot of fun. John Smith came into the lagoon and tied up alongside us with his *Mermaid of Carriacou*, his only companion the bright green parrot Banaca, whose mantra was diplomatically changed by Clara to, "Where the heck are we?" In a Caribbean Sea littered with individualists, scammers, drifters and millionaire yachtsmen, John stood out. A rough diamond of a poet and writer who self-published his book *Letters from Sinking Ships*, he was forever down to his last buck, but knew how to move with the wind and tide, to catch fish and survive. Clara loved to hangout on board the *Mermaid* with this unique sailing philosopher, whose loud, raucous laugh had a personality all its own.

Another hurricane season came around, and we strapped ourselves down and got ready for it. The year seemed to have passed quickly, but for the first time in a long while I didn't really have an idea where we were going or what we were going to do. It was all well and good marking time at Snoopy Island, but there was no future in it. We had done what we had come there for, but I felt like it was time to move on. Having the boys with us also put the pressure on. Family is family, and you do what you can for them, but there has to be a point where you draw the line. This arrangement seemed to have no end in sight.

Clara on board the Mermaid.

It was in late August when I received a call over the radio. "Hey Chris, I got a message here for you to call your partner in New York," Paul Marshall said over the radio. I jumped into our dinghy and whipped around to the other side of the lagoon and walked into Paul's office at Island Water World, where he let me use his phone. A little while later I was tying the dinghy back up alongside. Vanessa was under the awning sanding the skylight hatch, getting it ready to varnish. "How would you like to go to Europe?" I asked.

It was good news for us, but the sad part about it was Brahm and Aurio had to return to California. Once again, they would have to move on. It was a cruel turn of events for them because I think for the first time in many years, they had started to feel like they were a part of a real family, and just when they began to feel secure the rug was pulled out from under them. Again. At the airport they turned stone cold and wouldn't even say goodbye. I guess I don't blame them, though. They were flying back to an uncertain future with no idea where they were going to eventually end up. I felt for them, but there wasn't much else I could do. We had done our best, and only hoped that some part of what we had taught them might stick.

Aurio, Clara and Brahm enjoy a sail together.

10
Temples in Flames Part I

Far between sundown's finish an' midnight's broken toll
We ducked inside the doorway, thunder crashing
As majestic bells of bolts struck shadows in the sounds
Seeming to be the chimes of freedom flashing
Flashing for the warriors whose strength is not to fight
Flashing for the refugees on the unarmed road of flight
An' for each an' ev'ry underdog soldier in the night
An' we gazed upon the chimes of freedom flashing
- Bob Dylan, "Chimes of Freedom"

I walked through an open door into the suite of the glitzy New York City hotel. Gary Shafner, Bob's tour manager, was sitting with a fellow I didn't recognize, and I had the feeling they were waiting on me. I dropped my bags near the door, sat down and poured myself a coffee. Gary lit up another cigarette and introduced me to his companion. He was a big, tall man with a mane of jet-black hair. Perched in the center of his well-lined face was a most roman of noses. "Victor Maymudes," he said as he extended his hand with a smile and a mischievous flicker in his dark eyes.

"Okay. Now we're all here I'll tell you what's happening," Gary said. "As you know, Bob is starting this European tour in Israel, which will be huge because he has never played there before. We're leaving a few days early because Bob wants to go through Egypt to check out the pyramids. Everyone else is going to meet us in Tel Aviv, but we're flying to Cairo this afternoon. We should be leaving for the airport in an hour or so. We're just waiting on Bob."

"Cairo, eh?" I said to myself. "This sounds exciting." Bob had originally told me we were starting in Israel, and suggested Vanessa and Clara meet us in Zurich after the first couple of shows. Now we were making a slight detour to Egypt.

"I've got bags and tickets still to organize out at the airport, so I'll leave you guys to hang out here and ride to the airport with Bob when he's ready to go," Gary said, and after one more spin around the room he was gone. Victor and I settled in and waited for the phone to ring, and as we did, I found out the two of them went all the way back to the early sixties. "I was with Bob when he made his first trip to England," he told me. "I was there when he met the Beatles. What's your connection?"

"Oh, me and Bob own a boat down in the Caribbean," is about all I said. We continued to wait on Bob's call. He was leaving it tight. Finally, the phone rang around three thirty, which we both knew didn't give us much time to get to Kennedy and catch our flight. We picked up Bob at his room and rushed down to catch a cab. The ride to the airport was nuts. Our cab driver was from Nigeria, and he was a most willing ally. "We've got to get to Kennedy in a hurry," Victor said from the front seat. "I'll give you a hundred bucks if you can get us there by five."

"This is not a good time of day, sir, but I will try," he answered.

And we were off. The guy drove like a maniac with his co-pilot Victor urging him on. He drove down side streets and took every short-cut he knew. When we got out of Manhattan and on to the expressway, we found it bumper to bumper with rush hour traffic. Victor encouraged him to pull over and drive in the emergency lane, and he was game enough to do it. How we never got stopped by the cops I'll never know, but somehow, we got to the airport just in the nick of time. Gary was waiting outside as we arrived. Victor gave our cabbie his well-deserved tip and Gary then rushed us through to the VIP lounge.

Chaotic Cairo, the biggest city in Africa. Our hotel was an old fashioned five-star oasis located in the heart of this bustling, overcrowded, noisy, polluted but somehow enchanting city. Everyone seemed to be on the hustle, an obvious necessity for survival in that crazy place, but it was all done with a smile and a sense of humor. It was mid-morning when the three of us climbed into the beat-up Mercedes taxi for our tour of the pyramids. If you think New York City traffic is crazy, you should try driving in Cairo. Our jovial, rotund driver never took his hand off the horn.

Me, Bob and the Pyramid of Saqqara.

The first place we visited was the pyramid of Saqqara, where we wandered around for a while. The "don't climb the pyramid" sign only encouraged Bob to do exactly that. It was a very hot day, close to one hundred degrees, but Bob was dressed for the Nordic winter, wearing a jacket over the ever-present grey hoodie, a beret and fingerless leather gloves. He wouldn't have been mistaken for an archaeologist, let's put it that way. Later, we hired some scrawny horses from some young kids and rode around the much larger pyramids of Giza, and took a good look at the Sphinx. That night we went out to dinner at a famous local restaurant, a dark, cellar-like establishment which was memorable more for the huge rat we saw scurrying along the cobblestone wall than its renowned fare.

Now that we had seen the pyramids and done the tourist thing it was time to move on to Israel, but as many things in the Life of Bob, this wasn't going to be a straightforward proposition. On the morning of our scheduled departure for Tel Aviv, Gary asked Victor and me to come up to his room. "There's been a change of plans," he told us as he paced the room. "We're not going to fly into Tel Aviv like we're supposed to. This trip of Bob's is front page news over there in Israel. They're planning a massive welcome for him when we arrive – red carpet, government officials, the works. The press is camping out at the airport and at our hotel. There are paparazzi everywhere. The last thing Bob wants to do is fly into this mess."

"Like Daniel into the lion's den," I said.

"Something like that. Anyway, I'm checking out the overland route. There don't seem to be a lot of options, but I'll give you guys a call as soon as I know anything." Later that day I got the call from Gary. "I know this sounds crazy, but this is all I can find," he said. And it was. At three o'clock the next morning we found ourselves pulling our mountain of gear out of the trunks of two taxis at a random street corner in the middle of Cairo alongside a handful of sleepy locals, who we joined in waiting for a bus to take us to Gaza and Israel.

"Well this is different," I said to Bob, hands shoved into my pockets in the early chill of the desert morning. "After all of the wars I wouldn't have thought you could get to Israel by bus."

"I think it's kind of a new thing, like a part of the latest peace deal. At least you'll have a story to tell your grandkids," Bob chuckled. It wasn't long before our transport arrived, a local bus with its destination written in Arabic on its brow. The driver stepped out and opened the baggage department, and amidst the general confusion and heated Arabic arguments we loaded our pile of leather bags and Bob's guitar into the hold before joining the free-for-all push to get aboard. In the meantime, Gary attempted to sort out the ticket situation with the driver who didn't speak English, while a passenger who sort of did tried to translate. Eventually we took our seats, the doors blew closed, and we rumbled off towards the Suez Canal, Gaza, and Israel.

As the sun rose over the desert, the crowded bus rolled east. Local Egyptian music blared over the radio. At one point we pulled over to the side of the road where the driver and passengers all disembarked to face Mecca and pray. On a beautiful Mediterranean morning we arrived at Suez and drove on to a car ferry which took us across the canal to the Sinai, where we turned north and drove towards Gaza. Around noon we arrived at the border and disembarked. Once off the bus we retrieved our gear, and after clearing out through Egyptian immigration staggered across a one-hundred-meter strip of no-man's-land in the baking hot sun surrounded by high fences topped with coils of razor wire under the watchful eye of the Israeli army. After a thorough inspection by Israeli customs and immigration, we boarded another bus and drove on towards Tel Aviv, where we arrived in the late afternoon.

The crowded bus terminal was like a scene out of a Mel Brooks movie. No one had a clue who we were as we lumped our insane amount of luggage from the bus to the taxi stand, and after stacking it all atop of two taxis we drove off for our hotel. As we neared the hotel, we were met by a member of Bob's security team and directed to the underground carpark, where Bob slipped invisibly up to his room without any of the hungry paparazzi any the wiser. The first concert was two days away and still the bamboozled press continued to stake out the airport waiting for Dylan's arrival, not knowing we had already slipped into town through the back door.

Ah, the press. They're the same everywhere. Bob's trip to Israel was front page news, and a hungry mob of reporters was turning over every stone for a story. He had already pissed everyone off by not turning up at the airport when he was supposed to, so they were out for his blood. Before the first show, a meeting was scheduled between Dylan and the Israeli Foreign Minister. For his own reasons, and there were reasons, Bob decided to cancel the meeting. "Dylan Snubs Peres!" screamed the headlines. He'd surely stirred up a hornet's nest by not playing their game, but he'd been doing that forever, and no one could have a thicker skin than Bob Dylan. Another point which had the press on fire was Bob's religious view of the world. After *Slow Train Comin'* the world considered Dylan to be a born-again Christian. In Israel they wanted to claim him as a Jew. The press demanded to know the answer. They wanted a shot at him to ask point blank just exactly what it was he did believe. Get him to lay his cards on the table. After all, they figured, the world had a right to know! Bob gave them no joy whatsoever and let them stew in their own juices, so of course all they could come up with was pure fiction, which they made up in lieu of any substantiated facts. Once on the boat I asked him about that album, and he just shrugged and simply said, "Every country singer does a gospel album and that's mine." These hyenas would never be happy with such an answer, so he simply left them to make up what they wanted.

The first two shows at Hayarkon Park were jammed with forty thousand punters, but for some reason the gears weren't meshing properly, things were not yet in the groove and the press had a field day panning the show. The reviews had me more upset than Bob would ever be. I'd seen the effort and feeling that had gone into the shows; I'd seen the crowds screaming with joy. But the papers took views like this from a piece by Robert Hilburn of the Los Angeles Times entitled "Bad Vibes": "Hundreds left the Tel Aviv concert complaining Dylan did not interact with his audience or play the protest songs that brought him his fame in the sixties.

Israeli pop singer Shalon Hanoch wrote in the daily *Haldeshot* that he expected more substance, more contact. So many people came to hear him and he didn't even relate to them. It was as if he wasn't even there."

*Note to Bob - imagine where your career would be today if you had only taken the advice of people like Shalon Hanoch.

I opened the broad French doors and stepped out onto my jasmine scented balcony at the old British colonial King David Hotel and gazed over biblical Jerusalem, the afternoon sun reflecting off the white spires and ancient walls as they jumbled off towards the dry, barren hills in the distance. We had just arrived by bus from Tel Aviv in preparation for the outdoor sunset show, and even then, I could feel there was magic in the air.

The performance at the Sultan's Pools would have to go down, in my book at least, as one of the all-time greats. The difference between this tour and True Confessions was that Roger McGuinn of old Byrds fame had been added to the bill. In Tel Aviv, he opened the show with ten or so songs, followed by the Heartbreakers and then Dylan. Tom Petty decided to change this format, so after a couple of acoustic numbers he and his band joined McGuinn and charged into rip-roaring versions of the Byrds great old hits like "Eight Miles High", "Turn, Turn, Turn", "Mr. Tambourine Man", and "Rock and Roll Star" before cranking into their own high-octane set. The crowd was well primed and revved up by the time Dylan stepped onto the stage to join Petty, along with his three sequined, hip swinging, tambourine shaking, kick-out-the-jams Queens of Rhythm, when the tempo lifted yet again. After a dozen or so songs the Heartbreakers took a break and Bob did a solo acoustic set, with "Girl of the North Country" being a standout. The band then came back on stage and finished the show with Dylan. For the encore they played

"Knockin' On Heaven's Door", "Blowin' in the Wind", and then to the surprise of all, "Go Down Moses". Nine thousand people rose as one next to the walled city of Old Jerusalem, screaming and cheering for more as we meandered off stage into waiting limos and drove off into the night. It had been a three-hour long ripper of a show.

There weren't many nights I witnessed Bob turn up to an after-show party, but he did that night in Jerusalem. It was put on in a suite at the hotel, and the room was packed. Elliott Roberts, who managed the tour, was there along with all the band members and associated entourage as well as a lot of other people I didn't know. Kurt Loder was hanging out waiting to do an interview for *Rolling Stone* magazine. Bob was in an effusive mood, and it was good to see him relaxing with a drink and having a good time. At one point he told me to make sure I hung around until after his interview because he wanted to check something out. It was close to three in the morning when Bob and I slipped out of the room along with Victor Maymudes and Jim Callaghan, the old pro of a security hand who had been taken on for this tour. "Do you guys know how to get to the Wailing Wall?" Bob asked as we stepped into the lift.

And so there we were, the four of us walking under a full moon through the dark, deserted, cobblestone streets of the Old City with very little idea where exactly we were going. Finally, we asked directions from some machinegun-toting Israeli Army personnel manning a sandbagged security checkpoint. They weren't going to let us through, but in the end decided we weren't terrorists and pointed out the way. We finally reached that hallowed place, totally deserted and eerily quiet. We crossed a broad plaza and reached a low railing which separated us from the remains of this revered limestone structure, parts of which are said to date back to the time of King Solomon. Victor and Jim followed Bob in putting on the traditional Jewish headgear they found in a box next to the gate which led to the wall. "You coming?" Victor asked. "No, I'll watch from here," I replied. I figured I wasn't Jewish and knew very little about the wall and what it meant, so I just stayed put and watched with interest. After a while the guys wandered back and we all returned up the hill to the hotel.

That afternoon on the flight to Zurich I read a newspaper review of Bob's visit to Israel. I showed it to my partner sitting next to me.

Dylan's Ways Disgust Israelis

Jerusalem – American singer Bob Dylan was panned for his music and his manners after performing listlessly in Tel Aviv and rejecting the red-carpet welcome for his first concert tour in Israel.

Dylan had been stepping on toes since he arrived last Friday.

He did not show up for a traditional Sabbath meal held in his honor, missed an appearance on a television talk show and failed to turn up for a guided tour of Tel Aviv by mayor Shlomo Lahat.

Then he cancelled meetings with Israeli Foreign Minister Simon Peres.

"Dylan just said he couldn't make it and that was it," a Foreign Ministry spokesman said.

Dylan also cancelled a visit to the Wailing Wall – the last remnant of the ancient Jewish temple destroyed by the Romans in AD 70.

His behavior in Israel has drawn scathing reviews in the Israeli press, which panned the singer's performance before 40,000 fans on Saturday night, using words such as "boring", "monotonous", "flat" and "withdrawn".

> Before seeing reviews, Dylan acknowledged his performance had been sluggish. "I just couldn't get things rolling on stage," said the bearded singer, who had travelled for twelve hours by private bus from Egypt so he could see the country.
>
> "Maybe it was just that I was tired – jet lagged or something. But it happens some nights when you feel like you are on a sinking boat."
>
> Dylan wasn't so willing to concede a problem in the area of song selection. "I don't understand this 'hits' business," he said forcibly. "I never think about whether a song is a hit. I don't even know what has been a hit in some places. Besides, you can't guess what an audience wants to hear."
>
> However, on Monday night he was cheered by 9,000 at an outdoor concert in Jerusalem when he sang such favorites as "The Times They Are a-Changing" and "Like a Rolling Stone".
>
> Dylan has visited Israel before, but always in secret.

"You see what I mean? Like I told you before...if they can't find the real story, they'll just make things up to suit themselves." Later on, in the Rolling Stone interview he did that night at the King David, Kurt Loder quoted Bob as saying, "I don't do those kind of things anyway — meeting dignitaries and stuff. Television's not my thing, so I wouldn't do that, either. I can't see why everybody gets so mad over something that never would have happened anyway."

11
Temples in Flames Part II

Starry-eyed an' laughing as I recall when we were caught
Trapped by no track of hours for they hanged suspended
As we listened one last time an' we watched with one last look
Spellbound an' swallowed 'til the tolling ended
Tolling for the aching whose wounds cannot be nursed
For the countless confused, accused, misused, strung-out ones an' worse
An' for every hung-up person in the whole wide universe
An' we gazed upon the chimes of freedom flashing
- Bob Dylan, "Chimes of Freedom"

Arriving in Zurich, everyone seemed to breathe a collective sigh of relief. In Israel it was like we were bugs under a microscope. "It feels like the tour is finally starting," said Stan Lynch, the drummer. I went to the airport and picked up Vanessa and Clara, who ran to meet me, her clear little beach sandals slapping on the shiny floor, her tattered Nanny held in one of her outstretched hands as she bubbled and chirped about her big adventure on the plane. The following morning, we stepped out of our hotel to where the five big black tour coaches were waiting. Bob had his own bus, as did Tom Petty. The Queens of Rhythm had a bus and the band and tour managers had theirs. The last one was technically to be used for visiting VIP's but soon became known as "Vanessa's Bus", and this is the coach the three of us settled into.

And so started our once in a lifetime tour of Europe, where we crisscrossed the continent from north to south and east to west, staying at nothing but the most elegant of five star hotels. We played a show in still-communist East Berlin in front of at least one hundred thousand people. We played in Scandinavia and in Italy. We traversed the Alps several times, and had days off in many of the most interesting cities in Europe, with Bob more than once asking me how Vanessa and Clara were enjoying the trip.

The shows only got better each night. For anyone like me who grew up in the sixties and were into the Byrds, the performances were even more scintillating, as many of their best songs were originally written by Dylan. Tom Petty also had a soft spot for the music of the Byrds, and the Heartbreakers set was filled with their songs. Dylan would also do a solo acoustic set mid-show, which only added to the variety. My personal highlight was in Rotterdam, when Bob, Roger McGuinn and I were chatting next to the stage. "Would you mind if I put in a request?" I asked.

"Sure...what is it?" Bob replied.

"I'd love to hear you guys do "Chimes of Freedom"," I said. After a brief discussion between themselves Bob said, "Sure, why not?" And then later on in the night Roger joined Bob, and they played it.

And still the reviews were mostly negative. I just had to shake my head in disbelief. "What do these people want," I thought to myself, "egg in their beer?"

This was a big tour, and it really was like a travelling circus. The road crew who made all of this happen were an entity all to their own. They rode on their own buses, stayed at different hotels, and moved at separate times. When the last encore was played and we were long gone, they remained to break down the set and load it all into the trucks before high-tailing it to the next venue where it all had to be set up again. Catering played a huge part, because this army of technicians, worker-bees, drivers, runners, producers, managers, hair stylists, wardrobe personnel, accountants, musicians and schooner crew all had to be fed. These guys were all hardened pros who had seen it all before and weren't charmed by big names or fancy reputations. They just got on with their work, kept to themselves, and basically accepted their position in the over-all scheme of things. Vanessa, Clara and I, however, were a sort of mystery to them all. They could never really figure us out. For a start, I wasn't on the payroll; I wasn't an employee who was hired to do a certain task. All they knew was we were there because Bob wanted us to be, and so we were treated with a certain kind of courteous respect.

Then there was the intrigue. Whenever any group of people are put together for a length of time, you are going to have personality conflicts, rumor and innuendo. The Temples in Flames Tour had more maneuvering, plotting, and conspiracy than a mediaeval court. And naturally it all started at the top. We are talking about Bob Dylan, after all, who is as complex a character as will ever be found striding the surface of this planet. Back in the days of our first voyages together I had no idea of the other dimensions of the man. We just took each other at face value; we were partners plain and simple. But in the other world of Bob, and especially on this particular tour, I came to see the power he wielded and the position he held in the ranks of modern men. He could pick up a phone and anyone from princes to presidents would stop whatever they were doing to take the call. And so, in the background, simmering on the back burner, were various individuals in his personal entourage who for whatever reason had access to Bob and attempted to leverage their position to try and get to the top of the totem pole. At one level things were friendly and respectful, but beneath the surface there was an undercurrent of Machiavellian machinations and maneuvering which was hard to escape. Personally, I tried not to get involved. For his part I almost think Bob enjoyed what was going on, and in fact every now and then when things got a bit dull, he would give the pot a stir just to liven up proceedings.

So, what was my job? It was a sort of undefined role, I suppose. Mostly I was there as a sort of occasional sidekick. Sometimes after a show Bob might simply want to take a late-night stroll through an empty city, so he would call me and we'd slip out of the hotel for an hour or two. Or on a day off we might visit a quiet bar I had located where I knew he wouldn't be hassled. Otherwise, I just fit in where I could. Jim Callaghan was Bob's main security man. A good-natured Englishman, he had been around rock and roll for years, and had done a lot of big tours. He worked for the Rolling Stones, and had also done security for Queen as well as many others. Rumor had it he was ex-SAS - I'm sure he knew how to look after himself - but his greatest gift was his way with people. Jim had a knack of getting straight to the heart of someone's nature from the moment he met them, whether weirdo or rock star. He respected people, and rarely had a bad word to say about anyone. He was an expert at defusing a tense situation, which he always did with a smile. Anyway, on show days and when travelling I would give Jim a hand. If, for example, the caravan stopped in the middle of the night in the heart of the Alps to fuel up, and Bob decided to check out the souvenir shop or sit down and have a cup of coffee, Jim and I would be there. I learned there was a skill to knowing how to look out for Bob without being aggressive or obnoxious. There was an art to being relaxed and casual, but also being aware. For me, being around Jim was a real education. One thing Jim did well was deal with the wackos, and on the road with Bob I learned there are a lot of them out there. There was a woman who called herself Sarah Dylan and was in the front row of almost every show. Many times, she would stay at the same hotel as us, even in places like East Berlin. If we would go for a walk, she could be seen mysteriously following us. When there were people around like this, the first thing Jim would do was introduce himself to them. He was on a first name basis with these sorts, almost like he was trying to get inside their heads.

Callaghan also had a mischievous sense of humor. We were in Copenhagen in this classic little mahogany paneled hotel, and we had just finished a show and everyone was tucked in for the night. I had just stepped out of the lift heading to the bar for a nightcap, when I ran into Jim and he said there was someone outside I should have a chat with. I walked out the front door with him and he introduced me to a young dark-haired Dane. "Hello," the fellow said, "I am Oscar. Oscar Presley."

"Oh," I remarked, catching a glimpse of Callaghan's effort to keep a straight face, "any relation to Elvis?"

"Yes, as a matter of fact. I am his son."

"What can I do to help, Oscar?" I ask, trying my best to look serious.

"Well, this gentleman here told me you were the person I should approach on the matter of a check. Mr. Dylan owes me some money," he said quite seriously.

"A check?" I responded, raising my eyebrows. "And what would this payment be for?"

"Didn't the gentleman tell you? For writing 'Blowin' in the Wind'. I wrote the song for him and he never paid me." I took a piece of paper out of my pocket and scribbled a note. "And 'The Times They Are a-Changing'. I wrote that as well," he added.

"So, you would like to be paid for these two songs. Anything else?" I asked, using all of my self-control to keep a straight face.

"No, just those two," Oscar answered cheerily.

"Well, I'll have to check with our accountants," I said in a business-like tone.

"I was told you are the accountant," he stated questioningly.

"Oh yes, of course. What I meant was, I will have to discuss the matter with my associates. I have your details here, and we will get back to you," I said before making a hasty retreat. Inside the lobby Jim finally cracked. "Thanks for the introduction, mate," I said with a smile. "Now before I was interrupted, I was on my way to the bar. And after that little episode, I think you owe me a drink."

From Copenhagen the tour headed north to Sweden, crossed the Baltic Sea by ferry to Helsinki, turned south and wound its way across Germany, before traversing the Alps. After a few shows in the north of Italy we eventually checked into the Rome Hilton, famous for its lofty perch overlooking the Eternal City. A day off was scheduled, so Vanessa, Clara and I went out to see the Spanish Steps, the Colosseum, and the Vatican before ending up in a long queue of German tourists waiting to enter the Sistine Chapel. When it comes to long lines, I am not a patient man, and throughout the day I had encountered enough of them. When I spotted a comfy-looking taverna across the road, I told the girls they could meet me there afterwards.

A little while later they found me anchored in my little cove underneath the grape vines. They sat down and I ordered a round of drinks. "How was it, Clara?" I asked my daughter. "Did you find it interesting?"

"Yes, it was beautiful. And you know what? I spoke to God, and he told me I was going to have a little sister!"

Vanessa and I looked at each other with masked surprise. After everything Vanessa had been through, specialists in Australia had told us the odds of her getting pregnant again naturally were a million to one. "I know you really want a little sister, Clara, but sometimes in life you have to learn that things don't always happen as you want them to," Vanessa replied. Clara only smiled and shook her head.

"Don't worry, mummy. Everything will be okay; you just wait and see."

Clara was so sure that we didn't have the heart to dissuade her. But as the saying goes, "God works in mysterious ways", and this little incident will play a major part in the ultimate unfolding of this tale, as you will see.

After stopping in Milan, we wound back up into the Alps again to do a concert in Locarno, Switzerland. It was an outdoor show performed in a cobblestone piazza in the heart of this medieval city, and that night it happened to be freezing cold and raining. It was a strange night, to be sure, a night with peculiar energies riding the storm gusts through the dark narrow streets of that ancient burg, and even before the show started, I could feel something strange was afoot. Bob had caught a cold, his voice sounded raw and raspy, but beyond that he was in a squally mood the likes of which I had never seen before. Years later I read Bob's own account of what happened in the middle of the concert that night. In his book *Chronicles*, he talks about a sort of revelation that took place which no one else could see. It was a metamorphosis, a whole new energy "coming from a hundred different angles, completely unpredictable ones." This transformation occurred right in front of everyone, yet no one would have noticed. I was standing only a few meters away, and I can say in all honesty I didn't see it. I do remember it stood out as a dark and stormy night, the kind of a night when strange riders could have been approaching as the wind began to howl.

We walked off the stage in Locarno and straight onto the bus, drove all night and checked into our quaint Paris hotel in the early hours of the morning. After back-to-back shows in Paris and Brussels we crossed the channel to London, encamping ourselves at the very posh Mayfair Hotel. Seven shows were booked for the UK, and all of them were sold out. He probably could have played a few more if he wanted to. Three gigs were played in Birmingham followed by the last four performed at Wembley Arena in London. In Birmingham

George Harrison and Jeff Lynne turned up to see the show, and it was all very casual. No fanfare, no minders, no big deal - just a couple of old friends turning up to check out the show.

Backstage in London, Ringo Starr told me he collected tour laminates, and politely asked me if I would give him mine. I could hardly refuse. I had a hell of a time getting another one out of Al Santos,

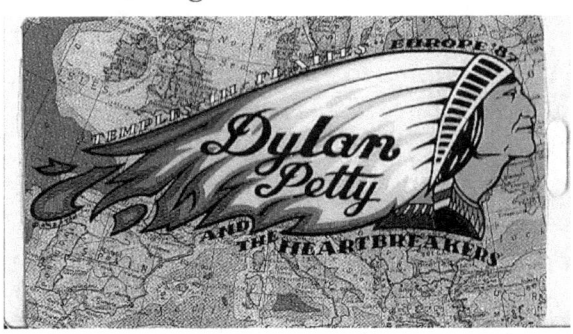

The Magic Passport...Access All Areas.

though. "What was I supposed to do, tell Ringo...no?" I asked. Al shook his head and scowled, but eventually gave me another one. On the last night at Wembley, George showed up again, and along with Ronnie Wood joined Bob on stage for the encore. And that was it. The last show was played, the band left the stage for the last time, the gear was broken down and packed away and everyone scattered with the wind. I was kind of expecting some sort of end of tour party, but there wasn't one. It wasn't exactly like the end of the last Queen tour Jim Callaghan told me about, when Freddie and the boys took the crew out to the most expensive brothel in London, all expenses paid. Now that was rock and roll!

Vanessa's parents had travelled to the UK from Australia for a holiday and had rented a flat on the South Coast, so she and Clara said goodbye to everyone and caught the train to the seaside town of Worthing. Bob told me he wanted to hang out in London for a while and asked me to stick around, so I did.

Nothing happened for the first couple of days, and I just lounged about my room waiting for the phone to ring.

Like Charlie Watts said, life on the road isn't all rock and roll. On the afternoon of the second day over a game of chess Bob mentioned that someone had given him the name of a great little Indian restaurant in Soho. He was keen to get out, so I made a booking. At the appointed time, Victor went to the lobby to organize a cab while I met Bob at his room. I could never have predicted what was going to happen next. Instead of walking through the lobby as we stepped out of the elevator, Bob made a sharp turn to his left towards the hotel restaurant. "Can we get to the street this way?" he asked.

"It's the restaurant, but yeah, you can get to the street," I answered. So off we went on one of Bob's patented detours. Heads turned as we wandered through the eatery; we exited out onto the street on a cool October night. Looking to my left I noticed a swarm of people crushed together outside the Mayfair Theatre, and then remembered there was a charity benefit on that night with stars like Eric Clapton and Mark Knofler attending. I quickly realized it was a gaggle of paparazzi waiting at the entrance for the celebrities to arrive. My next thought was to get Bob back inside the hotel before he was spotted, but I was too late. The first to notice was a balding swarthy Mediterranean type with a close-cropped beard. I saw him turn his head, do a double take, and then come churning towards us like a Mako shark coming in for the kill. In an instant the others were hot on his heels in pursuit.

Now this is where it got weird. Instead of just going back into the safety of the hotel, Bob clutched the top of his grey hoodie, and bending over at the waist started staggering down the sidewalk like the Elephant Man with this feeding frenzy of camera-flashing paparazzi surrounding us. I, of course, was freaking right out. I kept thinking about what Callaghan would do in such a situation. "Whatever you do, don't hit the bastards," he had said to me once. "Don't even touch them - they'll sue your ass off!" So as much as I wanted to, I at least refrained from getting overly physical. Bob continued staggering down the sidewalk like a prize fighter covering up in the clenches, performing a sort of Dylanesque rope-a-dope with this rolling maul of photographers squeezing us like Black Friday shoppers fighting for a bargain. Next, he staggered out into the middle of the street with this demented mob continuing to push and shove and shout and cuss, and all I could do was keep next to him and try and get him some breathing space. This went on for close to ten minutes. Every now and then Bob would call out in a muffled voice asking if the car was anywhere in sight, when I could only say no. I was between a rock and a hard place. I couldn't leave him alone, but I desperately needed an escape vehicle. Finally, Victor noticed what was going on and pulled up with the cab. The door flew open and we piled Bob in, covering him as if he were the President of the USA, flashes continuing to go off as we drove away. Between them they would have taken a hundred rolls of film, but I doubt they got one decent shot. (Years later a saw one of those shots in a magazine in my doctors waiting room. It could have been anyone.)

Not much was said afterwards. Just another night in the life of Bob Dylan, I suppose. We went and had our curry, and then I suggested we take the underground back to the hotel, which we did without any further untoward incidents. The people on the train couldn't believe their eyes, but they were very well behaved.

The morning after our curry-night adventure, Victor rang me. He told me Bob had arranged to see someone in the afternoon and would like me to come along. Meet him at his room at two, he told me. If Victor knew anything more about it, he wasn't letting on. This time when we stepped out of the lift there were no detours; we walked straight through the lobby into a waiting limousine. It was a grey October day in London; a black and white day devoid of color, like something you'd see in a 1930's movie. Raindrops trickled down the limo's crystal-clear windows as we splashed our way out of town. Nobody was saying much as Bob stared passively out through his black Ray Bans. He was in one of his pensive moods, and both Victor and I knew enough to keep ourselves quiet. I had no idea where we were bound, what our course was or when our landfall would be. All I knew was we were heading west. I didn't really care anyway. At least we were going for a drive.

We left London behind and after an hour or so emerged into the green residential countryside. Eventually there was some discussion as to which turning to take, and a little while later we entered through the gates of what looked to be an extensive estate. The limo wound slowly through the beautifully manicured grounds interspersed with tall stands of oak before finally pulling up before a classical Victorian mansion with spires and steeples and stained glass. As we stepped out of the car and I looked around the lush surroundings, something in the back of my mind told me I had seen this place before. And then I remembered the cover of the album *All Things Must Pass*, and somehow, I just knew. We were at George Harrison's house.

We were all greeted cordially by George's lovely American wife Olivia, who after exchanging pleasantries invited us inside and offered us tea, which we took in a cozy little nook off the kitchen. She told us George wasn't actually in at the moment, but we should feel free to have a good look around the place. She gave us a brief history of the one hundred and twenty room manor known as Friar Park, which George had bought back in the early days of the Beatles when an order of nuns had allowed the place to fall into disrepair. Since those heady days of the sixties the estate had become a passion for George, she said, where he had spent untold hours (and money) getting it up to its current elegant standard. I wasn't simply impressed...I was blown away. The dining hall was massive, with a table and seating for maybe twenty-four people. Outside there were neat pathways which led off in every direction and little signs which implored visitors to "Please walk on the grass." The estate covered sixty-four acres, so there was plenty to explore. There was even an underground sea grotto with a secret entrance and a miniature sandstone model of the Matterhorn. But what I was most interested in, besides the stunning architecture and the overall grandeur of the place, was George's in-house recording studio and its centerpiece, a giant glass cabinet which covered one whole wall displaying every guitar he had ever owned.

After an hour or so Bob was getting antsy. I knew the signs well. He wasn't used to waiting around for anyone...not even a member of the Beatles. He tried to make an exit, saying he had to be somewhere, but Olivia would hear nothing of the kind. She was cooking a roast lamb, George would be home shortly, and they both would be most put out if we all didn't stay and join them for dinner. It wasn't often that Bob didn't get his way, but he had come up against a formidable opponent and had to do the gentlemanly thing and acquiesce.

The dull pewter sky was quickly fading into the autumn night when a pair of headlights wound their way up the drive. George was home, accompanied by his ever-present mate Jeff Lynne. We met in the entry hall and George was most apologetic for being late. Dressed in dark corduroys, a white tee-shirt and tweed jacket, hair tending towards long and greying and clean shaven, he smiled and shook hands all-round - his Liverpudlian accent as thick as ever. Jeff was well mannered and quiet and seemed to be happy to stay in the background.

Bob smiled and was immediately at ease as we headed off upstairs towards the studio. Victor, Jeff and I followed along but gave them space. Meetings like this are something confined to history books and should not be interfered with. George was full of youthful exuberance as he showed us his studio and guitars, telling us excitedly about the projects Jeff and he were working on. After a while the call came from downstairs that supper was ready, and we all made our way back down to the dining hall.

The long dinner table had been laid out immaculately. Table cloth, silverware, candelabra…the works. The centerpiece was a huge leg of lamb laid out on a silver serving tray. Olivia seated us, with George at the head of the table, then me to his immediate left and Bob next to me. And so there I was, ensconced between these two heroes of modern-day culture. I tried not to get too carried away. After all it was only a dinner party; there was food to eat and wine to drink and conversation to be made, and what else could I do but join in and be part of it, have fun but at all costs make sure to keep my foot out of my mouth.

Olivia was overjoyed to be able to entertain guests in that fabulous room. George was engaging and light hearted, bringing the best out in Bob, who could be difficult when caught up in foreign surroundings. But George wouldn't let him, and soon had us all charmed with his sharp sense of humor. I'm sure there are those who would like to know what lofty conversations took place between those two on this special night, but to be truthful there wasn't much of anything earth-shatteringly significant, except a sort of brief nod towards certain powerful forces that pull the strings of the world, and how you take them on at your own peril. This passed over us like a dark shadow, but it was my feeling that these two knew far more about this subject than they were willing to let pass around a casual dinner party. Finally, it was time to go, and it was quite late when we headed off in our limo.

As we drove into the night, I tried to fathom what I had just experienced. Superficially I felt humbled and incredibly privileged to have been there. But there was something beyond those feelings, something far deeper. For the first time in my life I felt as if I had been brought down to earth, that my own mortality was laid out before my very eyes.

I suddenly had been shown a glimpse of a level I realized I would never reach, no matter how hard I tried. Not in a material sense…material things had never meant much to me. Up to that moment I had always had the confidence that anything in life was within my reach; all I needed was the desire to go and get it. I was where I was only because that is where I wanted to be. The previous few hours had highlighted my limitations to me, and it was a shock to the system. After a long silence, as we sped through the night. I tried to express these feelings to Bob. He quietly listened and did nothing more than stare at me through the darkness before gazing out the window once more. Never before would I have conceded that I had an allocated slot in the pecking order of things, but that night I was put in my place. And I knew it. My youthful arrogance and idealistic visions had been left in tatters. I would have to get used to it. There was more to come.

And that was it. Bob flew off to the States, and I took the train down to Worthing. As I rode through the English countryside, I reflected back to that hotel room in New York, and all that had happened since. Thirty shows over forty-nine days in twenty-eight cities and a lot of miles in between. As I looked around the graffiti-covered carriage at the lager-swilling louts and old man reading the paper next to me, I knew that not one of these people would believe me if I told them what I had just been doing. And why would I want to tell them anyway? For Vanessa, Clara, and I it would be a trip we would never forget, and forever appreciate what a great gesture it was to be included as we were. And Bob? More than likely he would have filed it away in the back pages of his memory before he got to Heathrow.

12

Against All Odds

*"It is certain my conviction gains infinitely,
The moment another soul believes in it."*
- Novalis

From Mayfair to Worthing is a big jump. Talk about instant reality check! One minute I was living in a thousand-pound-a-night cocooned world of protected luxury, and the next eating greasy fish and chips in a dreary seaside rental with worn carpets that smelled of too many summer holidays. Frank and Jean, my in-laws, were the greatest; I loved them to death. They were doing their best to give us a good time. They had returned to their homeland on holiday, and they were equally disappointed with our situation. English weather in bitterly cold and grey late October is a far cry from balmy Western Australia. After a couple of bone-numbing days and freezing nights huddled around an electric bar heater, we left that strange seaside town and went to visit some old family friends who resided in a cottage in Bridgnorth, a quaint village nestled on the banks of the Severn River in the Shropshire countryside.

This was more like it! John and Shirley Baldie were fantastic hosts. They reminded me of oversized Hobbits. They did their best to fatten us up with big country breakfasts and cakes and scones and fresh cream and endless cups of tea. Clara and Vanessa and I took long walks in those late autumn days, skies blue and crisp and windblown, the fallen red oak leaves crunching underfoot. Frank smiled with youthful exuberance as we strolled to the ancient local pub for a pint or two and a game of cribbage next to the roaring open fire.

Amidst all of this good cheer, however, a drama began to unfold. Something we all had believed to be an impossibility became a distinct reality. Vanessa began to exhibit all the symptoms of being pregnant. But try as we may she couldn't be made to accept it. She had good reason to doubt the evidence: she had only one fallopian tube left, and it was severely damaged. She'd been told the chances of her getting pregnant naturally again were astronomical. Yet she was displaying all the signs. Vanessa's parents and I persuaded her to do a test. "Okay, I'll do it just to show you are all wrong," she said. Then, when it came up positive, she wouldn't believe it. The thing is, even a cheap off-the-shelf drugstore pregnancy test is rarely wrong when showing positive. This was fantastic news, something we should all be celebrating. But no matter how hard we tried to convince her, she remained in denial. Eventually we took her to the local hospital, where a doctor did another test which confirmed what we all knew. Vanessa was indeed pregnant. And still she said they were wrong.

Even Clara had a go. "I told you in Rome that God said he was giving me a sister, Mummy," she said. "Why don't you believe it?" This made us all stop and scratch our heads. Yes, the timing was right... she could have indeed conceived in Rome. And yet, try as we may to convince her, Vanessa refused to acknowledge the irrefutable fact she was going to have another child.

I tried to distance myself from this emotional irrationality. Time was on my side. There would come a point when Vanessa would have no choice but to accept the facts. What I had to do was figure out how we would deal with this unexpected situation. First of all, I knew it would be insanity for Vanessa to return to the West Indies to have this child. To me the answer was obvious - she had to return to Australia with her parents and have the baby there. She not only had plenty of friends and family to support her, but she also had one of the best public health systems in the world to look after her, and it wouldn't cost a cent. To me it was completely logical, a real no-brainer. Unfortunately, clear thinking was not an attribute of Vanessa's at that particular moment in time.

The situation dragged on for several days, and made what should have been something great into a war of wills. "Our home is with you on the boat!" Vanessa would argue. "I'm not bloody pregnant, and it's only a waste of money for me to go back to Australia. You'll see. I'll be flying back to the boat within a month." Obviously, her hormones were going haywire and there was no possibility of a rational conversation. I had never seen her like this. Talk about headstrong! It got to the point where I figured the only way I could get her on the plane was to knock her out and carry her on board myself.

In the end we persuaded her to go, and I flew back to the West Indies on my own. There were tears and hugs and promises and that hollow feeling of separation as I left my family and went to board my plane. For them it would have been equally as upsetting; their life was aboard a schooner on the other side of the Atlantic Ocean and they were not returning to it. With nothing more than the few things they brought with them in their suitcase they were leaving all they knew behind and were travelling to the opposite end of the earth. Granted it was to the warmth and safety of her parent's home, but it was as far away as you could get from all they had come to love and treasure.

Vanessa and Clara...happy days.

Stepping off the plane in St. Maarten the humid tropical blast instantly let me know I was no longer in England. A taxi dropped me off and I walked across the shallows to Snoopy Island. All was well aboard *Water Pearl*; my good friend and part time crew member Bert Jones had kept a good eye on her. And now, for the first time in years, I was alone. Not only that, I had no idea what was going to happen next. The day-charter business had been good while it lasted, but that was now yesterday's news. I missed Vanessa and Clara, and wondered when I would see them again. So, there I sat, night after night down below in the golden glow of our new interior, searching for a sign as to what was going to happen next.

Two things were certain. The boat couldn't just sit around and do nothing. I would have to work it to pay the bills. And there would be no way we could live aboard with a newborn child. It was tough enough with a five-year-old. It was obvious we would have to find a place ashore, which was yet another expense. And where would that be? St. Maarten? Bequia? I'd been there, done that. I had the feeling that the walls were closing in, like I had ridden up a box canyon and noticed I was being surrounded by Indians.

There were other possibilities. I could try and convince Bob to buy me out, but I didn't like my chances. After all, he was batting on a good wicket. He knew and trusted me and never had to worry about the boat as he knew it was in my interest to look after it. To be fair, our partnership had worked well for both of us, but life is fluid. Things change, and what was good yesterday is not always desirable tomorrow. The last option, of course, would be to sell the boat, but it was one which neither of us really wanted to consider. Bob liked the idea of the boat being there for him when he had time to use it. I probably looked at it a little more romantically. It just didn't feel like the story should simply end with a handful of cash.

What was left? The only thing I could think of was to use the boat for what she was built for and go sailing, have an adventure, and keep the movie rolling. The more I thought about it, the more it became clear. The South Pacific was beckoning. One night in early December I sat down and wrote a letter to my friend Gary Danielson from the schooner *Aafe*, who I heard had married a Tahitian girl and was running a charter business out of Huahine in the Society Islands. It was a shot in the dark, but "you can't catch fish if you don't put out a line," as Bamu would say. Maybe there was a way we could work together. I had to explore the options.

It wasn't long before I received a reply. Gary was surprised to have heard from me after all the years, and was very positive in his response. He had indeed married a local girl, had two children, and was making ends meet by chartering in Huahine. "I can't promise anything, but I think we could work something out for you here," he said. "If you knew how cool this place was you would be here already." Was this the sign I was looking for? I wasn't sure, but it was the first hint I'd had in a while. Many pieces of the puzzle still had to be found, but at least it was a positive indication.

Christmas came and went and it was a very lonely experience. Bamu returned from Bequia, and we did the occasional day trip for La Samana to keep some cash coming in. As the days passed the thought of sailing west began to take root. We remained moored to our little spot in the lagoon, and in between charters I started to make serious preparations for the five-thousand-mile trip through the Panama Canal to Tahiti. We overhauled the rigging, replacing blocks and halyards where needed, and Bamu continued to keep the paint and varnish up. As the days rolled by, I felt more and more confident the logjam was beginning to break up and my course was becoming clear.

Then one evening came the shout of a familiar voice from the shore only a few meters away. "Ahoy *Water Pearl*!

Permission to come aboard!" I walked up to the bow and looked down at the person standing knee deep in the calm water. I recognized the tall figure straight away. "Damn...if it isn't John Degnar," I thought. I pulled myself ashore in the dinghy and brought my friend aboard.

How could I forget the first time I met "Johnny Danger"? It was at Antigua Race week in '77, and I was visiting the schooner *Lusty* for afternoon cocktails with RP, Capt. Crank, and crew aboard that classic, round-the-world Alden schooner when this tall, longhaired Apache appeared on the quay at Nelson's Dockyard. "Who let you off the reservation?" was all RP said as the smiling, turquoise adorned character climbed aboard amidst other jocular greetings from the rest of the crew. It came to pass that Danger had sailed at various times aboard the *Lusty* as she slowly circumnavigated the globe. He fit right in with these hard-partying rascals, and sailed on with them from Antigua to St. Barths, where we shared many a drink at Le Select. I hadn't seen him for several years, and it was good to catch up with him again. "So, what's been going on?" I asked as he climbed aboard.

"Oh, nothing serious," he smiled with a flash of white teeth. "I decided to take a break from New Mexico and check out the Caribbean again. I was over at the bar at the Kim Sha when one of the boys mentioned you were tied up here, so I thought I'd drop in to say hello. I even brought along a bottle of rum...if you're interested." I didn't need much encouragement. We settled in for the night telling yarns and having a laugh. John was looking for a place to stay, so I invited him aboard. Danger came aboard for a couple of days, which turned into weeks. He fitted right in, paid his way, helped out where he could, and kept the good times rolling. As the days passed by, I began to sound him out on his thoughts of sailing to the Pacific, and he was all for it. For me to make this trip I needed a crew that was going to contribute to the expenses, and John fit the bill perfectly. He was single, knew his way around a boat, had a bit of loose change in his pocket, and was up for the adventure. In the evenings over a few drinks we began to put a plan together.

What we needed were a couple more free spirits like Danger to turn this plan into a reality. It might have been during the party frenzy of the new version of the St. Barths Regatta, or maybe it was at the bar at the Kim Sha - the details are a bit foggy - but somewhere along the line Willy Halsey found out we were working up a voyage to the Pacific and said he was keen to jump on board. He sat down with John and me and we worked out a potential departure date. It seemed like everything was falling into place. It was time for me to talk to Bob.

I flew to LA, rented a car, and drove out to Bob's place in Malibu. This was not something we could discuss over the phone. We were partners, after all, and if this trip was going to happen, I needed Bob to go along with it. It was near the end of February and the Malibu skies were clear and cool. I hung out for a couple of days and we kicked things around.

The afternoon sun canted west over the Pacific, throwing a soft light through the kitchen windows as we sat drinking strong coffee at his old pinewood table. "You know, the Caribbean has been great, but after fourteen years it is time for a change of direction," I said. "With Vanessa now pregnant again I need to get closer to Australia and get more serious about raising a family. Clara needs to start school and we will need a place ashore. I can't keep doing the same old thing forever. It's time for one last adventure, one last hurrah. The boat is as ready as it will ever be; I've got the makings of a good crew as well as good business possibilities in Huahine, so to me the Pacific is the only answer."

"Yeah, man, but Tahiti is such a long way to get to, you know?" he replied after a while. I could see that Bob wasn't too excited about the idea, and it would take some convincing on my part to win this argument. We went back and forth for a while. We had reached a Mexican standoff.

"I guess the only other option, then, is to sell the boat," I sighed.

"Oh man…you don't really want to sell the boat, do you?" he stated, more than asked.

"Not really. But to me it's the only alternative." And so this is how the discussion went. In the end Bob came around to the Pacific idea, but somewhat reluctantly. He agreed to come on board for the voyage, if not physically, then at least in spirit. We shook hands on the deal. *Water Pearl* was bound for the South Seas!

13
Castles Made of Sand...

"Twenty years from now you will be more disappointed by the things you didn't do than by the ones you did do. So throw off the bowlines. Sail away from the safe harbor. Catch the Tradewinds in your sails. Explore. Dream. Discover."
~ Mark Twain

"If you cannot arrive in daylight, then stand-off well clear, and wait until dawn. After all, that's one of the things God made boats for- to wait in."
- Tristan Jones

Now comes the hard part. For thirty years I've thought about how to write this. For thirty years I've played it all back through my mind. On countless nights I'd wake up in cold sweats; I've beat myself up innumerable times. I've reconciled. I've tried to forget. In the end, all I could do is move on with my life. The how's and whys and what ifs could drive you crazy if you let them. For a while I dealt with it like Ray Bowman after a deal had fallen through, but soon found whiskey to be only a Band-Aid over a gaping wound. I eventually discovered that there is no other way out but to stand up, look in the mirror and accept responsibility. There are only a handful of people who know the facts about what really transpired in Panama, and as painful as it is, I must see things through to the end and tell what I remember of it. Then everyone can stop guessing as to what actually happened.

Willy and John were committed. Now all we needed were a couple more crew members and we could be on our way, and in Bequia at the Easter Regatta we found them. David Goldhill had circumnavigated the Caribbean with John Smith aboard the *Mermaid of Carriacou;* Trisha Mulligan was an experienced sailor out looking for adventure. Within a matter of hours everything had come together nicely. It was only Bamu who wasn't too happy about the turn of events. He would have loved to come along, and I certainly would have taken him, but he had a wife and child in Bequia and needed an income to support them, and unfortunately, I couldn't afford to pay him wages. Maybe if he had been aboard the boat still might be in Tahiti. But he wasn't.

Water Pearl sailed from Bequia in the late afternoon. I had spent the final two days saying goodbye to all the people who had been so close to me and had done so much to get me where I was. Son Mitchell, Loren, Bluesy, Athneal, Uncle Linkie, Gilbert, Herbie, Nero…the list went on and on. I even caught up with Crosby, who gave me a drunken hug. The only person I didn't see before I left was Nolly, who drifted about like a ghost and did his best to avoid me.

Kingsley and Mackie Simmons were the last to say goodbye to me. We shook hands under the almond tree in the spot where I built *Just Now*. It was a very somber and subdued send-off. It was if somehow those islanders had received a premonition of the future. I shrugged it off and went aboard, they let go the bow lines, we backed out and slowly turned west. I was disappointed I hadn't seen Bamu to say goodbye, but it was time to go. As we slowly came head to wind to hoist the sails an inflatable dinghy roared up alongside. It was Bamu. He jumped up on deck and gave us a hand in hoisting and setting the sails. Then I turned the wheel, the bow fell away towards West Cay and Bamu and I shook hands, and after a moment hugged. "Good luck," is all he said before jumping back into his dinghy. He motored off, paralleling our course for a while, checking that all was set properly and in order. And then, with one more wave he spun the dinghy around and powered back into the harbor without looking back.

I turned and gazed into the amphitheater of Admiralty Bay and watched it drop astern until we rounded West Cay and it disappeared from sight. The crew had been quiet until then, but it was Willy who broke the silence. "Hey Cappy, how about a green one?" he asked with his roguish grin.

"Sounds good to me," I smiled, and there were Heineken's all 'round as we toasted our luck and our voyage. There was a sweet Tradewind blowing through the cays, and as we eased our sheets, I took one last look over my shoulder. It would be my last glimpse of Bequia for a long, long time.

"Tahiti here we come," said John. We drank our beers and enjoyed a glorious sunset. I set the watches and we sailed south for Grenada. We were on our way.

The boat was hauled out on the big synchro-lift in Grenada. There wasn't much more to do other than giving her a clean and roll on some anti-fouling. After a couple of days, we were back in the water and I cleared for Isla Margarita, where I wanted to stock up on cheap fuel and basic foodstuffs. The crew was working out great. Everyone was getting along and did their fair share, whether it was cooking or doing any of the other daily chores. Trish took being the only girl on board very well. She was a tough cookie and took John and Willy's ribbing in her stride. David worked in well as a second navigator, and the boat herself loved sailing in the open ocean as we reached across the Galion's Passage to Isla Margarita, averaging close to nine knots.

Isla Margarita was a duty-free port, so we rented a car and stocked up on everything we thought we might need between there and Tahiti. Canned goods, rice, oats, tea, coffee, frozen sides of beef - we didn't skimp on anything. Our liquor supplies were topped up, with everything from French wine to Russian Vodka. The last stores to be brought aboard were the fresh fruits and vegies, which we organized in the shower compartment next to the galley for easy access. The final chore was to fill up on duty-free diesel. This we acquired through a grimy Dutchman who supplied us the fuel in steel jerry cans we had to transport and load while at anchor, which was a messy, tedious job. It was worth it though, because eight hundred gallons of fuel cost us the grand total of one-hundred- and sixty-dollars US.

Water Pearl felt the weight of the added stores, and settled into the water nicely. After a couple of busy but fun-filled days anchored off this laid-back Venezuelan island (the local rum was a big hit with the crew), we picked up our anchor and set sail for Panama, but with one added crew member. The crew had conspired together to acquire the boat a mascot - a beautiful green parrot, who being a female we took no time in naming Margarita.

To the northwest of Margarita lay a group of islands known as Los Roques. Although noted to be a beautiful place to visit, I didn't have any detailed charts of those islands. In fact, my charts of the whole of the Western Caribbean were very scanty indeed. On my way back to the boat from California I stopped in Miami and bought an extensive set of charts for the South Pacific, but I neglected the Caribbean. At the last minute I found I didn't even have charts for the eastern coast of Panama, so I hustled around St. Barths looking for some. Finally, it was Lulu who gave me a few he had of the approaches to Colon and the Panama Canal. Further west of the Venezuelan islands lay the notorious drug running area of Colombia known as the Guajira Peninsula, and we wanted to give this area a wide berth due to its bloodthirsty reputation of yacht hijackings and other illegal activities. Because of all these reasons we decided to shape our course clear of Los Roques and out into the middle of the Caribbean Sea on starboard tack, where we planned to then gybe onto port and reach into Panama. The broad reach, when the wind is over the helmsman's shoulder, is the most comfortable point of sail for a schooner. We were not on a straight-line course, but our extra speed and added comfort more than made up for the extra miles.

And who was in a hurry anyway? Those were the finest days of sailing I ever experienced. The boat was made for those conditions. Being close to seventy feet long and weighing over sixty tons, she reveled in that Tradewind weather. The wind blew a steady fifteen to twenty knots from the east, the seas were hardly felt by the big wooden schooner, and the skies were sunny and clear. We were averaging one hundred and eighty miles a day. The vessel felt like a lively spring colt let loose in the pasture, loping along and never wanting to stop. In the daytime we hoisted the big rectangular fisherman's stays'l, which filled most of the area between the two masts, and on those legs, we really felt like we were flying, the seawater hissing past to leeward.

During the day, when not at the wheel, the crew spent their time making "baggywrinkles". These were an old-time sailing device tied up into the rigging to prevent chafe. With our sheets well eased, the mainsail and foresail lay heavily onto the lee rigging, which after a time would cause the steel wire to chafe through the Dacron sails. The baggywrinkles formed a sort of cushion between wire and sail. We wove these bottlebrush-like contraptions out of short lengths of cheap Manila rope, and Willy was the best weaver in the crew, more than likely because it kept him busy. When we left Margarita, he decided to quit smoking, so he left with no cigarettes. He didn't hold out long, because after a day or so he started to "Jones" bigtime. No one else aboard smoked, so out of desperation he started rolling up the scraps of Manila and smoking them, which I'm sure did nothing more than give him a big headache.

After four perfect days of sailing we were nearing Panama. Our Sat Nav, which I had installed before we left St. Maarten, was working perfectly. Unlike a modern GPS, which will continually update a position, the Sat Nav of the eighties only identified your position when a satellite was passing overhead, which in our case was about every four hours. Our radar, on the other hand, was on the fritz and a top priority to be repaired while we were in Panama. On the morning of our fifth day out we spotted land to port, which was a tall range of mountains that ran to the south along the isthmus. All day long we ran before a light wind, expecting to reach the canal at any time. Sunset came, and it was one of the most dramatic any of us had ever seen. Large, jet black clouds banked up to the west. The water, too, seemed to fade into black. Underneath the clouds a blood-red sun stared at us like the Great Eye of Mordor. If this wasn't an omen of things to come then there never was one, but the five of us didn't pick up on it at all. I went below and put Hendrix's "Voodoo Chile" onto the stereo, and turned it up loud.

Just about that time we hooked a nice tuna, which Trish took below to cook up for dinner. About eight o'clock (20:00) we picked up the navigation lights of the canal. Numerous big ships were coming and going, and we were simply following them in. We decided to wait until we were anchored inside the harbor to eat, but began to rue that decision when it seemed like it was taking forever to get there. Willy was particularly anxious because he couldn't wait to get ashore to buy a pack of cigarettes.

Eventually we spotted the long breakwater which formed the entrance to the Panama Canal. A myriad of flashing lead lights greeted us, and it was all rather confusing. The wind had sprung up, and the night seemed particularly dark as there was no moon. There was also a lot of shipping traffic, which kept us on the lookout. Because of all this it took us a while to get all of the sails down and properly furled. It was finally around midnight when we were all squared away and turned towards the entrance of the canal. David and I then went below to check the chart. Back on deck we picked up a series of directional lights which seemed to be leading us into the canal. With the motor just ticking over we cautiously followed them in. The boys stood in the bow with our bright searchlight scanning the water ahead. "Come on ahead...it's like highway A1A," were the clear words from forward. Trish was standing aft, just forward of the mainmast. She wandered back next to me and said, "This doesn't look right." I tended to agree. We were moving very slowly, but ahead all I could see was darkness, with no sign of an entrance at all.

And then I saw it. "Holy shit!" I shouted as I threw the engine into full astern. It wasn't the entrance that caught my eye. Over my left shoulder I glimpsed a breaking wave. "We're going up on a fucking reef!" I yelled.

The boys quickly rushed to the stern. "We're okay Cappy...we're okay," Willy was saying. The 125 hp Gardner was giving all she was worth as we backed into the steep swells. I was at the point of almost believing it was just a close shave when it happened. The stern lifted high to a feathering wave, and when we dropped there was a crunching sound and the next thing I knew the wheel was lying at my feet on the deck. The rudder had been smashed off. "Oh fuck! The rudder's gone!" I screamed into the wind.

"It's okay...we're still alright," Willy yelled, trying to convince me.

But I knew different. We were screwed. With the rudder gone and no steerage, the stern of the boat swung hard to starboard, bringing us broadside to the waves. I threw the engine into full ahead. It was our last hope. But it didn't matter. The next wave broke and drove us broadside into the reef. And then all hell broke loose.

My first reaction was to do something to get us off the reef. But that wasn't my first thought. My first thought went deep down to the bottom of my soul, like an arrow through the heart. It was a clear realization, a straightforward shot to the brain, and as much as I didn't want to believe it, I knew it as Truth. I knew this was a mortal wound. "She's gone, Willy!" I cried.

"Don't say that Skip! We'll get her off!" was his hopeful reply.

I knew he was wrong, but I didn't dwell on it. We had to do what we had to do. It was crazy. It was total chaos. It was pitch dark except for the white foam of the relentless waves crashing over the bulwarks. We had to get an anchor out. *Number One*, our big dinghy that carried the 35hp outboard, was luckily on the leeward deck. I flew to it and got it untied. The crew quickly stowed an anchor, chain and rope in her bow, and together we slid her over the rail and I jumped in. With the vessel to windward I had a bit of protection, so I got the engine clamped on to the stern, and it was only a matter of minutes before I was crashing out through the waves like a man possessed to get an anchor set. The tail end of the line I left tied to the anchor post, and with the line properly coiled it flew out of the dinghy behind me. And then the next arrow struck. The outboard died, and I couldn't get it started again. I immediately began to drift back towards the stricken vessel. I shook the fuel can. It was full. As I drifted shoreward, I found the fault. The rubber fuel line had somehow been crimped and it was cut at that point. The crew saw what happened and slowly pulled me back to the boat.

I jumped back on board looking for a plan B. "Let's fire off some flares and get on the radio," I yelled as I jumped into the aft cabin. David found the flares and quickly shot one off while I grabbed the VHF mic. On channel 16 I spoke as calmly as I could. "Mayday, mayday, mayday. Vessel in distress. This is the schooner *Water Pearl*. Mayday, mayday, mayday."

The port pilot picked me up. "*Water Pearl*, this is the Colón pilot. What is your position?"

"If I knew my position sir, I wouldn't be aground," I answered. Eventually we figured out we were on the reef near the Point Toro lighthouse. The pilot said they would send a vessel as soon as possible to render assistance.

I took a breather to try and ascertain our situation. Things weren't good, but it could have been worse. Although we were hard aground and lying on our bilge at a steep angle, we weren't being pounded or being driven onto a deadly shore. Waves were smashing over our port side, but she wasn't breaking up. The spreader lights were on, illuminating the chaos before my eyes. The noise was horrific. And as I tried to somehow make sense out of this nightmarish scene a head appeared out of the darkness, and then someone was climbing over the bulwark. "Are you guys all right? Is anyone injured? Who is the captain?" the man was saying in an immediately recognizable American accent. Just then several more people materialized and began climbing aboard.

"I'm the captain; I'm the one who got us into this mess," I said.

"Lt. Colonel Corson Hilton, U.S. Army," the man said. "Is anyone injured?"

"No, everyone is okay. But where did you come from, and how did you get out here so quickly?" I stammered. I was still trying to come to grips with the surreal situation swirling around me.

"Your ship is lying on a shallow reef about one hundred yards from shore, just outside a U.S. Army Jungle Operations Training Center. You are lucky in that respect as no locals can get out here to rob you blind. You can easily walk out here from shore, so when one of my men saw your flares, we came out immediately. What can we do to help?"

John and Willy were next to me listening to the Colonel's words. "Well we need to get the crew off along with whatever immediate possessions we can take with us," I said. "You guys pull the dinghy alongside and put whatever you can into it and get it ashore. I'll stay here and see if there is anything else I can do."

Just then the VHF radio came to life. The harbormaster had sent out the port pilot boat to assist us, and when I climbed up and peered over the windward bulwark, I could see their searchlight in the distance sweeping over the black water. There was no way they were going to get in close enough to help us, so I got back on the radio and told them so. I said we were being assisted by the U.S. Army, our crew was safe, and thanked them for their offer of assistance. They acknowledged and I watched as their lights faded into the darkness.

The crew wasted no time in filling up the dinghy with their gear. I went below for my passport and gave it to John. While I was there, I grabbed a bottle of whiskey from the liquor cabinet. "Are you coming ashore now, Skip?" Willy called from out of the dinghy.

"No, you guys go along. I'm going to hang out here for a while," I said.

Trish was the last to go. "Come on Chris…there's nothing you can do here. Come ashore with us and then see what you can do in the morning."

"No, you guys go ahead. I'll be okay. I just want to stay here for a while," I repeated. The Colonel assured me the crew would be well looked after. A sentry would be posted ashore so no looters could get aboard. He also tried to coerce me to go ashore with the crew, but I refused.

The Colonel and his men slipped back over the rail into the water, the dinghy disappeared into the darkness, and I was alone. I turned off the spreader lights and sat down on deck with my back to the cabin side and started to pour that Johnny

Walker down my throat. How could this be happening? This hellish nightmare couldn't be real. The waves boomed and crashed over the rail, soaking me to the bone, but I drank on and screamed into the uncaring wind. My boat lay panting like a giant wounded animal beneath me. The voice in my head tried to convince me there was something we could do to save her, but deep down I knew there was no way out. A realization as undeniable as the morning sunrise showed me there would be no miracle salvations this time.

14
Panama - the Final Chapter

"Outside of that, Mrs. Kennedy, how did you like Dallas?"
- Ray Bowman

Eventually I finished the whiskey, gave in and found my way ashore. The sentry saw me stagger up the beach, and the next thing I knew I was being helped into a brightly lit room full of people. I was put in a hot shower and given some dry clothes to put on. I was in a sorry state, but everyone in the room sounded positive. Voices and faces were coming at me like in a dream, saying things like, "don't worry, buddy, we're going to get you off," and "they say they can do it, Skip." Finally, someone threw a blanket over me and I closed my eyes.

Next thing I knew I was being gently shaken. "Wake up, Cappy," I could hear Willy saying. "We're getting ready to go." I opened my eyes and jumped to my feet. The realization of where I was and what had happened flashed through my brain like a white light. I was awake and moving in an instant. We all piled into a jeep and roared off into the early morning light. Over the noise of the engine Capt. Bart Mollet proceeded to tell me the plan he and his men had come up with to get *Water Pearl* off the reef.

It wasn't long before we arrived at a small harbor which was part of the base. Several military vessels were tied up there, including two large square-bowed landing craft, or LTC's. I was directed into a Boston Whaler with Sargent First Class Robert Smith. "Call me Smitty," he said as I jumped on board and he started up the engines. The rest of the crew went aboard one of the LTC's, and moments later the two vessels pulled away from the dock and motored slowly through the mirror-like calm, which was reflecting the pastel hues of the coming sunrise.

It was a couple of miles from the mouth of the breakwater to the spot where *Water Pearl* lay stranded. It didn't take the whaler long to skip out there, but the landing craft was a half an hour behind us. In the pre-dawn light, the running lights still glowed brightly from their boxes in the rigging aboard the stricken schooner. For some reason it had slipped my mind to turn them off, and as crazy as it sounds, I was worried about the batteries. When we got closer it wasn't a pretty sight. *Water Pearl* was heeled to almost forty-five degrees, the red anti-fouling of her bottom standing out well above the white foam of the breaking waves, her varnished masts canting radically towards the dark green shoreline. There were breakers and coral heads everywhere. How we ever got as far in as we did was something I couldn't understand.

Smitty and I picked our way through the coral heads as we waited for the bigger vessel to arrive. When it was finally in place, he maneuvered the whaler as close as he could get and I jumped over the side into the grey water with the end of a light half-inch nylon line tied to my foot. (Smitty didn't mention until later that the son of famous undersea explorer Jacques Cousteau had only recently died from a shark attack in these same infested waters). I swam across the reef and pulled myself aboard. Going to the bow I pulled the small line which was joined to the heavy towing hawser until the spliced eye came aboard. I passed it through the hawse pipe and looped it over the Sampson post and signaled to the crew. The landing craft slowly went astern, taking up the slack. The rope whipped across the water and began to squeak and moan as it tightened up. The skipper put the power on and black smoke began to belch out of the exhaust stack and the rope stretched bar tight. The twin GM diesels were screaming across the water as he gave her all he had. The tension was palpable...something had to give. And then it did. The vessel moved! The bow of *Water Pearl* started to swing slowly seaward. Inch by inch her head began to turn. Gradually the boat began to stand up. My heart raced! She was coming off!

Unfortunately, that was as far as we got. Try as we may she just wouldn't move any further. For a half of an hour he gave it all he had, but she just wouldn't budge. Eventually it was decided to give up. The tow line was tied to a big anchor and dropped over the side to try and keep her in position. The two boats turned for home. I dejectedly slipped over the side, waded ashore and walked around to the dock to meet the boats as they arrived back. Once alongside I stepped aboard and spoke to the skipper, who was very positive. "Hey listen, at fifteen hundred it'll be high tide and we'll go out there with both of these LTC's and we'll get that sombitch off...don't you worry!" He had shifted her and it was low tide. At least we had some hope.

First light and the LTC almost has us off.

As the adrenaline of the last twelve hours started to wear off, the reality of the situation began to sink in. I was in a sort of shock. I WAS in shock. I just kept saying to myself, "I can't believe I fucked up. I can't believe it. I just can't believe it..." The crew were in a sorry state as well. We had all been kicked in the guts, and it hurt. The colonel had given us a couple of rooms in the barracks to stay in. At lunchtime we were directed to the mess where we stood in line with green uniformed soldiers, trays in hand, waiting for our chow. I couldn't eat a thing. Afterwards we wandered back to the barracks, stretched out on our bunks and tried to rest. I could only lay there and stare at the ceiling in total disbelief. A million thoughts spun through my head. Why didn't we just wait a few hours until daylight and then go in? What would I do if we did get the boat off? What about Vanessa and our plans? What about Bob? For sure I knew the crew would all bail. I heard John and Willy talking about flights out already. I took a deep breath and tried to gather myself. "One thing at a time…one thing at a time," I said to myself. "Wait until three o'clock and see what happens."

A few minutes later there was a knock on the door. A polite young soldier with a crewcut stood outside. "Colonel Hilton would like to see you, sir," he said. I accompanied him to an air conditioned, wood-paneled office. The Colonel sat behind a big desk, and stood as we entered. With a slight resemblance to Oliver North, he looked far different from the man in a swimming suit I met the night before. A uniform can do a lot to change a person.

"How are you holding up, Mr. Bowman? Sorry about the accommodation, but we are not really set up for visitors, if you know what I mean," he said with a hint of a smile.

"I'm bearing up all right, sir. I can't thank you enough for all the help you and your men have given us. I just can't wait until three o'clock to see what happens."

"That is why I have asked to see you," Colonel Hilton said, his steely blue eyes looking straight into mine. "The first thing I did this morning was contact General Pearce, my commanding officer, and advise him of the situation. The action we took this morning was well within the scope of my command. It was my decision to send our LTC out there to render assistance, and I'm only sorry there wasn't a better result. Any further action to be taken, however, has to be cleared by my superiors, and believe me I have gone right to the top. It is my unpleasant duty to inform you that the General will not allow me to offer you any more assistance other than give you food and shelter here on the base until you resolve your unfortunate situation. He unequivocally refused to allow me any use of military vessels to assist a civilian. Anything else that is in my power I will do, but as far as sending boats out my hands are tied."

I was crestfallen. Knocked out loaded. The nightmare, it seemed, was going from bad to worse. "If I may ask, what were the reasons given by the General?" I queried.

"There were several. First of all, it is not in the framework of the military to give assistance to civilians unless in an emergency. Sometimes things can even be difficult between branches of our own military. Last year a US Navy patrol boat ran up on the reef only a few hundred yards away from where you did. Eventually we were allowed to help, but a lot of strings had to be pulled in high places before we could do so. Luckily the vessel was steel, and there was little damage sustained, but they made a good job of it and ran high up onto the reef at full speed, if that makes you feel any better. Secondly, the political situation here in Panama is quite tenuous. This Noriega thing has everyone jumpy. For any Americans to operate outside of the Canal Zone we would need special permission from the Panamanian authorities, and that could take weeks. Finally, there is the issue of liability. What if we pull you off and you sink? Who is responsible?"

"What if I personally go and talk to the General myself? Do you think that would help?" I hopefully enquired.

"You are more than welcome to try. However, General Pearce is a very busy man, and I don't know how quickly you could get to see him. Secondly, he is over on the Pacific side, in Panama City, and that is several hours away. You may be better served to try and find someone in the Canal Zone to help you. You could be wasting precious time trying to convince him to change his mind, which in my personal opinion I doubt he would do."

The writing was on the wall, and I didn't need to be convinced. The Colonel was a genuine person and was doing all he could to help. I had no other choice but to try and find another solution. Colonel Hilton must have read my mind. "What I suggest you do is go and see the Canal Zone people. They are an independent American company, and they have a multitude of tugs working the Canal. I will give you a car and driver, and he is yours for as long as you need him. He knows his way around and will be ready to go as soon as you want."

"There is a lot of gear I would like to get off the boat before it gets ruined, and that is something my crew can do while I'm gone. Do you have a place where I can temporarily store these things?" I asked.

"Of course, that won't be a problem. And I will ask for volunteers to help you as well." The Colonel stood and put out his hand. "As I said, I will do all in my power to help. You are Americans in a tough situation. I only wish I could do more."

The door closed; I took a deep breath and tried to regroup before descending the stairs. Things were getting more difficult by the minute. I didn't know how much deeper I could dig.

Outside in the tropical Panamanian heat and humidity I attempted to regain my bearings, tried to put one foot in front of the next and balance myself. Scotty, my driver, was waiting for me in his souped-up Bronco. I went back to the rooms to tell everyone the latest development. Just then Smitty drove up with a platoon of helpers in the back of an olive-green army truck. My crew jumped in with them, I climbed in with Scotty and we went our separate ways. Off through the base checkpoint and down a lonely bitumen road walled by thick jungle we drove, eventually coming to a halt at the Canal, where we were held up as a giant ship maneuvered through the lock. I couldn't help thinking that we should have been anchored snuggly in Colón Harbor, waiting to go through ourselves. My gut wrenched, like someone had stuck me and was twisting the knife. The big tugs I saw operating there did raise my hopes, though. With that amount of horsepower, they could easily haul my vessel off. After a couple of false turns, we found the office we were looking for, and following a prolonged wait I was ushered in to meet the man in charge of canal tugboat movements. I began to relate my story but was cut short. This middle-aged American had no time to listen to stories. "Sorry, can't help you. First of all, there's nothing in it for us. These tugs are our bread and butter and there is no way we would risk one of them out there amongst the reefs. But even if we wanted to, we couldn't go out there because of the damned treaty Carter signed handing everything outside of the Canal Zone over to the Panamanians. The only ships who would be allowed to help you would have to be locally registered. So sorry, but no dice."

That was it. Meeting over. I tried to plead my case but the man looked at me as if I were deaf. "Well is there any local company you know of who might be able to help?" I asked from the doorway.

"There is a guy in Colón by the name of Gomez. Owns a supply vessel and a tug, I think. He's the only one I know of on that side of the Canal."

Things were going from bad to worse. It was early afternoon by the time we drove into the broken-down Caribbean port of Colón. Renowned as one of the roughest places in the Caribbean, the town's appearance did little to dispel its vicious reputation. Garbage littered the curb-sides and overflowed into the streets, the roads were potholed and in disrepair, and its once grand Spanish architecture was dilapidated and falling apart. The place had definitely seen better days.

Scotty found the office of PAMAR, whose proprietor luckily enough was in attendance. On the inside, the office was modern and well-staffed. Pedro Gomez was a heavyset man who wore a lot of gold. Behind his desk he had a team photo of the LA Dodgers, with him in it. He told me he once played for them as a relief pitcher. He may well have, but he would have been far more suited to play for the Pirates, as I was soon to discover. After relating to him the precarious situation I was in, Pedro thought for a few minutes. "Well, we have an ocean-going tug that would easily pull you off, but my partner is presently hauling a barge from Cartagena to Baltimore and isn't due back for two weeks. I've got a flat-bottomed supply ship with two engines of a thousand horsepower each that should be able to do it - that is if the terms are suitable," Pedro said with a pearly white smile.

And so began our negotiations. I didn't really have much of a position from which to bargain. There was nothing else on the Caribbean side of the Canal that was big enough to do the job. Pedro held all of the aces. When he said, "I'll do it for ten thousand US dollars, SOF," which I discovered meant "Succeed or Fail", there wasn't much else I could say except I would have to get the go-ahead from my Lloyds insurance broker in London, whose offices were closed at that hour of the day.

"You get your agent to telex me the go-ahead and I can be out there tomorrow afternoon. Don't worry amigo. I'll do my utmost to help you out," my new-found compadre said, slapping me on the shoulder as we walked to the door. The guy was slippery, there were no two ways about it, but you couldn't help liking him. I only hoped that he could deliver. I didn't have much choice.

Scotty drove me back on to the base just before dark. The crew's room was littered with clothes and other assorted gear; Willy sat shirtless on the edge of his bed, the smoke from a cigarette curling up from between his fingers. The others all sat up as I walked in. "How did it all go, Cappy? Are the guys from the canal going to help us out?" Willy asked. I told everyone about the events of the afternoon and how our hopes were now in the hands of an ex-Dodger relief pitcher.

"What about you guys? How did it go?"

They told me close to thirty volunteers turned up to help, and how they had formed a human chain and passed virtually everything ashore and into the truck. "Don't worry Skip, everything's safe. It's all been locked up in an old ammunition bunker," Willy said.

The next morning, I was up at first light to see if I had received a reply from my insurance broker. The night before, Colonel Hilton had taken me to the communications room, where I was given my own desk with a phone and access to a telex machine. I had sent David Paine, my Lloyds broker in London, the bad news the night before and asked him for the go-ahead to get Pedro moving. As I walked into the office, one of the orderlies handed me a torn-off telex stating the Underwriters had agreed to Pedro's terms. David also asked me to contact the local Lloyds agent, a Mr. Horst Schmitz, for whom I was given a Panama City number.

There were a couple of other calls that I had to make, neither of them pleasant. I had to call Bob. And I had to call Vanessa. I decided to wait and see what transpired later that afternoon. I picked up the phone and dialed Pedro's number, and he told me he had received the go-ahead from London. He told me his ship had commitments that morning, but later in the day when the tide was high, he would come out to Point Toro and have a go. For my part I just hoped he would actually make a genuine attempt and not just go through the motions to scam a quick ten thousand bucks. Finally, I called Mr. Schmitz, who told me to expect him sometime in the afternoon.

I left the office and walked across the manicured lawns to the road which led out to the beach. This was not a chore I was looking forward to. Revisiting the greatest disaster of my life would not be a pleasant undertaking. The road bent around a stand of tropical bush and ended on the sand. I stood in the shade of a coconut tree and looked out at the boat two hundred yards off shore. She looked everything like she was heeled over and sailing; only no sails were up. It was low tide, and outcroppings of coral showed themselves between me and the stricken schooner. The sea was calm, with only tiny wavelets rolling gently in and dispersing themselves around the hull. I walked through the knee-deep water towards the boat. As I did a colorful object lying on the reef attracted my eye, and as I got closer, I recognized it immediately. It was Clara's piggybank in the shape of a clown. Someone must have dropped it the day before. I picked it up and continued on. I reached the rail and climbed up on deck. Words alone cannot express how I was feeling at that moment. I pressed on and clambered down below and could tell immediately that she had withstood the grounding well up to that point. There was no seawater over the floorboards, no sloshing of water in her bilges. I could smell diesel and old bilge water, but that was about it. Otherwise the interior was a disheveled mess. Our uneaten dinner still sat on the stove. Back in our cabin I took down my pictures of Vanessa and Clara. The drawers and lockers had all been cleared out the day before, but the chart was still on the chart table. I rolled it up and took it with me. I wanted to know how we ended up three miles from the harbor entrance and somehow thought we were on course. I still couldn't figure that one out.

Early that afternoon the Lloyds assessor turned up, and I didn't like him from the moment I laid eyes on him. He was a very officious German, and it was immediately obvious he was not on my side. He questioned my account repeatedly, as if searching for contradictions. I told him straight it wasn't my intention to put my boat on the rocks, and that once it happened, I had done everything within my power, including swimming through shark-infested waters, to try and save her. I was still doing all I could to get her off, I said, and wouldn't stop until I had exhausted every possibility. This placated him a little bit.

Then we took a look at the chart. I showed him our last known position, and where we dropped our sails and so on. As I looked more closely at it, I immediately began to pick up major differences between what was on the chart and actual reality. And then I saw something that made everything fall into place. The chart was published in 1965! In the twenty-three years since its publication the lights had obviously been changed. The ranges we were looking for that night didn't exist anymore. We had made the most serious error any navigator could make; we tried to make the land fit into our preconceived idea of where we thought it should be. Later on, I was to discover that the lead lights I thought were taking us into the canal had only been recently installed to guide helicopter pilots into the base. They were more than likely the same lights which put the Navy patrol vessel aground. The more I looked at it, the more I just shook my head and asked, "Why didn't we just hove-to and wait until daylight?"

Anyway, Herr Schmitz left to file his report, and I stood by to see if a Panamanian ex-relief pitcher could, as Vin Scully, the famous LA Dodger commentator, would say, "Pull this one out of the fire."

It was a little after four o'clock when we saw Pedro's blue supply ship heading our way. "He's leaving it a bit late," I thought. "He won't be able to see much in this light." We had *Number One* working again, and we picked out a channel through the reef so we could carry a tow line aboard. Willy and I were in the dinghy and the others were on board *Water Pearl*. We ran out to meet the slowly moving vessel. Pedro was at the helm, and he was taking it slowly, working in as close as he could get while keeping a close eye on his depth sounder. He was moving steadily, inching his way in, until he got within five hundred yards or so of the boat, when he suddenly stopped. We wondered why. He wasn't close enough yet. As we turned around and drove back, we saw the reason. He was aground.

"Oh no," I thought. "Here we go again."

When we circled around the big supply ship, we could see he hadn't just bumped the bottom, either. He was stuck fast. The momentum the vessel had been carrying, even at a slow speed, was more than enough to get him wedged hard onto the reef. At first, we thought that using his big engines he would be able to back off easily, but that wasn't the case. We hung out there for more than an hour, but when it began to get dark, we picked our way back ashore. Sitting on the beach, the five of us watched the ship's running lights get brighter as darkness overtook us. Finally, around nine o'clock, we saw the lights moving again, and it didn't take them long to disappear around the breakwater as Pedro headed back into the harbor. Once again, my heart sank. "What do I do know?" I thought as we turned and walked dejectedly back to the barracks. I was running out of options. It was like I was getting sucked deeper and deeper into a horrendous nightmare, and try as I may I just couldn't wake up. The crew was very disheartened as well. But to be truthful, they had other things on their minds.

Morning came and everyone was extremely quiet as we walked to the canteen for our army breakfast. They didn't have to say anything. I knew what was coming. They had decided to leave, and I didn't blame them.

15
Aftermath

*Sometimes my burden
Is more than I can bear.
It's not dark yet,
But it's getting there.*
- Bob Dylan, "Not Dark Yet"

I guess that's about it then. If a story has a beginning, it must have an end. I'll just tie off a few loose ends and we'll be done. Pedro Gomez got the ten grand for his "SOF". He may have been a pirate, but he was true to his word. When his tug returned to Panama, he promised he and his partner would give it one more shot. I had to wait two weeks for the tug to arrive, but the weather was kind. There was hardly a breath of wind, the sea was calm and flat and *Water Pearl* was holding up well. The tug only had twenty-four-hours in Panama before the next job, but in that time, Pedro said they would do all they could. Then on the day of our final attempt it blew up a gale, and we couldn't even get a line onto the boat. We struggled from first light until well after dark, and the wind and seas never let up. Finally, I had to tell the captain to stop because either he or one of his men was going to get hurt. In the morning the tug was gone, and so was all hope.

It was only then when I went to Pedro's office to call Vanessa and Bob. They weren't easy phone calls to make. Vanessa and Clara were naturally in tears. They had just found out they'd lost their home. Vanessa was getting close to delivery, and I promised to be there for the birth. Bob took the news okay. It was not what he was expecting to hear, he was disappointed, but there were no hard feelings. He told me he was in New York and I said I would come and see him on the way to Australia and fill him in on the details.

The insurance company paid up, but not without a fight. At a meeting in Panama City, there were six of them against me trying to turn the screw by saying I was negligent and they were only going to dole out a partial payment. I had been there before; I had been assaulted by experts. I had to pull out my ace in the hole. "You gentlemen have seen the documents...you know who my partner is. Bob Dylan has on retainer the best New York attorney's money can buy. Now if you want to take them on, you are more than welcome, but I don't like your chances." They asked me to leave the room, and after their private discussion miraculously changed their tune and agreed to pay up.

A Lloyds surveyor had flown in from England, and he stood on the reef with me as I looked at the boat for the last time. "I know only too well what is going through your mind right now, Mr. Bowman. I have seen it more times than I could count. You have been paid out and now the vessel is there free for you to attempt to salvage. My advice to you is to get on a plane and leave. Take the money and move on with your life. I think you have been through enough."

It was true. It was if he were reading my mind. "Maybe I could fly in Athneal and the boys," I was thinking. "There'd be no 'Succeed or Fail' with him." Some of the Army guys suggested we get a couple of D9 Cats and drag her ashore over the reef. A demolition sergeant even told me he could dynamite a channel through the coral for her, no problem. I didn't think there was much of a chance of either of those ideas happening, but even if they did, then what? Where would I put her? How much work would there be to get her sailing again? How much money would that eat up? And what about my wife and kids? Guyana and its choke and rob was minor league compared to Panama. At least in Guyana they didn't have guns. Added to the mix was the fact Vanessa was about to deliver, and I knew I must be in Australia for the birth.

But to be honest, I was done. The well had run dry. I wasn't Henry Wakelam. In the words of the famous Panamanian boxer Roberto Duran when he failed to answer the bell in his epic fight with Sugar Ray Leonard, "No mas." Taking the surveyor's advice, I turned around, walked off the beach, and never looked back.

Bob was in New York auditioning musicians for an upcoming tour. He was staying at his favorite Manhattan hotel, and as we often did, we met at his room and then went for a swim in the hotel pool, where I told him the whole story between laps. He didn't say much until the end. We were sitting on the edge of the pool and he turned to me and said, "Man, it's like that reef has been sitting there waiting for you since the very beginning." And that was about it. I knew Bob had loved the boat in his own way, but he had a knack of accepting things and moving on, which is exactly what he did.

I flew to Perth, where Vanessa had rented an apartment overlooking the sea near Fremantle. I arrived on the seventeenth of June, and it was mid-winter. I sat at the window and watched the storms blow in over the angry Indian Ocean. The baby was due at any moment, and I think she had only been holding on until I got there. Vanessa went in to labor two days later, and after another birthing marathon delivered us a beautiful girl, who we named Faye after the faith Clara had shown that she would have a sister. I was a mess, and it was a trying time. It was in that cold, dog-eared apartment after Vanessa and the kids had gone home to stay with her parents when I experienced my moments of whiskey-fueled angst. It took a few days for me to work out that alcohol wasn't the answer. Eventually I came to, levelled off, rejoined the girls, took a deep breath and faced an uncertain future.

We settled in Western Australia and I began a second life building wooden boats. Starting out all over as a stranger in a strange land wasn't easy, but everything worked out pretty well in the end. Vanessa even miraculously got pregnant again and had a son we named Glenn, who along with Faye grew up to be strong and healthy. We bought a little house near Fremantle where I could build my boats and Vanessa grow her garden and fruit trees. Clara went to school and became a lawyer and now runs a renewable energy company in Santiago, Chile.

Ray continued to fight those windmills, and much like Don Quixote, never succeeded in defeating them. He didn't become the world's richest man or save the world from acid rain, nor did he buy Australia. He never gave up, though. Blinded by diabetes and suffering from acute prostate cancer, he still kept charging to the bitter end.

I always had a dream to return to Bequia in a boat which I had built myself. Eventually I got there, but kind of cheated. While working in Sri Lanka I built *Taru,* a classic gaff sloop which just fit into a forty-foot container. I shipped it to St. Maarten and in April of 2010 finally sailed back in to Bequia with my bro Mark and my son Glenn. Walking in to the Frangipani Hotel on the morning of arrival we found Nolen and three rum punches waiting for us. It was quite a reunion. George Harrison once said, "No sunset lasts forever." Life is fluid, things change, and Bequia had moved on, just like everywhere else. Son Mitchell was there, writing his memoirs, and Nolly was still around, as ephemeral as ever, but Loren, Bluesy, Gilbert, Crosby, Herbie, Athneal… most of the old heroes had passed on. Only Uncle Linkie was still hanging in there, and he was well into his nineties when we paid him a visit at his neat little cottage in La Pompe. I caught up with Bamu and Kingsley too, and we cooked up a fish 'broff' for old time's sake.

Just Now, renamed *Bequia* by Bob Gilbert, is alive and well in California. Bob Dylan even owned her for a time, which is just another twist in a very twisty tale. No other big vessels were built in Bequia again. *Water Pearl* was the culmination of over one hundred years of heritage, an incredible creation empowered by the heart and soul of an island lost in time. Beautiful boats will always continue to be built, but there never will be another one like her.

Maybe the Hindus are right, and there are no coincidences. Maybe Bob Dylan was right, and that reef had been lying in wait for me from the very beginning. Or perhaps the Dutch hippie living in that cave in Crete was correct when he said you know when you are on the right path when things fall into place. Be that as it may, I have had to live for thirty years with the fact I was at the helm when everything fell into place on that fateful night. If that is indeed how things work, then maybe bad things are meant to be, just as well as good. Or maybe things that seem bad at the time are necessary for the universe to unfold as it should. In any case, my life was changed dramatically, and I'd have to say everything worked out for the best in the end. "Every disappointment leads to success," is how Loren would put it.

As for Bob, well as most people would know he is still making records and doing what he does. And the Never-Ending Tour just keeps rolling on. He and I catch up every few years, but our orbits are light years apart now, careening off on different vectors through time and space. There was a time, however, when our stars aligned, and for a brief moment we were able to share a very special experience. As you get on in life and the years drift by, it is sometimes hard to believe that all those things really did happen. Now that it's done, I'm glad I finally took the time to get it all down on paper. It's like a weight has been lifted off my shoulders. It is just another story, but one that deserved to be told.

Most of the time
I'm clear focused all around
Most of the time
I can keep both feet on the ground
I can follow the path
I can read the signs
Stay right with it
When the road unwinds
I can handle whatever
I stumble upon
I don't even notice
She's gone…
Most of the time
- Bob Dylan, "Most of the Time"

The End

Acknowledgments

I would especially like to thank my family for all of their love, support, and invaluable editorial input which helped make this book what it is. I would also like to tip my hat to my good friend Simon Hadlow, whose harsh encouragement kept me polishing, polishing, polishing...

The artwork for the cover is from an oil painting of *Water Pearl* under construction by Australian artist Peter Carr. I greatly appreciate his contribution to this book.

Photography Credits

Page I: Ray Bowman
Page 17: Ed Norgard, Independent Star-News July 5, 1964
Page 66: Francisco Encalada
Page 104: Ray Bowman
Page 108: Tad Brady
Page 113: Mel Grundy
Page 128: C.E. Bowman
Page 134: C.E. Bowman
Page 138: C.E. Bowman
Page 141: C.E. Bowman
Page 145: Mac Simmons
Page 147: C.E. Bowman
Page 164: C.E. Bowman
Page 172: C.E. Bowman
Page 182: C.E. Bowman
Page 185: Ray Bowman
Page 187: Ray Bowman
Page 188: Billy Weaver
Page 208: Ray Bowman
Page 210: C.E. Bowman
Page 217: C.E. Bowman
Page 261: Vanessa Pope
Page 262: Vanessa Pope
Page 263: Vanessa Pope
Page 266: Ray Bowman
Page 267: Ray Bowman
Page 269: Ray Bowman
Page 270: Ray Bowman
Page 271: Ray Bowman
Page 272: Vanessa Pope
Page 278: C.E. Bowman
Page 279: C.E. Bowman
Page 288: Mac Simmons
Page 296: Vanessa Bowman
Page 306: Vanessa Bowman
Page 322: Mel Grundy

Page 323: C.E. Bowman
Page 324: Vanessa Bowman
Page 325: Vanessa Bowman
Page 330: Vanessa Bowman
Page 351: C.E. Bowman
Page 353: Steve Lloyd-Smith
Page 356: Vanessa Bowman
Page 358: Vanessa Bowman
Page 365: Unknown
Page 370: Jennifer Devantier
Page 371: Vanessa Bowman
Page 372: Vanessa Bowman
Page 375: Victor Maymudes
Page 399: C.E. Bowman
Page 418: Unknown *Water Pearl* crew member
Page 433: C.E. Bowman

Also by C.E. BOWMAN

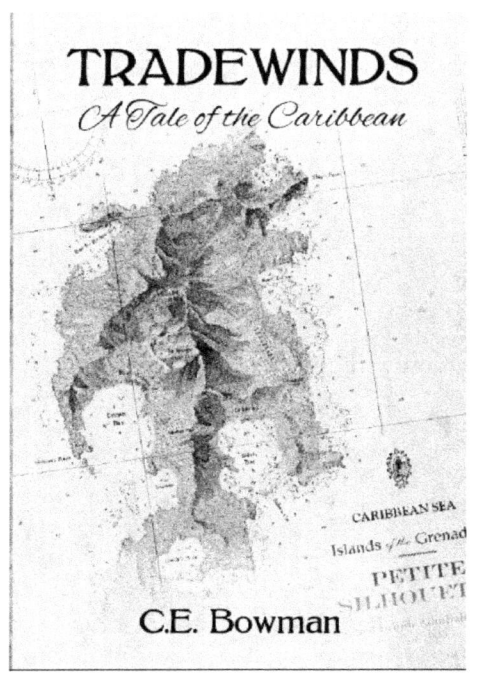

Shipwrecked on the small Caribbean island of Petite Silhouette after the Great War, Australian sailor Jack McLeod makes a new life as a bootlegger, island trader, ship builder, and family man. But storm clouds are looming on the horizon. WWII sees the West Indies become a battleground between the Allied Forces and the marauding U-boats of Hitler's Nazi Germany. Embroiled in espionage and intrigue, the crew of the schooner *ROULETTE* must call upon all of their skill and experience to battle a ruthless and unseen foe.

Splicing historical fact with fiction, TRADEWINDS takes the reader on a thrilling ride through the exotic Caribbean at a time when the outside world invades these idyllic islands, changing them forever.

"Tradewinds is a remarkable piece of work…a beautiful tribute to the people, their islands, and their way of life."
-Douglas Pyle, author of *Clean Sweet Wind*

To discover more about the author or purchase his books, visit:
www.tradewindpublishing.com

The Author

C. E. Bowman lives near Fremantle in Western Australia. He continues to sail and build the occasional boat. This is his second book.

www.ingramcontent.com/pod-product-compliance
Lightning Source LLC
Chambersburg PA
CBHW070522010526
44118CB00012B/1048